Fancy

Pictures

Mark Neville

Fancy Pictures

Steidl

The

Port Glasgow

Book Project

2004

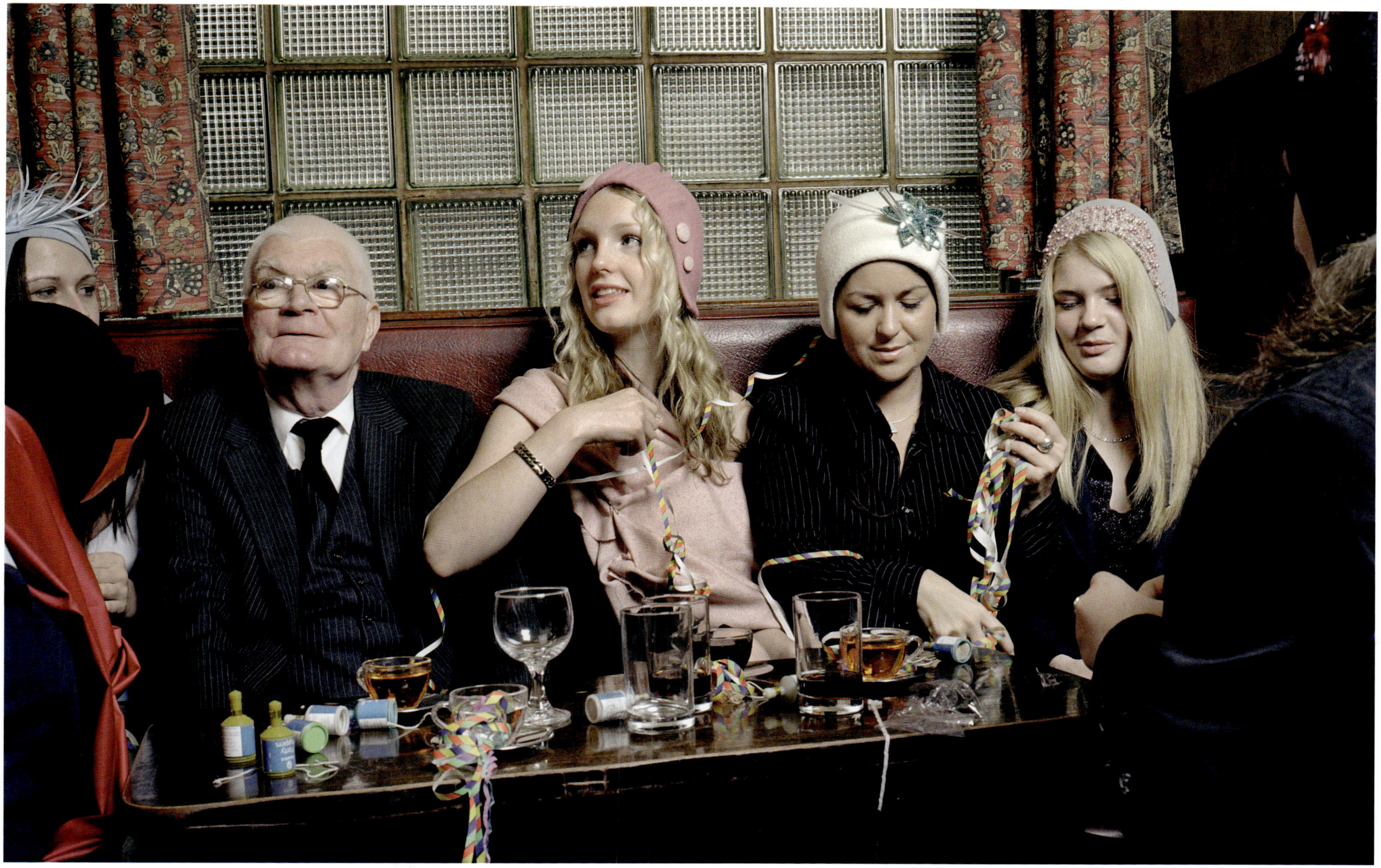

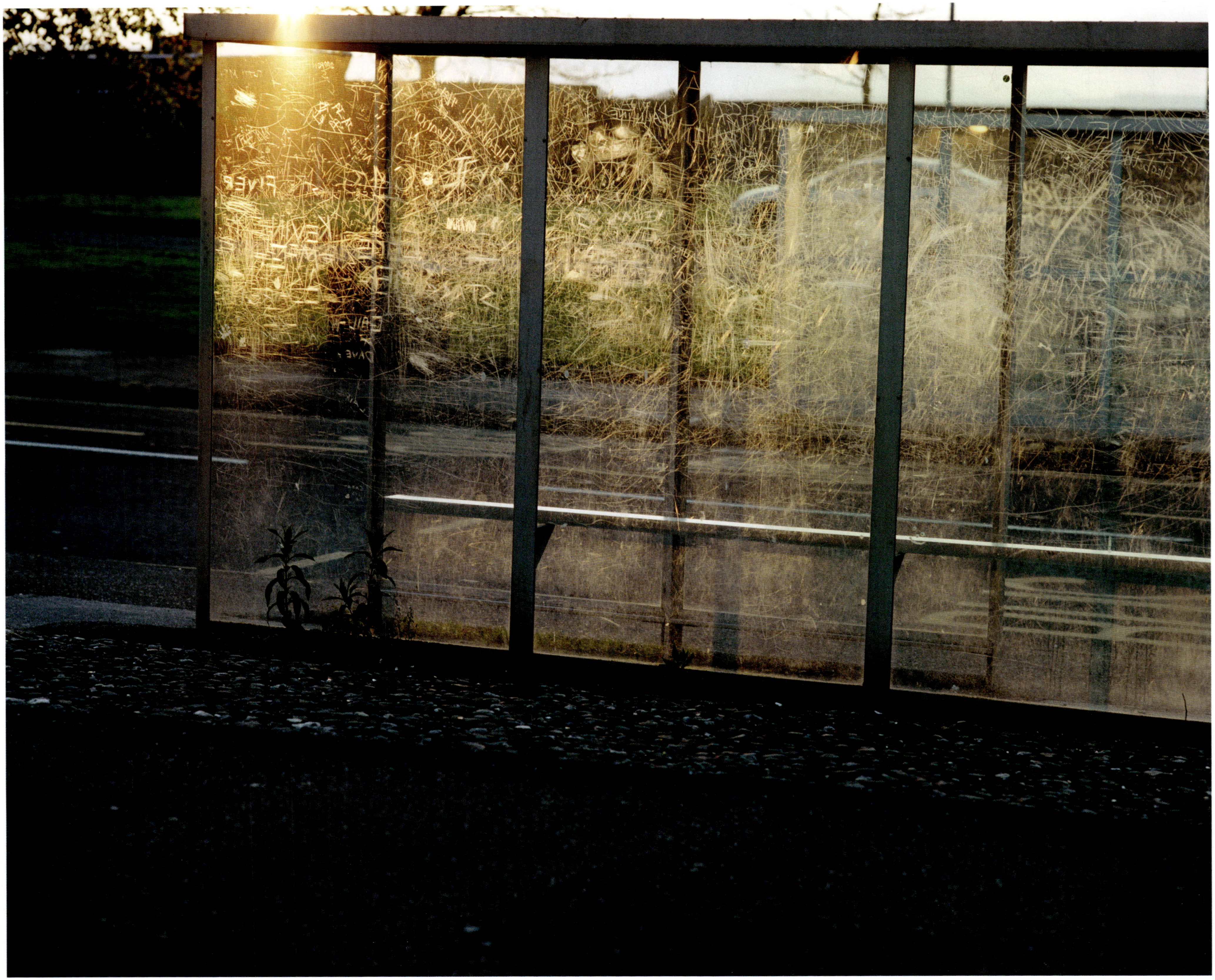

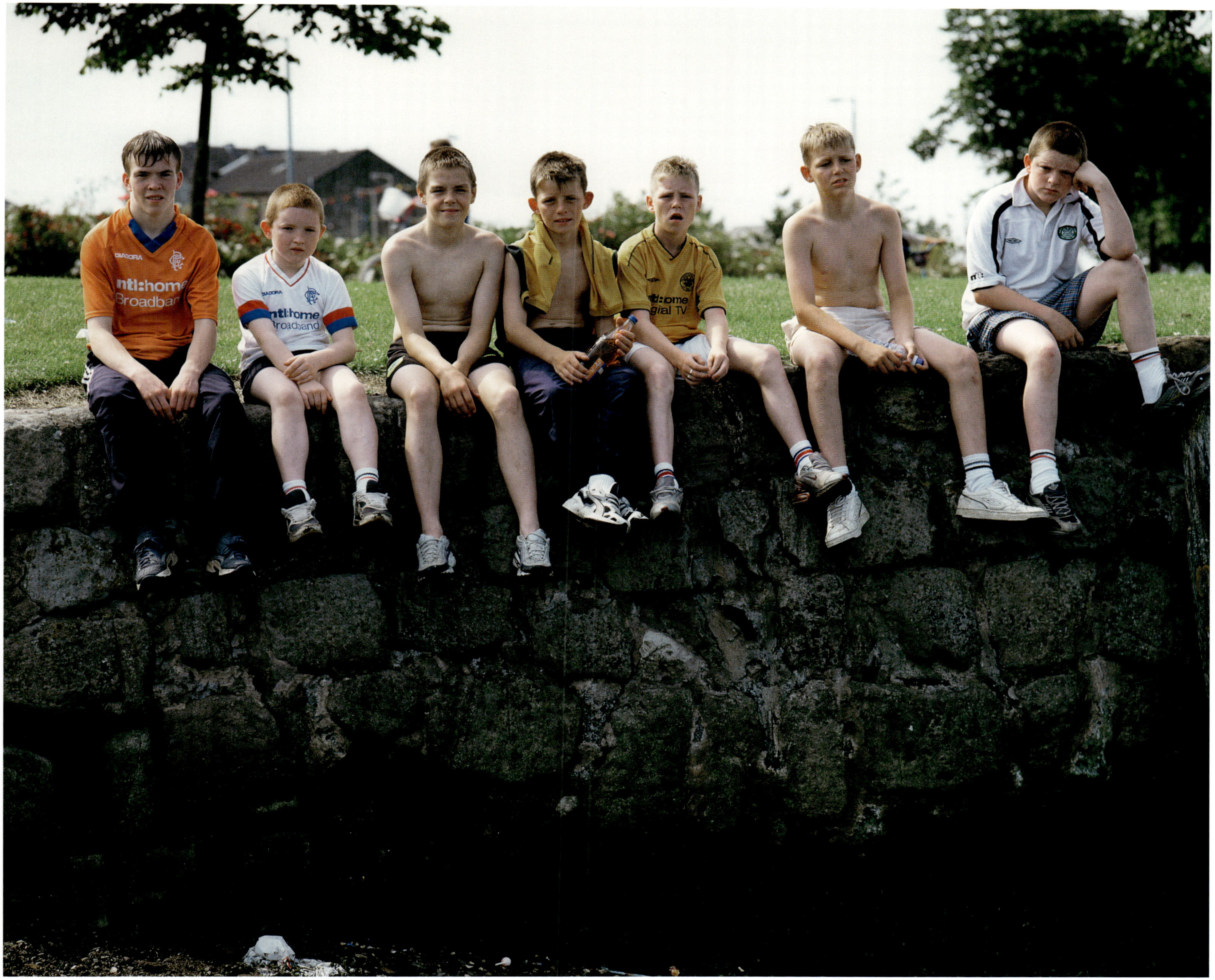
DIADORA
ntl:home

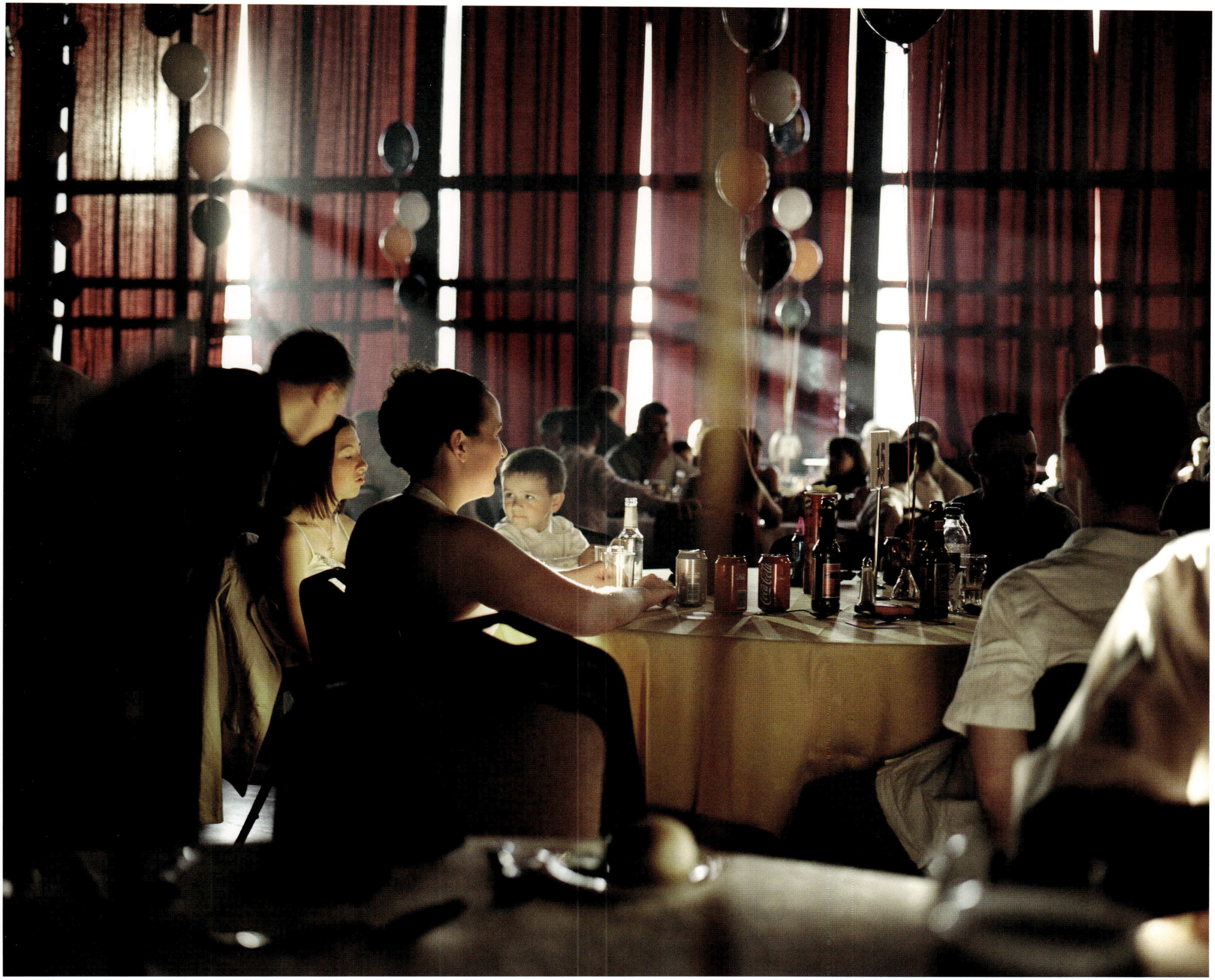
15
Coca-Cola

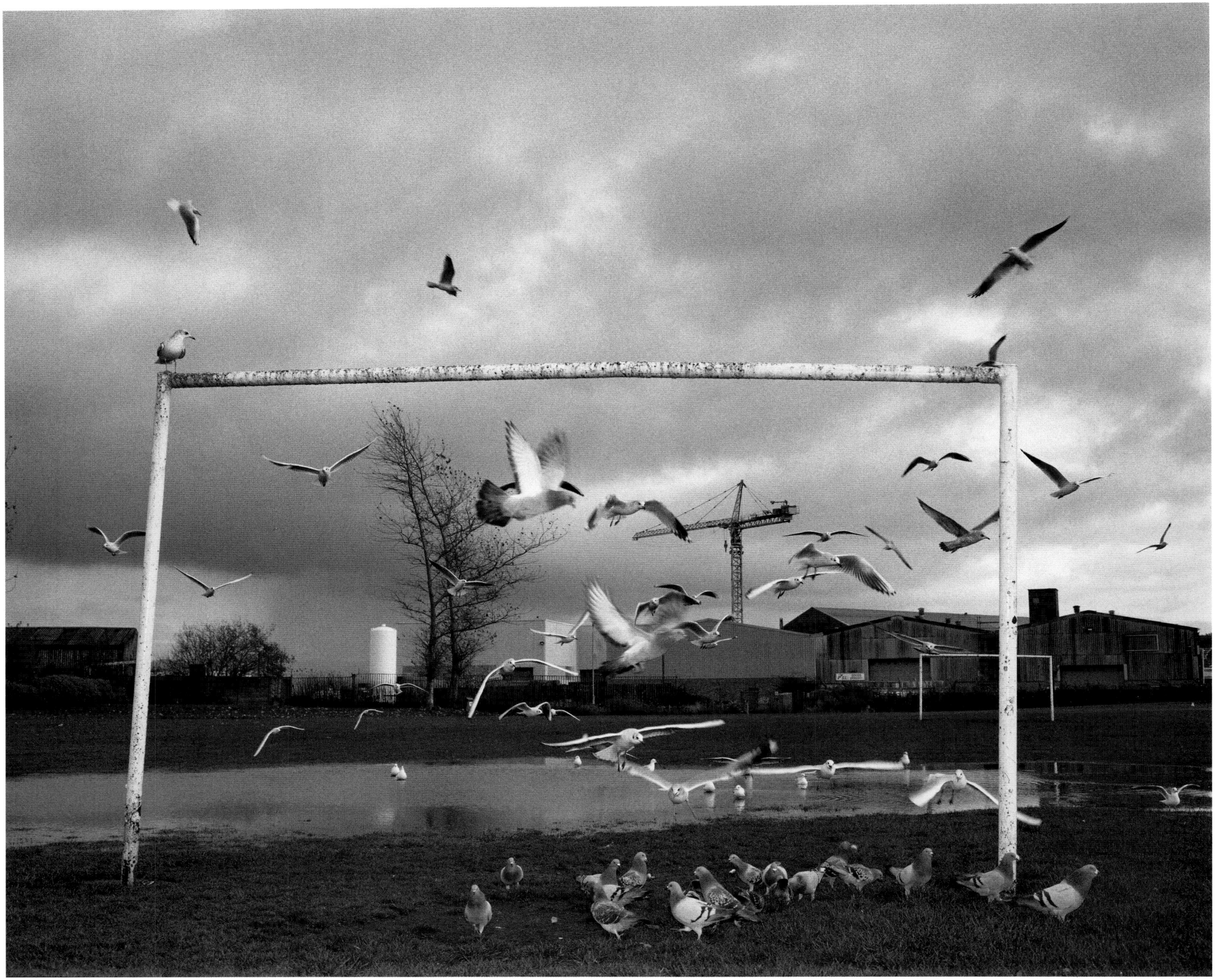

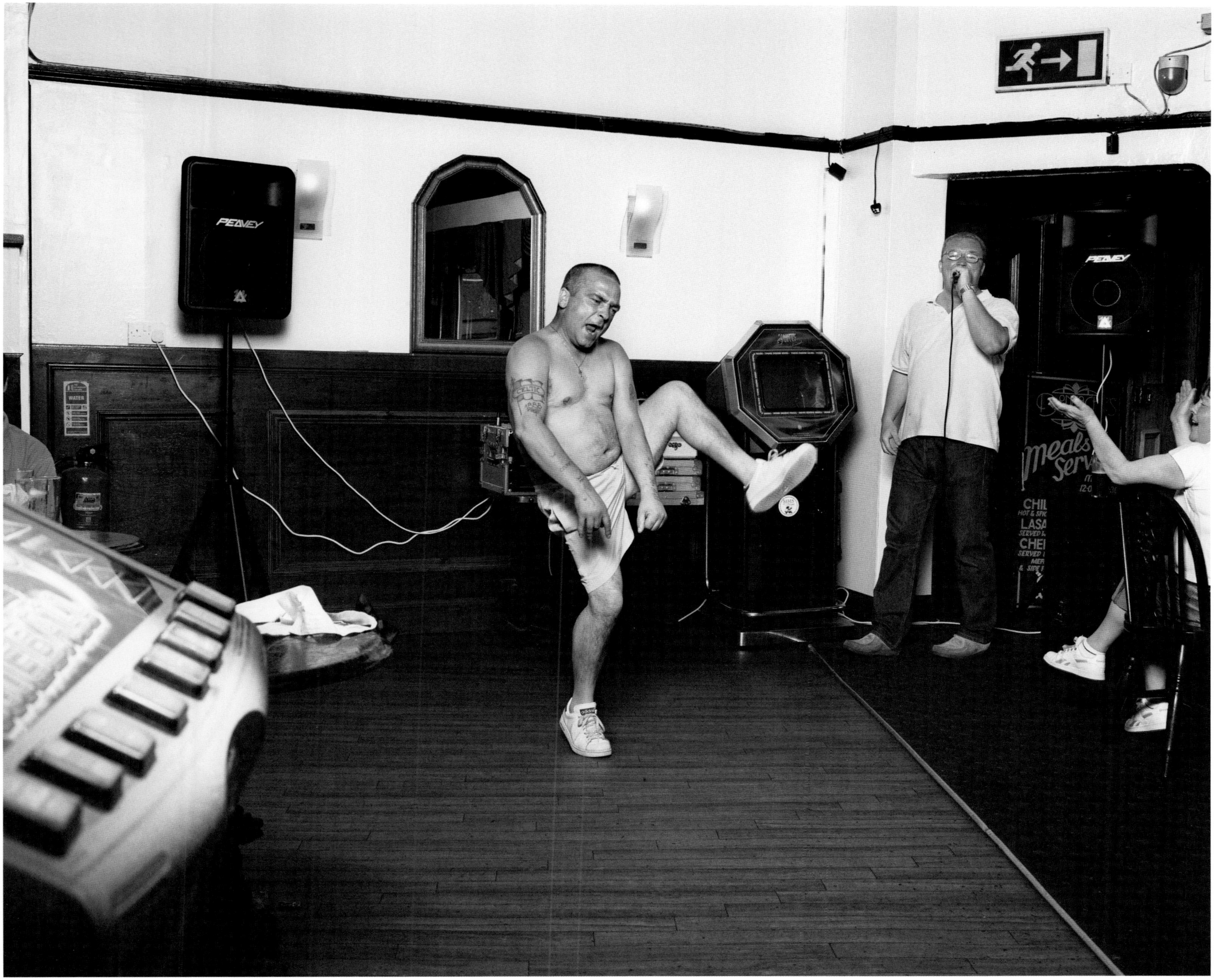
PEAVEY
PEAVEY

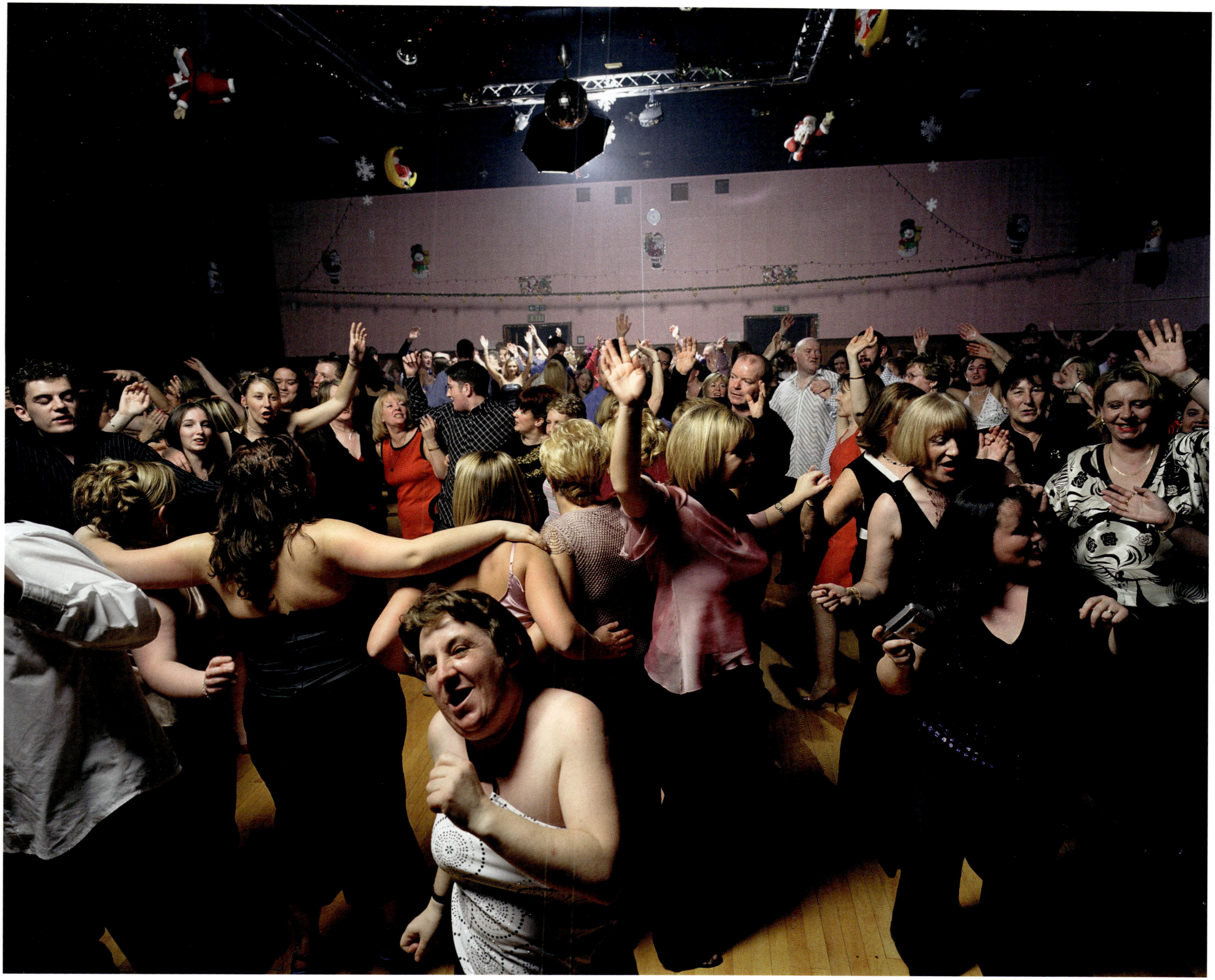

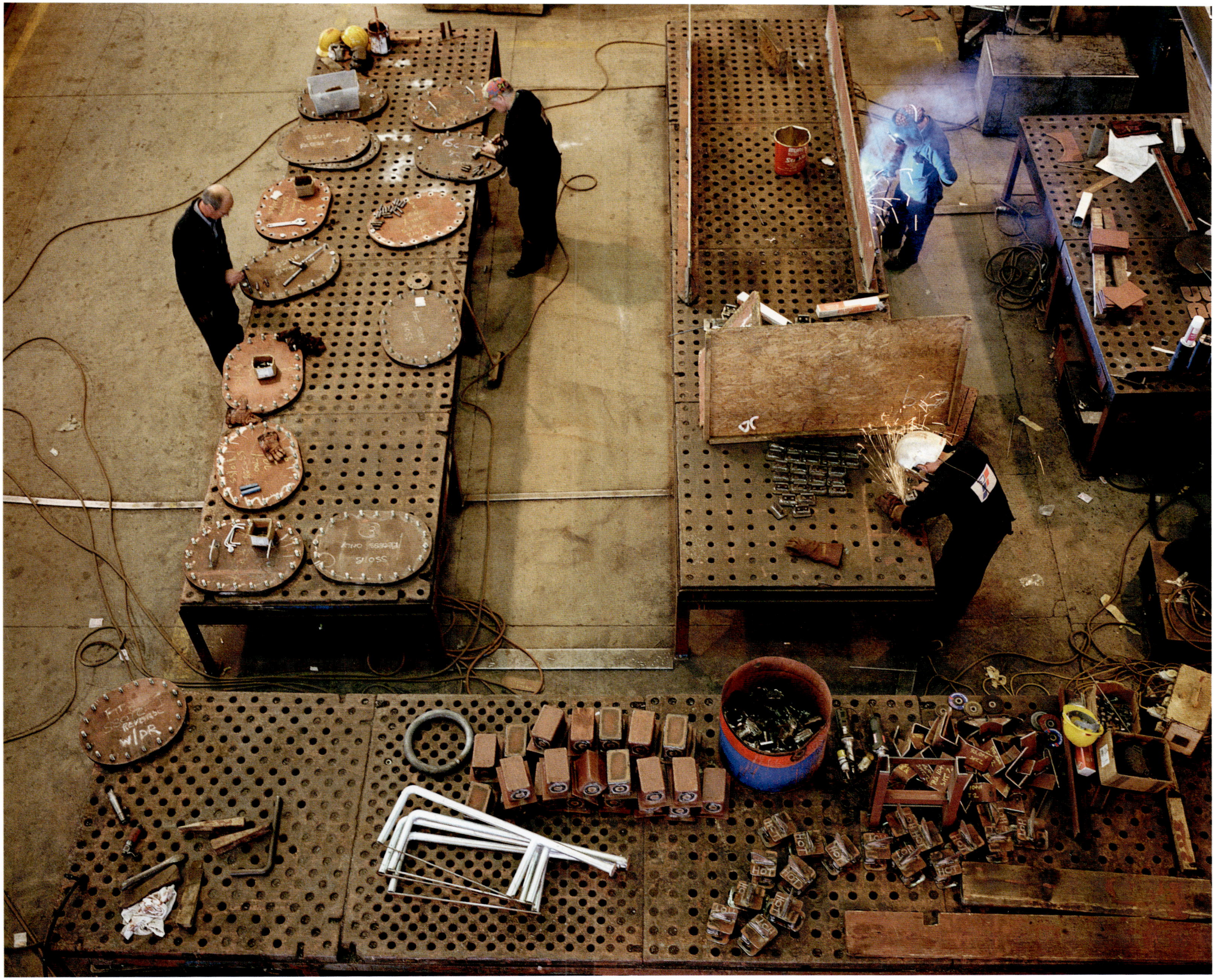

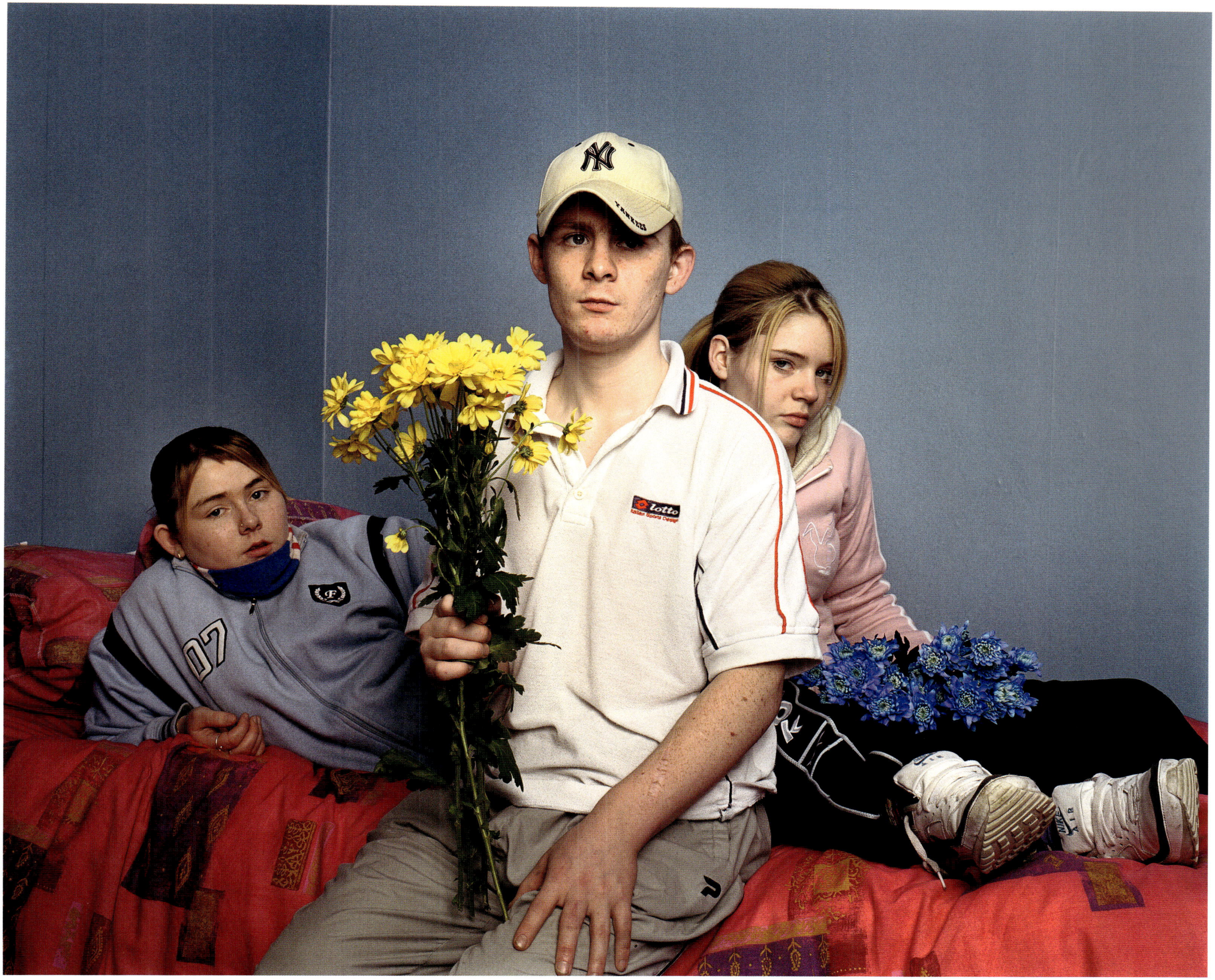
lotto
07

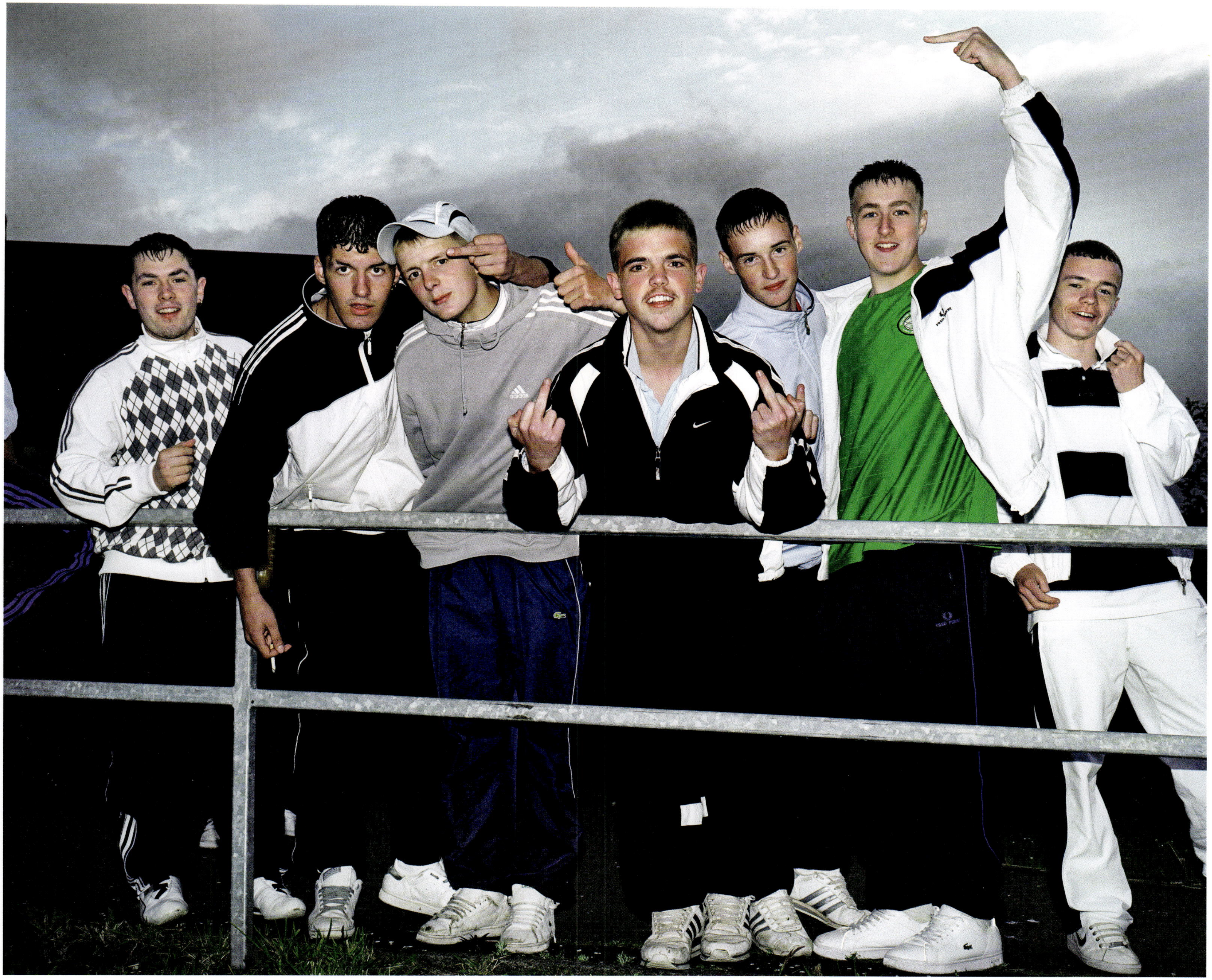

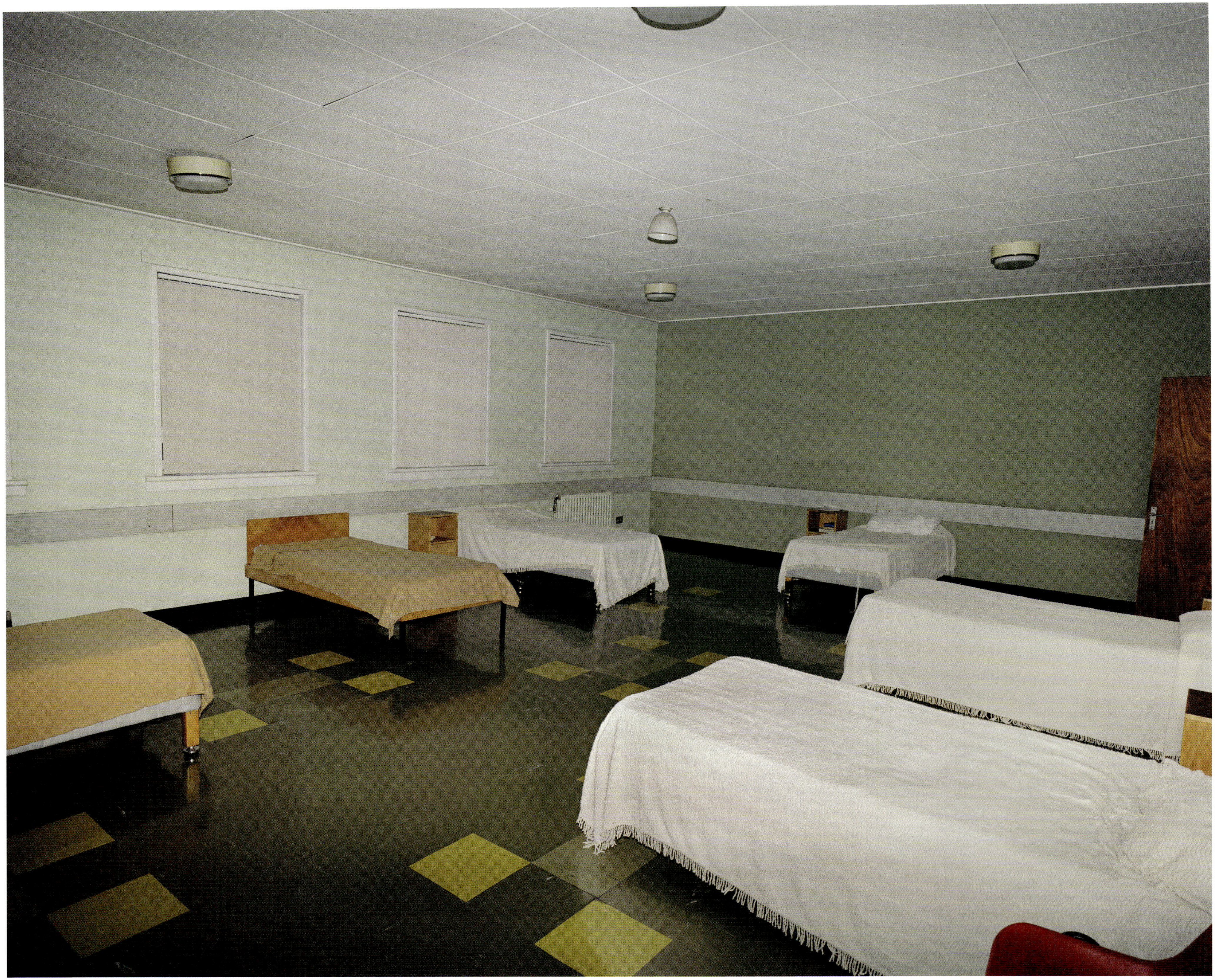

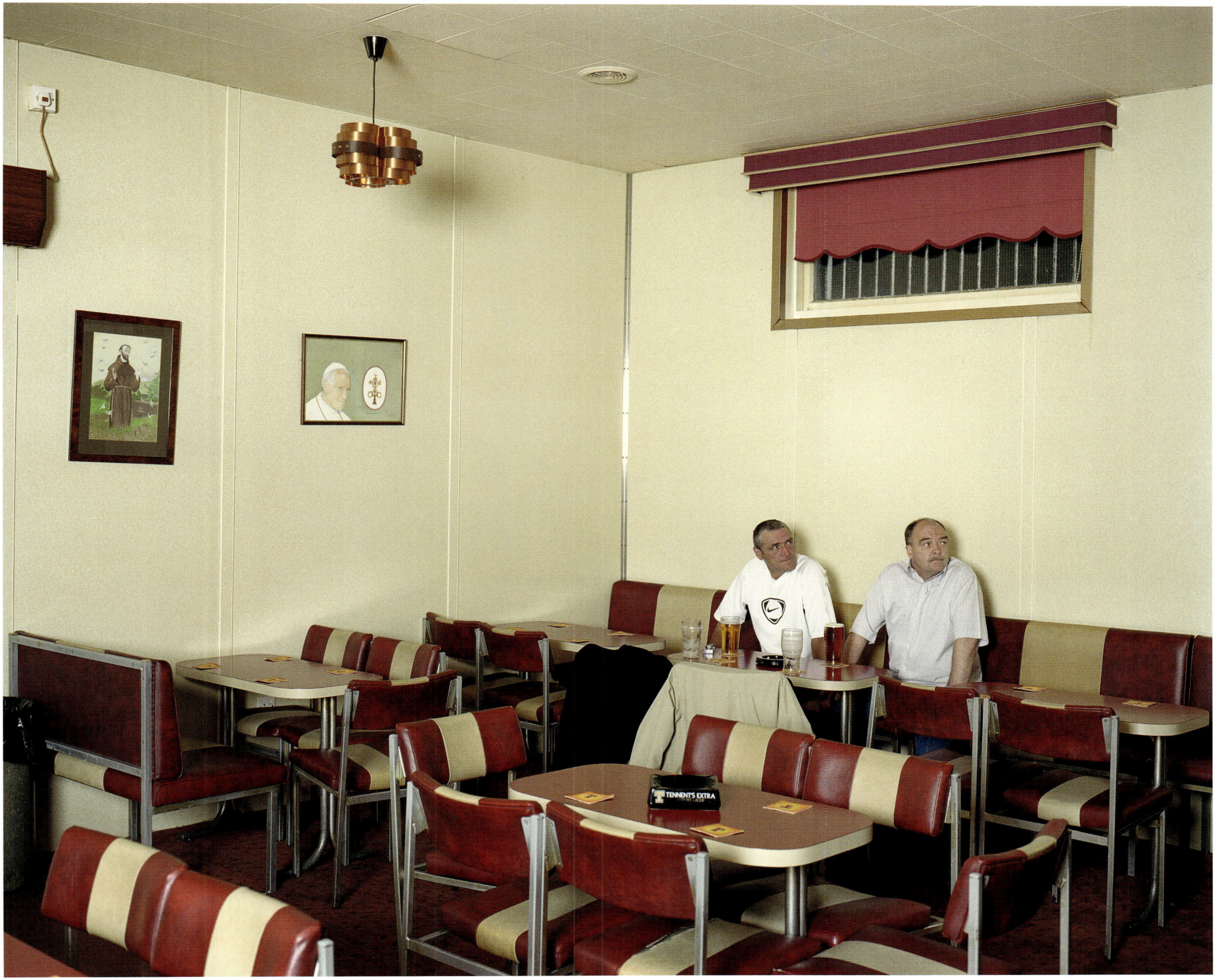
TENNENT'S EXTRA

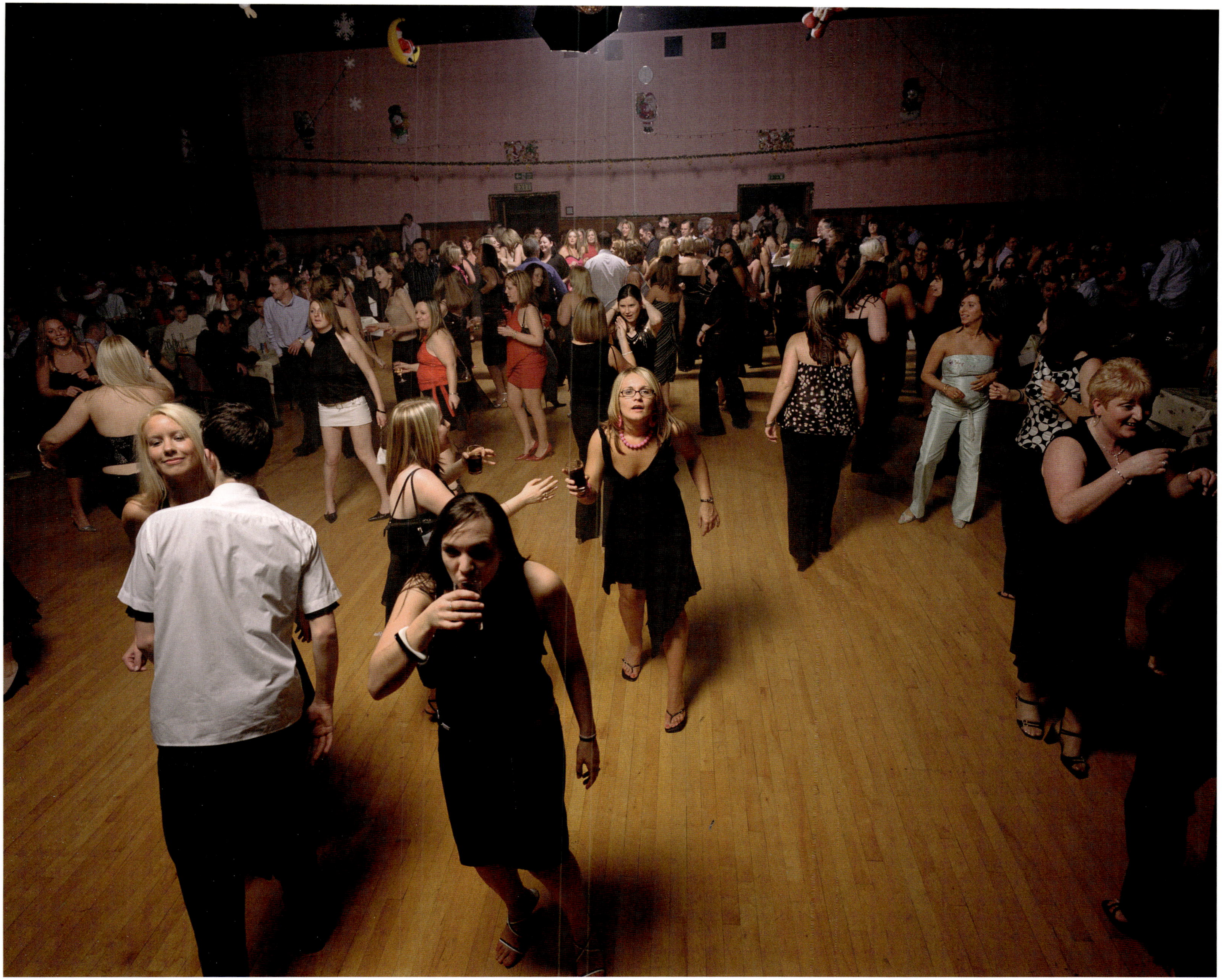

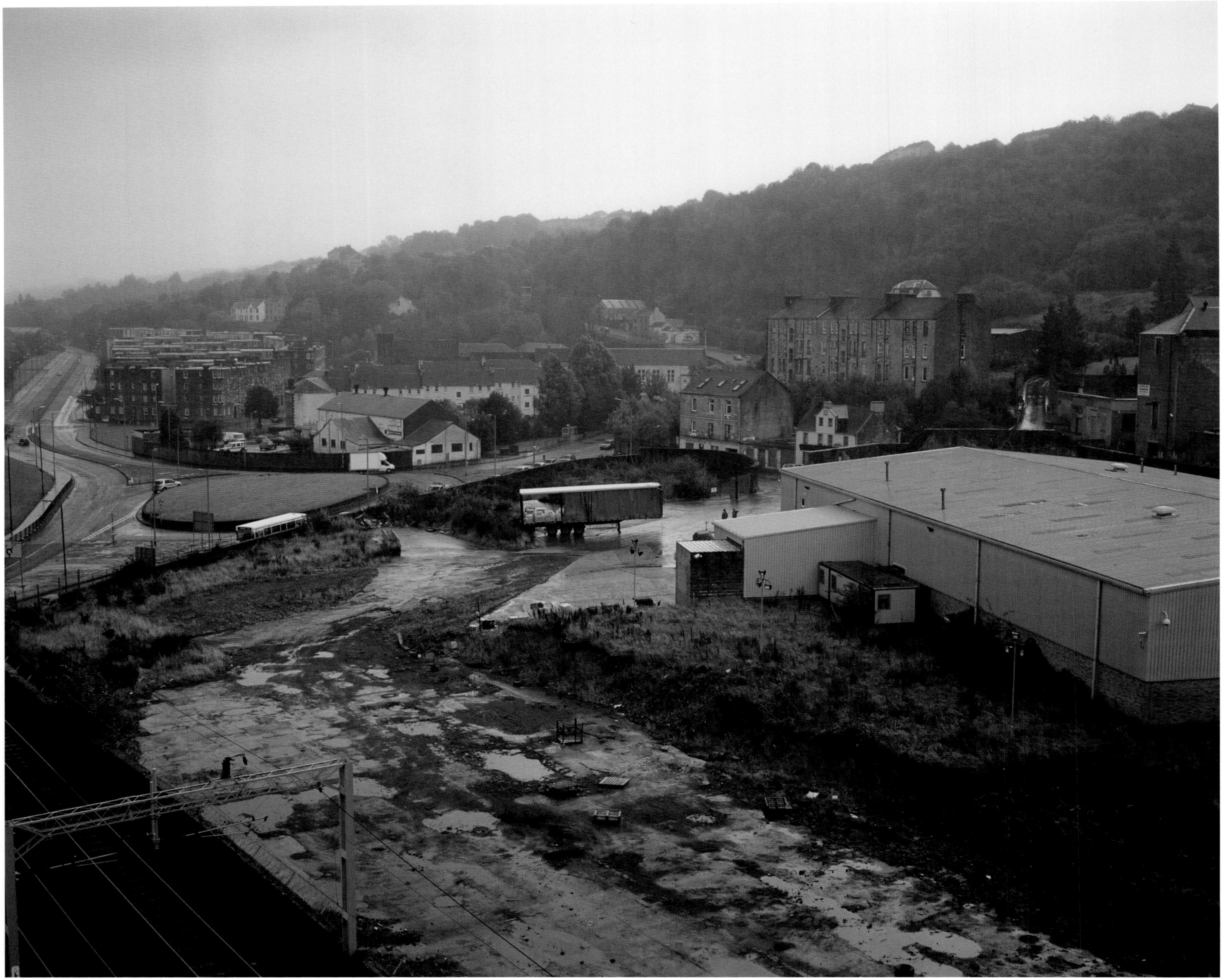

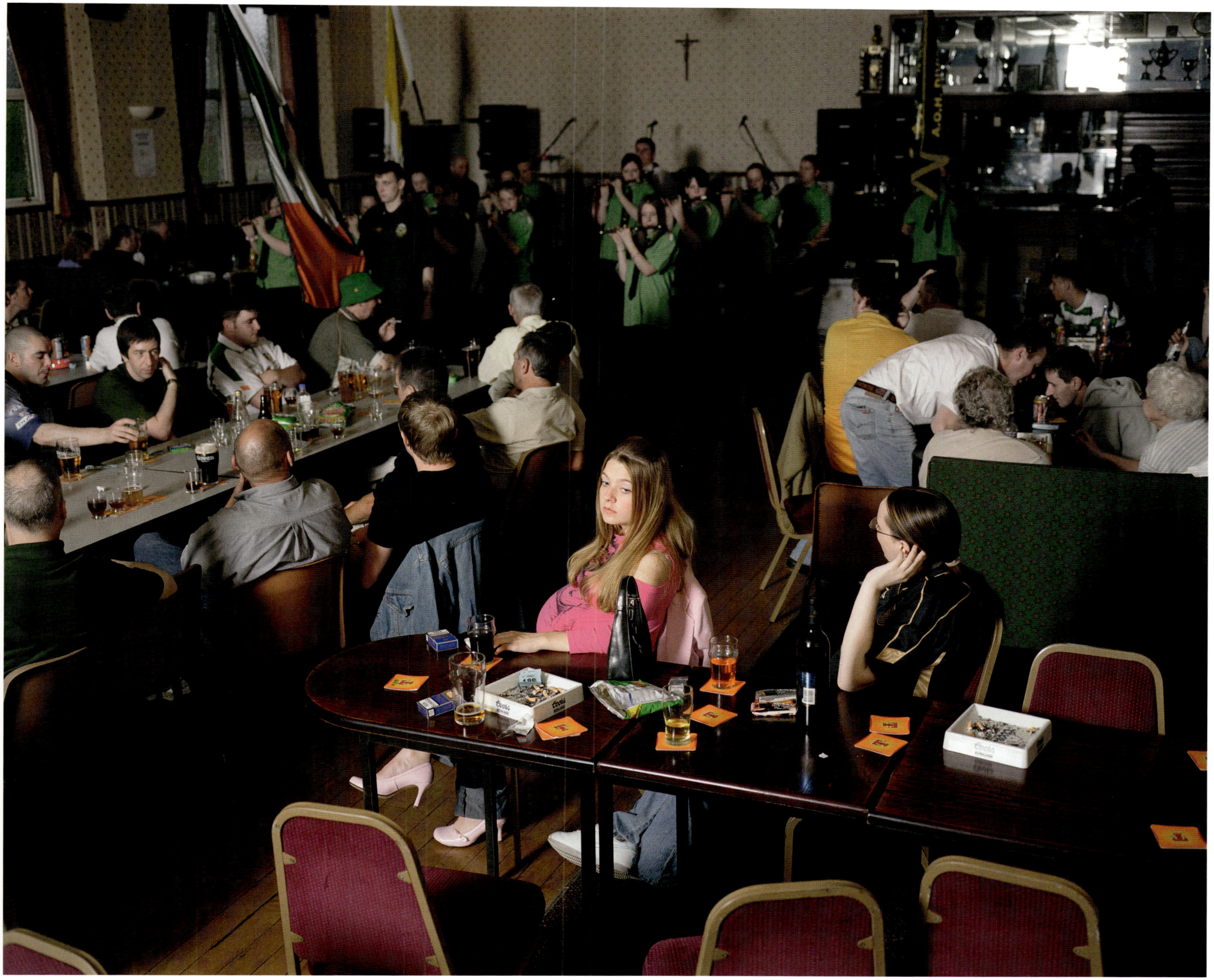

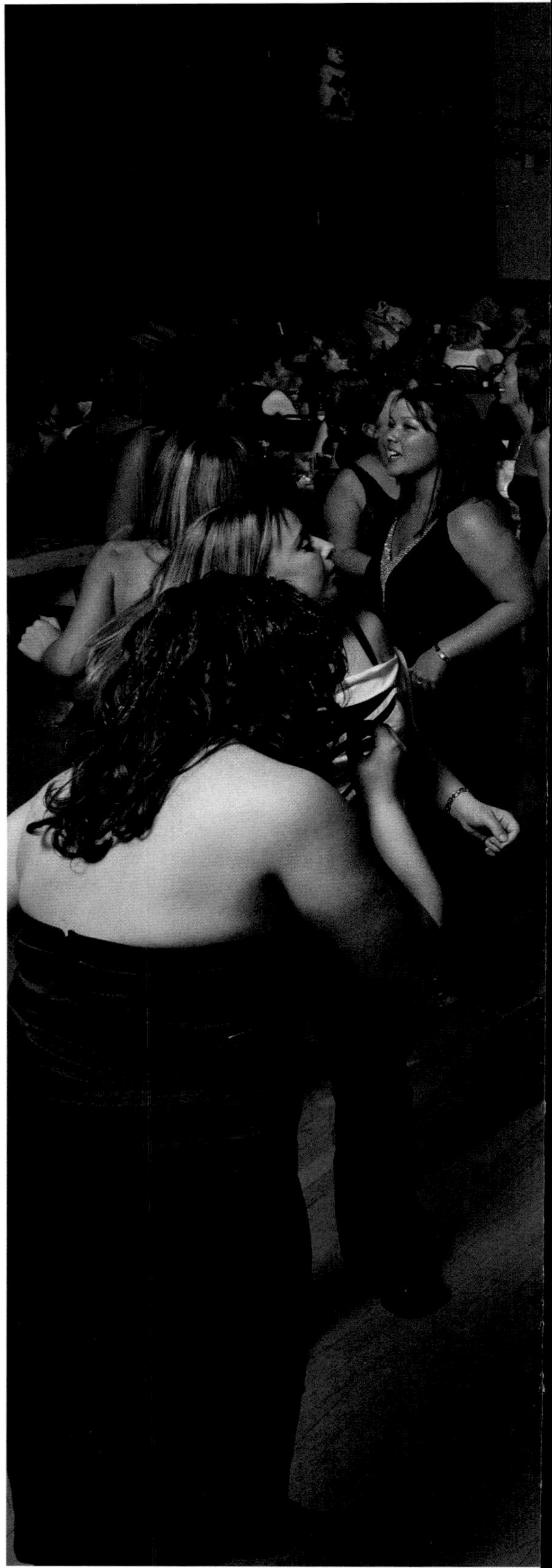

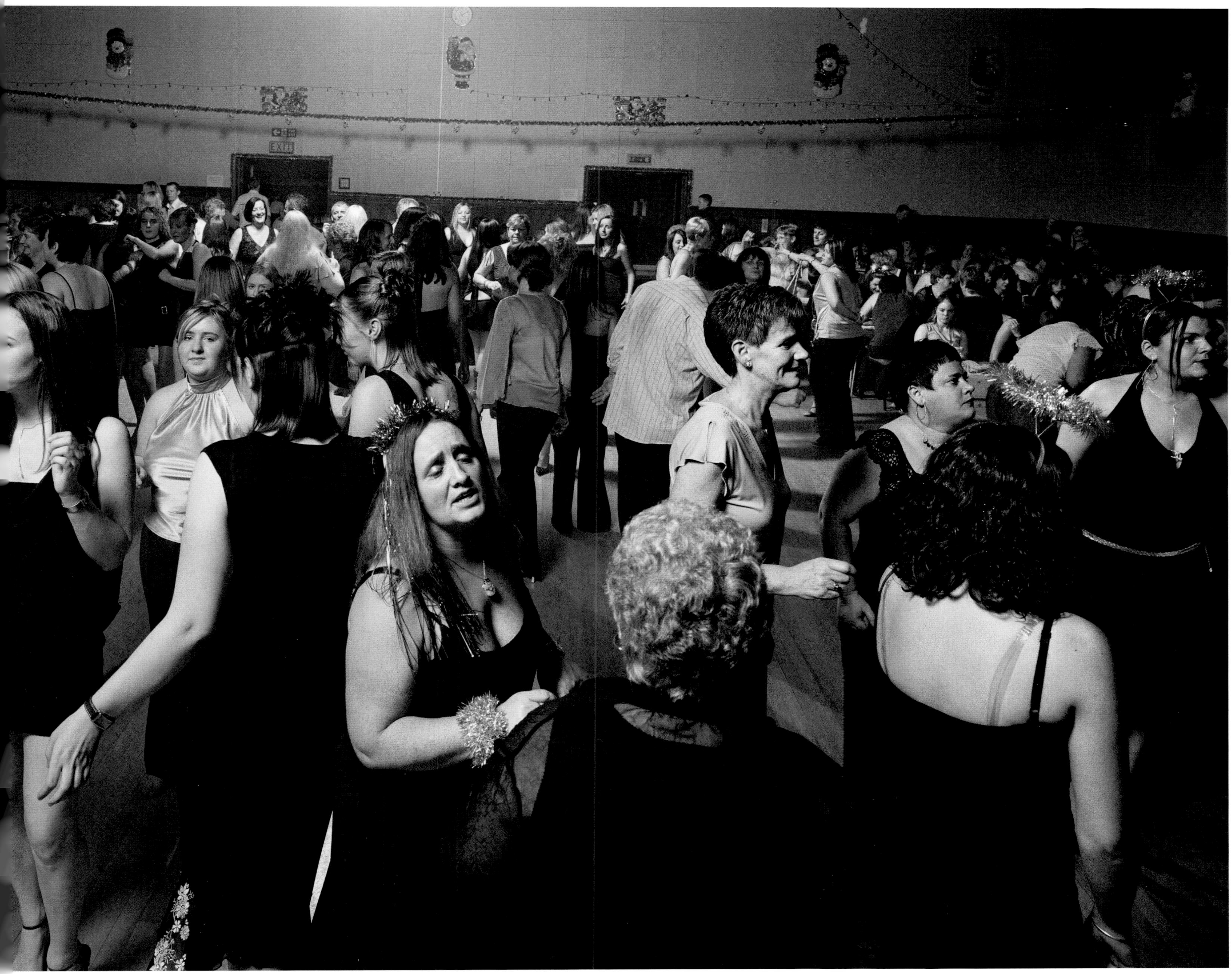
EXIT

Titles

5. The Star Hotel, John Wood Street, 2004
6. Shore Street Bus Shelter, 2004
7. Coronation Park, August, 2004
9. Greenock Sports Personality of the Year Award, 2004
10. Coronation Park, 2004
11. Donnachie's Cafe Bar, 2004
13. Betty at Port Glasgow Town Hall Xmas Party, 2004
15. Ferguson's Shipyard, 2004
17. Mark's New Flat, 2004
19. Boys at Devol, 2004
20. Port Glasgow Fire Station, 2004
21. St.Francis Social Centre, 2004
23. Christmas Party, 2004
24. View from the Ropeworks Building, 2004
25. Ancient Order of the Hibernian Social Club (Donna), 2004
27. Town Hall Christmas Party, 2004

Mark Neville

in Conversation

with David Campany

Difficult

Begginings

David Campany: Mark, this book covers your projects from the last twelve years (2004-2016). Could you say a little about what you were doing before this? How did you come to the very distinctive kinds of approach you now make? And what was the first encounter with photography that mattered to you?

Mark Neville: My grandfather was captain of a ship during the Second World War and he came back in 1945 after four years at sea. I got to know him in my early teens. He was an aggressive, formidable character…I now realise that he was almost certainly suffering from severe PTSD [Post-Traumatic Stress Disorder]. Very scary, and he was around in my youth quite a lot. But when he wasn't shouting at people he was taking pictures of them, with a waist-level box camera. Medium-format slide film, so he was actually quite a serious photographer. I've seen some of his photographs. They're not technically great but I think it was his way of accommodating himself to civilian life, re-adjusting in some way. It was his way of mediating and communicating because he wasn't able to do that in conventional ways. That had a lasting impression on me, I think, and now I can make the connection between what he was doing and what I do. That was definitely a formative experience.

I can see that. Much of your work involves you figuring out a relation to the world, how to negotiate it.

Absolutely. My work is intensely personal. Many artists strive to make a separation between their personal life and their work but I can't do that. It's not obviously autobiographical, but I am aware that every time I embark on one of my projects it involves me living with a community for quite a long time, becoming part of that community. It's a search, although I've only come to figure this out recently, for a sense of belonging, a family, and quite often one finds very strong family units within working-class communities. There's a desire to be accepted as one would be by a family, and a desire to mediate that relationship somehow, which is always a negotiation, a collaboration, as opposed to an objectification.

Did you go to art school?

I went to a lot of art schools. At Reading University I was in a department called Painting and Construction, doing wall-based relief work. In my year there were people like Mike Nelson who went on to have significant careers. It was a well-respected course. After that I did other things for a while, and then did an MA at Goldsmiths in Fine Art. It wasn't photography yet. I was making installations using light systems. Thomas Demand was in my year, and Michael Raedecker. This was in the early 1990s.

Some great art came out of that period but there was definitely a move away from social and political engagement of the kind that had been such a strong legacy of conceptual art and documentary practice in the UK.

Very much so. I did another MA at the Rijksakademie in Holland. There I began to feel that I wanted my work to be about something that was happening in the real world. I didn't know how to realise that desire but it was there.

Did that desire come from looking at works by others, or was it just a feeling about how you wanted to live your life?

It was to do with how I wanted to live my life, and feeling I wanted this connection between my art and my real life experiences. I'd had a lot of experience for someone in his early twenties. I'd also been a fashion model…

Really?

When I was at Reading I was completely broke. I had no parental support. A friend was modelling in London and suggested I do it. I was tall and skinny with curly hair and was told that look would do well in Milan, so I went to Milan. I was with an agency that took 30%, so better than the art world's 50%! But it was difficult. At first I was drawing on the street to survive. You know, pre-Raphaelite paintings in chalk on the sidewalk outside the Duomo. I was window cleaning too. Then I did get picked up for modelling work. So the same Milanese snobs who were walking by me on the sidewalk were now applauding me for walking up and down a catwalk for two minutes.

Those are stark experiences of your own body and the gazes of others.

Definitely. And those experiences are at the root of my own work now—how photography commodifies people. What came to interest me in my mature practice was finding ways in which I could interrupt or subvert that commodification of people and their bodies.

What else happened for you at the Rijksakademie?

I was always in the library, reading quite a lot and what struck me the most was the art of people like Bas Jan Ader, Yves Klein and other "heroic" male performance artists. All I was seeing of their performances were these grainy little reproductions in art history books. But even those images could evoke a whole series of dreams and impressions. They were still images of real, live actions. I wondered if I could make my own performances. So I shot with a very high-speed film camera that could slow down an action that took seconds in real life into something that lasted minutes, and the relation to stillness could be even more pronounced.

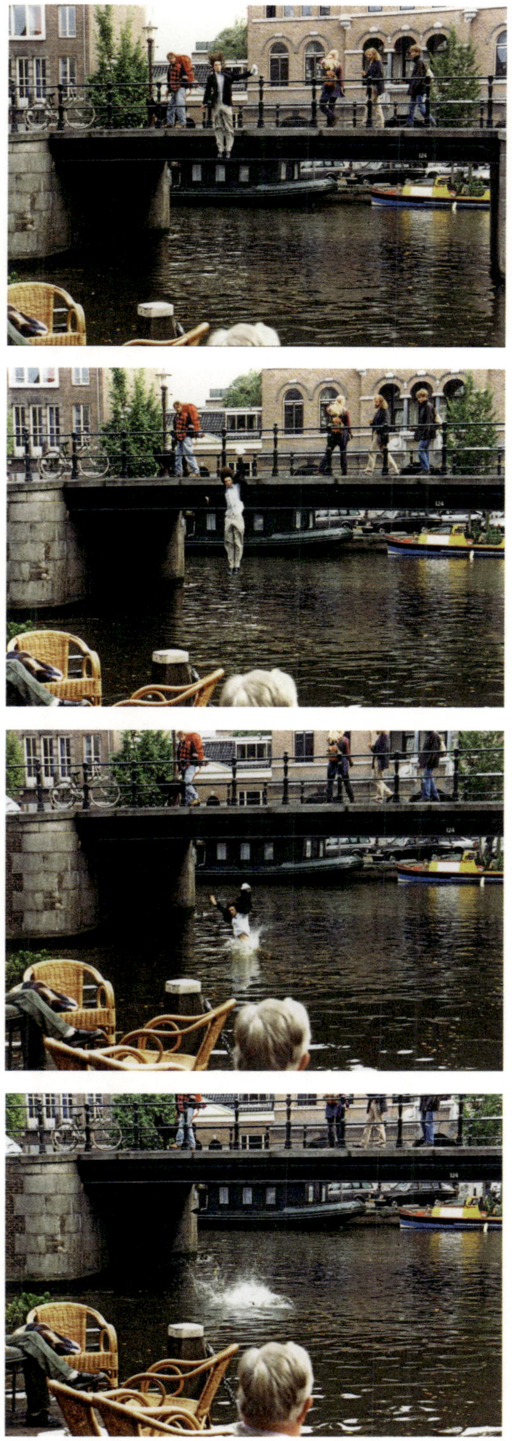

Production Stills from *The Jump Films*, 1994

For one of those films you jumped into a canal.

Yes, because Bas Jan Ader had cycled into a Dutch canal. In the photos the camera is quite a way from him, he is like a little figure plunging into a picture postcard view of Amsterdam. I made a few movies, the best of which is one of me jumping from a bridge. I am wearing a suit, it's shot from a distance, and in the film it takes five minutes for me to hit the water. Meanwhile, a big Amstel beer truck passes in the background, like a perverse advertisement synchronised with an abortive suicide attempt.

So you were already thinking about the body as a centre of meaning.

Yes. A productive line of enquiry was really opening up for me. And even today there's a very strong element of performance in what I do. I physically go into communities and, over time, I negotiate some kind of performance from the people I'm with.

You decided at a certain point that there was something in the documentary approach, although you have serious problems with the conventions and assumptions of mainstream documentary.

Although *The Jump Films* were eventually shown at Tate in a programme of artists' films, generally speaking I wasn't getting much of an audience, despite my best efforts. I carried on making work, in a very committed way, but I was not represented by a gallery and I was not showing much at all. Soon I began to ask for whom I was making the work. Who was I trying to communicate with? Who was my audience? While *The Jump Films* had a visceral visual quality, they were quite clearly for a knowing art world familiar with the references. I got very frustrated with that. Could I think about a different audience and maybe let that inform or direct the work? So my biggest "jump" was from thinking of the gallery or museum as the ultimate audience to thinking "isn't it more interesting to find out what other communities and audiences think about work that is for them, but also challenging for them?" I'd done enough art school theory, and I was as well-versed as anyone in the arguments about audiences, but none of those arguments could tell me how a community in, say, a working-class shipbuilding town might respond to photographs I made with them. I was really excited about what might be possible.

The

Port Glasgow

Book Project

I was 34 or 35 years old. I was living in Belgium but moved to Glasgow in 2001. I saw an advertisement in an art magazine inviting proposals for a "public art" project on the west coast of Scotland. It didn't specify anything more than that. It was a totally open call. I had discovered Port Glasgow, which is up the coast from Glasgow. I had always been an admirer of Stanley Spencer's war commission paintings of Port Glasgow. I loved the place immediately. It's a former shipbuilding town, full of character, visually stunning, with a great view out to sea. Only one shipyard remains. It was hanging on to its former glory. In the 1950s more ships were built in Port Glasgow than anywhere in the world. Now it's clinging to a post-industrial identity.

And what was your public art proposal?

Well, it had to be something that was available to the whole town. I remember being in a bookshop that had a large photography section, looking at expensive coffee-table books of social documentary photography. I would sit down and look through these things. It struck me immediately, and amazingly clearly, that these books were not aimed at the kinds of people who were in the pictures. That seemed wrong. They were images of poverty and hardship made for comfortable people. It made me feel awkward but I was fascinated looking at this material, packaged nicely in glossy, hardback books. I got very interested in how those kinds of images are disseminated. There was a real contradiction, a hierarchy, an exploitation. From my art school background I had been very interested in artists thinking about context, people like Hans Haacke who has made many works that addressed or critiqued something of the institutions in which they were presented. Could I extend that idea of "institutional critique" to social documentary photography and, indeed, books and book selling? So the idea was to produce a book about Port Glasgow that was directly for the people of Port Glasgow. I would be the photographer but I would give as much authorial control as I had to the community. I would ask them what I should photograph. I would ask them to collaborate. Even to help me make costumes. I would shoot in a mix of black-and-white and colour. And I would make the book only available to people who lived in the town. I would print eight thousand copies: one for each household. The book would never be commercially available. It would never be in the bookshops where I had realised what was so wrong with social documentary photography. These coffee table photo books always end up on the coffee tables of white, middle class people like

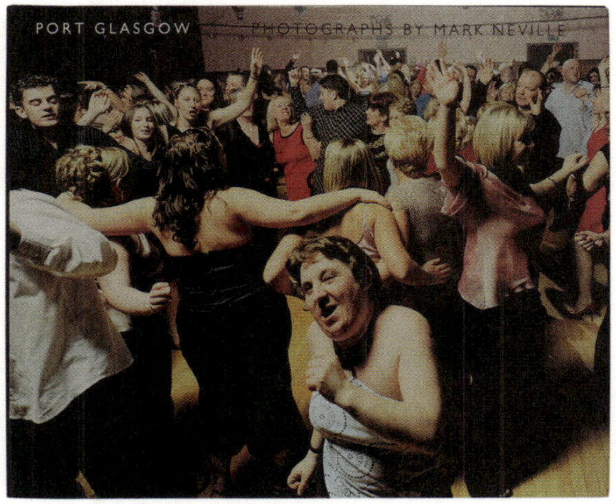

Cover of *Port Glasgow*, 2004

me and not on the coffee tables of those communities they represent.. I wanted to challenge that.

And your proposal was accepted. That was brave of the decision makers!

Yes, it was really brave.

What you ended up doing was very different from the familiar idea of "community photography" which, although it came out of that critique of the unhelpful power relations of much social documentary, is often very worthy but dull and unimaginative, despite the best intentions. There's a fine line between "community" and "committee" when it comes to art practice.

I didn't want to go down that route. The term "community artist" is often regarded as almost an insult, at least by the art world. I never saw it like that.

But you did see it as something that needed to be wildly imaginative, technically sophisticated and visually intelligent.

Well, community work often lacks proper funds, so things end up being less than they could be, put it that way. I knew my project needed to be well-funded.

What was the budget for *The Port Glasgow Book Project*?

The total was £106,000. Once I'd been told my concept was approved, I worked out the budget and it was accepted.

This was very unlike the conventional "public art" project…public sculpture, billboards, a mural, or performances. What you were proposing really hadn't been attempted before.

Yes, I thought of the book as a sort of symbolic gift. The people of the town might like it, or not like it, but it was a direct return of something to them. Unlike a bronze sculpture in the town centre, they had control over it; both in its creation, and as an object when it was complete.

This was the beginning of you really immersing yourself in a community for a long period of time something you now do with nearly all your projects.

I was ready to do that. I had already cut quite a lot of ties with the art world. I wasn't following it. I wasn't going to gallery openings. I was completely ready for a new approach. I had a budget and I could really try a new way of being, living, working and making images. I gave myself two years to focus just on this project. I got to know lots of people in the Port, developed new relationships. I found that if you show no fear, if you are honest and open about what you're doing, it's fine. But in a tight community, where everyone talks to everyone, if you upset someone, you upset everything.

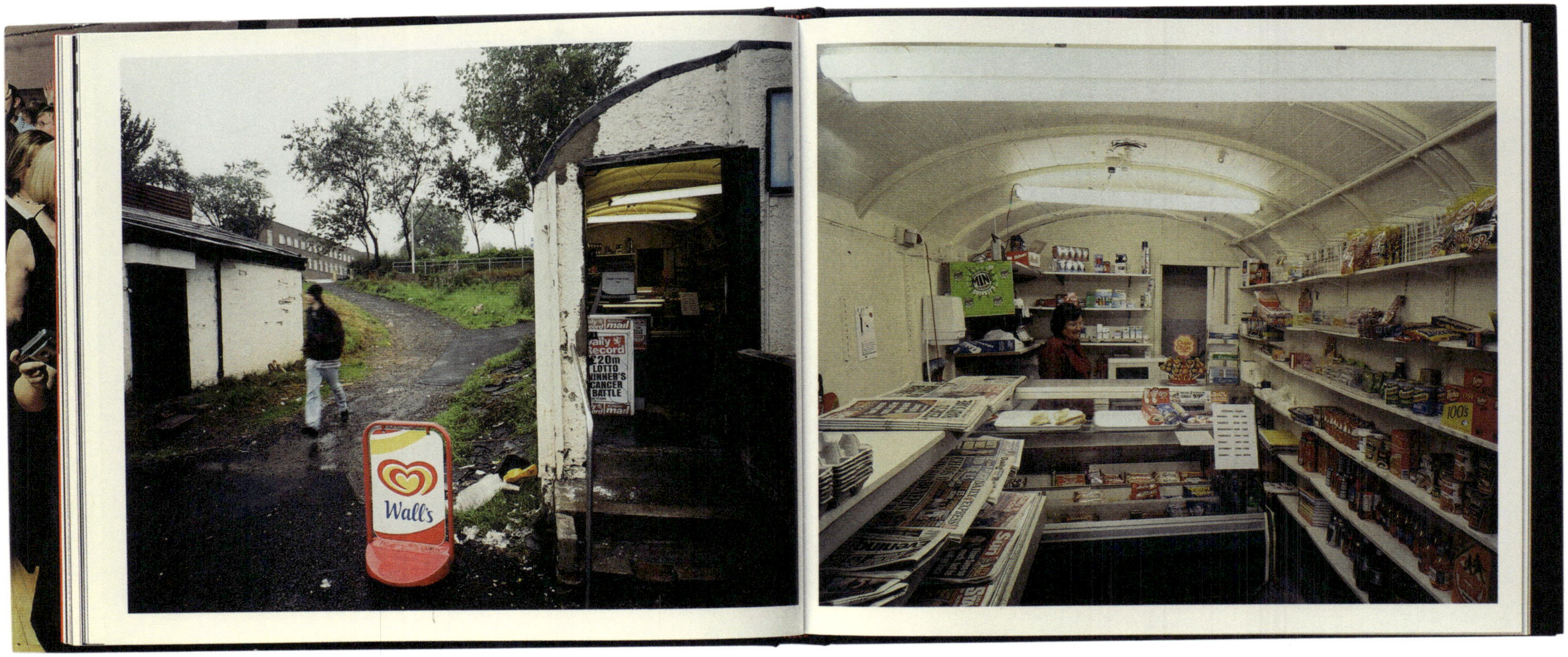

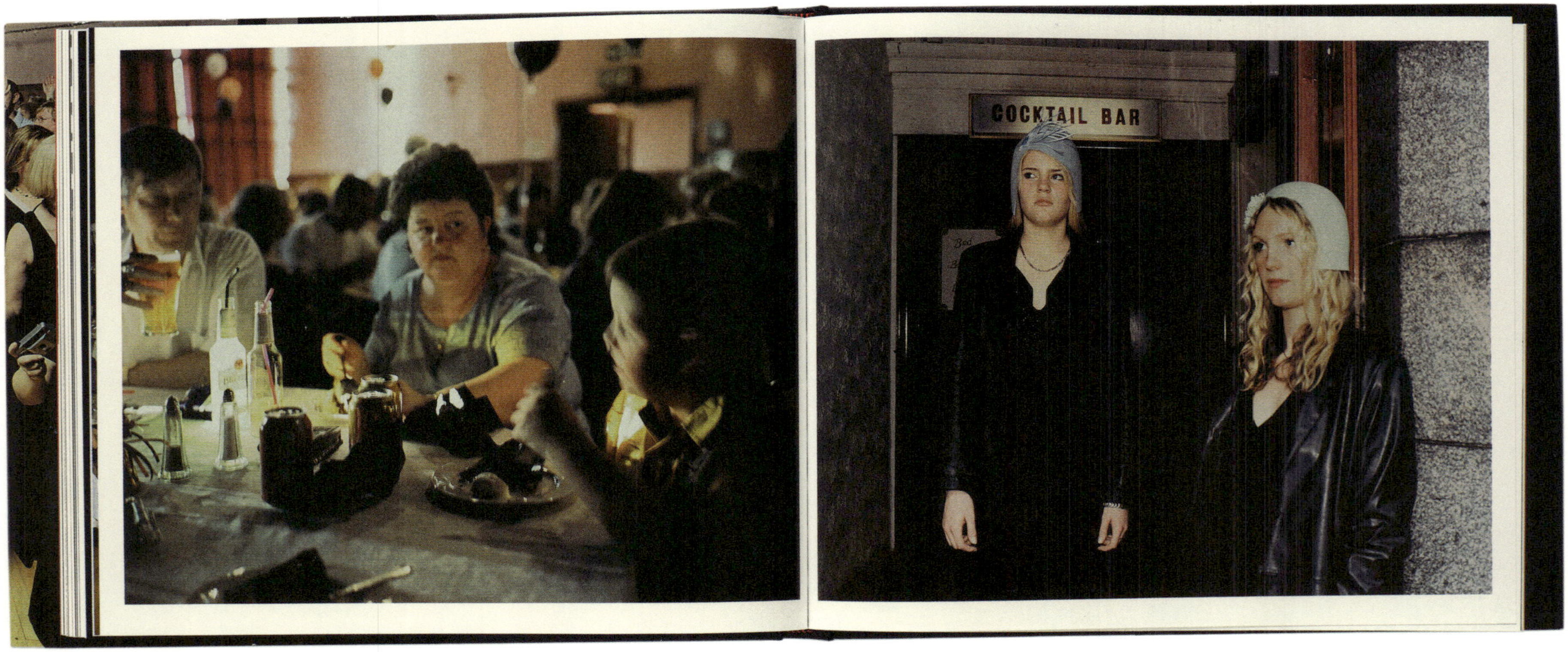

Spreads from *Port Glasgow*, 2004

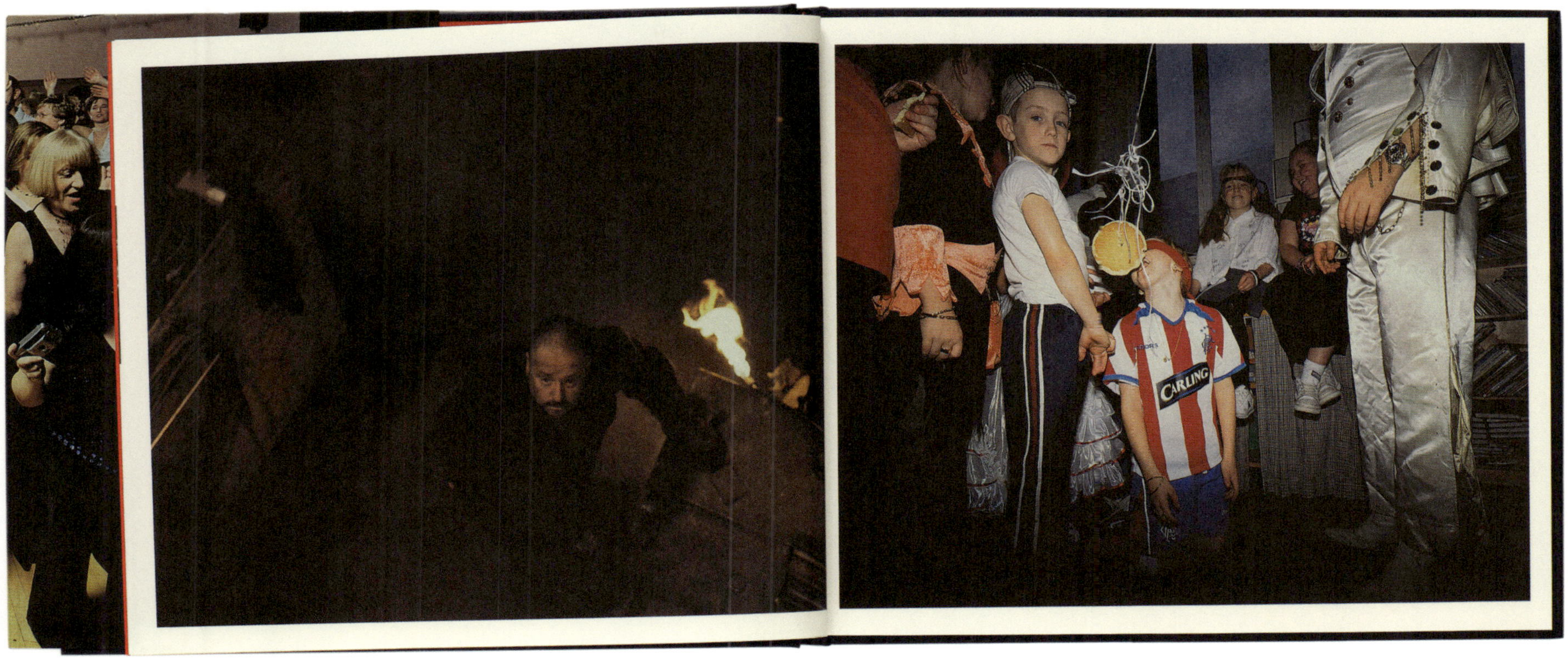

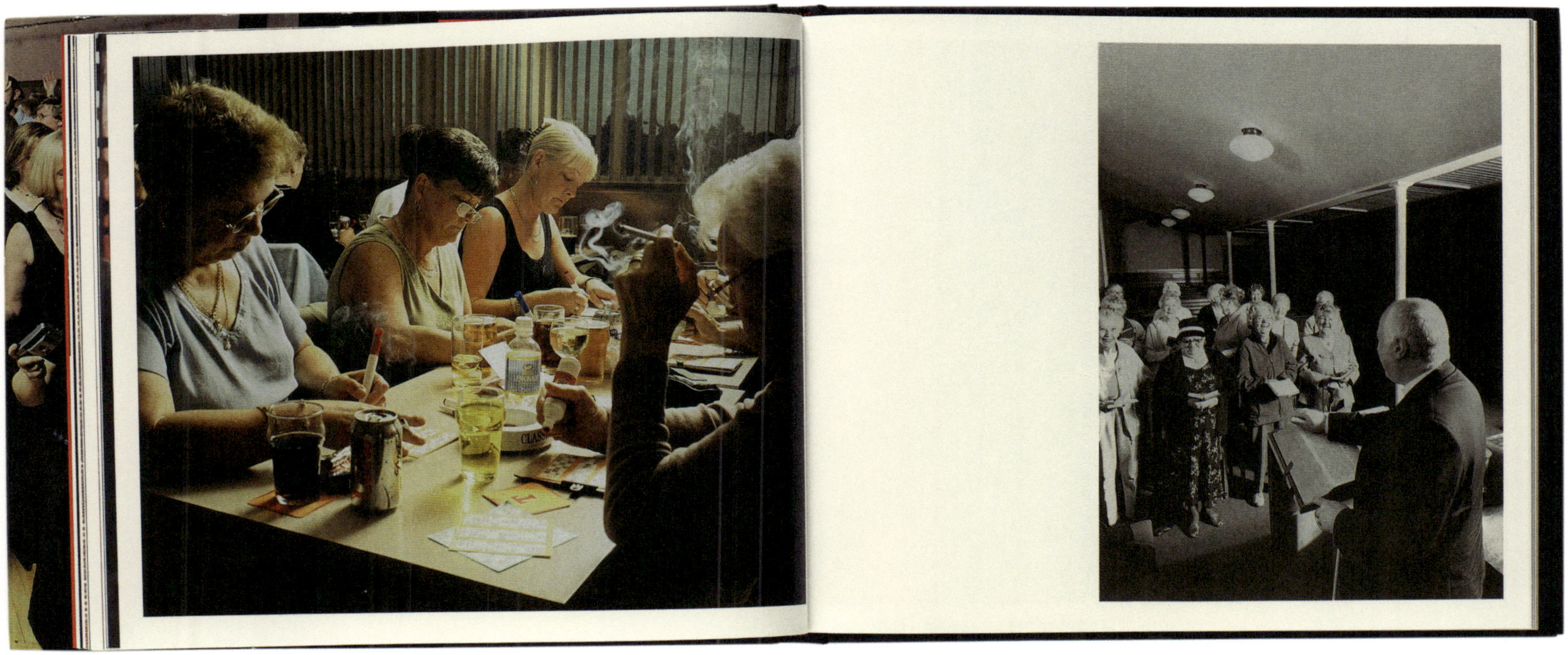

Spreads from *Port Glasgow*, 2004

Did people see the pictures as your project progressed?

Yes. I had small exhibitions throughout the two years. I paused every month or two to show what I was doing and have an exhibit in the window of the butcher's shop. And when I was ready to print the book I showed my whole edit and asked if anyone objected to anything. That was very important.

Your photography is enormously ambitious technically, pictorially. Some of your pictures fit with what we would recognise as social documentary but there are also staged moments, there is very elaborate lighting, the black-and-white / colour switch, you even use a sports photo-finish camera. Is all this an attempt to disturb the expectations around how certain subjects "should" be photographed?

Absolutely. Disturb the expectations, break the habits, disrupt the conventions.

But without losing the impulse to make richly descriptive photographs…

Right. I want people to be able to see the conventions but also to be able to relate to the photographs as documents of some kind. To do that you can't be complacent or lazy or unambitious. I had to attack on all sort of levels. So yes—different cameras, different kinds of collaboration, different kinds of lighting and composition. Sometimes I would be installing and testing complicated flash lighting for several days before shooting. I even found an old analogue chemical photo-finish camera—the kind used to photograph Olympic runners as they cross the finish line. I also found Raymond, a great technician who worked at a Glasgow sports hall and who used to operate the camera back in the 1970s. It's an amazing machine. A strip of 35mm film races past a fixed-slot lens so anything moving in front is clear, while the background just becomes horizontal streaks. The film passes straight into developing chemicals. You can see the results in a few minutes. We used it to photograph people as they came out of pubs. I remember someone thought it was a surveillance camera, and that I was a government benefits informer.

The results are fascinating and they still have the chemical stains and splodges on the negatives. Throughout the project you switch between naturalism and artifice.

Elsewhere in the project some of my pictures are unstaged observations—just me walking around snapping—while others are very staged and took a lot of planning. For example, I employed a fashion designer friend to make hats that looked historically indeterminate: a bit 1920s flapper girl but a bit futuristic. I went into a pub called the Star Hotel where Stanley Spencer had stayed, and I photographed some young women wearing them. I liked the idea that, in fifty years time, these pictures might look really confusing. The reader would think: "Gosh,

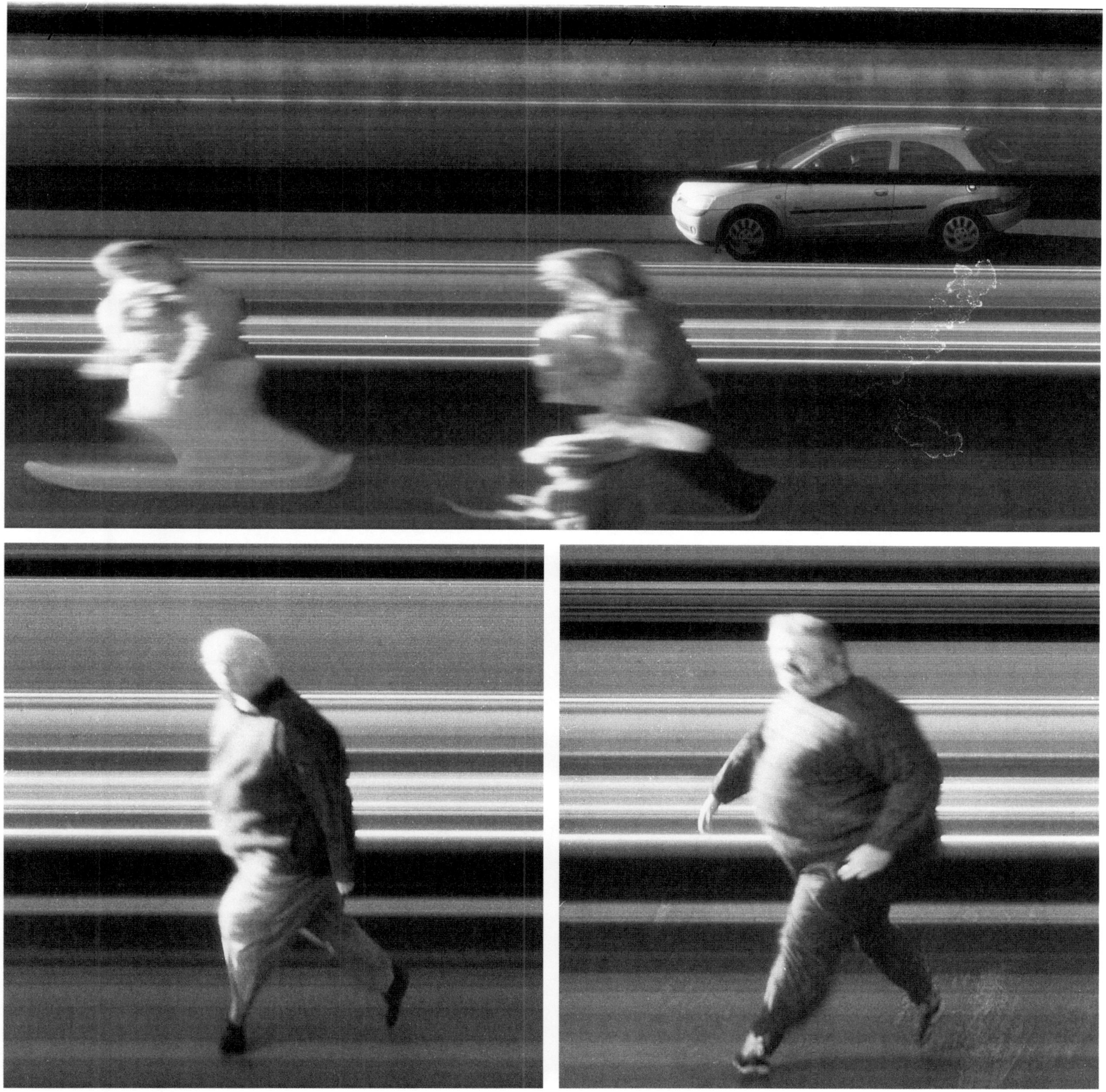

Customers exiting the Star Bar (taken
with a photofinish camera), 2004

GREENOCK TELEGRAPH, Friday, 7 January, 2005

Book cash aid for young footballers

By Lorraine Tinney

A CONTROVERSIAL book about Port Glasgow is helping to kick-start the careers of budding football stars.

More than 100 boys from cash-strapped Port Glasgow Boys' Club, will be able to take part in competitions down south after they earned thousands of pounds for delivering Mark Neville's hardback of photographs.

The book, titled Port Glasgow, featured images of the town and its people, received a mixed response when it came out late last year.

But the project, funded by the Scottish Arts Council, has been a lifeline for Port Glasgow Boys' Club, which raked in a wad of cash after its members delivered copies of the book to every house in the town.

Around 180 youngsters aged between nine and 19 in 11 separate teams are members of the club, which was set up 19 years ago.

Secretary John Watson said: "The club is very important to Port Glasgow because so many boys are involved. Raising money is a constant struggle. We rely on parents buying a lottery ticket. We also do a lot of fund-raising. It costs us £500 a week to run the club, including halls, referees and transport, and last year we couldn't afford to take the boys to the competition."

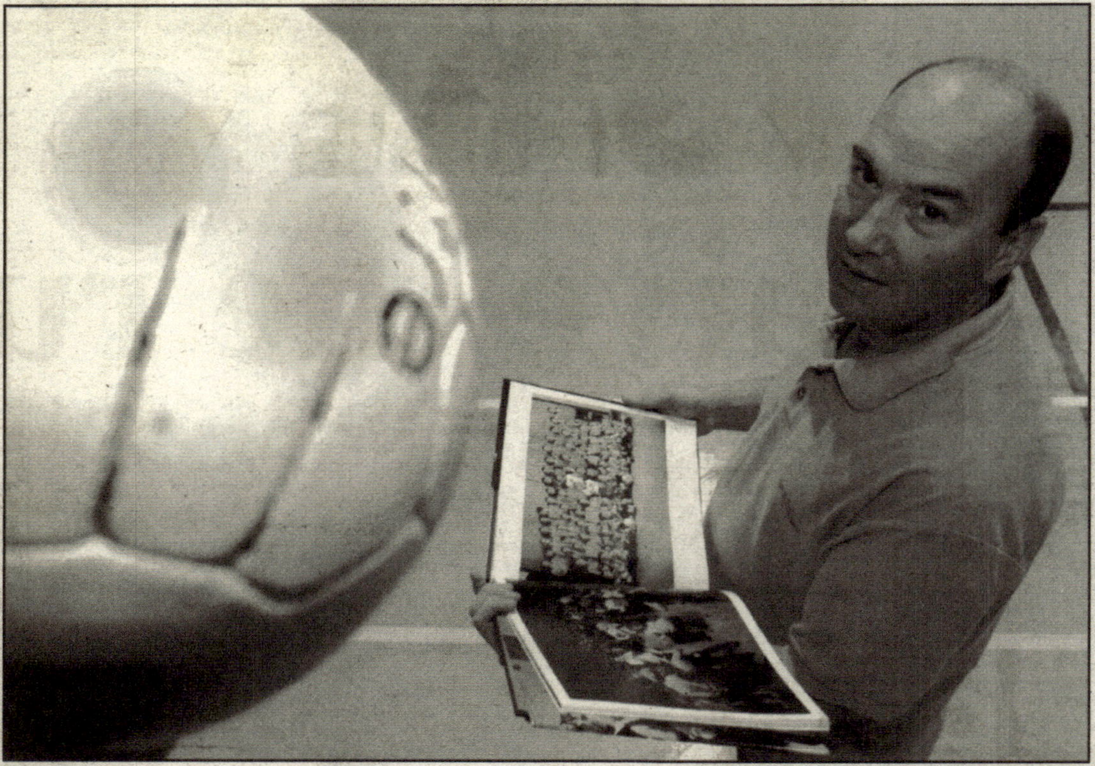

ON the ball: Secretary John Watson is happy the club will be able to take part in competitions. Picture: George Munro

The extra cash means the club can pay £50 towards the boys' trip to the Preston and Morecambe Easter Cup competition and another tournament for older players in Blackpool.

John added: "Some families have two or three boys in the club and couldn't afford to fork out £130.

"I've got mixed feelings about the book. The quality of photographs is excellent.

"When we were delivering them people were asking for extra copies to send abroad but I know some people have put them in the bin.

"It's been a lifeline for the club but we still have to raise funds to keep going."

If anyone would like to make a donation they should contact John on 715771.

The Greenock Telegraph,
7/1/2005

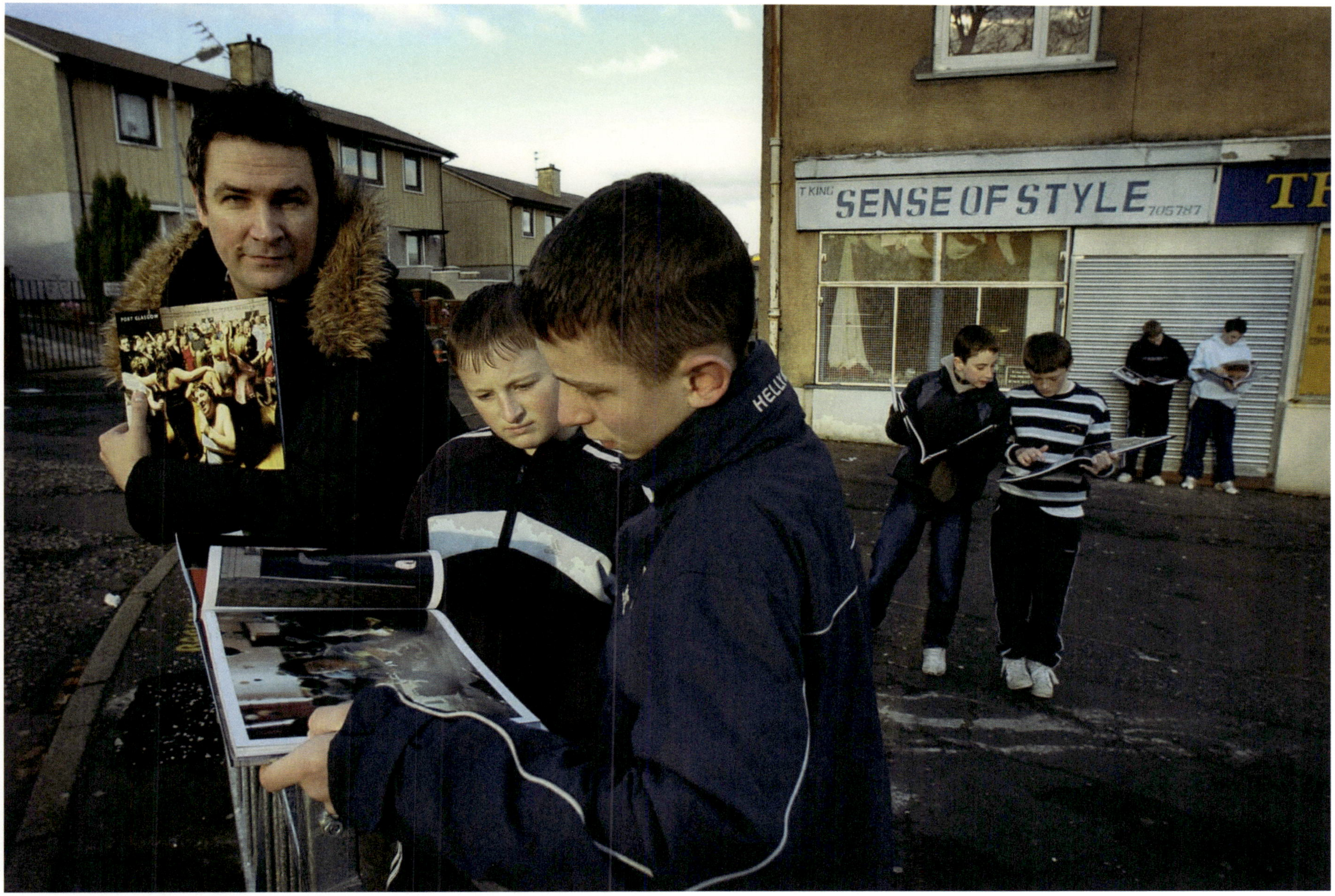

Port Glasgow Boys Football Team who delivered all eight thousand copies of the book to each home in the town, 2004

look at the hats they used to wear in Port Glasgow in 2004", and it would be a total lie. You can't trust a photographic image, at least, not in an immediate way.

How long did you shoot for this whole project?

Just over a year. I came up with an edit and a design, and got it printed. All eight thousand copies. After much bureaucratic struggle I got permission to allow the local boys football team to deliver the book. That way I could give *them*, instead of Royal Mail, the £14,000 that I had budgeted for postage. Whenever possible I wanted to feed back into the community, and this idea fitted beautifully, both ethically and conceptually.

How did it feel seeing the book in the hands of the people of Port Glasgow?

It was one of the best days of my life watching these swarms of kids chapping on doors of the council estates and handing over the books.

Were you nervous? Although you had been collaborating all along it was, in the end, a book with your name on it and you were taking responsibility for it.

I was exhausted by then. It had been a long, long process. The first people to see it were the staff at Port Glasgow Town Hall, where I stored the book (and where I had photographed people dancing). I was petrified. But actually they liked the book and were really pretty proud of it. And I think they were shocked at how high the production values were, and how substantial it was. I don't think they were quite expecting to see themselves historicised in a big, hardback book, and in such a respectful way. And all this was new experience for me. I didn't know what to expect.

I guess nobody did. It's not like any other project.

Right. But in a way that was what I had been seeking. Not everyone liked the book. The most extreme reaction I had was from the residents of Robert Street, who had a meeting and decided there were too many photographs taken in Catholic pubs and clubs and not enough taken in Protestant pubs and clubs. It's still a sectarian town in many ways. They decided to burn their copies of the book. I literally got a call from the fire station telling me a pile of my books was on fire. I looked at the book again: there were nine photos taken in Protestant pubs and clubs, and seven in Catholic pubs and clubs.

That slight imbalance hardly justifies a book burning.

Now I see it as an interesting thermometer of religious feeling and social tension. At the time I was just upset.

I wonder if that's really the truth of their motivation. It sounds more like a displaced response to actually being given something unusual

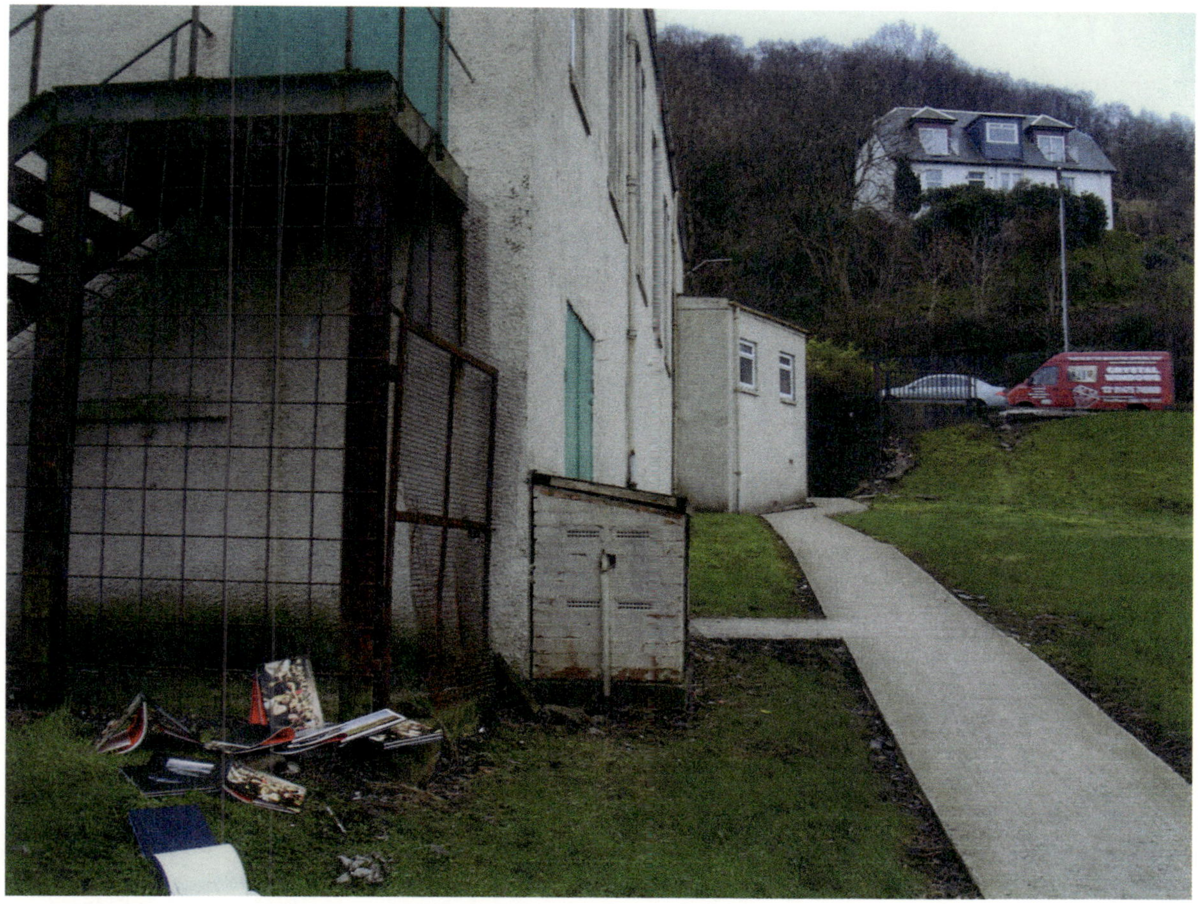

Copies of *Port Glasgow* dumped at the back of the Hibs Club, 2004

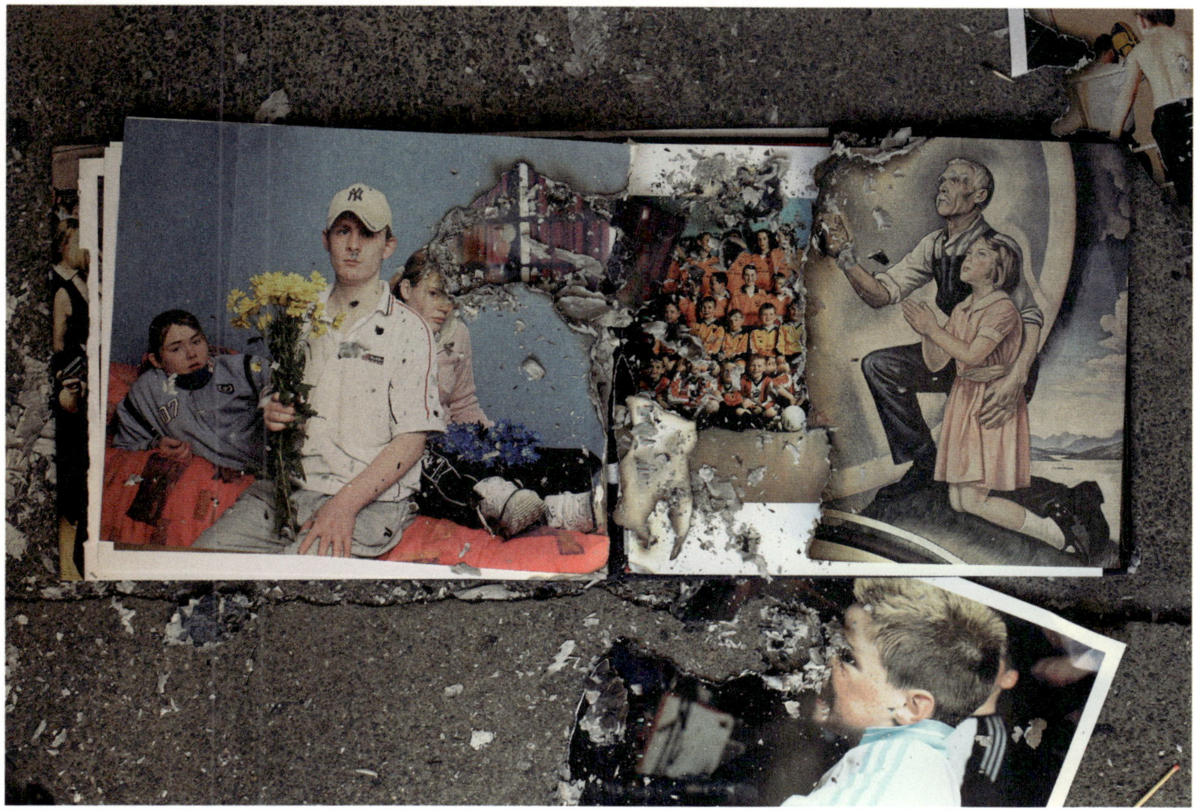

Copies of *Port Glasgow* burnt at the back of the Hibs Club, 2004

and maybe a bit confusing. Counting up the number of Protestants and Catholics seems a very mundane way of responding to such a complex book. The arrival of a book, even if it's a gift, is a little disorientating, no?

I think that is probably a part of it. Nevertheless, perceived sectarian bias was enforced through questionnaire forms and emails that I got back from people, so it certainly turned into a real objection. One person even called the book "pro-IRA". Some people objected that £106,000 was a lot of money when local services are being cut back. But in reality there was no way that money set aside for an arts project was ever going to be used for something else. A more common reaction was "What's the catch? Are you really giving this book to us for nothing?" More generally though, the response was positive and very open. People made the effort to articulate how they felt and what they liked about the book. They were pleased something of such quality had been made about their town.

That was a very intense project. And I imagine, while you learned a lot, the conclusions you could draw were complicated. That said, it's clear you felt that this immersive way of working and then giving back had great potential, and that the visual approaches you had begun there could be developed further.

Yes, but in a way the project was so specific to that community that I didn't have much to show for it afterwards. It had been made and consumed entirely in Port Glasgow and now it was over. I did keep back a few copies of the book. I sent it to a handful of art world people and sent one to you, as I liked your writing and thought you would understand what I was doing, although I didn't know you at the time.

I remember you sent the book with a note saying: "Dear David Campany, this book is not for you." It was a strange feeling looking at it because, as you say, it was a closed project. It wasn't "for me" or anyone else outside of the town, at least not in the primary sense.

But, paradoxically, it was precisely because the project was so closed that the art world got interested in it! The perversity of human nature. Museums and galleries wanted to make the work the subject of exhibitions. Also the book began to get a wider reputation and copies starting selling on eBay, sometimes for up to £500. So if you hadn't burned your copy you could sell it. The book cost £12 per copy to make, so that is quite an increase!

The art world interest is significant because, of course, within that world there has been a renewal of interest in experimental documentary work. Maybe we can come back to this point a little later.

Well, I've tried to continue with the attitude that the art world is only ever a secondary audience, even though secondary audiences are important.

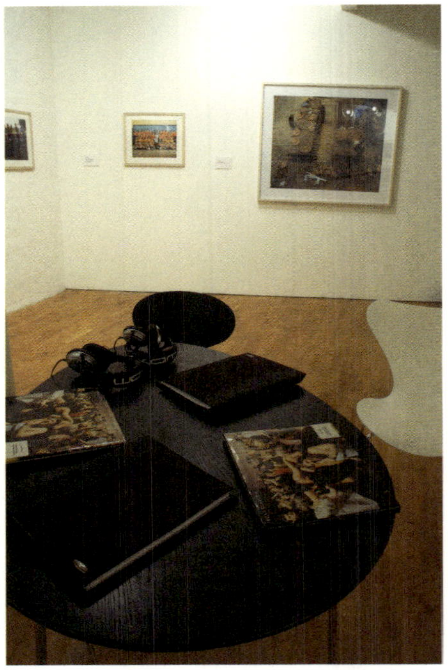

The Port Glasgow Book Project installed at Modern Art Oxford, 2006

From : rudi talacchia <rudirooster@hotmail.com>
Sent : 28 November 2004 13:48:53
To : markinportglasgow@hotmail.com
Subject : Port Glasgow

Hi Mark

Just to say thanks for brightening up my day when i received a free copy of your book titled Port Glasgow, it arrived on a Sunday morning by a young boy who i was about to chase away for walking on my garden when he said " its a free book big man, aboot tha port " i looked at him thinking wheres his wee mates probably eyeing up the back garden to see if there s anything worth stealing ..but as it turns out there was no hiddencatches, nothing went missing from the garden and i spent about an hour looking through your book, touching stuff as many of the photos i can relate to obviously coming from the area, and i suppose they mean something to us. avery nice gesture by yourself to ourselves, not sure what your trying to gain from this or what the reason behind it is but i wish you luck in acheiving it.

thanks again

Rudi

The first e-mail response to *Port Glasgow* from a Portonian, 2004

If this Book was intended to discredit P.G then it is a MASTERPIECE.

an ambitious artwork by mark neville
year in the port book project
only taking place in port glasgow

Thank you for spending a few minutes giving some comments on the Port Glasgow Book
PLEASE complete this form and hand it in to the Port Glasgow Town Hall

How and when did you first learn about the Book Project? LEAFLET THROUGH door.

What were your expectations of the Book Project? Very HigC.

How well do you feel that these expectations were met? DEPLORABLE

Please rank the following statement on a scale of 1 - 5
1 = strongly agree **2** = agree **3** = neither agree not disagree **4** = disagree **5** = strongly disagree

The Book Project made me think about the positive things Art can contribute	5
There is a sense of Community Ownership towards the Book Project NO DIVISIVE	5
The Book Project reinforces local peoples Confidence in the community NO	5
The idea to have the books delivered by the Boys Football Club was a positive contribution to the community YES	1
The Book Project reduces Isolation for some people in the Port 5	NO
The Book Project provides a platform for debating the changes to the Port and the Local Community 5 HEAVEN HELP US, IF THESE ARE "CHANGES"	[illegible].

Overall, do you like the book? Please mark in box

I think it's very good	
I think it's good	
I like only a few parts of the book	
I find it unsatisfactory	X.

Comment
1. The use of PRO-IRA (IRISH REPUBLICAN) PHOTOS is deplorable.
2. Photographing Hooligans is regrettable.
3. Not enough focus on Streets, Blds, Parks and the good things in P.G.
4. Overall gives out impression that P.G. is a Town of Drunks, Hooligans, & IRA sympathisers

Scottish Arts Council
PROJECT PART-FINANCED BY THE EUROPEAN UNION
URBAN II

Completed questionnaire returned to Port Glasgow Town Hall, 2004

PRIDE IN PORT GLASGOW . . . PRIDE IN PORT GLASGOW

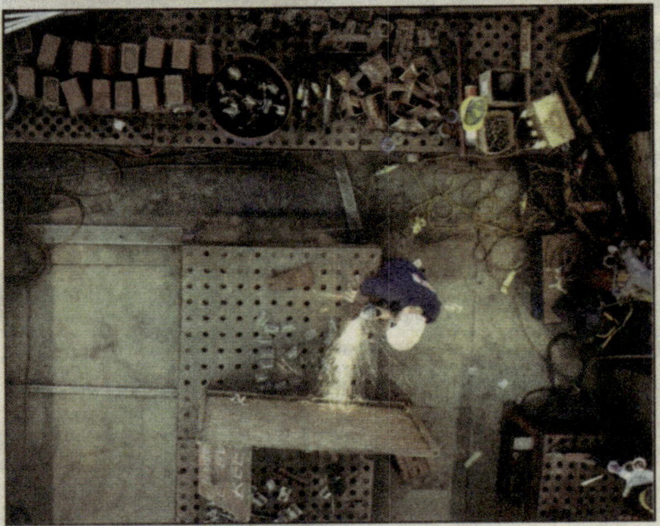

A WELDER at Ferguson's shipyard.

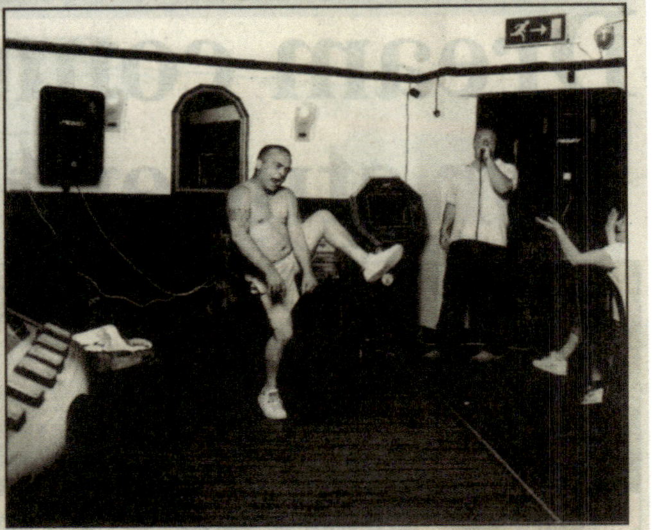

DANCING at Donnachie's Bar.

Job for the boys

PORT Glasgow Boys' football club are helping deliver Mark's book to 8,000 homes across the Port.

Over 120 boys aged five to 19 are in the club, and the older ones will be involved in delivering the books.

The club is being paid for their work, and all the money will go towards a trip to a football tournament in England next spring.

The club is organised by brothers Tom and John Watson. Tom said: "We were happy to get involved because the money raised will mean a trip away for our boys. For some of them it will be their first ever trip away from home, and a great experience."

The books will be delivered over five days from Sunday.

Photo finish

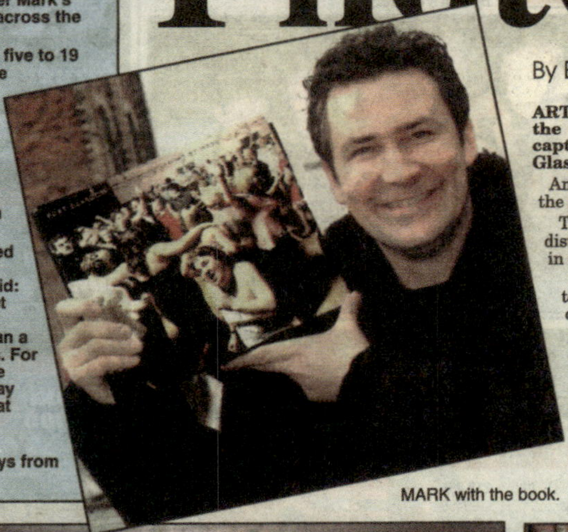

MARK with the book.

By Ewan Fergus

ARTIST Mark Neville has reached the end of his year-long project to capture the spirit and people of Port Glasgow in photographs.

And he is marking the occasion with the publication of a book of his work.

The book, called Port Glasgow, will be distributed free to all 8,000 households in the Port this week.

Mark (38) said: "Getting the book out to everybody will be the culmination of it all, and the best way of saying thank you to the people of Port Glasgow who have all been really brilliant throughout the project.

"Everybody was so friendly. I came to the town not knowing anyone and as an Englishman I thought there might be a few cultural barriers to get over.

"But I just explained to people what I was doing, and was simply overwhelmed at how friendly and supportive everybody was."

Mark won a competition organised by Inverclyde Council and the European regeneration project Urban II to choose an artist to brighten up parts of the town with art.

He took hundreds of pictures and used special slow-motion cameras to capture the lunching of the Minna at Ferguson's shipyard.

He photographed everything from church services to children's parties.

And he said he took real satisfaction from knowing everybody in the town would be getting a copy of the book.

He said: "It's a historical document now, which everybody will have for their children and the future. The project was about capturing that special sense of strong community in Port Glasgow and I think we achieved that."

And he added: "But Portonians will, I'm sure, be very quick to let me know what they think."

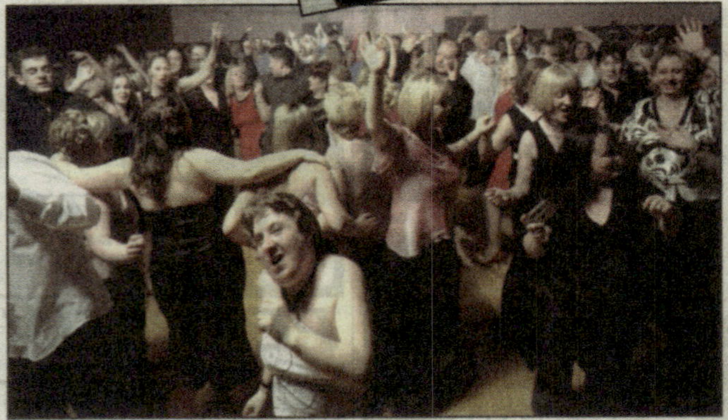

CHRISTMAS celebrations at Port Glasgow Town Hall.

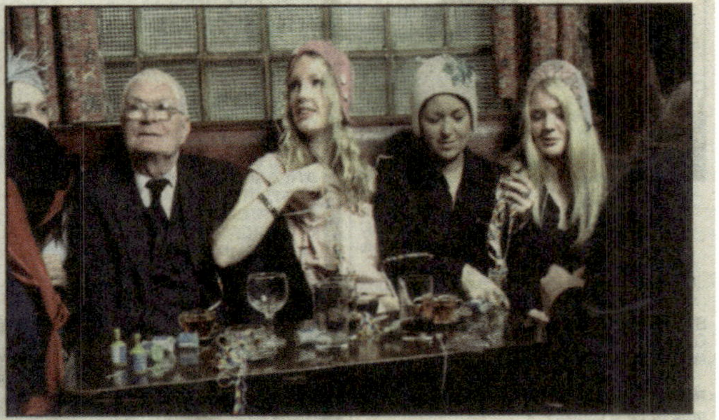

ENJOYING a drink at the Star Hotel.

The Greenock Telegraph,
26/11/2004

The Greenock Telegraph,
30/11/2004

GREENOCK TELEGRAPH, Tuesday, 30 November, 2004

New picture book gets town talking

Photos cause sensation as work hits the streets

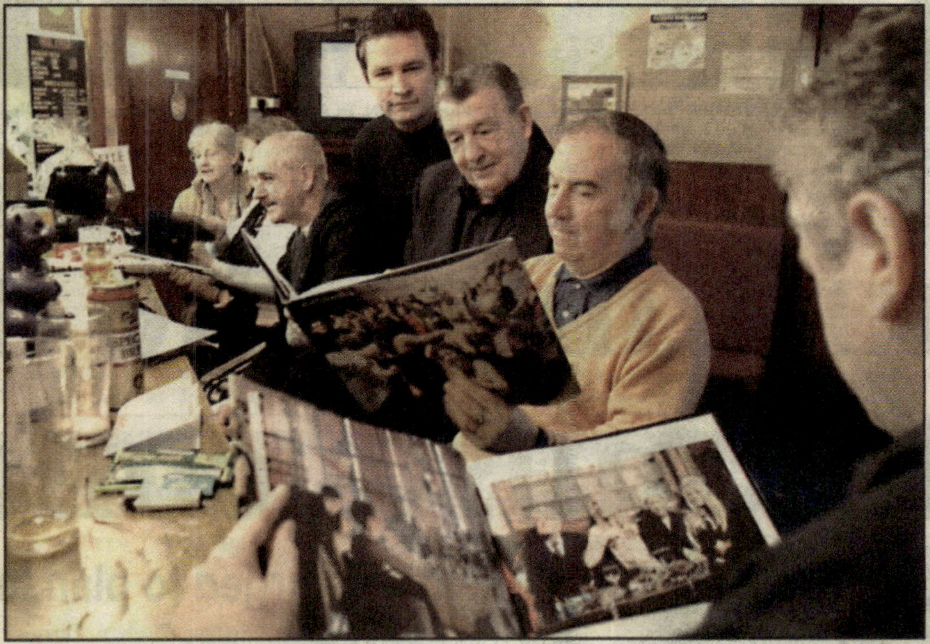

ALEX Lynn, front, and Robert McLaughlin get their first look at work from Mark Neville. Picture: George Munro

A NEW book portraying life in Port Glasgow through a lense is causing a sensation.

Artist Mark Neville put together his photographic impressions of the town during a year-long project.

His images are realistic and depict people in the town living their lives.

At a launch yesterday locals were given their first glimpse of 'Port Glasgow'.

The *Telegraph* caught up with residents to get their impressions.

Port Glasgow gran Betty McVey (64), Court Road. said: "It wasn't what I expected but I still like it. The book portrays Port Glasgow as it is now. People can identify with it and they'll know people in it.

"It is putting Port Glasgow, without the shipyards, on the map. It shows how life has moved on."

One of the most striking selection of photographs is of last year's Christmas party.

Robert McLaughlin (66), of West Barmoss Avenue, said: "It definitely shows we like a good party. It shows Port Glasgow like it is. I did think there would a picture of the castle in the book though.

Friend Alex Lynn (66), of Fyfe Park Terrace said: "It is brilliant, the presentation is lovely. I like everything about it."

The £106,000 art project was funded by both the Scottish Arts Council and the Lottery.

As part of the project youngsters from the local boys' club will be busy delivering a copy to every household.

Inverclyde Council's tourism and events organiser Helen Drummond, responsible for co-ordinating the project, believes it will be a real talking point.

She said: "It is a very high quality book and will cause a lot of discussion. It is the work of an artist. People who were looking for a promotional book may be quite surprised."

At the event in the Star Hotel artist Mark Neville thanked the people of Port Glasgow for their hospitality throughout his year-long residence.

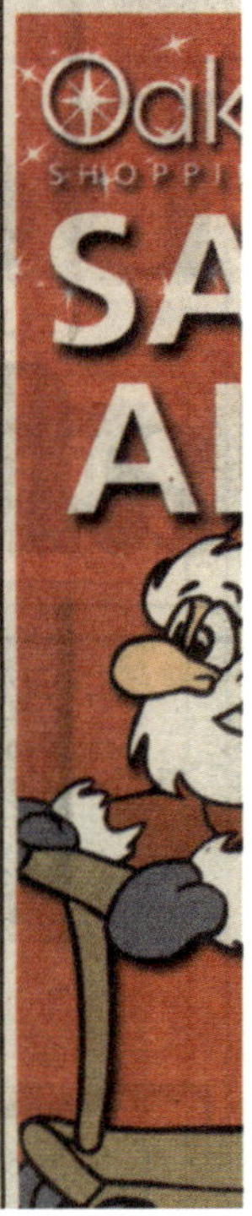

'He has exploited the people of Port Glasgow'

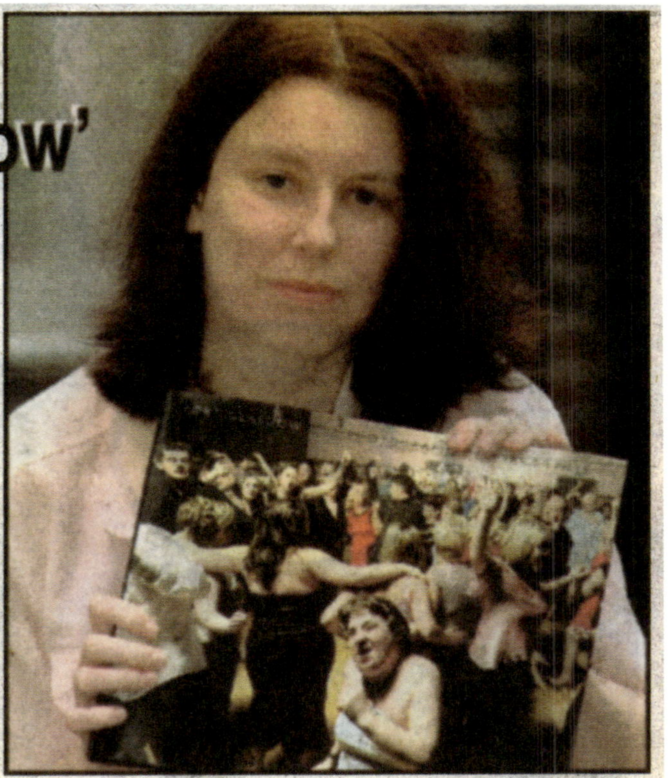

NURSERY teacher Claire Scott has hit out at the book "as a negative portrayal of Port Glasgow people and their town".

The mum-of-two was born and bred in the Port, but said she didn't recognise her home town in the glossy hardback.

"He has exploited the people of Port Glasgow and he is calling it art to get away with it. I don't recognise my town in that book and I have lived here all my life.

"It's a stereotype of what people expect it to be like. It would have been a braver thing to do to fight against the old image of "the dirty wee Port."

Claire (36), who works at Kelly Street Children's Centre, was incensed when she saw a group of teenagers making a rude sign titled Devol. She said: "It doesn't say much for a diverse housing scheme where a lot of decent people live.

"It's what's missing from the book — if you want to see Port Glasgow life you photograph the Comet Festival, or the Civic Art Exhibition, or a wedding coming out of St Andrew's Church, or people shopping. It is a missed opportunity."

"Port Glasgow is a vibrant community full of life and beauty. I choose to live here, I love the people, the humour and the way everybody knows each other."

She added: "This is an outsider looking in with a prejudiced view before he started. We are a real community, real people with feelings — we have to live here when his lens is gone."

The Greenock Telegraph,
1/12/2004

GREENOCK TELEGRAPH, Wednesday, 1 December, 2004

ARTIST Mark Neville spent a year photographing Port Glasgow and its people. All 8,000 households in the town have now been given a free copy of the book. It is a £106,000 project funded by the Scottish Arts Council and the Lottery. But it has provoked a strong reaction in the community with some people loving it and others being angered by the way he has portrayed the townsfolk. Here we hear opposing views. KATHLEEN MEARNS and LORRAINE TINNEY report.

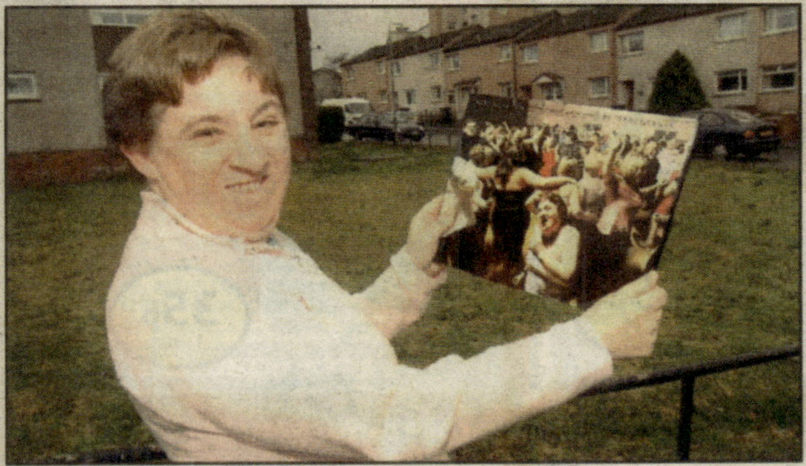

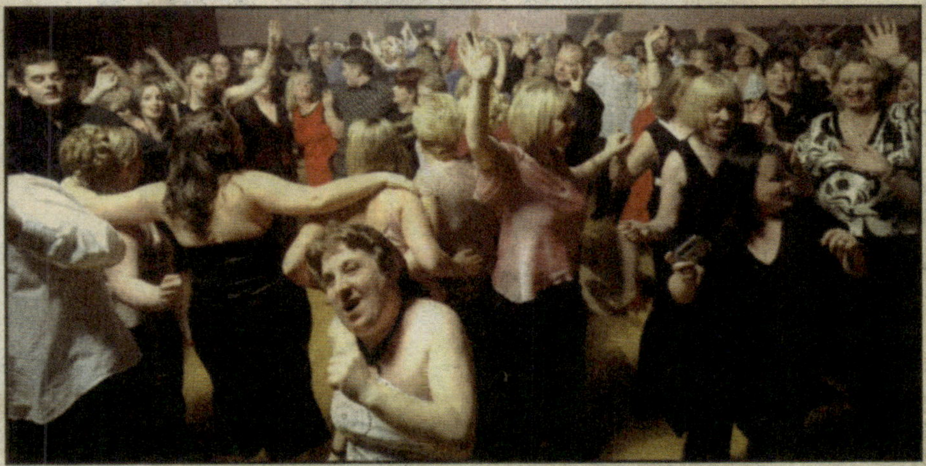

Talk of the town

'I can't get over how good the photos are'

BETTY Robertson will forever treasure the book of photographs of Port Glasgow by Mark Neville.

She has good reason to remember the book for a very long time as a picture of her takes pride of place on the front cover.

The 43-year-old is seen laughing and dancing at last year's Christmas party in the town hall.

Betty had been told beforehand the photograph would be on the book's cover — and is pleased by the decision. She loves the image and says it brings back good memories of her night out. "I like the photograph very much. It's nice. It's a very happy photograph. I'm enjoying myself dancing. It was a good night. I bought the top I'm wearing especially," she said.

Betty was at the party with her family, including sister Isabel Robertson. She moved to Port Glasgow's Oronsay Avenue in July to be closer to Isabel after living for most of her life in the Gibshill area of Greenock.

Her sister Isabel appears in the book too, along with nieces Tracey Miller and Janice and Donna Robertson. Betty said: "I love the book. I look through it every night — I know a lot of people in it. I can't get over how good the photos are."

The Greenock Telegraph, 1/12/2004

Fancy

Pictures

2008

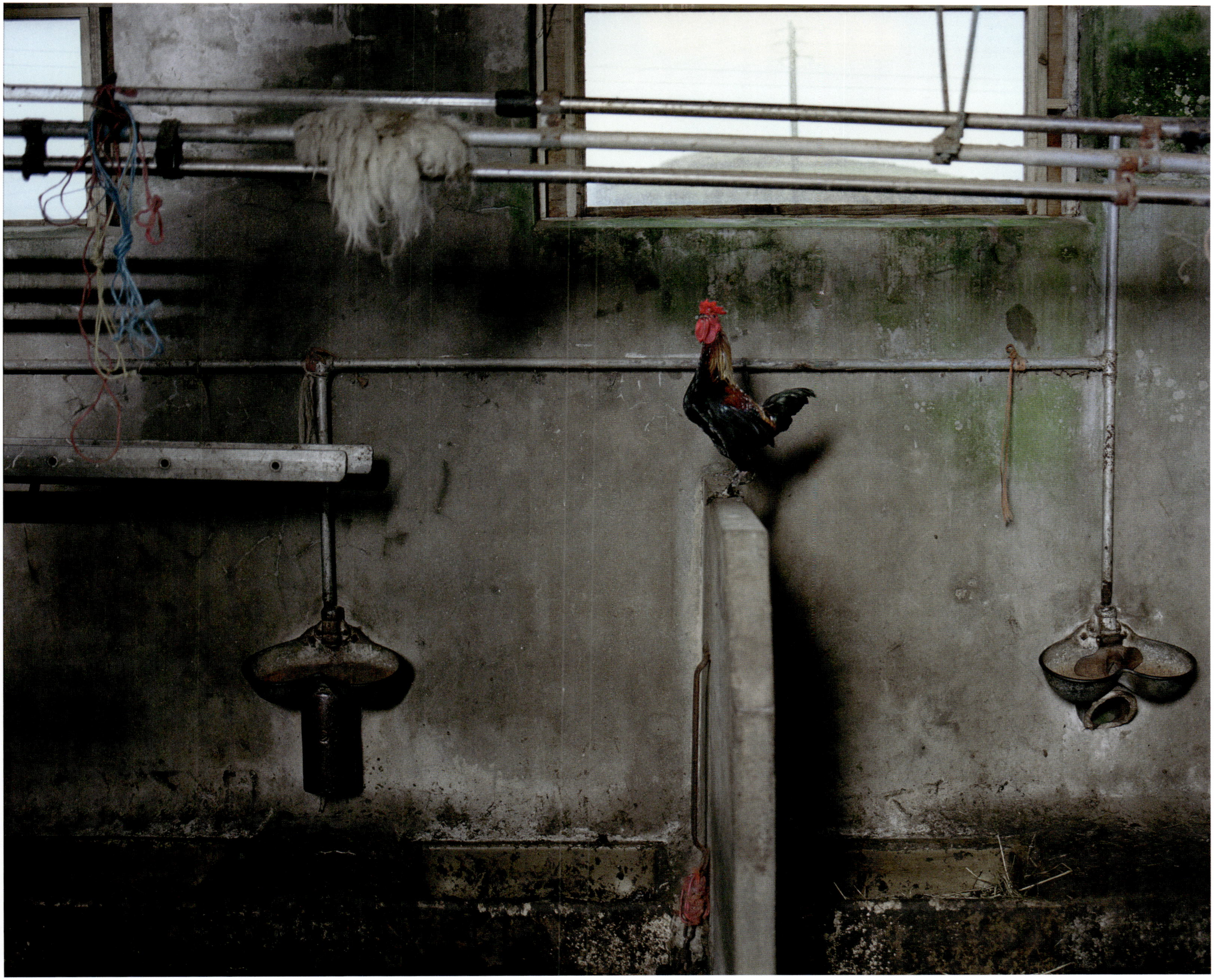

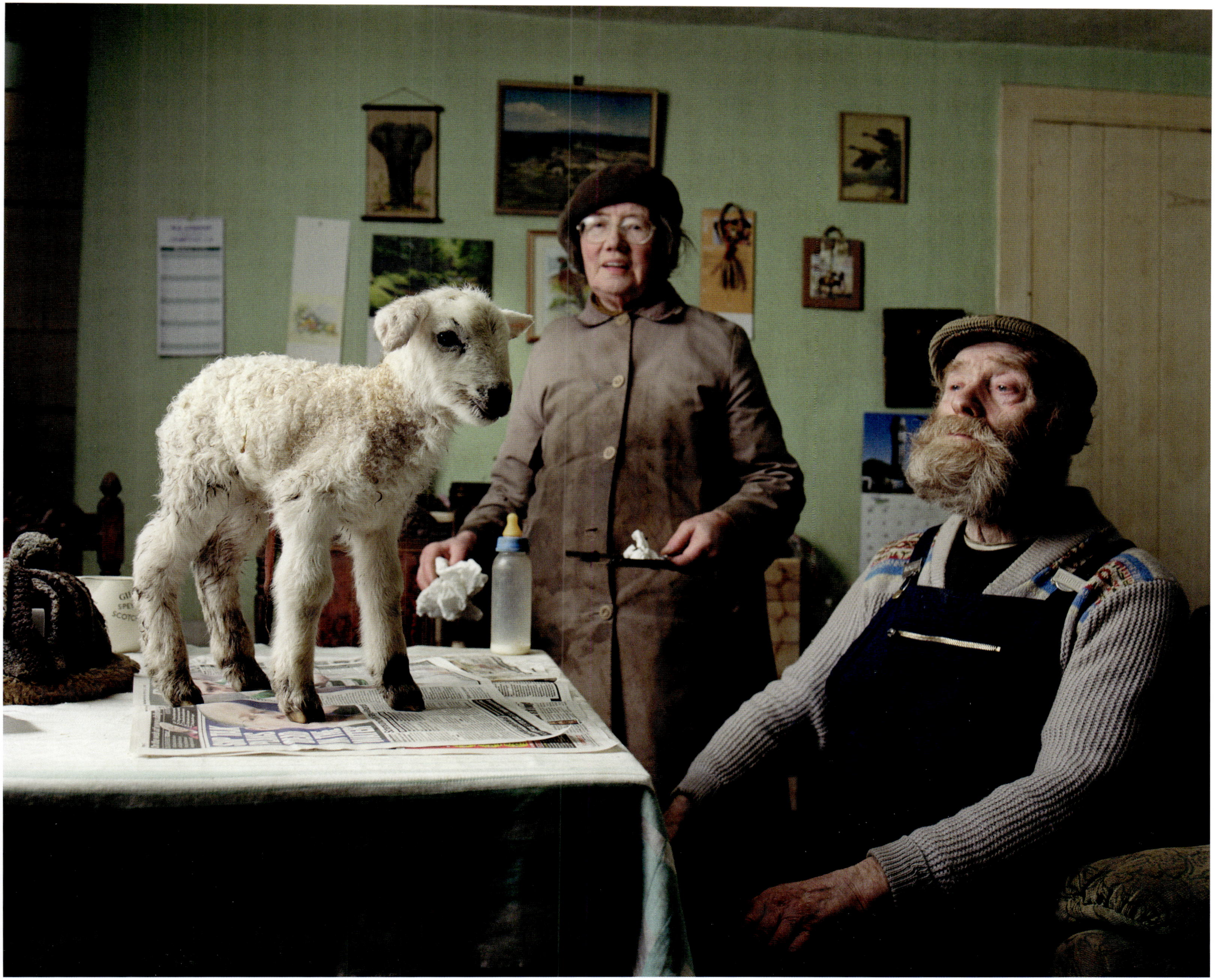

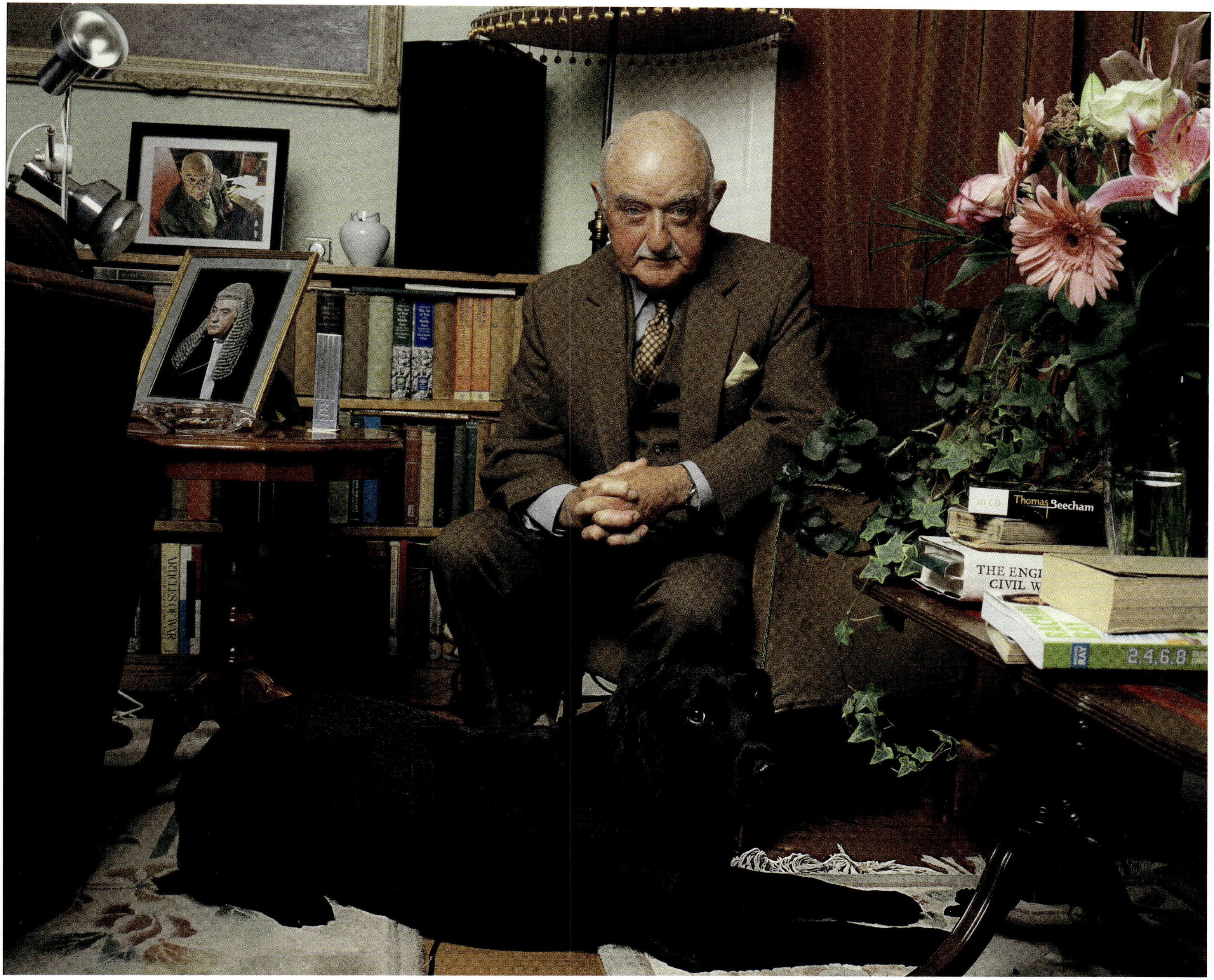
10 CD
Thomas Beecham
ARTICLES OF WAR
2.4.6.8

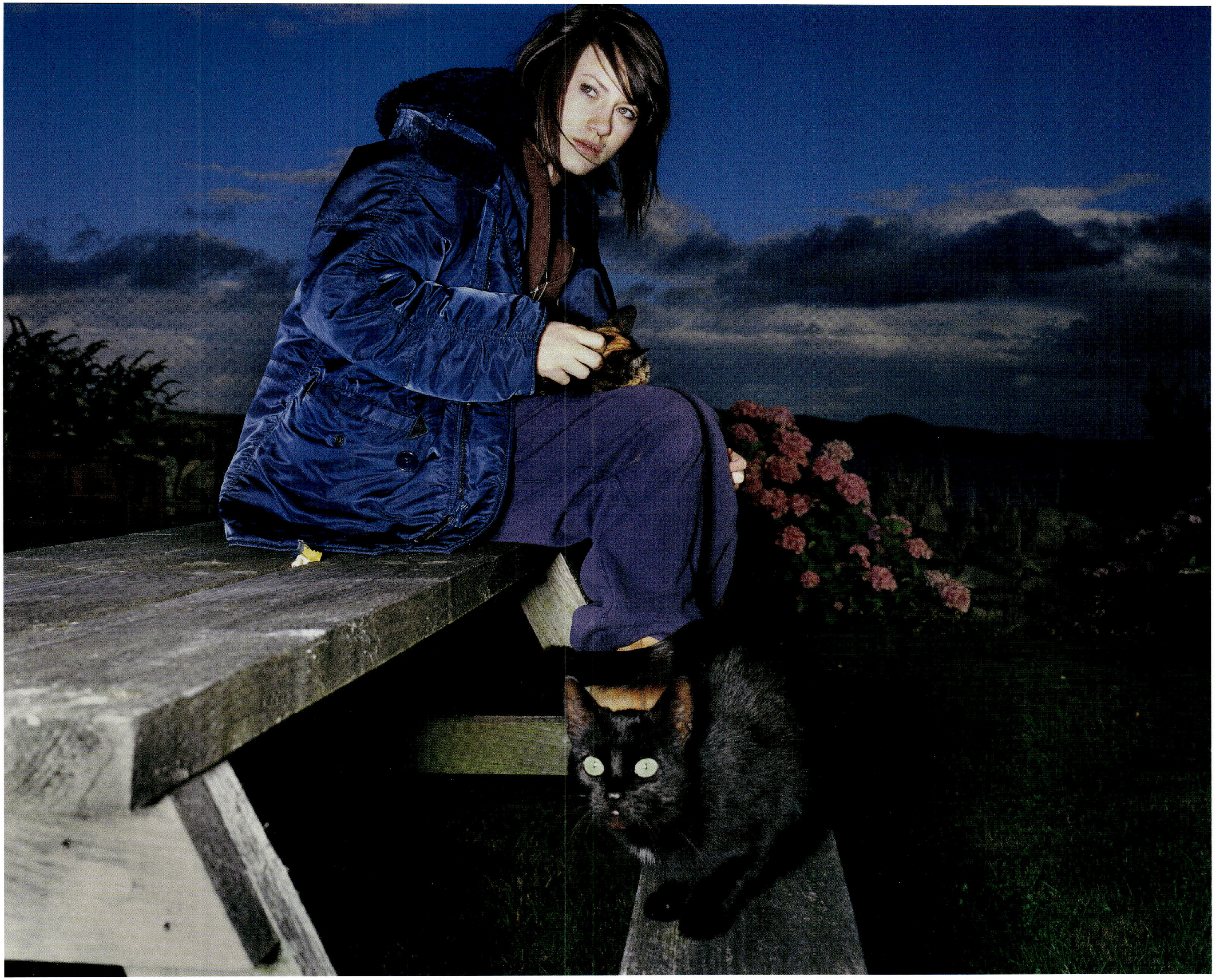

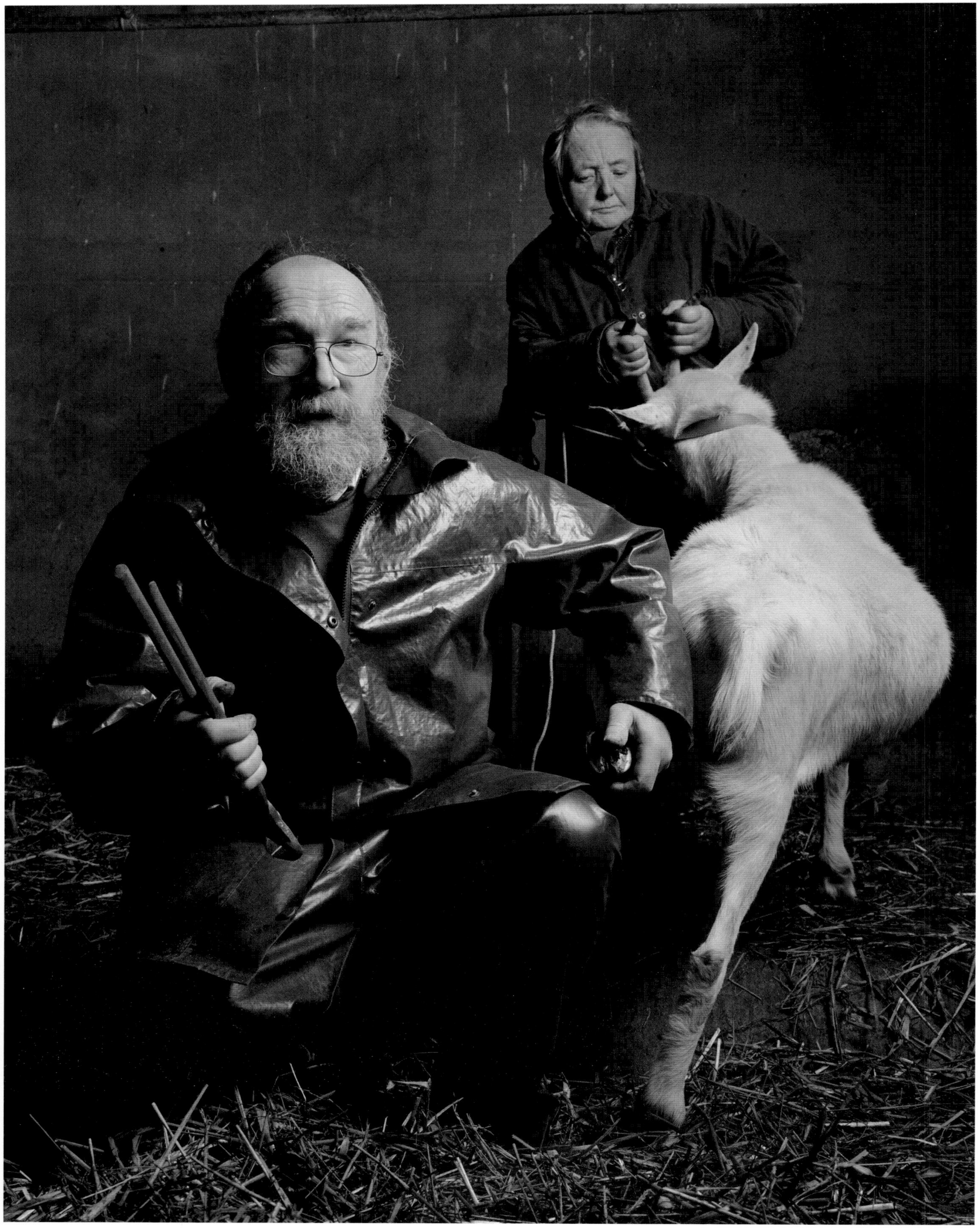

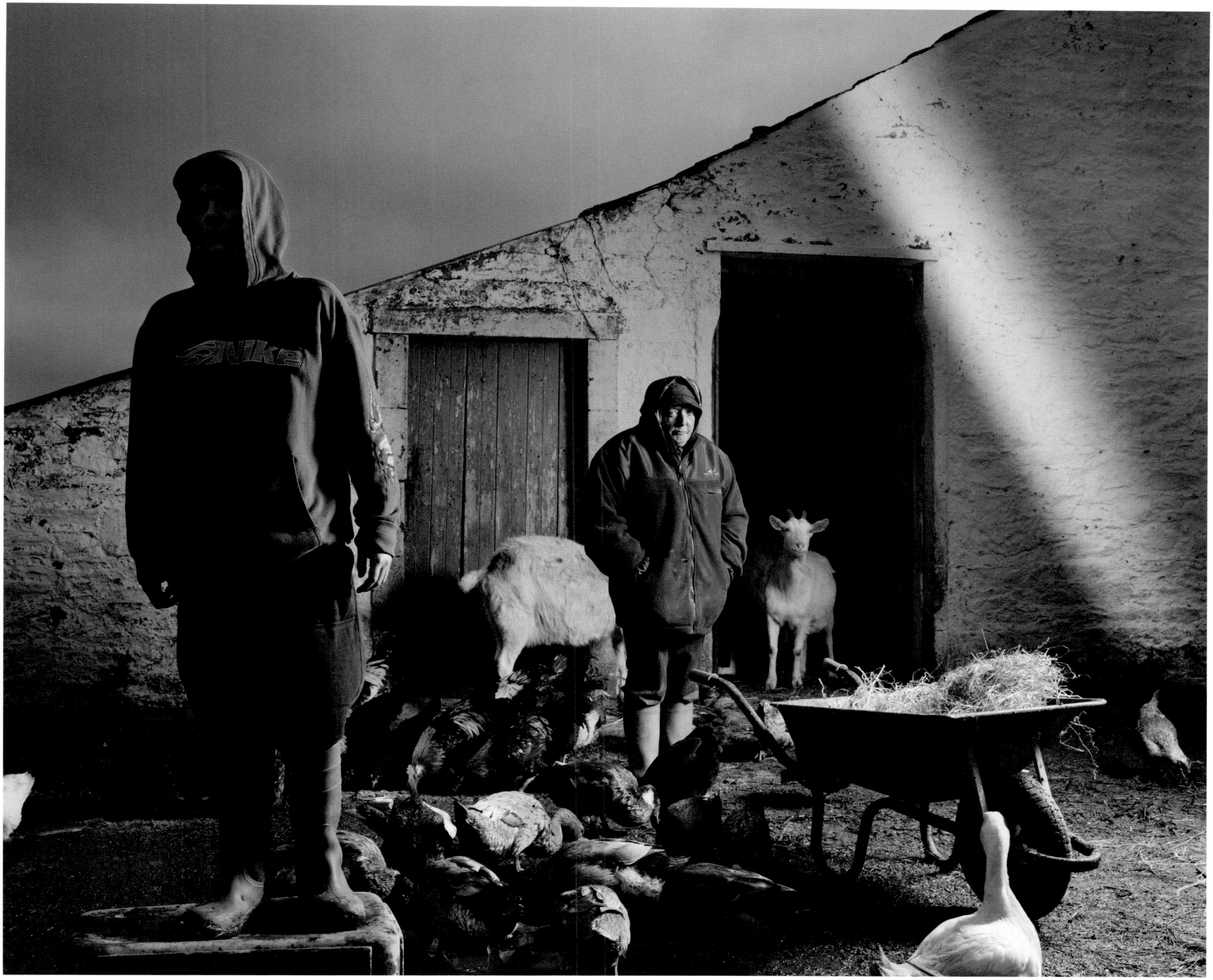
Nike

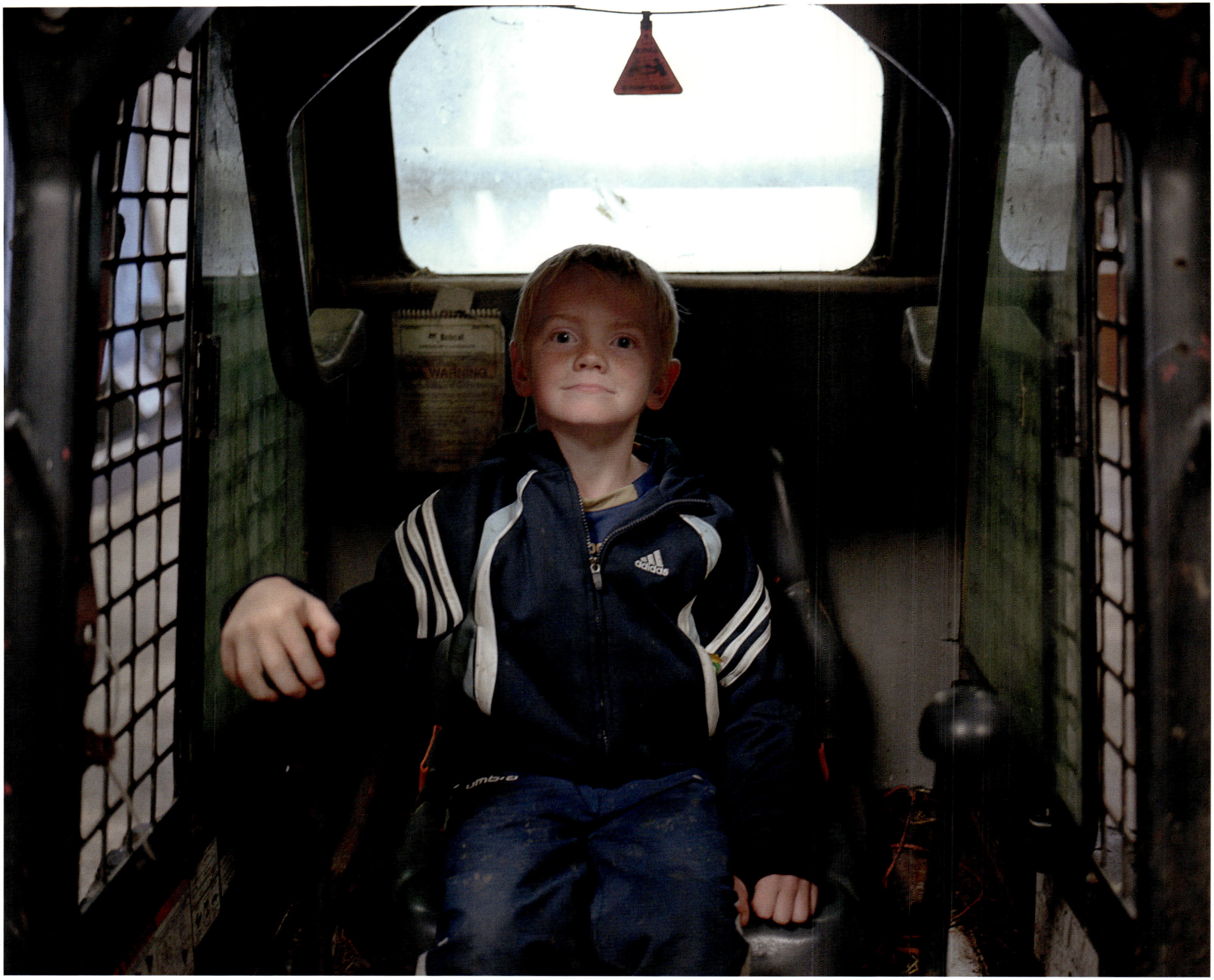
WARNING
adidas

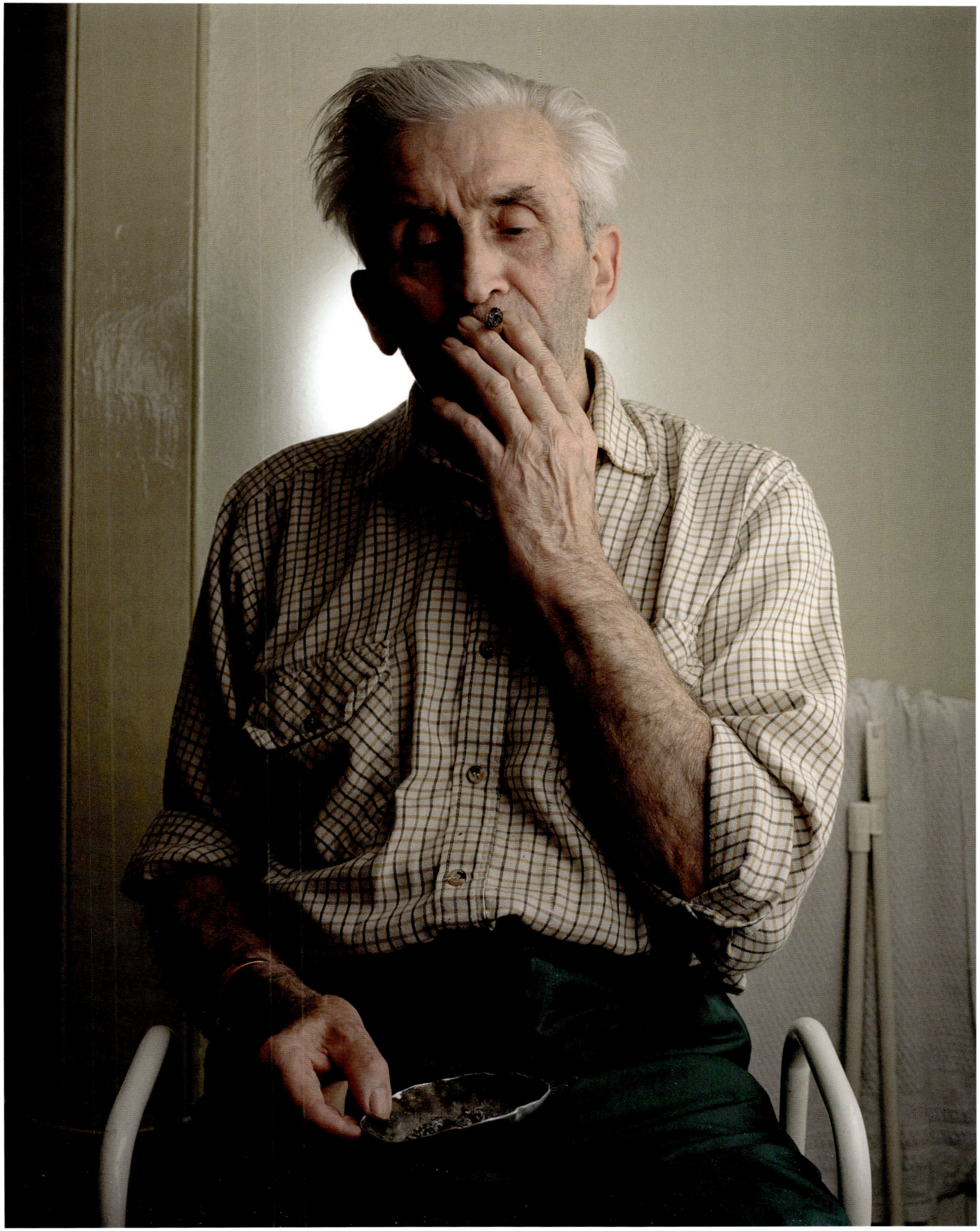

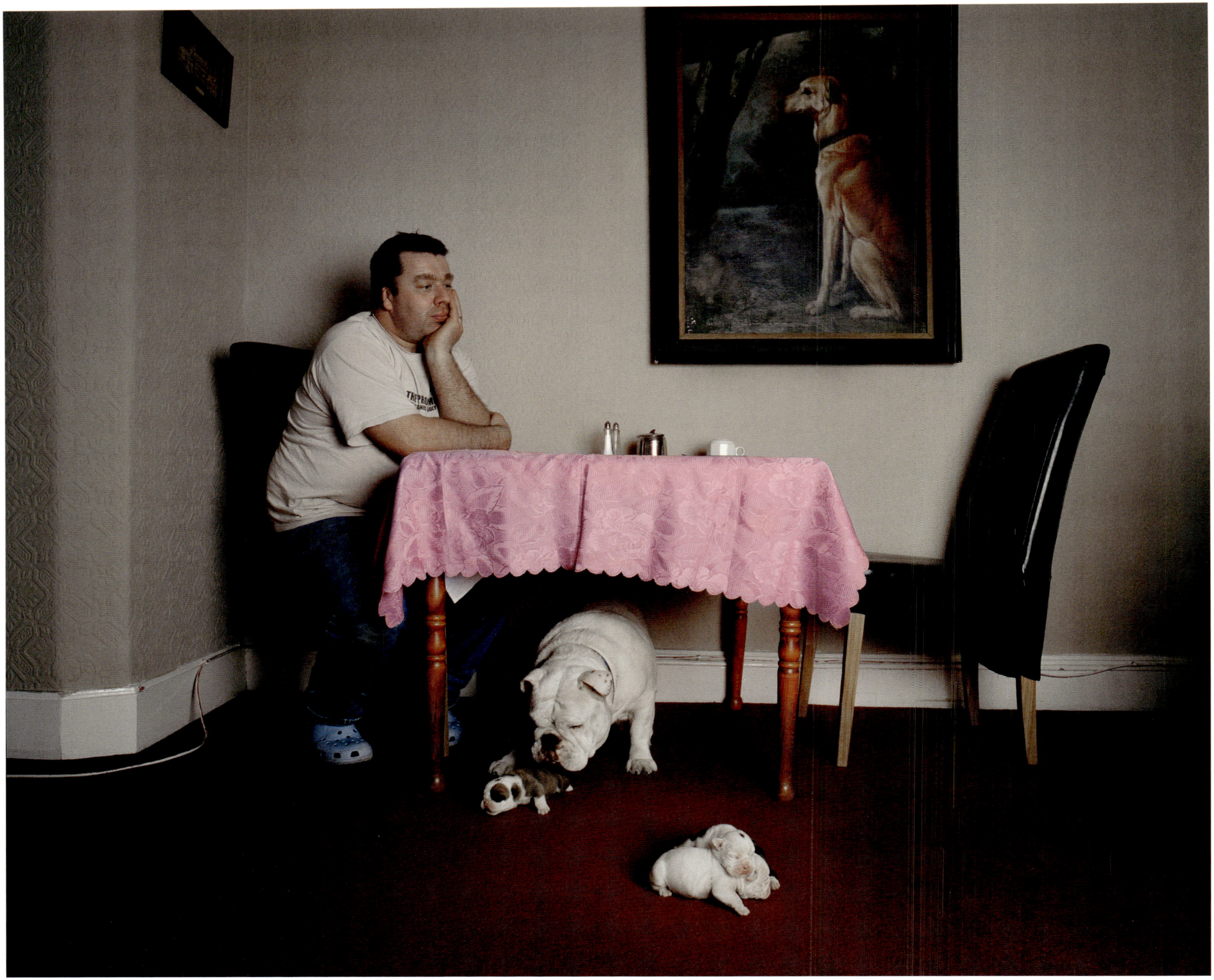

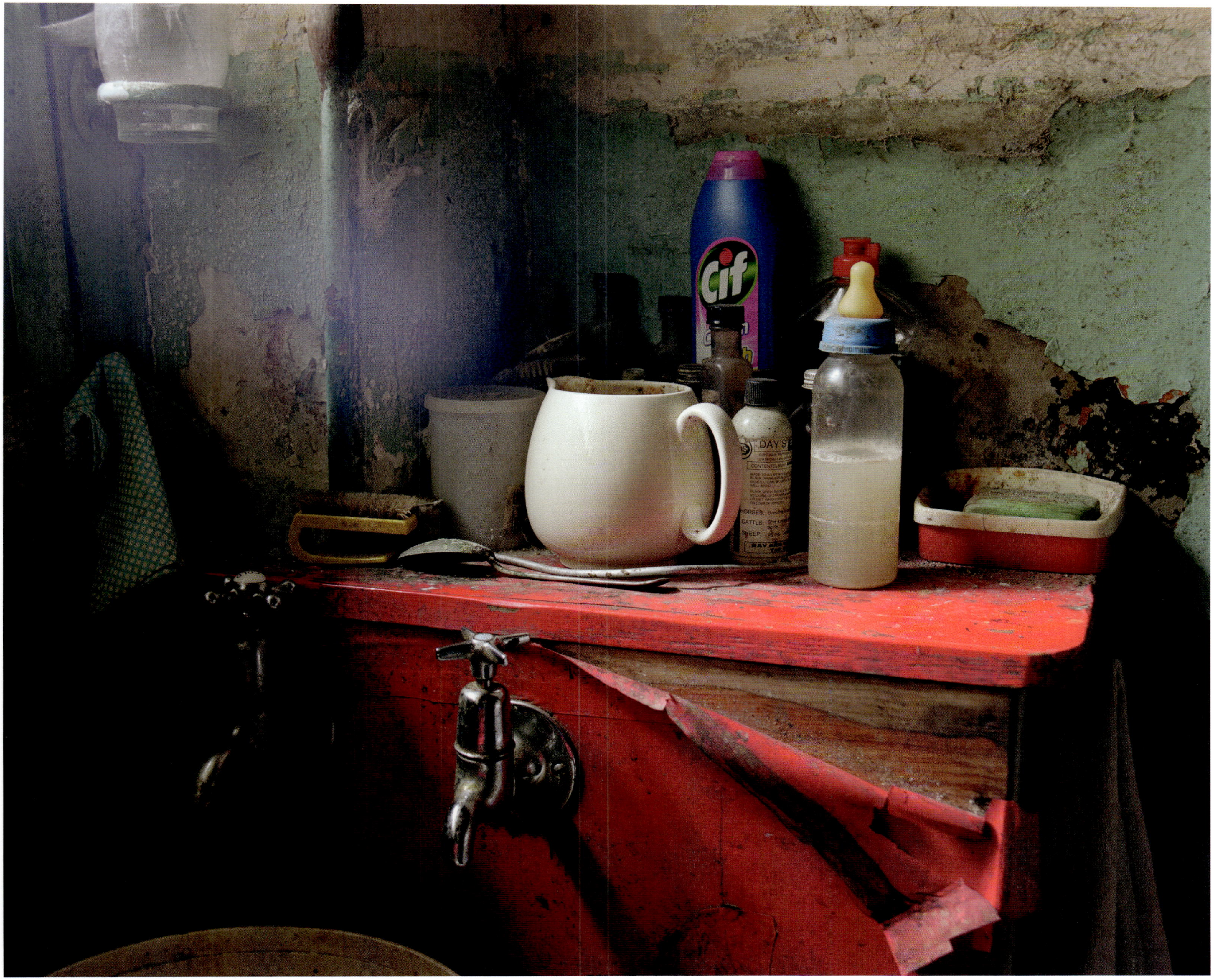
Cif
DAY'S
HORSES
CATTLE
SHEEP

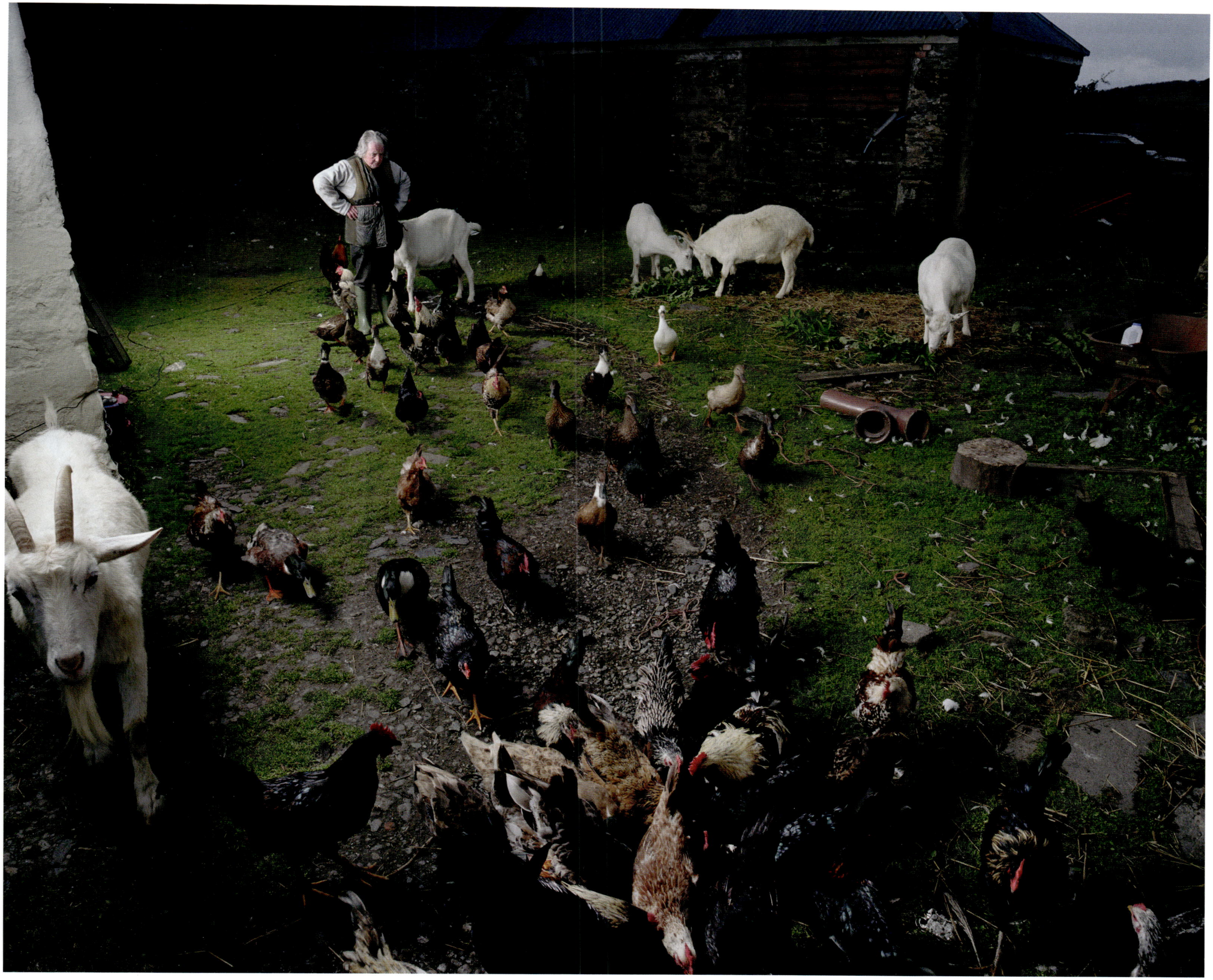

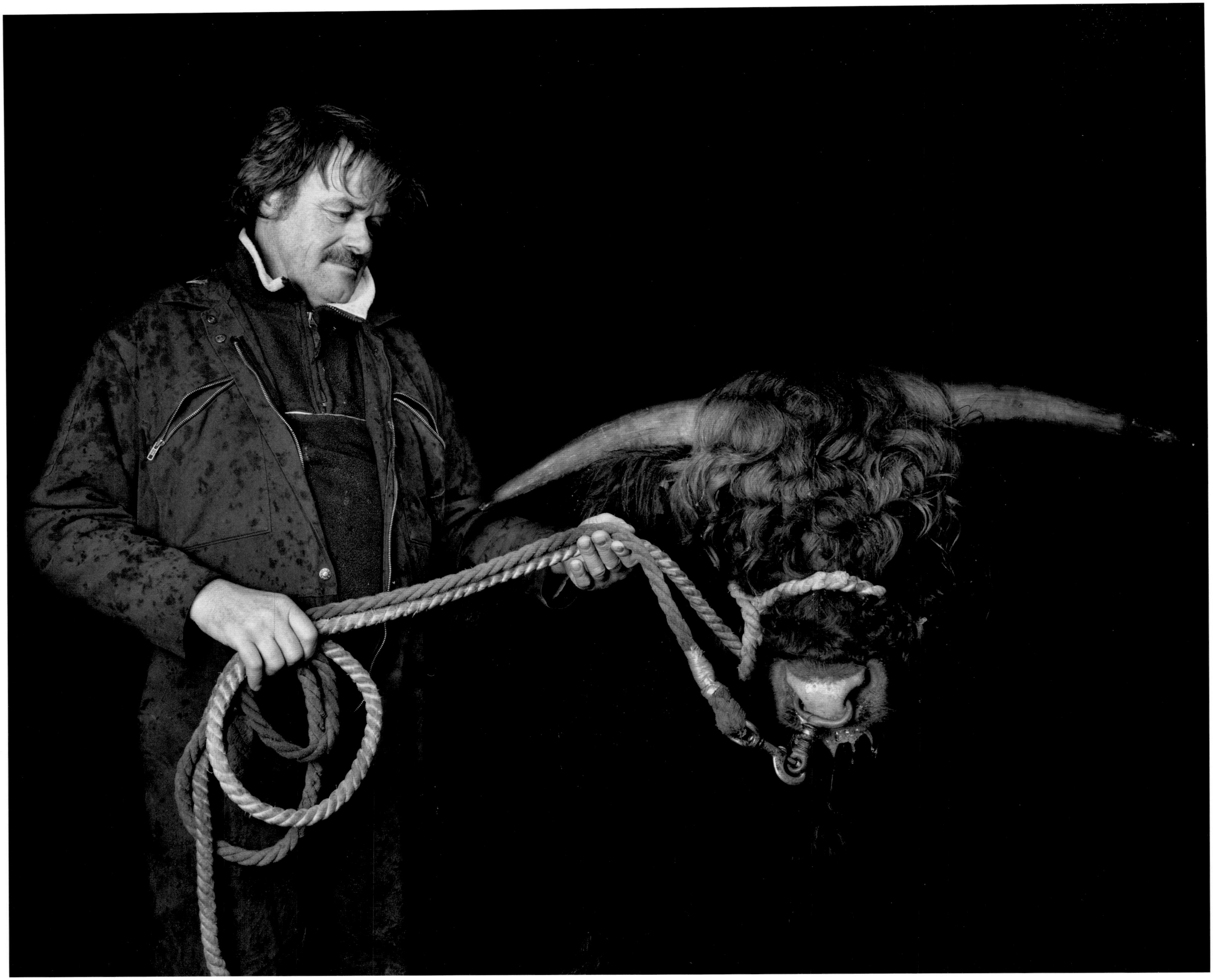

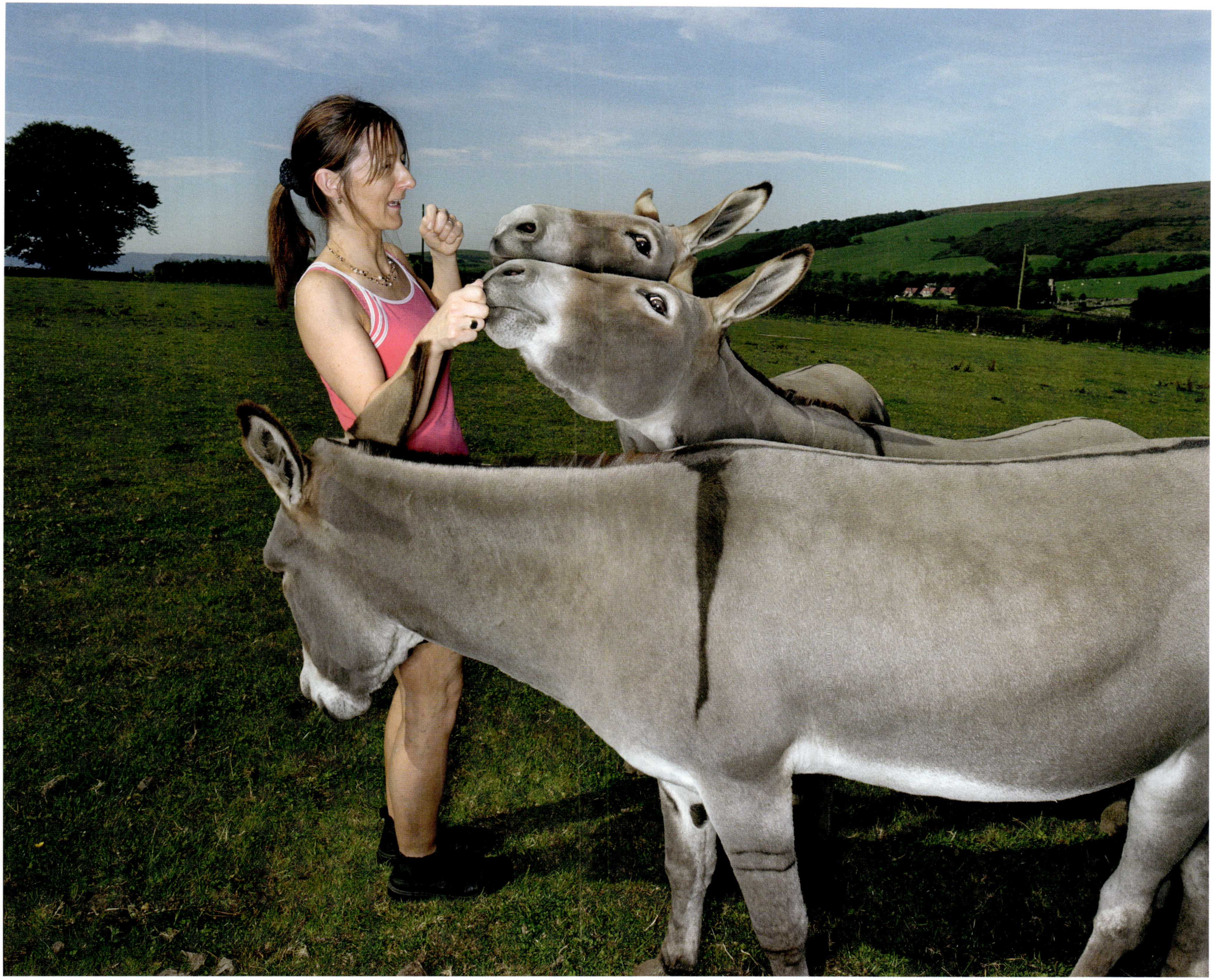

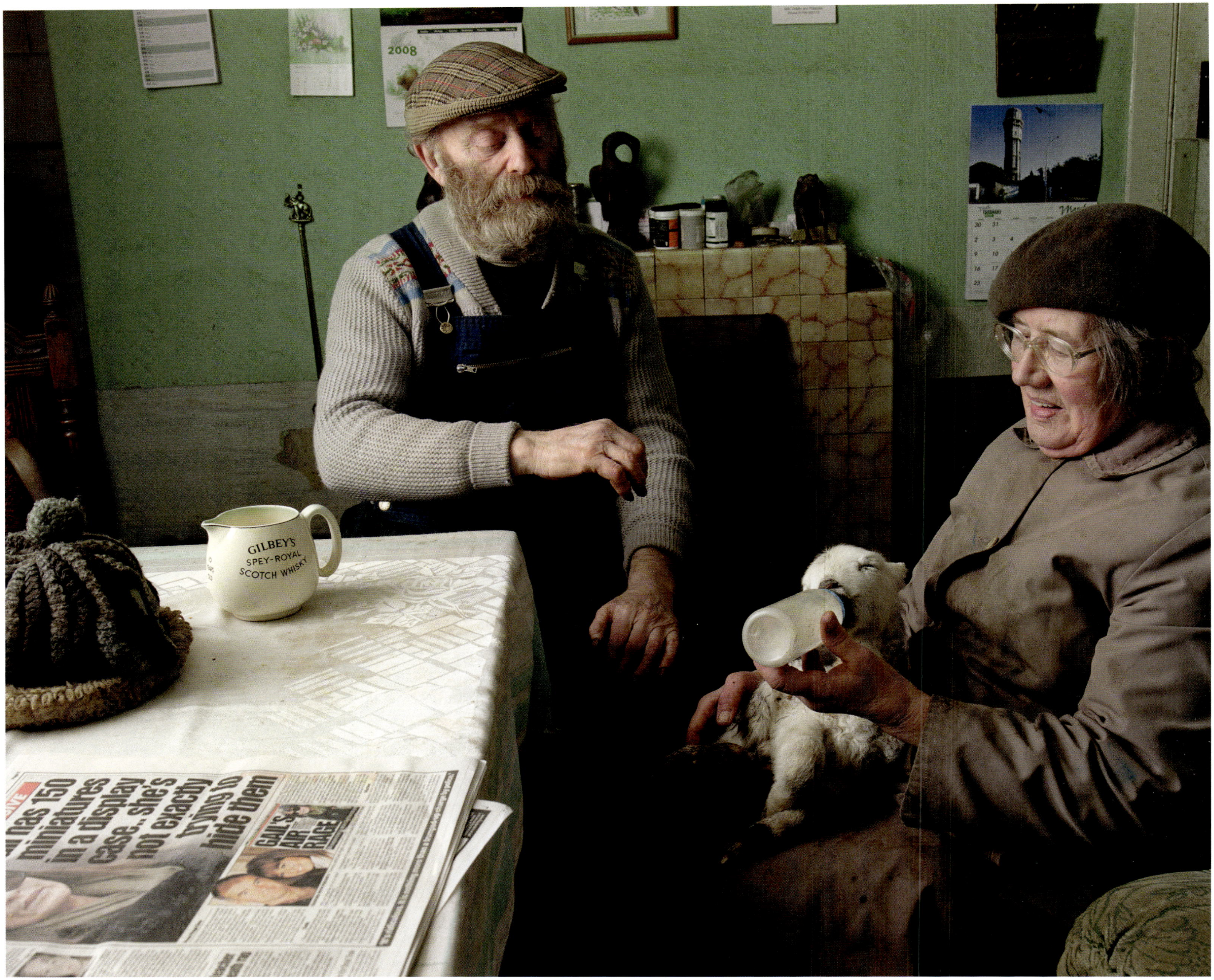
2008
GILBEY'S
SPEY-ROYAL
SCOTCH WHISKY
has 150
miniatures
in a display
case... she's
not exactly
trying to
hide them
GAIL'S
AIR
RAGE

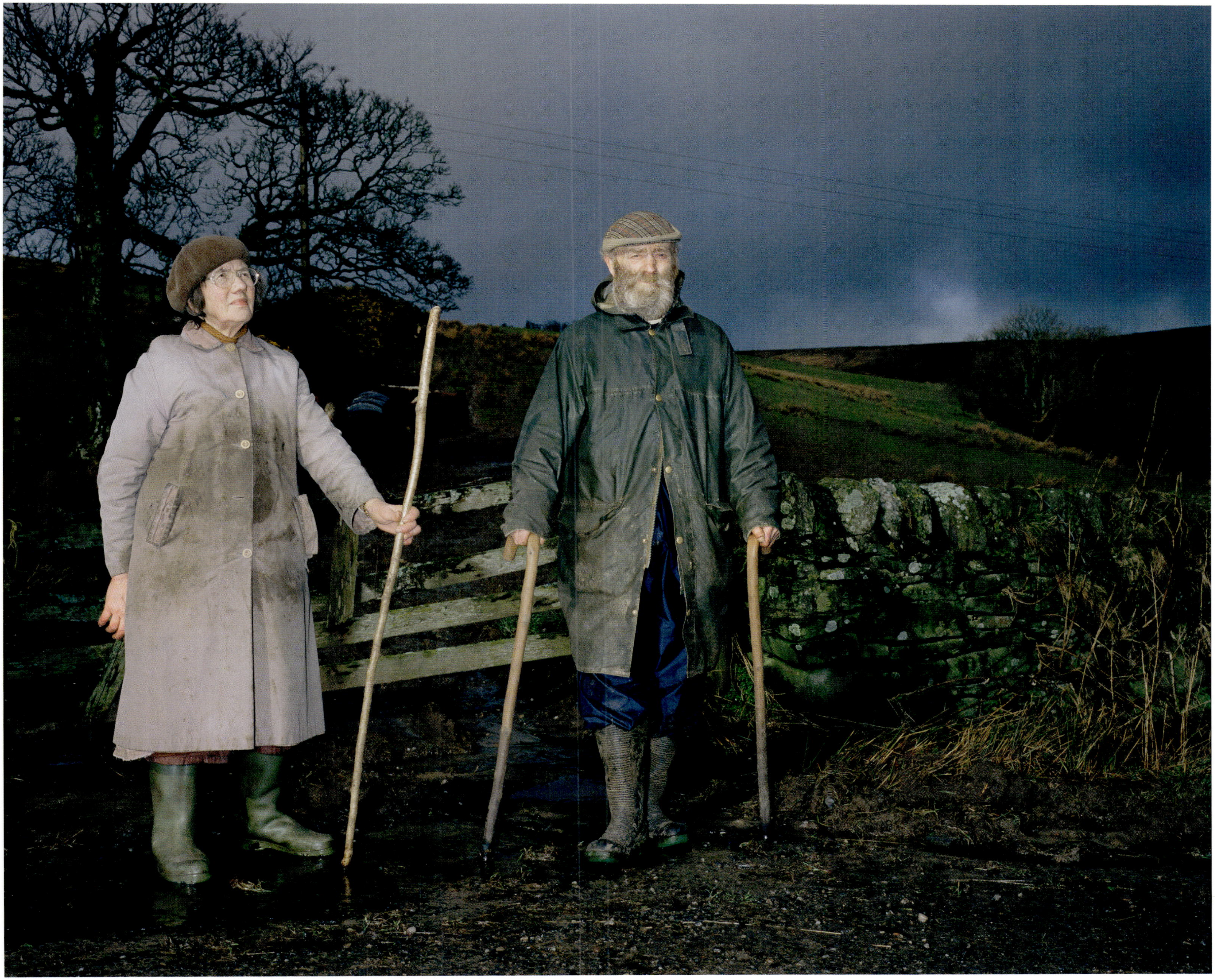

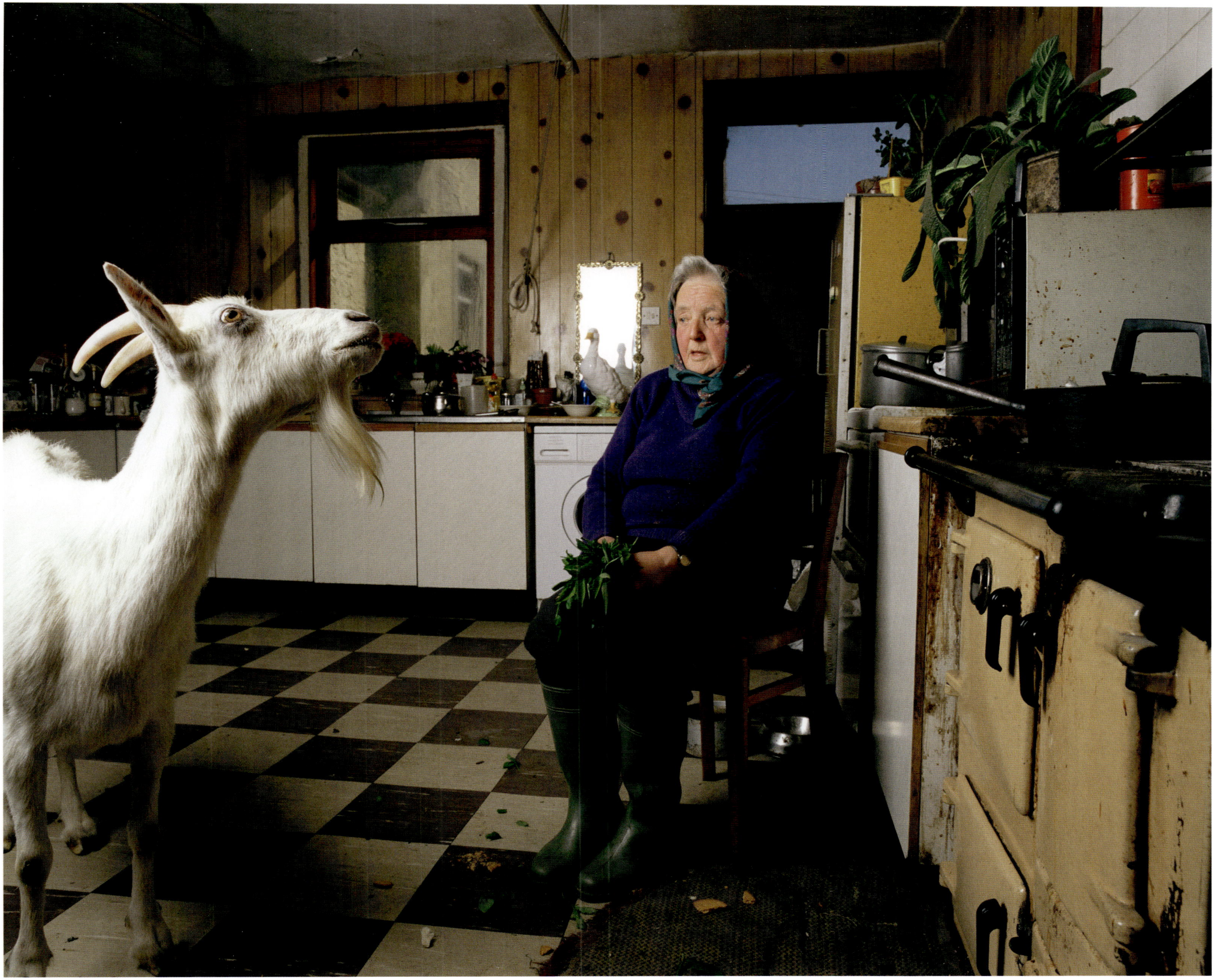

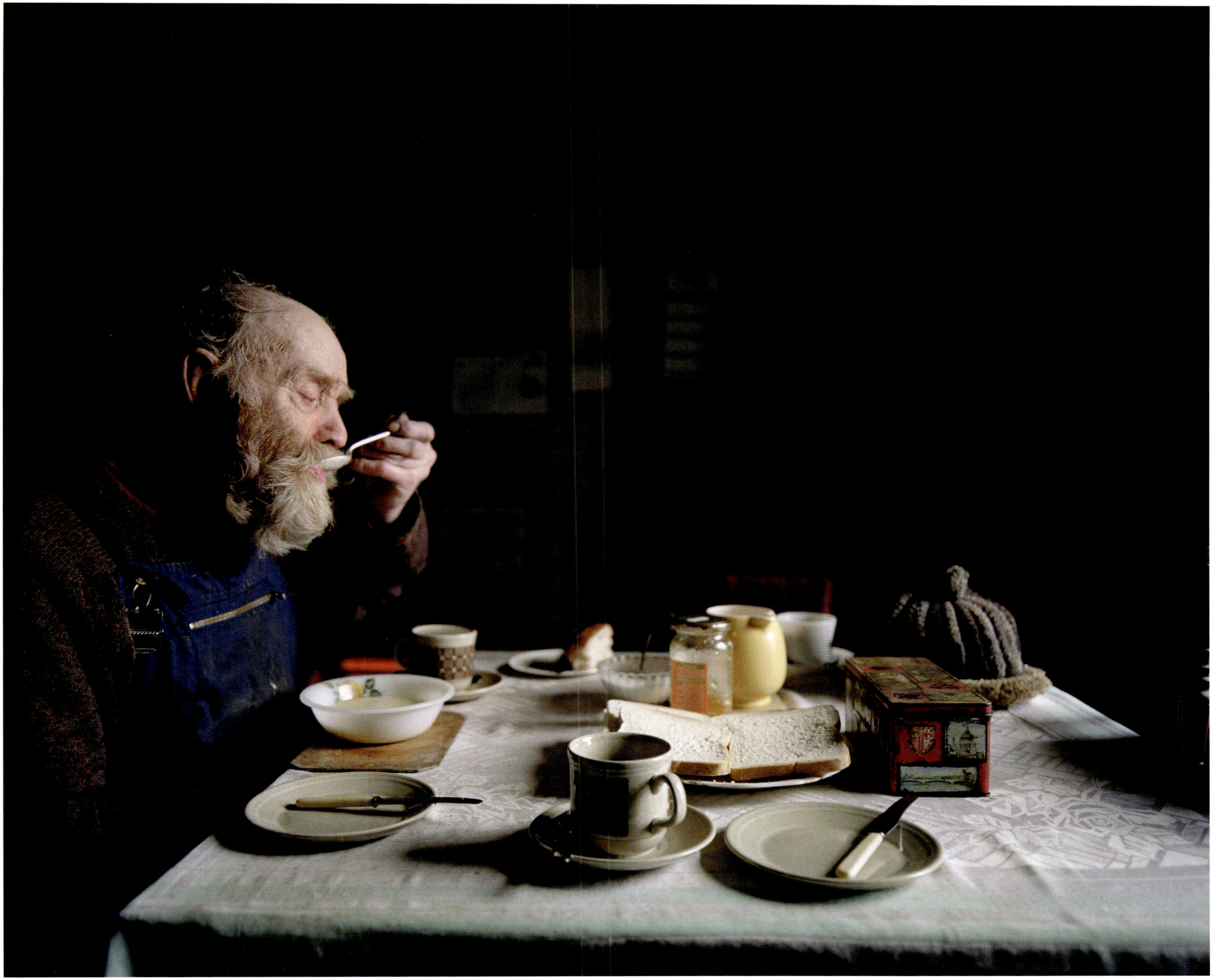

Titles

49. Still Life with Cock, 2008
51. Newborn Lamb, 2008
53. Sherriff Irvine Smith, 2008
55. Xenia with Cat, 2008
56. Goat Pedicure, 2008
57. Annie and Andrew, 2008
58. Robert, 2008
59. Smoking, 2008
60. Bulldog Breeder and Hotelier Amos, 2008
61. Still Life, 2008
63. Annie's Farm, 2008
64. Speedy with Highland Cow, 2008
65. Donkeys, 2008
66. Newborn Lamb, 2, 2008
67. The Currys, 2008
69. Annie and Snowy, 2008
71. Supper, 2008

David Campany: *The Port Glasgow Book Project* led to another encounter with a Scottish community.

Mark Neville: Sophie Crichton-Stuart, the curator at Mount Stuart had read about the Port Glasgow project. Mount Stuart is a large Victorian Gothic country house on the Isle of Bute, off the Scottish west coast. The island is a farming community and, like Port Glasgow, there are very roughly around eight thousand people. For generations on the island, people have been employed in certain ways to do certain types of work. So there are lots of similarities in outlook, humour, ideology and value systems. But the Isle has established working relations that haven't changed much in hundreds of years. The curator is the sister of the Marquis of Bute who owns the island and most of its farms. All the farms pay a rent to Mount Stuart. So these farmers have worked the land for generations, often without ever getting to own it. That said, the Marquis is a very benevolent landlord. The rents charged are low, he really is part of the community, and he is visible. But the model is essentially feudal. Interestingly, they've been commissioning artists for generations so Mount Stuart House has paintings by Thomas Gainsborough and Joshua Reynolds. It is a sort of aristocratic family album. But the farmers themselves are not really represented in much of the art and, when they are, they are not identified as individuals.

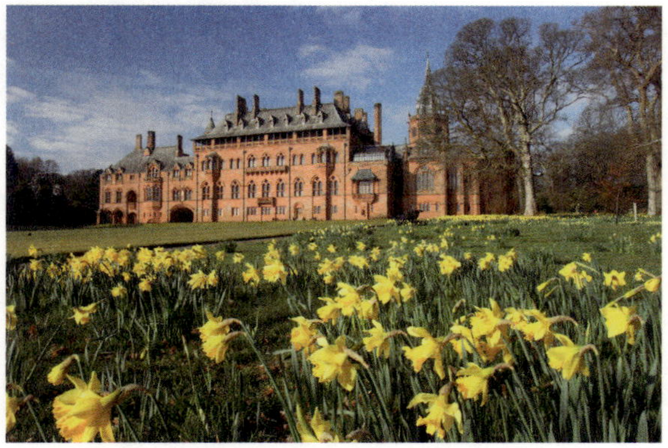

Mount Stuart House, Isle of Bute, 2008

In that kind of artistic patronage, there's always an assumption that the artist is somehow exempt from the social order, is outside the class structures. As if they float around without commitment to anything but art.

Socially indeterminate.

Sometimes very interesting work can be made in those circumstances. Bill Brandt was a wealthy foreigner when he made his great observations of insular British class rituals in the 1930s. His books *The English and Home* (1936) and *A Night in London* (1938) slide across all the social divides and class barriers. He finds everyone equally fascinating and strange, and maybe that's all we can expect from a rich artist. But questions of observation and class solidarity are always complicated for photographers and artists. Where did you stay on the island?

There was no point my staying in Mount Stuart. I'd be cut off from the farmers. I ended up staying with Annie MacDougall, who features in some of the photographs. She was a single woman in her sixties

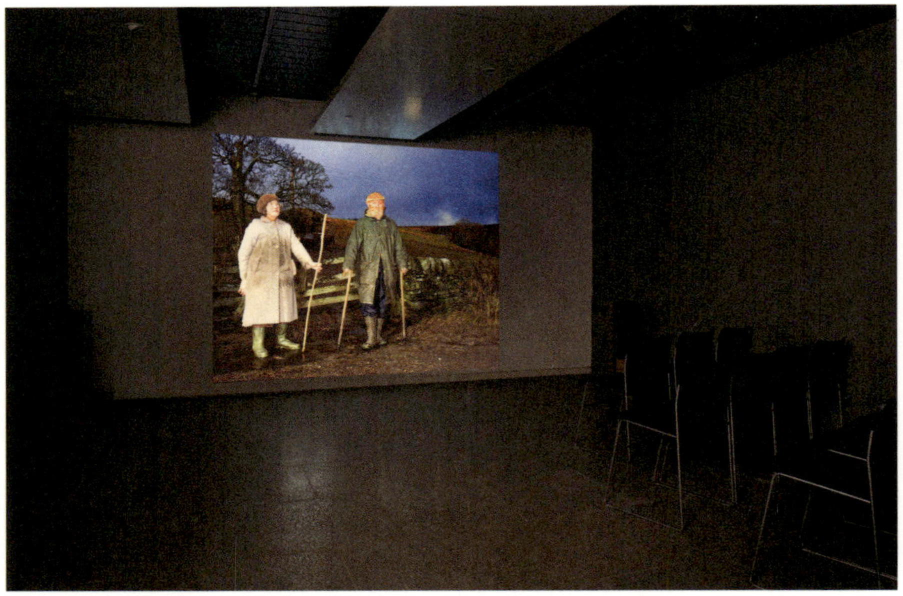

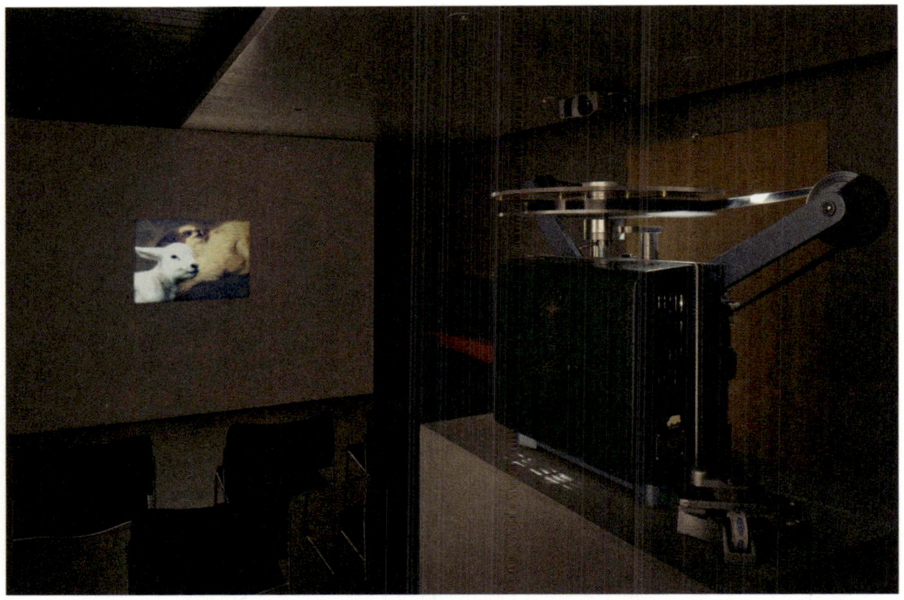

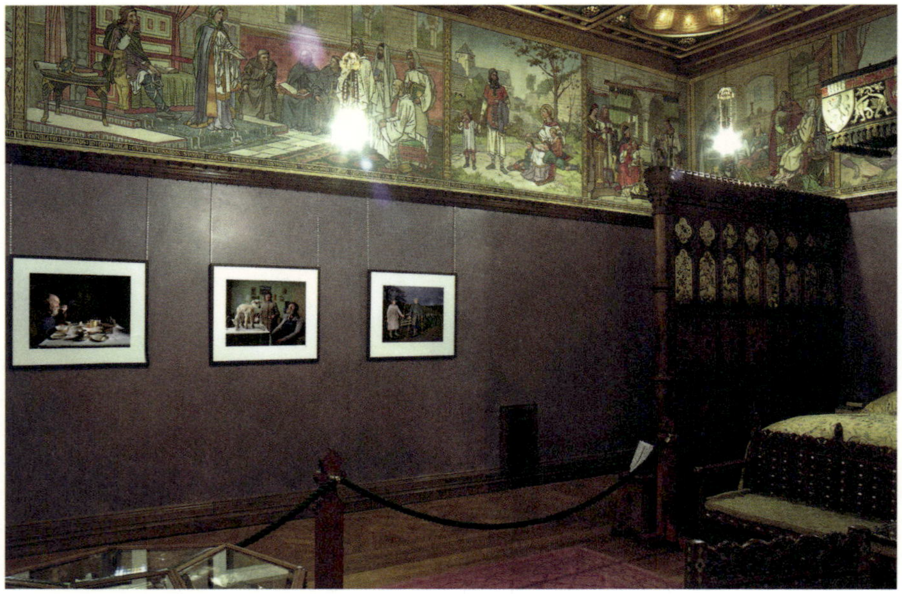

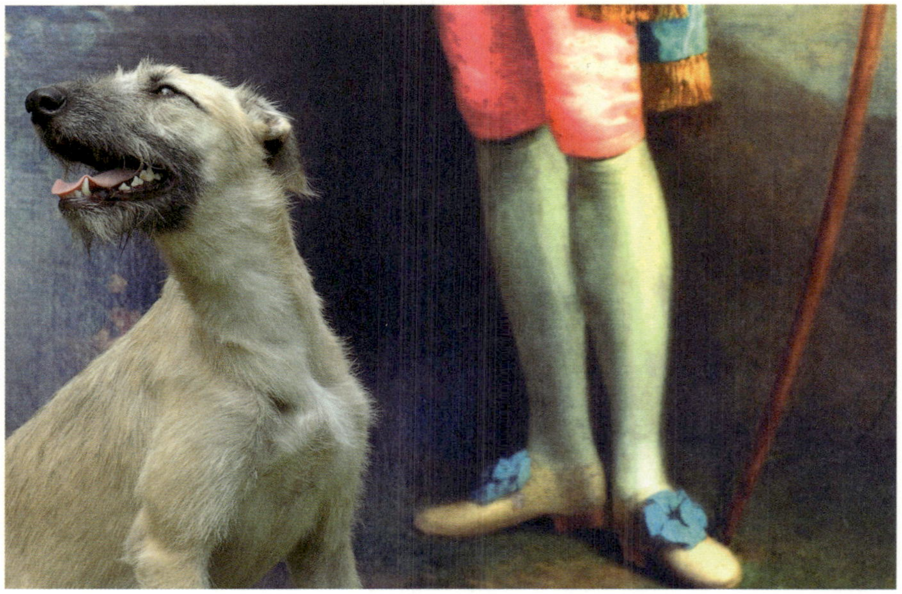

Tula Fancies slide installation at Mount Stuart Visitor Centre, 2008

Four Photographs installed in the bedroom of Mount Stuart House, 2008

Fancy Pictures, 16mm film loop, 18mins, installed at Mount Stuart Visitor Centre, 2008

Production still from *Fancy Pictures*, 16mm film,18mins, 2008

with little family (but many friends) and she more or less adopted me. She used to drive me around on her errands. She used to look after animals and she introduced me to people. She had a vulgar sense of humour which I loved. She was my way in to life on the island. Part of the reason I felt at home both in Port Glasgow and on the Isle of Bute amongst working communities, was that I was making far less money than most of the locals were. I think they could also see I was working really hard for the people I was documenting, as hard as a farmer or a steelworker, so I was seen to belong there. Of course there's an element of voyeurism but there's not a sense in which I could be seen to be exploiting anyone. I'm not making money and I'm caring about how they are represented.

I sense the people in front of your camera see that the kind of work you're engaged with is labour-intensive. Quite often the suspicion people have about photographers is based on the fact that taking pictures can be sly and very easy. Pictures can be made with almost no labour at all—the photographer arrives, with no real connection, takes what they want and leaves. As soon as there's a large-format camera, lights, a tripod and the slow deliberation that goes with them, the relation changes. It's an investment. Historically photographers have rarely been seen as workers at all.

Unfortunately I think that's particularly true in the UK, the refusal to see photography as proper work, or even a proper art form.

Is this related to the UK class structure?

I remember in the Isle of Bute it was the first time I'd ever met anyone from the aristocracy so I was apprehensive. But, in fact, Sophie and her brother Johnny were warm and easy-going, and knowledgeable about art and photography. And they really appreciated my work, despite the fact that it ended up being a critique of this kind of feudal relationship between the landowners and the land-workers. Sophie knew that's what it would be and she still went ahead and commissioned it, endorsed it.

Well there is a kind of critique that's not merely ideological but comes out of close observation of lives as they are lived, a nuanced observation of how circumstances shape people and how people shape circumstances. When we think of "critique" it's usually hard and blunt and lacking subtlety. But a very crude account of social situations only ever preaches to the converted.

Yes and something of the nuance comes through in the editing of the work too. *Fancy Pictures* ended up as a slide show, very high quality, using a medium-format projector. So again, another not-quite-standard documentary technology. The work ended up being partly about this mystical relationship between people and animals on the island. This is something I had seen in the arts and crafts within Mount Stuart House before I started. Carvings and tapestries depicted farmers in a generic, anonymous way, never named, just as workers with a deep connection to the land.

Then there is socialist realism of the Soviet era that depicts the farmer as heroic.

Yes. I deliberately referenced Soviet realism to suggest that real power comes from working the land, as opposed to owning it, which is the contrary message of 18th-century portrait painting. I tried to cut across those problems with my photography, doing something that the artworks, arts and crafts, and tapestries in the house were not doing. This carried through into how it was shown. I presented the slideshow at the house and invited all the farmers to come see it. It was the first time that some of them had actually been into their landlord's residence. Before that their relation to the house may have been to send a rent cheque every month.

How was that received?

Previous artists had made work "for the house", or its grounds, and the opening nights usually involved getting two hundred people up from the London art world. It's very appealing to the art jet-set to have a party in a Victorian Gothic mansion on a Scottish island. I was interested in communicating with a very different audience. Basically it was for the farmers. They could come to the house and see themselves in this high quality slideshow, projected very large, life-size. There they were, represented in the great house. So three hundred farmers came, and very few from the art world. The show ran for four months.

You called that work *Fancy Pictures*.

The term came form art history. In the 18th century it was used to denote a sentimental depiction of a peasant. My work was, in a way, an ironic reference to that genre of British painting.

By this time some of your pictures are being bought by collectors and presented in museums?

Yes. *Port Glasgow* had become part of an exhibition at Modern Art Oxford called *Local Stories*, which looked at an emerging pattern of artists working with communities. I really debated with myself whether I even wanted the work to be shown in that way. Eventually I decided that I could show some of the photographs alongside lots of supporting material, such as the community response that explained the nature of the project.

So museum visitors would understand that it was not work made primarily for them?

Exactly. And whenever there were print sales I would give a large percentage back to the community, via charities based in Port Glasgow, or individuals represented in the pictures. The Arts Council

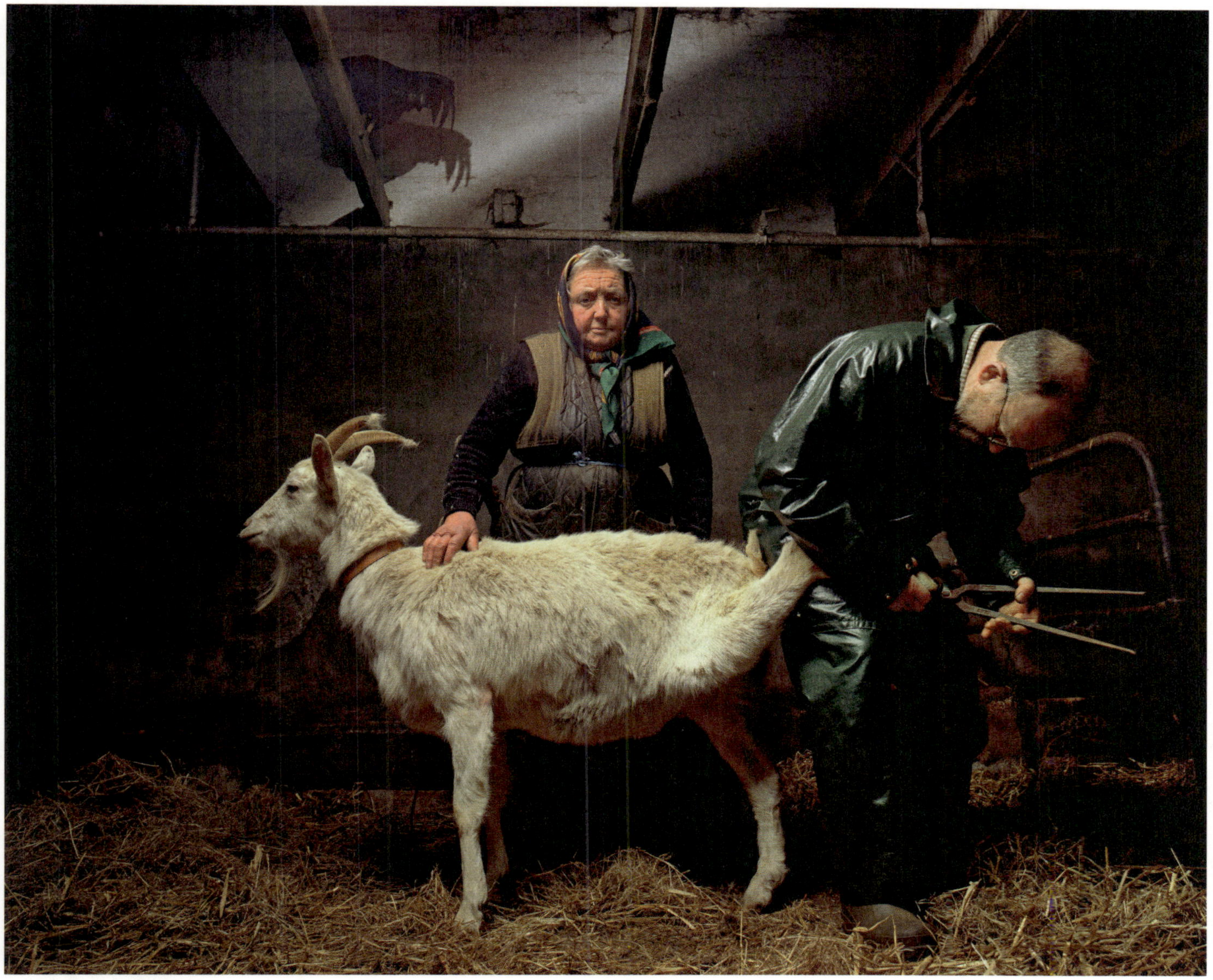

Annie Macdougall, *Goat Pedicure*, 2008

www.buteman.co.uk Friday, October 2, 2009 THE BUTEMAN - 9

Annie goes on display at Holyrood

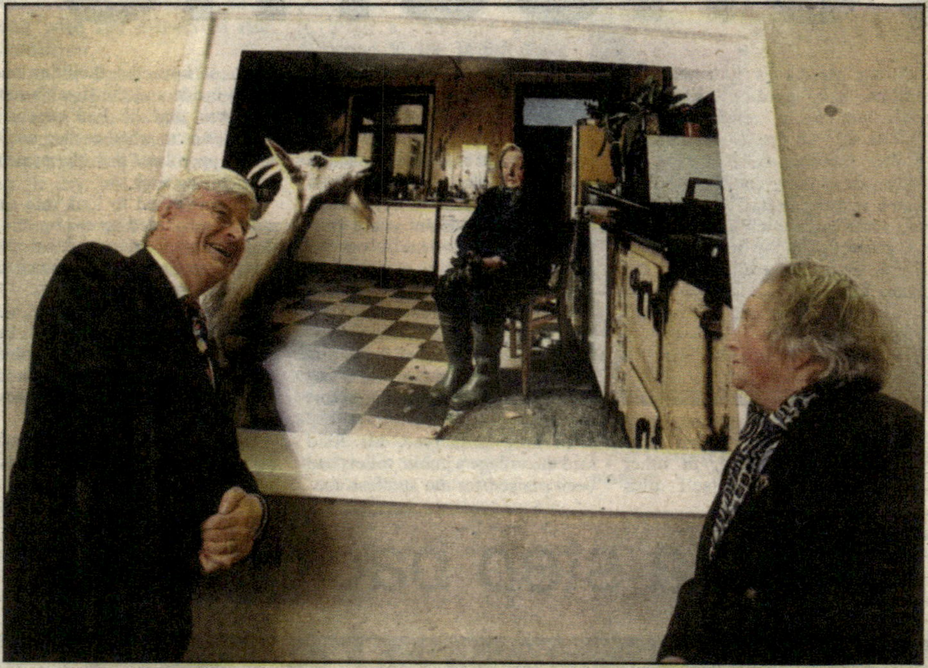

PHOTO FINISH: Robin Harper MSP and Annie Macdougall admire Mark Neville's photograph of Annie and Snowy at her Gortans home. The photograph is on public display in the Scottish Parliament building at Holyrood. (Picture courtesy of The Scottish Parliament.)

A PHOTOGRAPH of Bute resident Annie Macdougall and her goat Snowy at her Ardbeg home has gone on display at the Scottish Parliament - and Annie herself has paid a visit to see the work this week, 50 years after her last trip to Edinburgh.

Annie admitted that she couldn't resist making the journey from her home at the Gortans to see the picture – which shows her inside her farmhouse kitchen with her goat Snowy – hanging at Holyrood.

The photo, taken by artist Mark Neville and originally exhibited at Mount Stuart last year, is part of a collection designed to explore the complicated relationship between landowners and farmers who work the land on the west coast.

Said Annie: "I don't often leave Bute, let alone travel anywhere as far afield as Edinburgh but when the Parliament invited me over to come and see the photo on display I just could not say no.

"It was a long day getting through there and back, but it was well worth it.

"I had a lovely day and feel very, very honoured indeed.

"I'm not one for a fuss, and know there is not a thing special about me or my life, so it's lovely someone like Mark chose to take a photo like this of me - and for the Parliament to like it so much they have it on display is just unbelievable."

Mark Neville said: "This is the second time I have seen the picture at Holyrood and I think it looks great and think it really fits in with the rest of the building. It looks very at home where it is situated.

"It was an absolute joy meeting and working with Annie, who has become a very, very good friend of mine now.

"I'm so pleased she has been able to make it through to the Parliament to see this picture of her, in a place so many people - of all walks of life - will see it and see a little bit of her world."

Robin Harper MSP, chairman of the Parliament's art advisory group, said: "I love this photo. I love the unexpectedness of it.

"It was always the intention that the Scottish Parliament should reflect life in Scotland and this wonderful photo does just that.

"This is a bold photo that fits in with the bold and modern architecture of Holyrood.

"It is lovely Annie was able to make a rare trip from her home on Bute to come and see this image of her here at Holyrood, where it is a very popular photo.

"We are delighted to have the photo here and thrilled she could come to see it."

Report's praise for Careplus

A ROTHESAY-based care provider has received a glowing inspection report from the Care Commission - with two aspects of its service described as 'excellent' and a third as 'very good'.

supervision of staff and the involvement of the provider, manager, co-ordinator and employees in the inspection process.

Under 'quality of staffing', the only minor area for improvement found during the inspection recommended that the company's

The Buteman newspaper, 2/10/2009

of England bought work from *Port Glasgow* and *Fancy Pictures.* I didn't sell many and not for much money. But I'm always interested in feeding back into the community. At one point the Scottish Parliament bought one of the *Fancy Pictures* images of Annie MacDougall with her goat called Snowy. This was about two years after that project ended. I put in the contract that if the photograph was acquired and hung in the Scottish Parliament they would have to pay for Annie to come over from the Isle of Bute to Edinburgh in a chauffeur-driven Jaguar. It was the first time she had left the island in fifty years. She turned up at parliament, met the First Minister, was treated very well and taken back at the end of the day. It was one of these small ways in which I was able to give immense pleasure and receive immense pleasure from my work. If you follow one line of conceptual ethics it can pay great dividends.

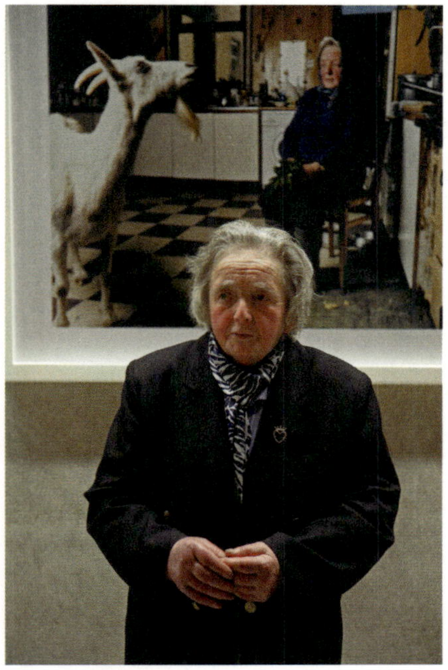

Annie Macdougall in front of her portrait exhibited at the Scottish Parliament, 2009

But not always in the ways one might expect. It's often unpredictable.

True.

Does the immersion in such projects and then their coming to an end feel strange to you?

I go back to my grandfather not being able to communicate except via a lens. The camera is a way for me to meet people, talk, get to know them and also express something of myself. It does work, at least on some levels. A tall white guy out of context, if he has a camera and he's taking his time, people will stop and talk to him, if he's open and honest, approachable, accessible and talkative. I've never been beaten up. Never had equipment stolen. I don't get on with everyone—nobody can—but on the whole there's a mutual respect at least. In twelve years of making these very involved and intense projects there's been almost no personal animosity. Maybe people sense that I feel the need to belong somewhere.

I'm able to mediate my place in the world and mediate this search for belonging, this search for family, for being accepted. The irony is, of course, that I'm never wholly accepted and the existential search goes on to the next community and the next. And of course the end of each project is invariably difficult for me. It's difficult to cut off or, at least, put it on hold for a long time as I move on to the next project. I'm still in touch with people in Port Glasgow and on the Isle of Bute.

Deeds 2010

Not

Words

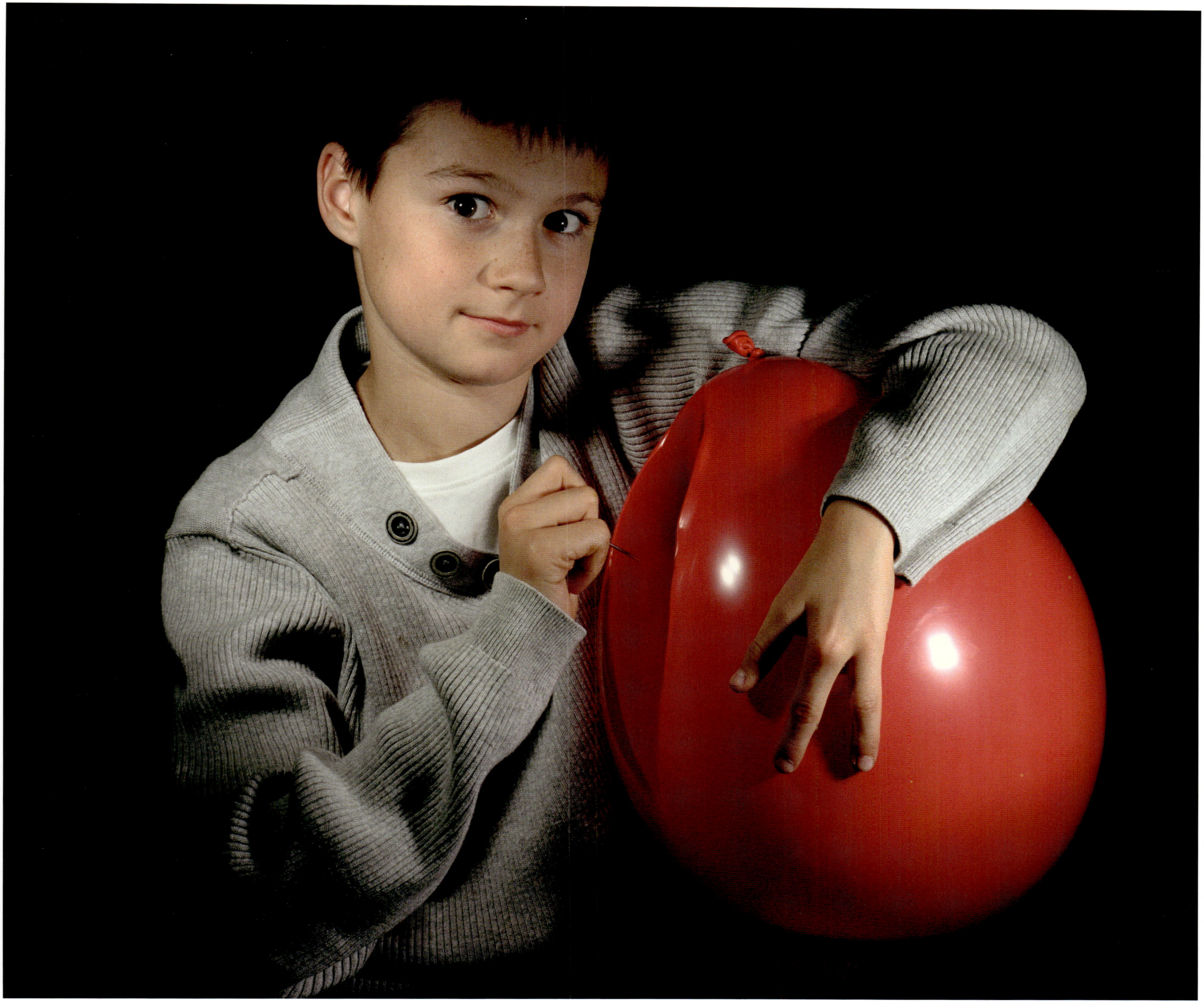

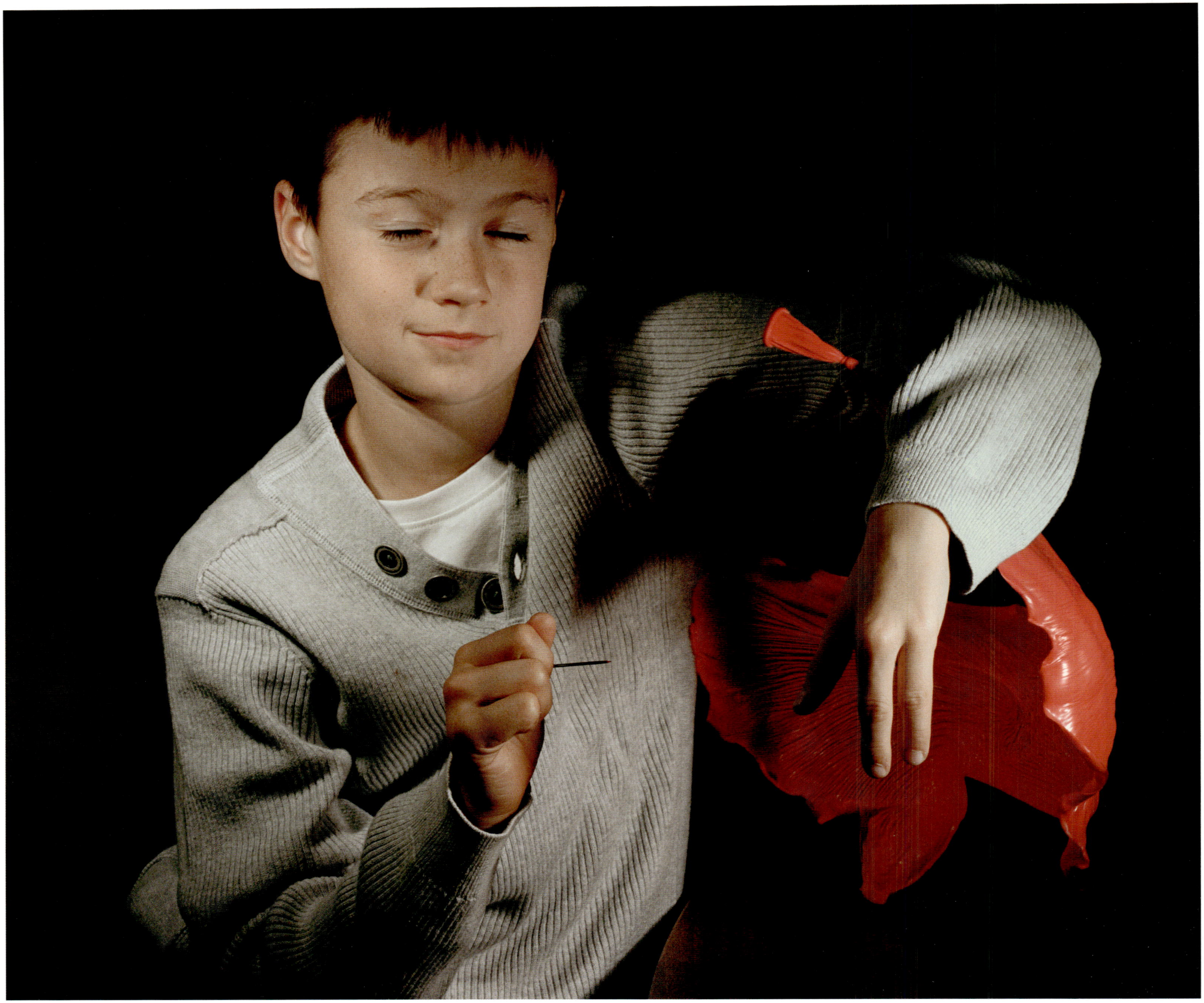

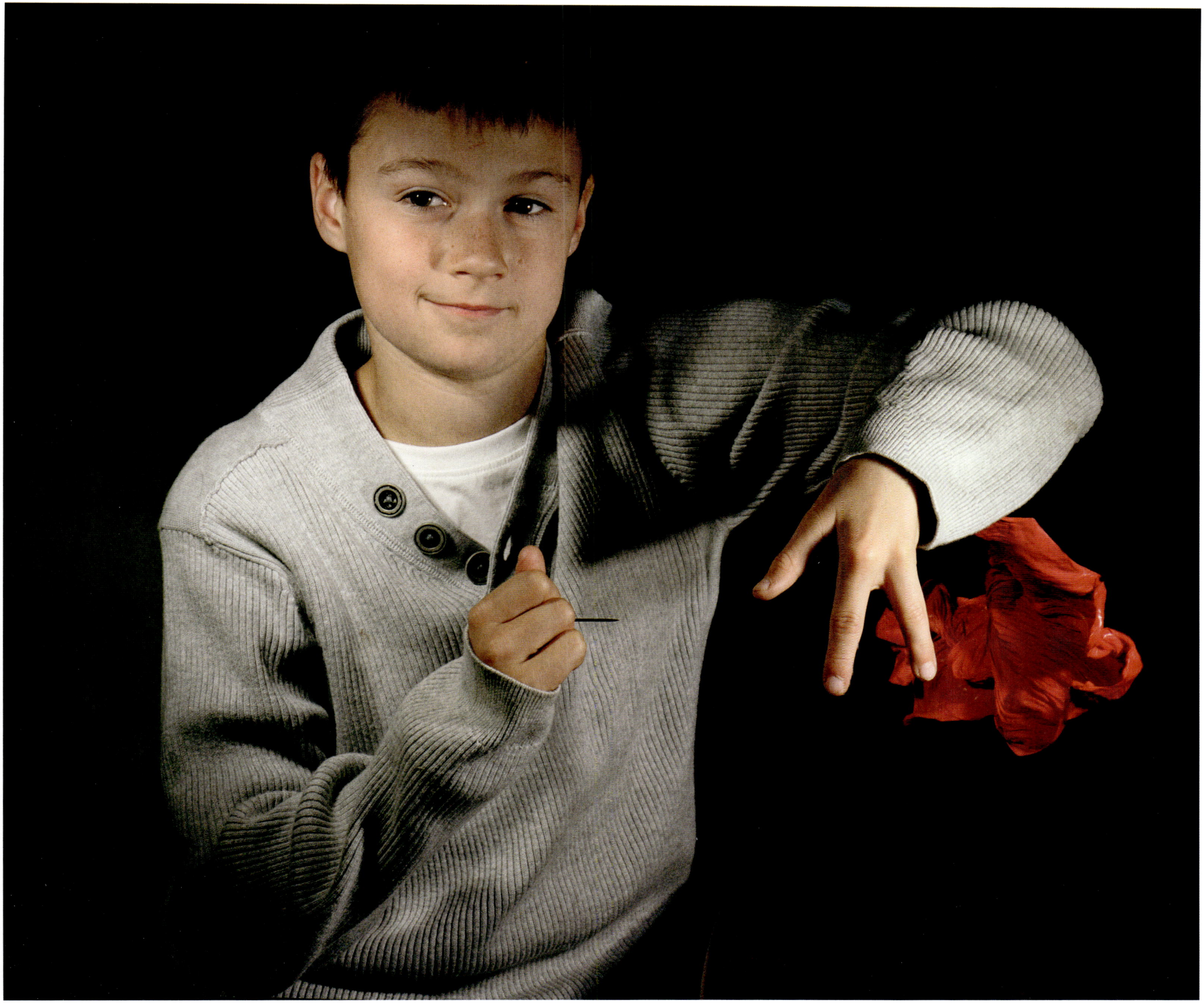

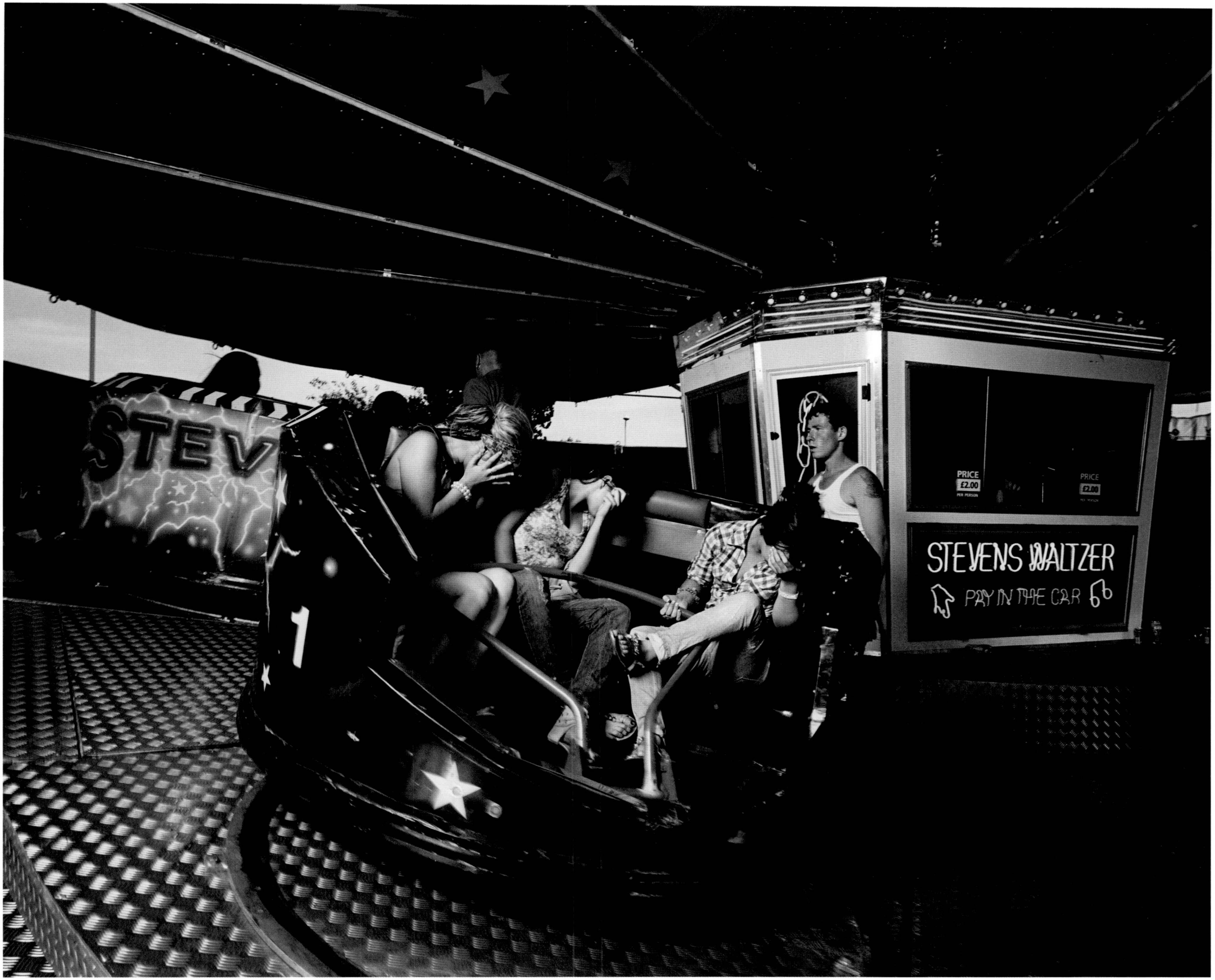
STEV
PRICE
£2.00
PRICE
£2.00
STEVENS WALTZER
PAY IN THE CAR

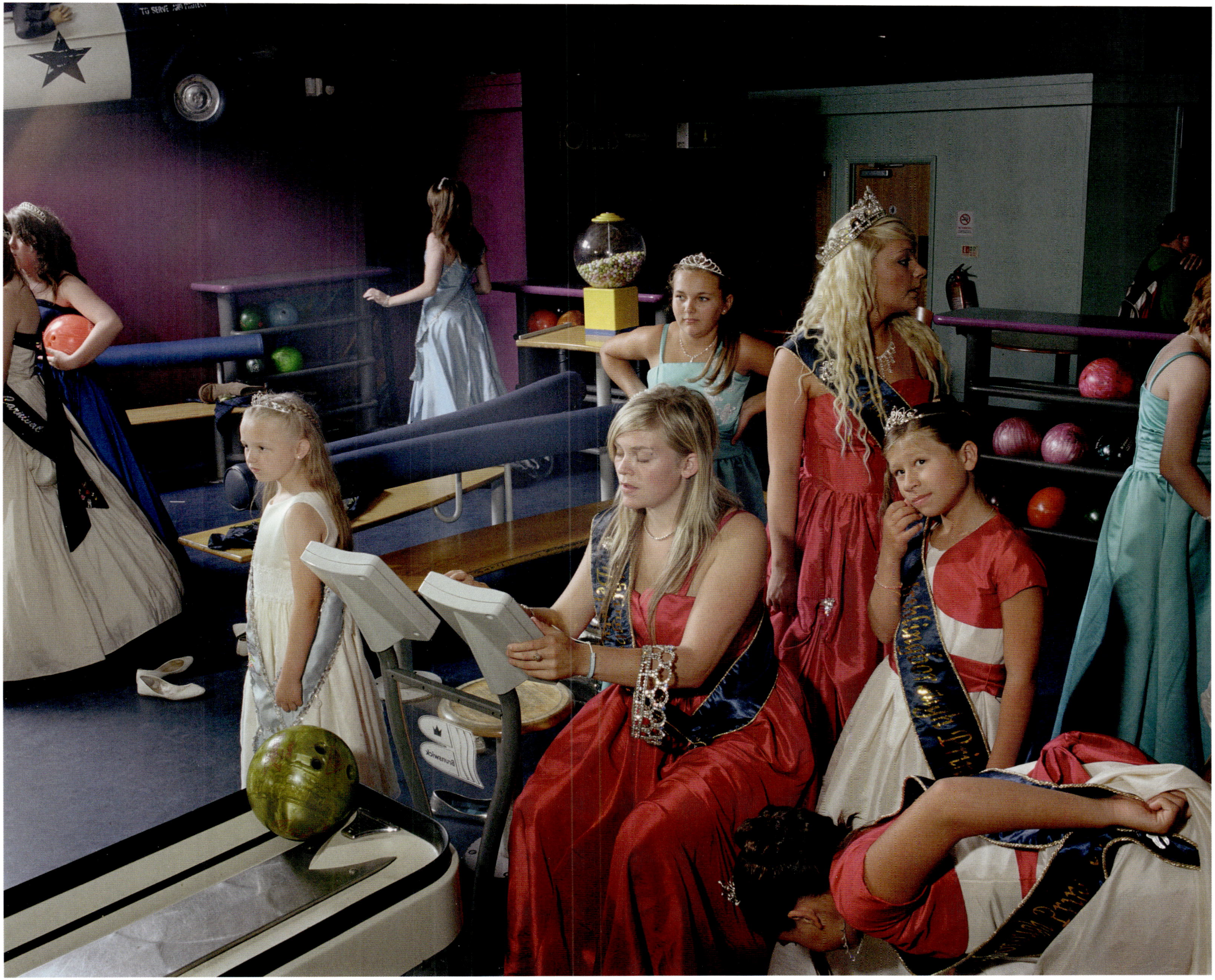
Carnival

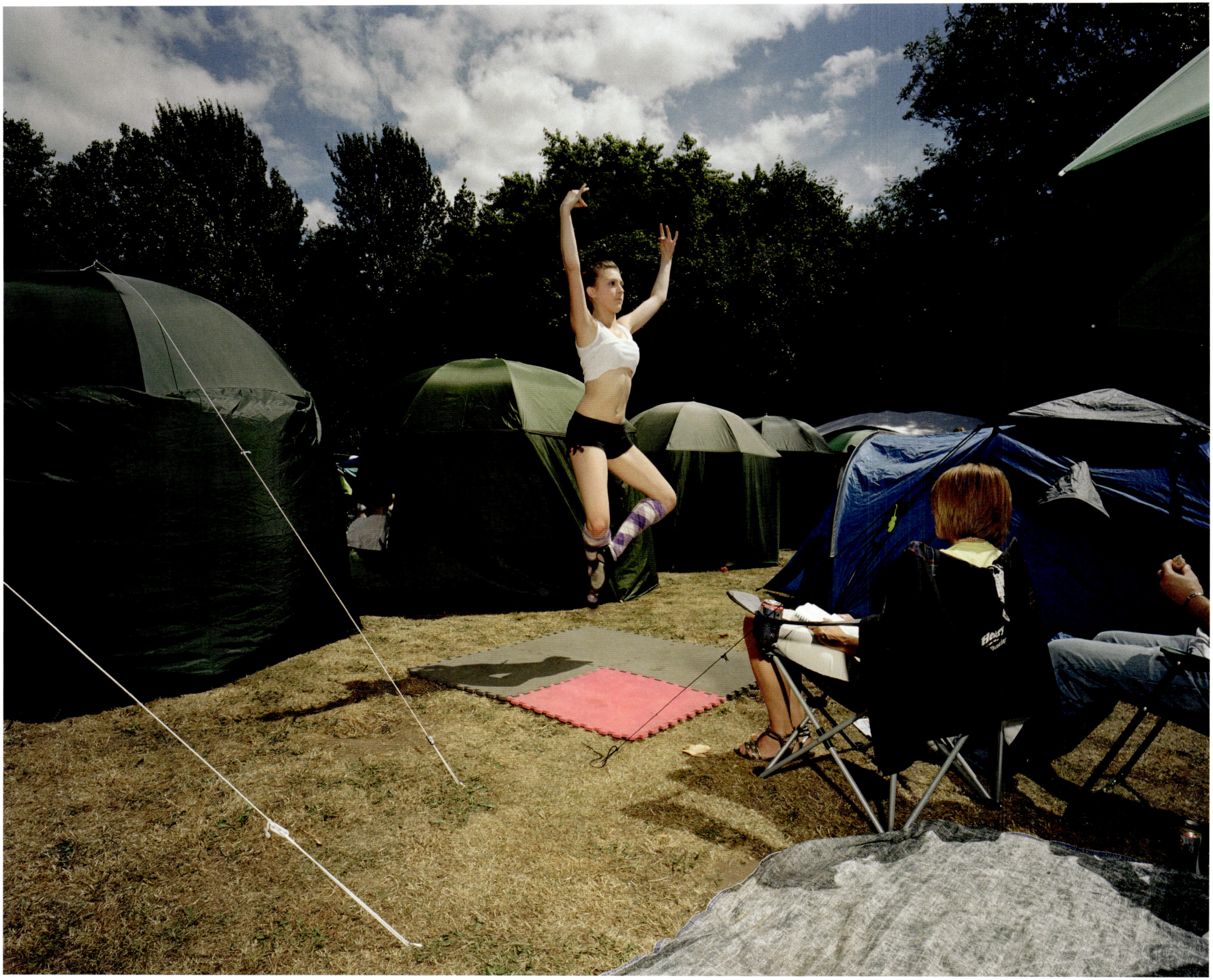

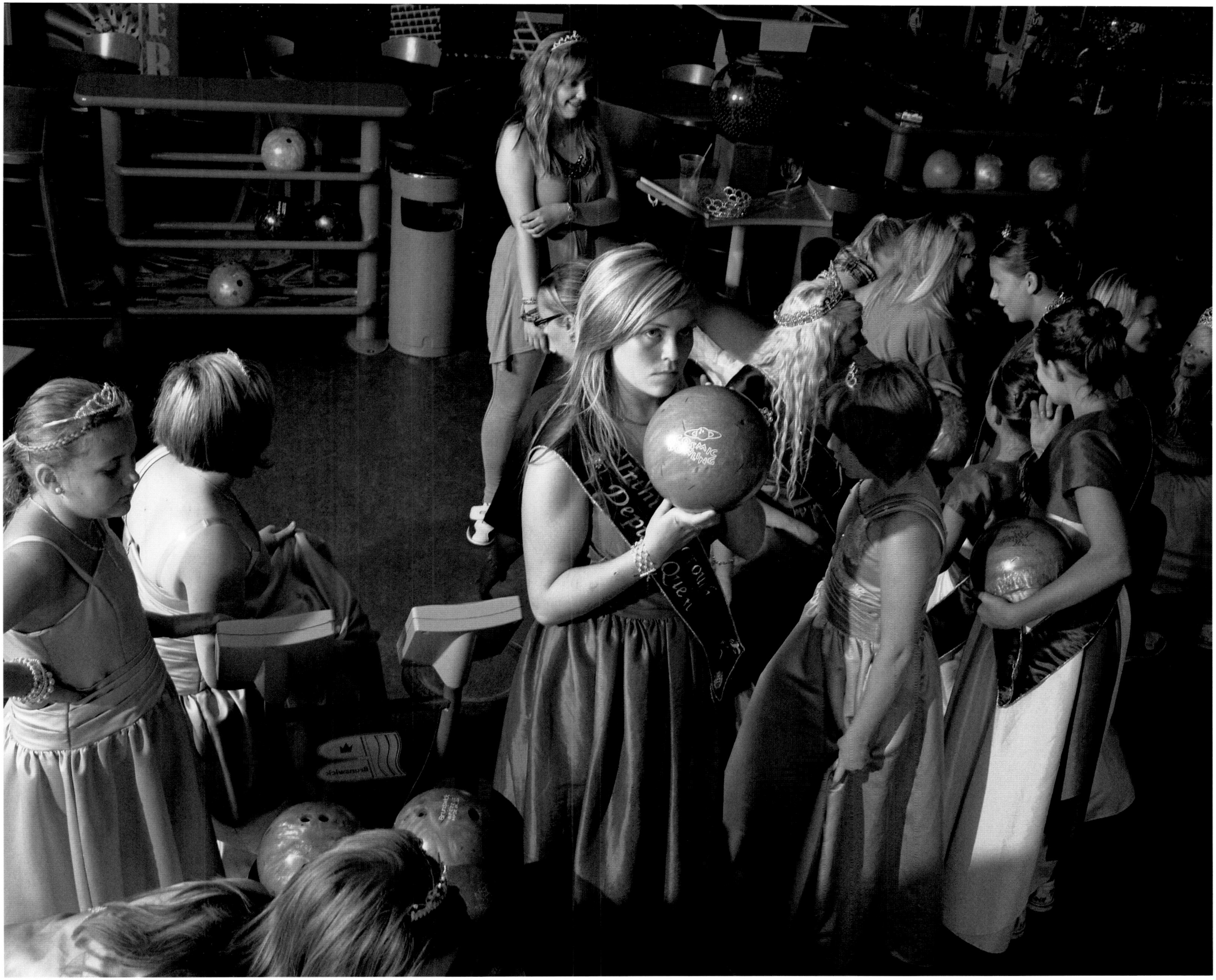

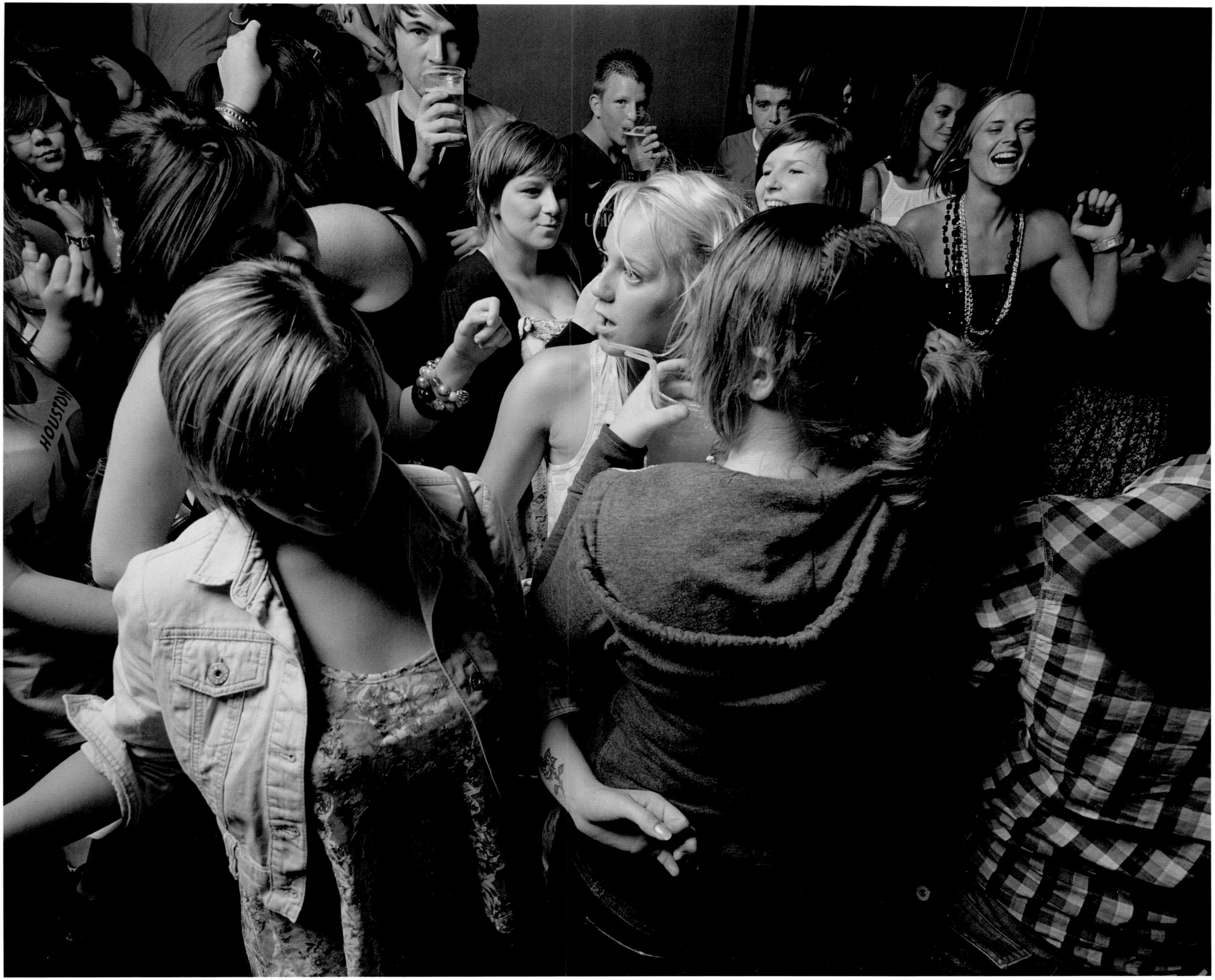
HOUSTON

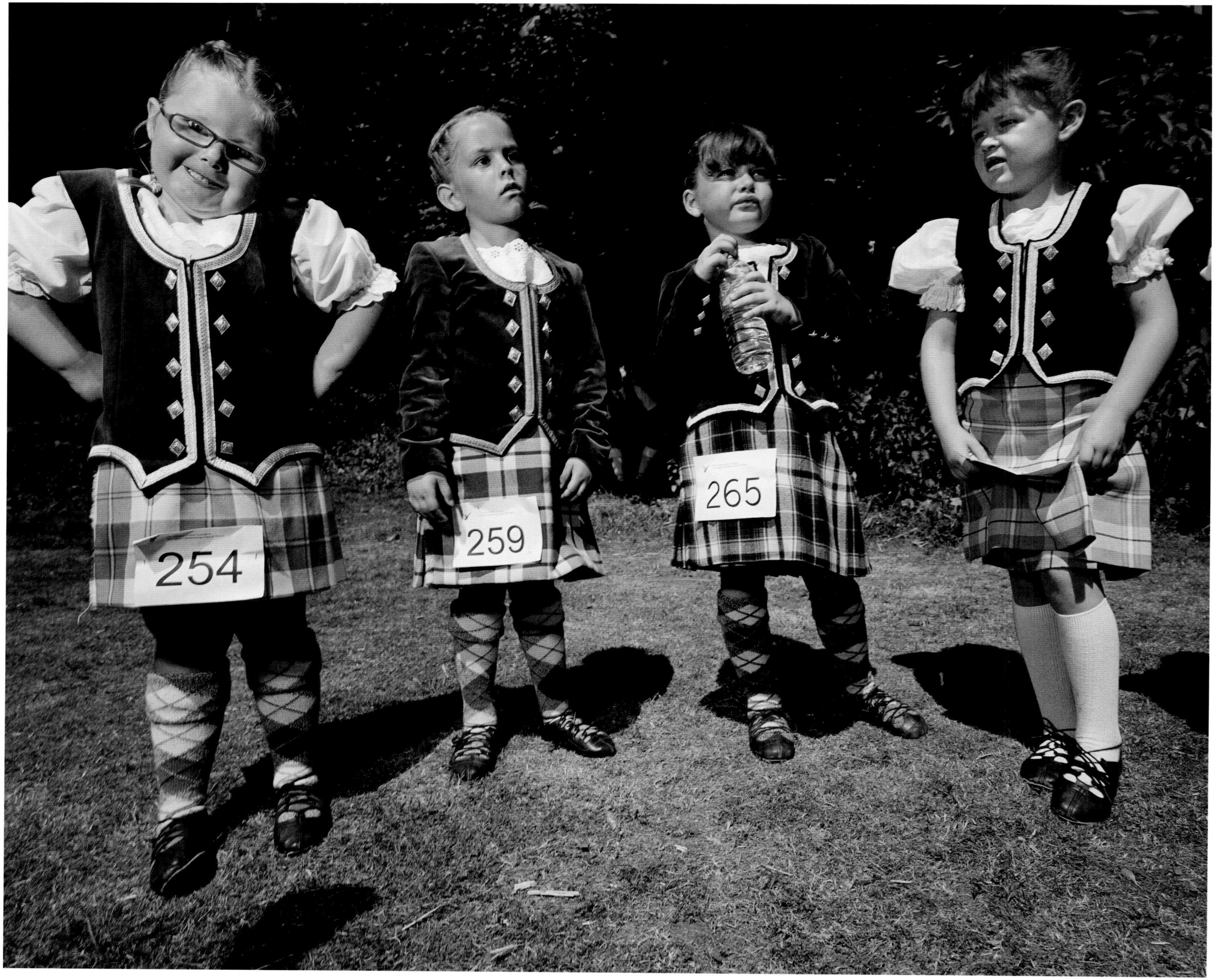
254
259
265

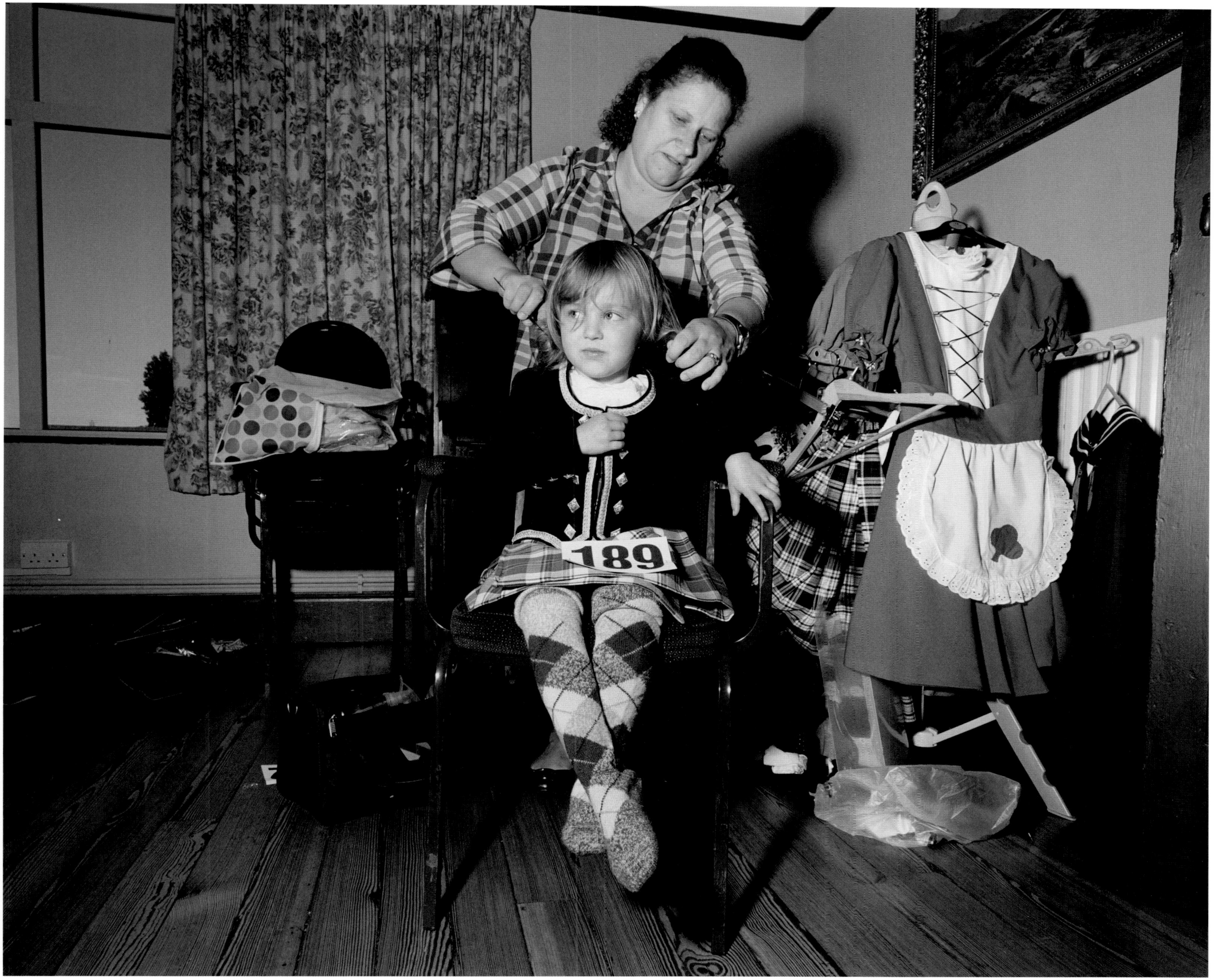
189

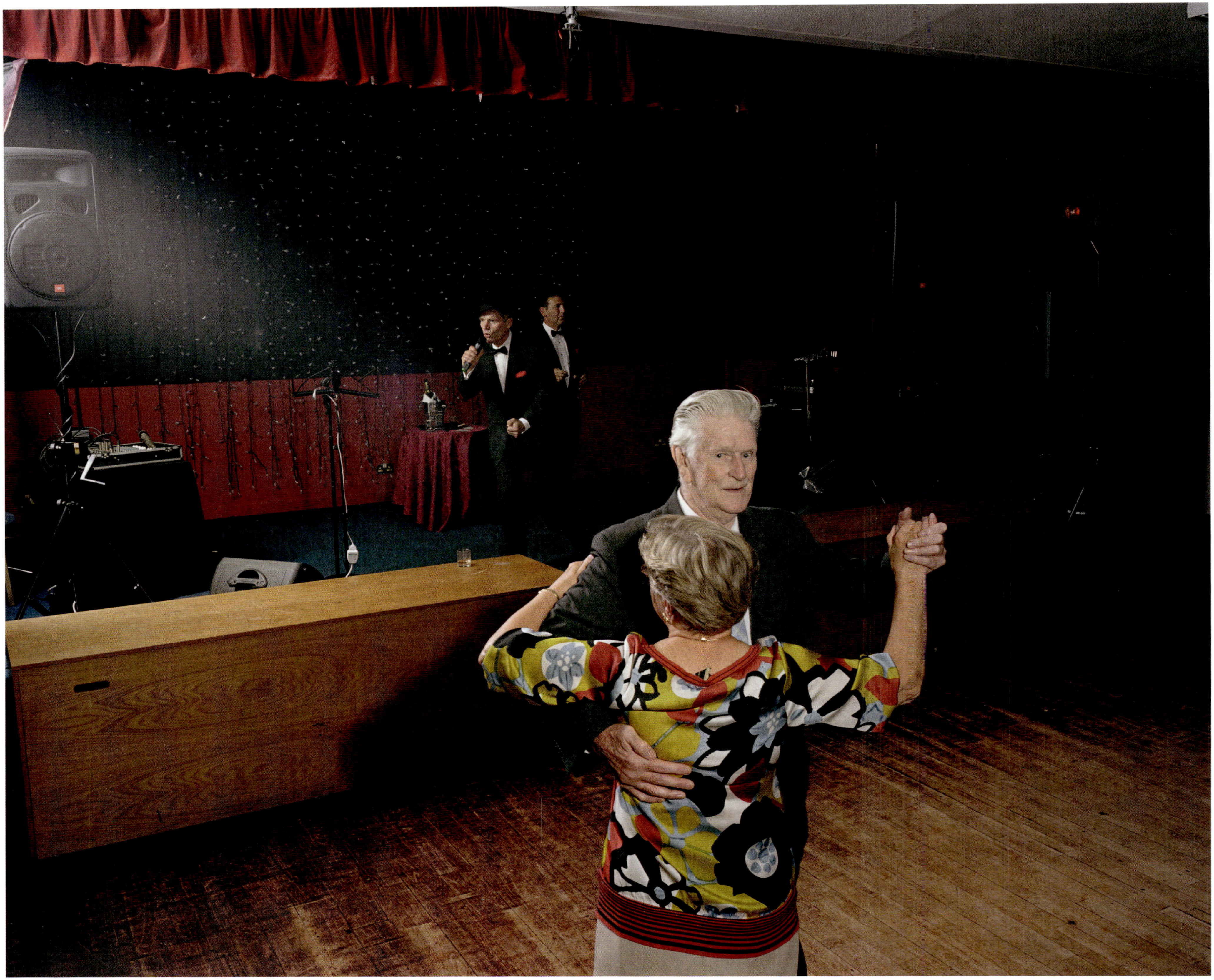

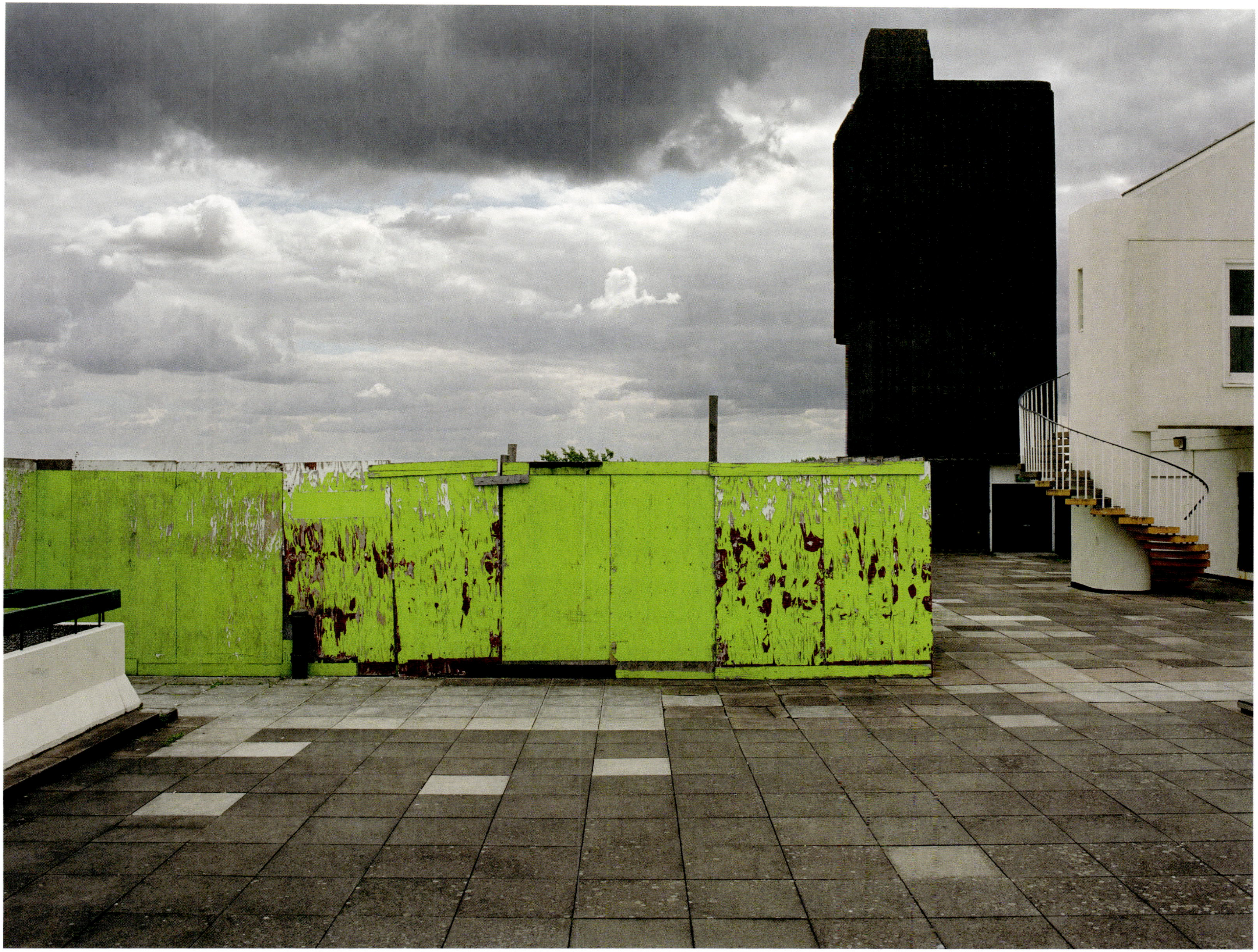

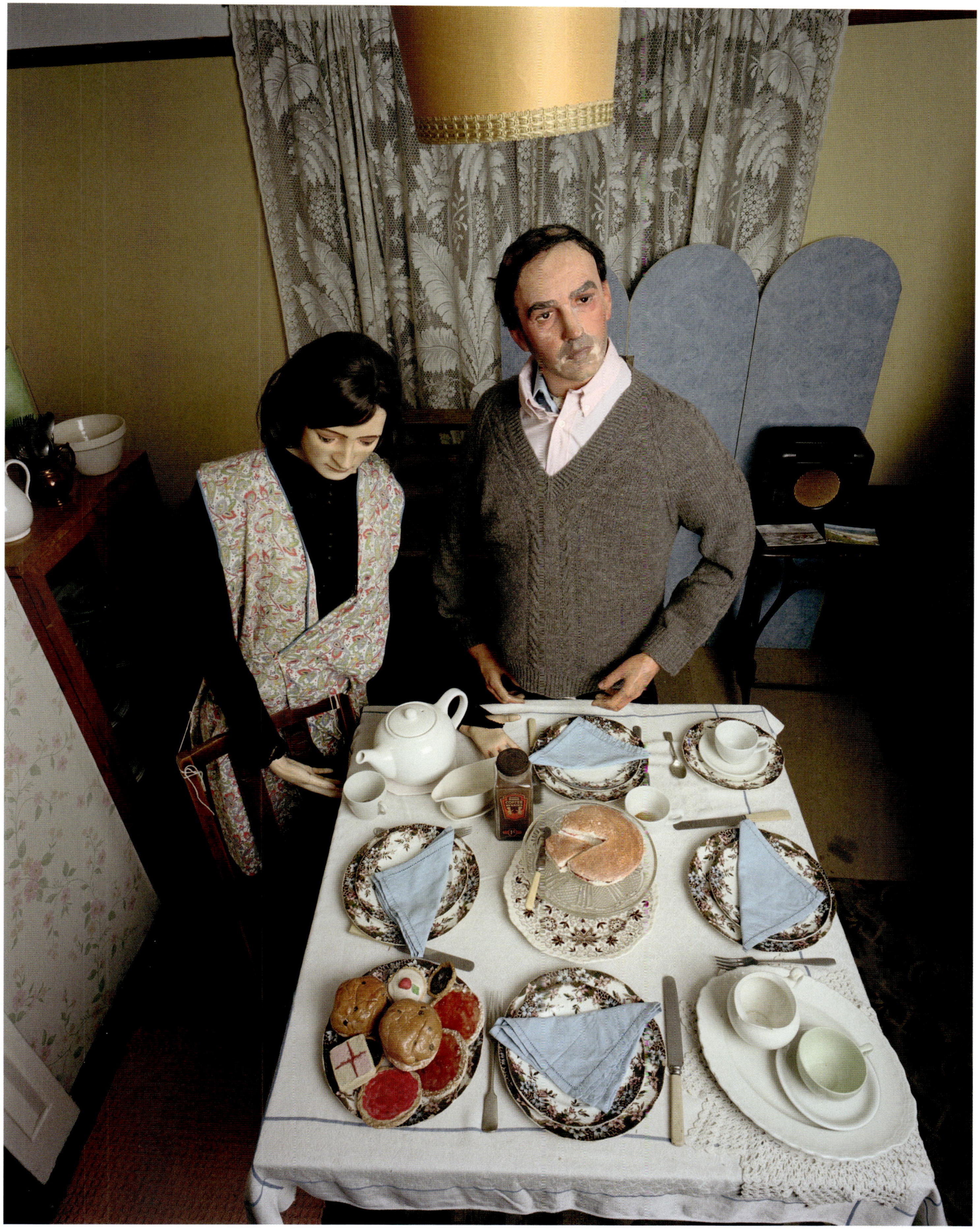

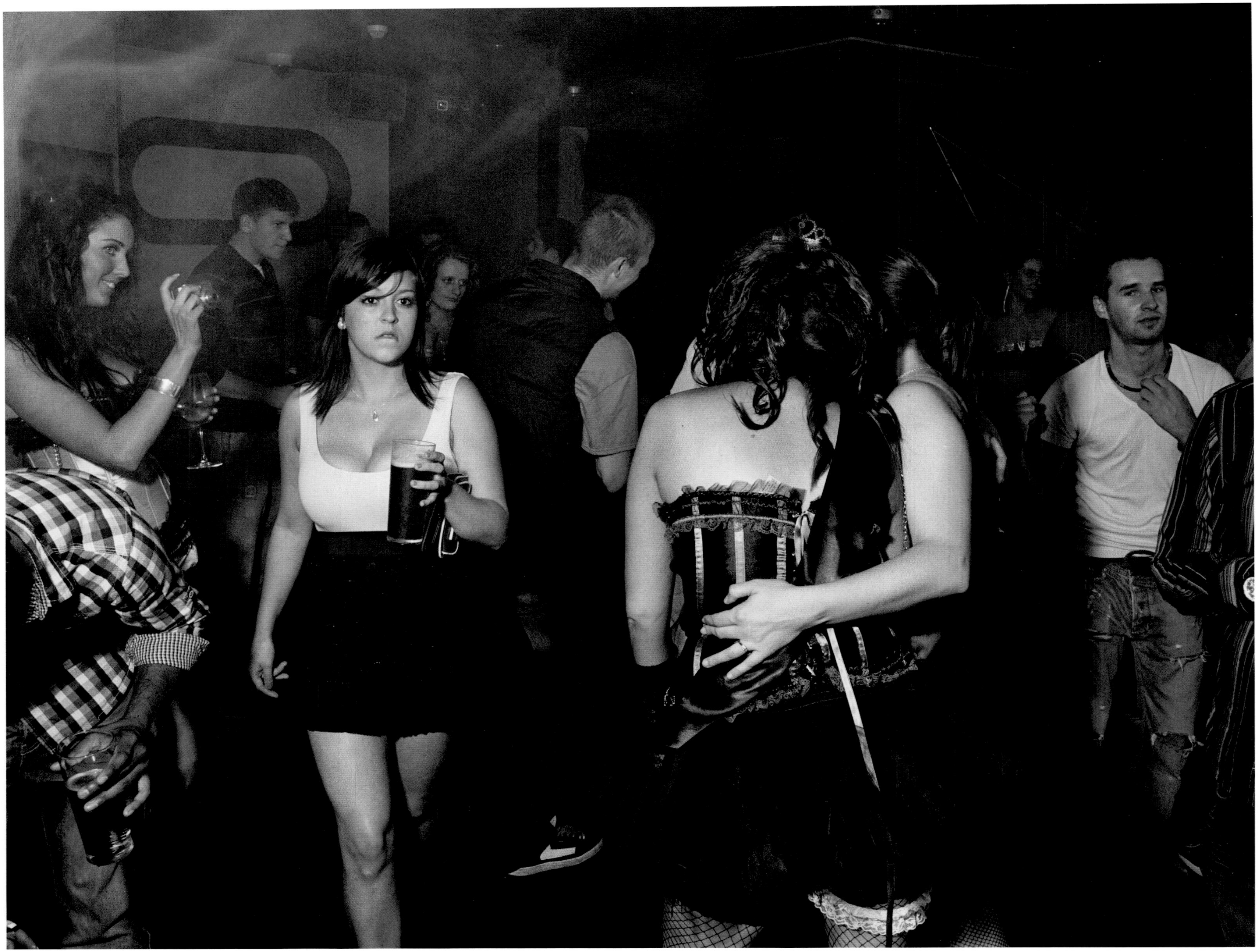

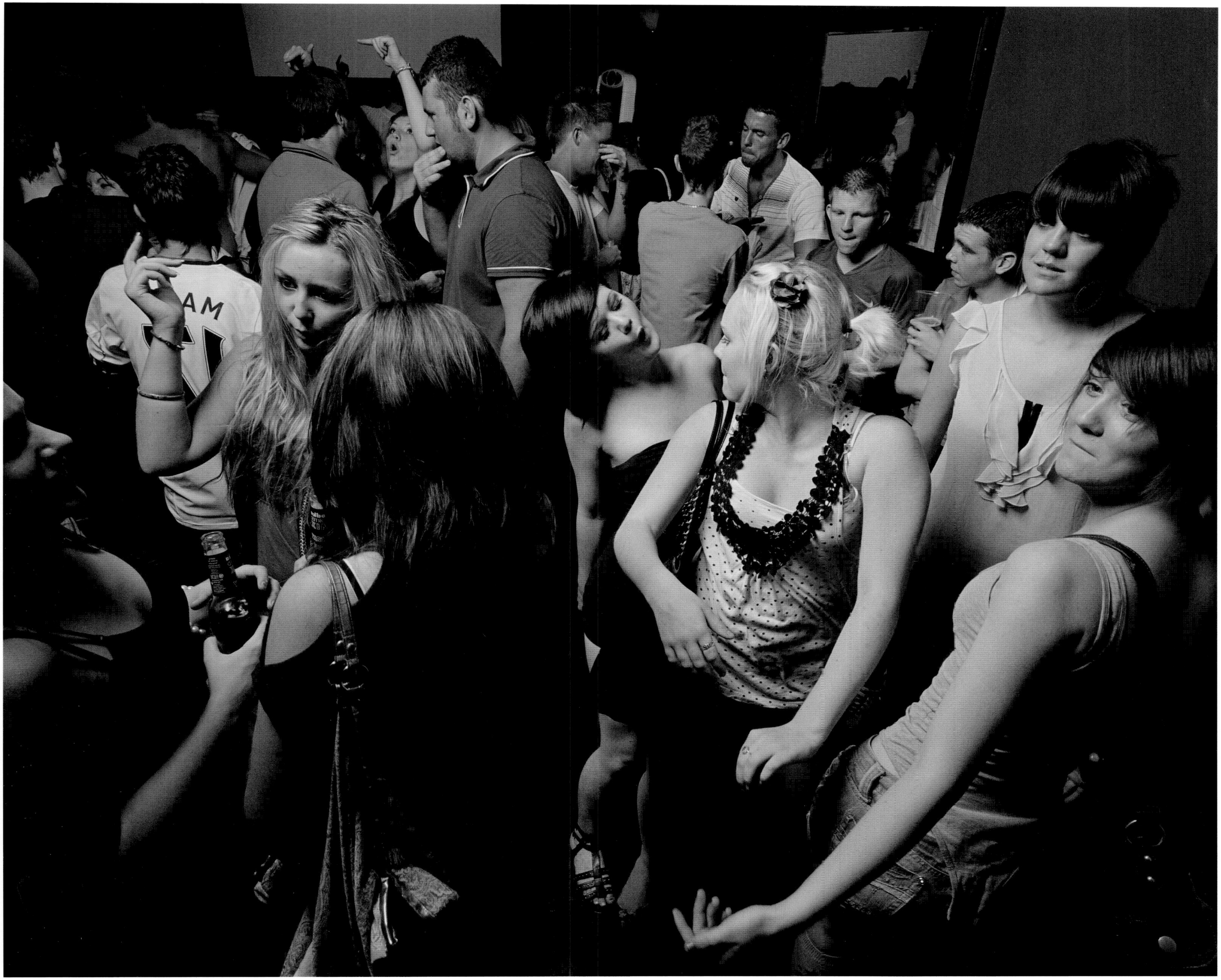

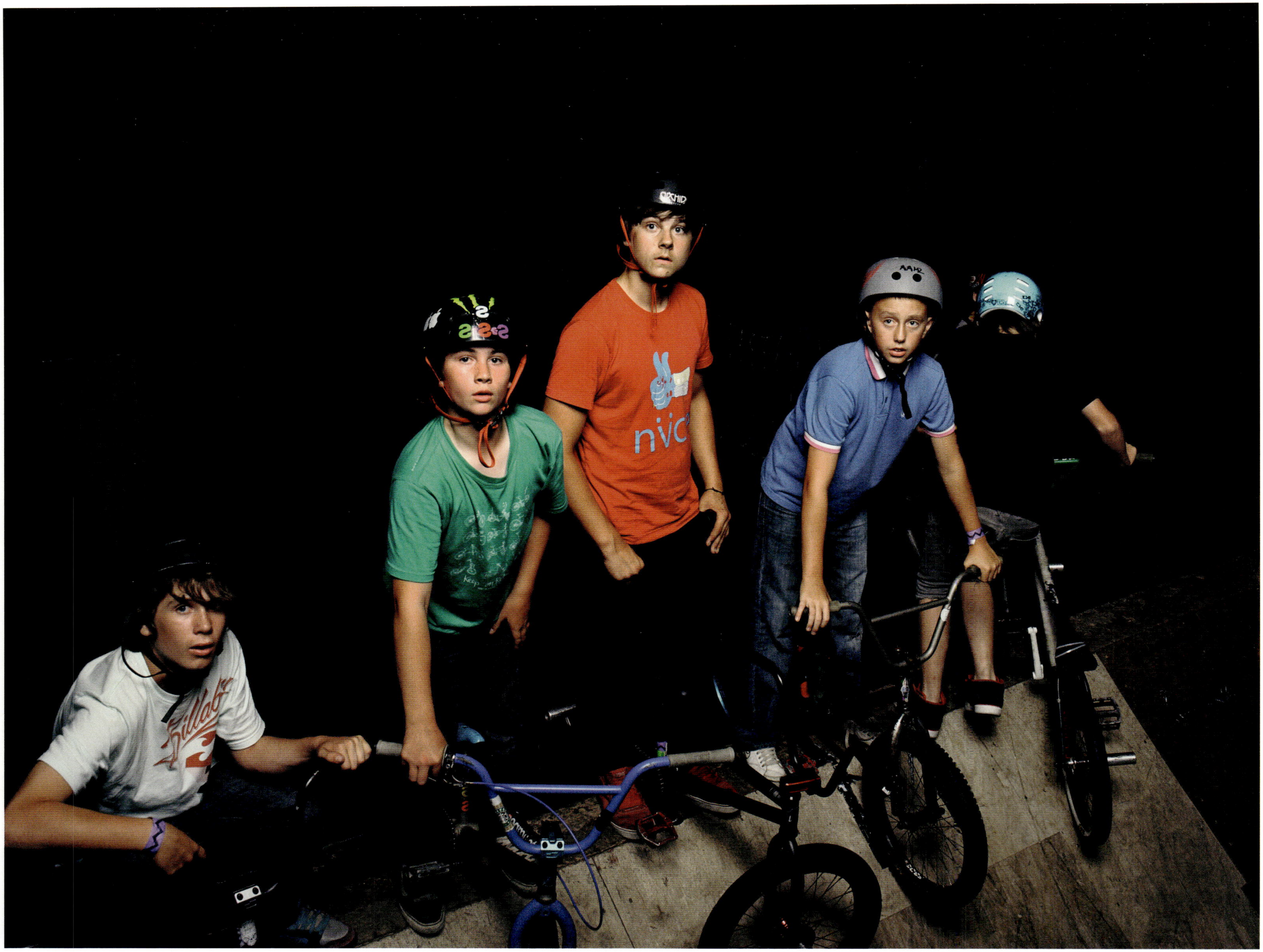

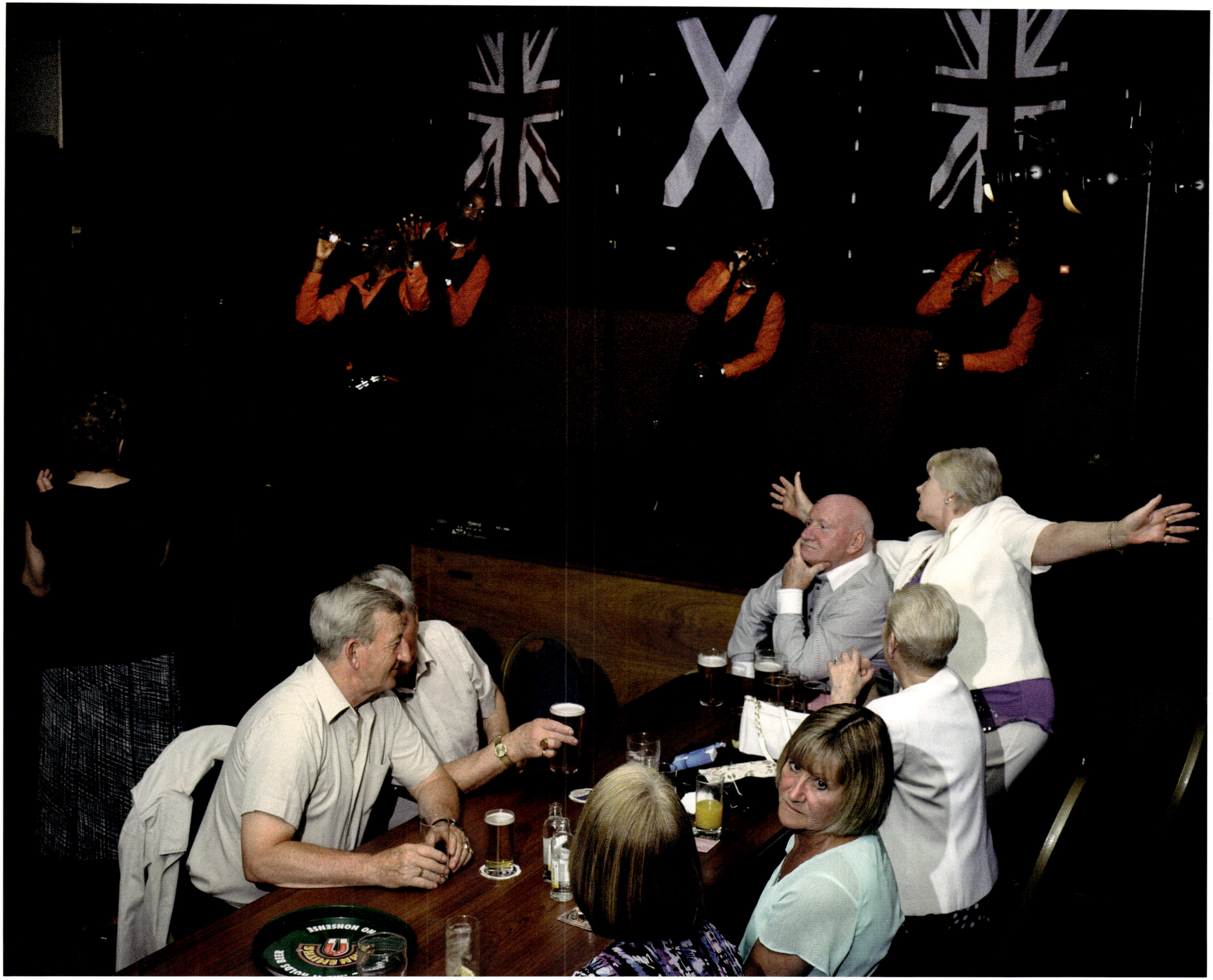

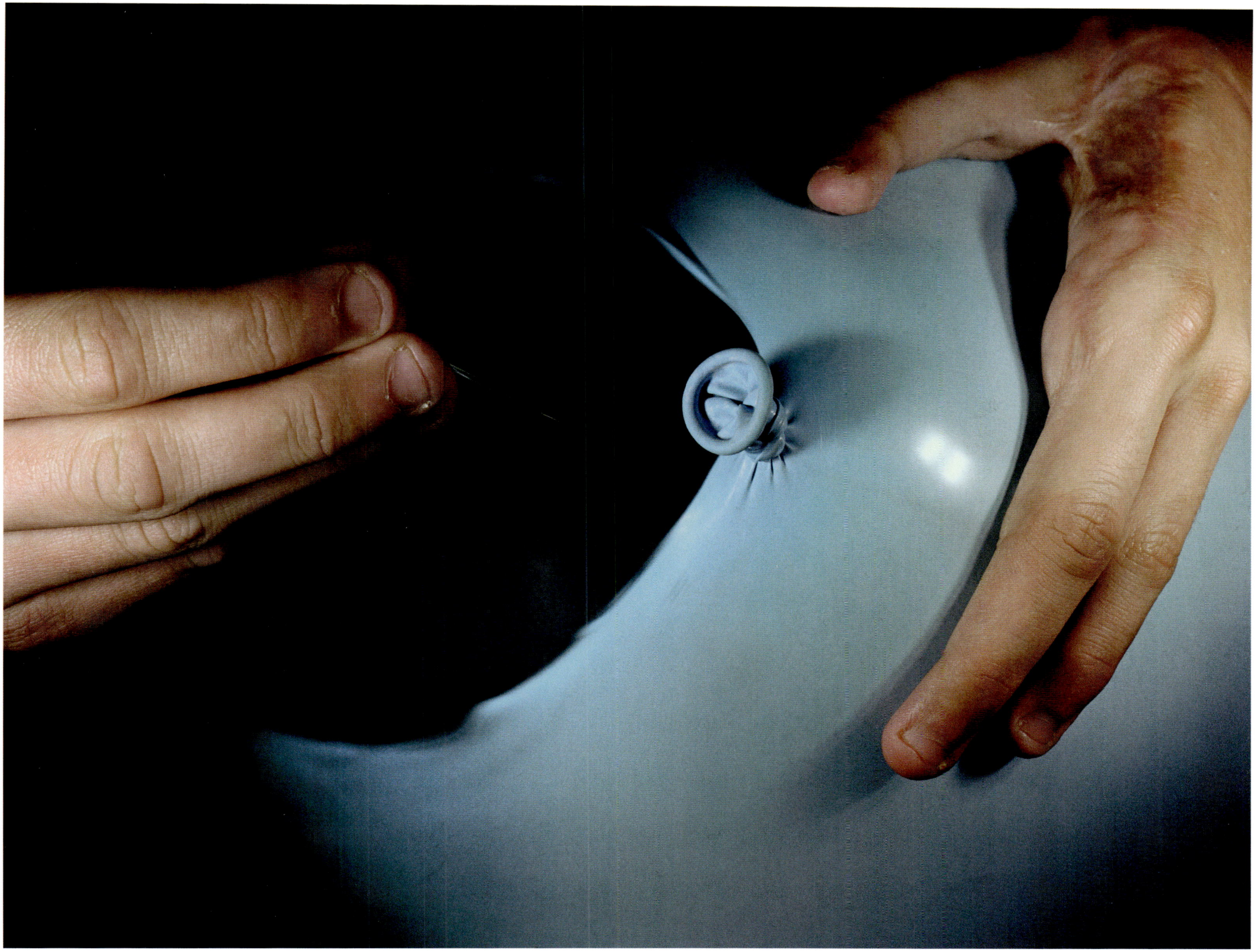

Titles

81. Ben Bursting a Balloon, 1, 2010
82. Ben Bursting a Balloon, 2, 2010
83. Ben Bursting a Balloon, 3, 2010
85. Stevens Funfair, 2010
87. Corby Carnival Queens Go Bowling, 1, 2010
88. Highland Dancer Among Tents, 2010
89. Corby Carnival Queens Go Bowling, 3, 2010
91. Madisons Nightclub, Rockingham Road, 2010
92. Highland Dancers, Corby Highland Games, 2010
93. Corby Highland Dancers preparing for competition, 2010
94. Frank Sinatra & Dean Martin Impersonators Play the Grampian Club, 2010
95. Willow Place Shopping Centre, 2010
97. Model of 1920's Domestic Scene of a Steel Worker, East Carlton Park Museum, 2010
98. Rockafellas Nightclub, Princewood Court, 2010
99. Madisons Nightclub, Rockingham Road, 2010
100. Adrenalin Alley, 2010
101. The Brothers of Soul play the Grampian Club, 2010
103. George Taylor Bursting a Balloon, 2010

Deeds
Not
Words

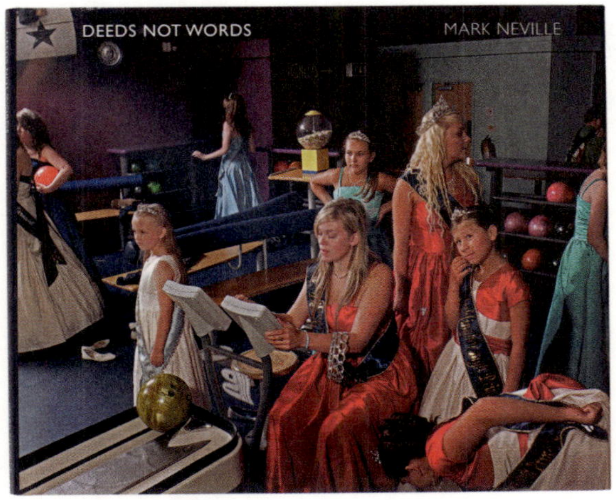

Cover of *Deeds Not Words*, 2010

David Campany: You never work to a great plan.

Mark Neville: No. When a project comes to an end I don't know what I'm going to do next.

While your next project wasn't in Scotland, it had a strong Scottish connection.

Someone on the Isle of Bute heard my English accent and asked if I knew anyone living in Corby. Actually this happened a few times and it prompted me to visit Corby. It's a town in the heart of the English countryside, surrounded by twee and conservative English places like Kettering and Huntingdon. But it has a very strong working-class Scottish identity. During the 1920s a big steel mill closed in Motherwell, near Glasgow. At the same time the owners Stewarts & Lloyds opened a new steel mill down in Corby, an area which has fantastically rich iron ore. The company invited the Scottish work force down to Corby and they came in large numbers. They were offered accommodation, an inside toilet. Wave upon wave, generation after generation, of Scottish people came between the 1920s and the 1970s. It has resulted in a unique culture in Corby. People speak with a Glaswegian twang in their voices. They sell more Irn Bru in Corby than they do in Glasgow, and all sorts of typically "Scottish" foods remain very popular. Even though the steel works closed in the early 1980s, the place has held onto this strong Scottish working-class identity. Actually the town has a very large eastern European demographic now, but still the culture remains Scottish.

I found all this really fascinating and started making regular visits to Corby. While I was there I heard about a very important court case. It was the Corby 16 case and it had already been going on for seven or eight years by this point. Essentially, a group of mothers had identified that their babies had been born with a similar type of birth defect: missing fingers or toes. It was almost always a defect of the limbs. This was what is called a "cluster" of defects: a higher than average number, in a small area, in a short space of time. This means there is probably a reason—an environmental reason—for it. During the 1980s, Corby council had undertaken a huge reclamation of the site of the former British Steel works, which involved digging up and removing vast quantities of the toxic waste that had been a by-product of steel making. This reclamation had been done very badly, employing people with little idea about the toxic waste. It was put on the back of open trucks and driven through the town uncovered. This happened for about a decade during which a fine red dust hung in the air of Corby. The mothers argued that during the first or second trimester of pregnancy, when the foetus is forming, if you inhale these dioxins there is a high chance the foetus can be damaged. We know that dioxins do this to animals but we can only extrapolate that it has the same effect on people. There is no way to prove absolutely the causal link between the dioxins and the birth defects. So it was a civil action brought by the mothers, arguing that it is *more likely than not* that there was a link. It was really a groundbreaking court case, not unlike the Erin Brockovich case in America. It was eventually successful.

You began to photograph before any kind of judgment was made in the case?

Oh yes. I was shooting even before I was aware of the case. But the court case started to help me form what I wanted to do in Corby. I decided to see if I could use the form of the photo book to impact upon the issue. I approached the Wellcome Trust, which funds medically-related arts projects, and they gave me a small grant to live, work, research and produce a book.

And who would be the audience this time?

The audience would be the environmental health departments of every single local council in the whole of the UK, all 433 of them. But also government policy makers, key opinion formers, people who are actively involved in shaping and making government policy around post-industrial land reclamation and toxic waste disposal. The Corby 16 case was concluded in favour of the families whilst I was still making the book. But even after that, and after the book had come out, nothing much had changed at the level of policy. In other words there was nothing to say that another council or a property developer might come along, dig up a site of a former factory, chemical plant or steel works and do exactly the same thing as happened in Corby. There are no lucid, consistent guidelines either for testing for these pollutants or controlling them.

But this project becomes a real test for what you had been thinking about: how photographs communicate and might have a direct impact. Photographs largely deal with appearances in the first instance.

And this project became very much about appearance. I focused on the youth of Corby, not just the teenagers with birth defects, but the youth in general. The photographs really explore adolescence—those years when young people are very self-conscious about their own appearance, their own "body-image". So the whole project has a heightened awareness about body-image and self-image. Two boys, Ben Vissian and George Taylor, who were born without fingers, were photographed with a high-speed flash. I made sequences of them popping balloons. Around those I made more typical social documentary

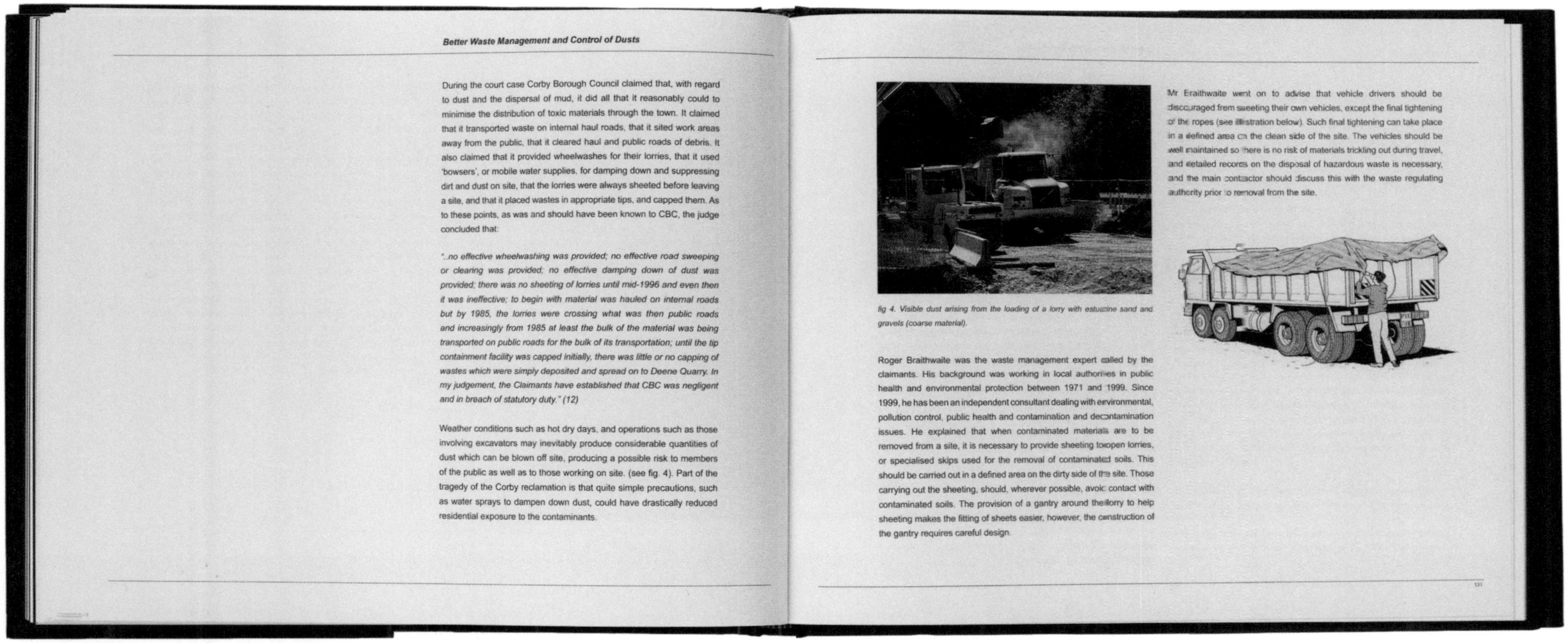

Better Waste Management and Control of Dusts

During the court case Corby Borough Council claimed that, with regard to dust and the dispersal of mud, it did all that it reasonably could to minimise the distribution of toxic materials through the town. It claimed that it transported waste on internal haul roads, that it sited work areas away from the public, that it cleared haul and public roads of debris. It also claimed that it provided wheelwashes for their lorries, that it used 'bowsers', or mobile water supplies, for damping down and suppressing dirt and dust on site, that the lorries were always sheeted before leaving a site, and that it placed wastes in appropriate tips, and capped them. As to these points, as was and should have been known to CBC, the judge concluded that:

"..no effective wheelwashing was provided; no effective road sweeping or clearing was provided; no effective damping down of dust was provided; there was no sheeting of lorries until mid-1996 and even then it was ineffective; to begin with material was hauled on internal roads but by 1985, the lorries were crossing what was then public roads and increasingly from 1985 at least the bulk of the material was being transported on public roads for the bulk of its transportation; until the tip containment facility was capped initially, there was little or no capping of wastes which were simply deposited and spread on to Deene Quarry. In my judgement, the Claimants have established that CBC was negligent and in breach of statutory duty." (12)

Weather conditions such as hot dry days, and operations such as those involving excavators may inevitably produce considerable quantities of dust which can be blown off site, producing a possible risk to members of the public as well as to those working on site. (see fig. 4). Part of the tragedy of the Corby reclamation is that quite simple precautions, such as water sprays to dampen down dust, could have drastically reduced residential exposure to the contaminants.

fig 4. Visible dust arising from the loading of a lorry with estuarine sand and gravels (coarse material).

Roger Braithwaite was the waste management expert called by the claimants. His background was working in local authorities in public health and environmental protection between 1971 and 1999. Since 1999, he has been an independent consultant dealing with environmental, pollution control, public health and contamination and decontamination issues. He explained that when contaminated materials are to be removed from a site, it is necessary to provide sheeting to open lorries, or specialised skips used for the removal of contaminated soils. This should be carried out in a defined area on the dirty side of the site. Those carrying out the sheeting, should, wherever possible, avoid contact with contaminated soils. The provision of a gantry around the lorry to help sheeting makes the fitting of sheets easier, however, the construction of the gantry requires careful design.

Mr Braithwaite went on to advise that vehicle drivers should be discouraged from sheeting their own vehicles, except the final tightening of the ropes (see illustration below). Such final tightening can take place in a defined area on the clean side of the site. The vehicles should be well maintained so there is no risk of materials trickling out during travel, and detailed records on the disposal of hazardous waste is necessary, and the main contractor should discuss this with the waste regulating authority prior to removal from the site.

Spread from *Deeds Not Words*, 2010

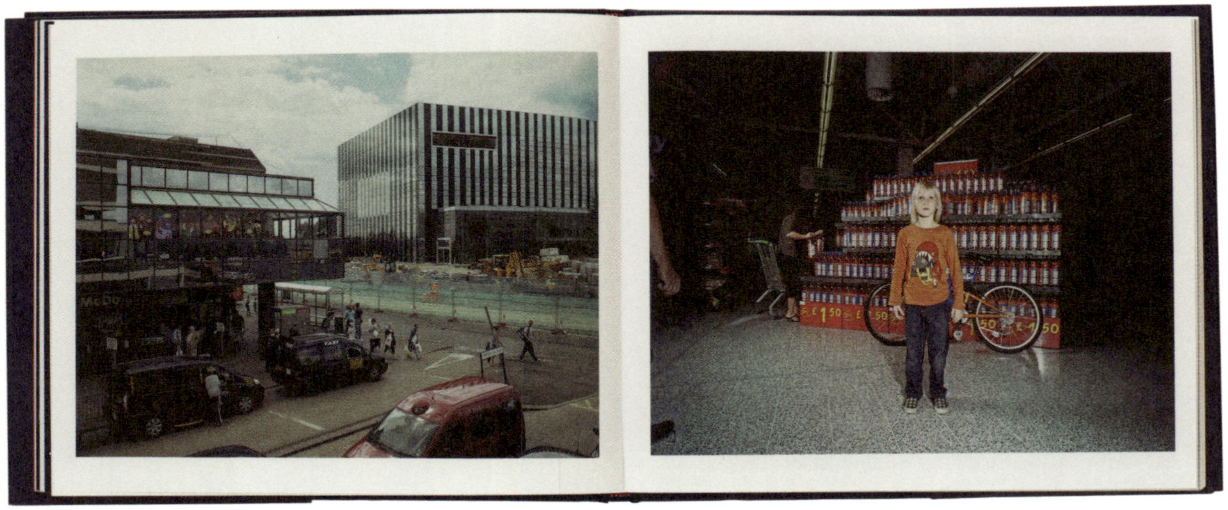

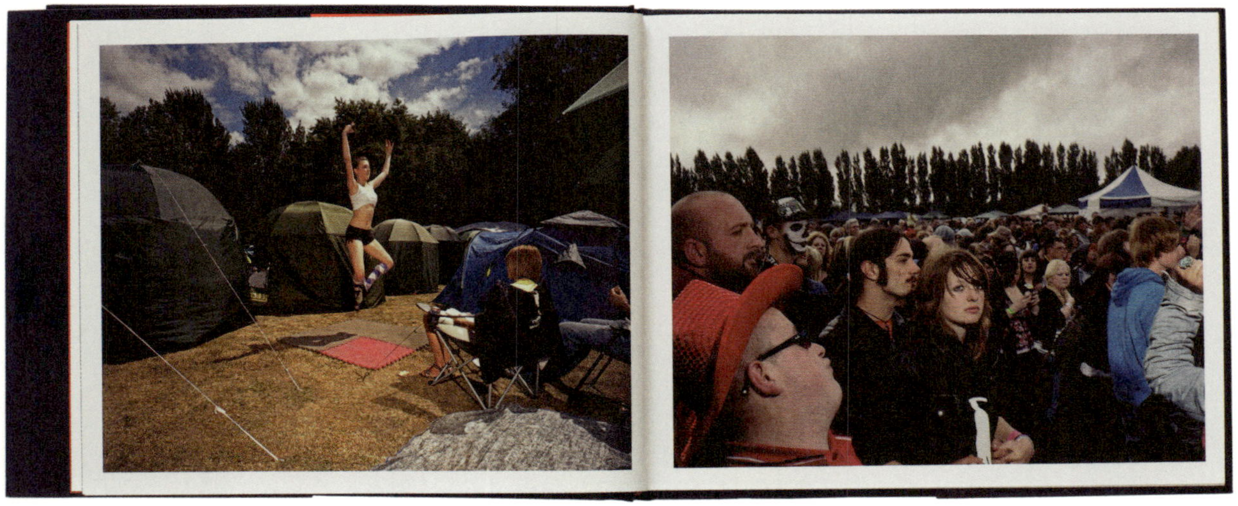

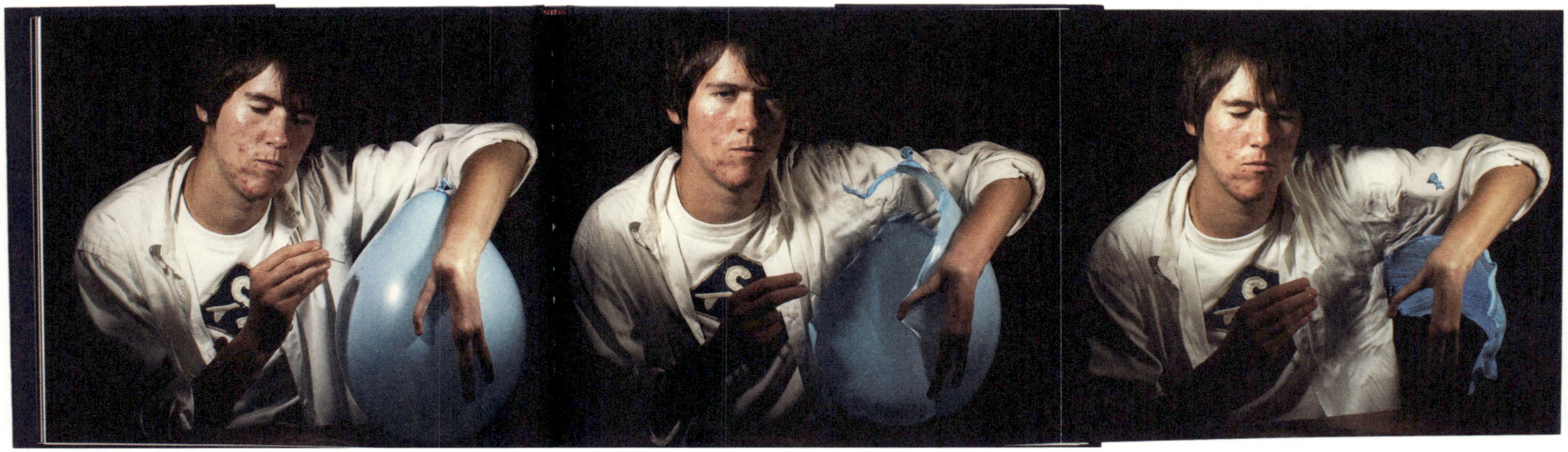

Spreads from *Deeds Not Words*, 2010

pictures of everything from carnival queens to highland dancers, and nightclubs for the youth of Corby. But it was all about appearance.

Those boys are really involved in those sequences.

That was very much the intention. I'd noticed that in previous representations of Ben and George, for example in newspapers, they were either asked to hold their hands up to be photographed in isolation, cut off at the wrist, or they were asked to hide their hands behind their backs. There was no sense of integration of the deformity into the whole body, personality and life of these children. We all have to deal with the physical packages we're in, don't we? I felt I wanted to make more complex, multi-layered portraits.

They defy easy reading I think, and that slows down a viewer.

That was the idea. The balloon burst pictures are done in complete darkness with high-speed flash. The sound of the burst triggers the flash. This technology reveals something that the naked eye cannot perceive. And in a way that was a metaphor for the whole court case. You couldn't actually *see* the dioxins having their effects. Ben loved the pictures. He took them into his science class at school. They discussed them. He was taking part in the whole process. He had ownership of the project.

I can see the pictures come out of what you were doing in the previous projects, but now you're asking those pictures to do some quite specific things, to work in the name of a quite specific outcome.

I did feel I had a particular question to ask when I made *Port Glasgow* and here in Corby I had a different question to ask.

But in *Port Glasgow* the "success" of the project was the making and delivery of the book. That's the fulfilment of your goal. Anything else that happened was a bonus. In Corby the goal is much more defined: you are looking for policy change.

I felt there had been no explicit manifestation of the court case—its outcomes and conclusions. So I made the book and titled it *Deed Not Words*, which is the motto of Corby Town Council. The first half of the book is photographic. The second half is nearly all text: a summary of the court case, the science involved, various testimonies from those affected. The book was distributed as I had planned and it seemed to have almost no effect. I got a couple of positive emails and letters in response but beyond that, almost nothing. And it was at that point that I approached you David, and we began to collaborate on a possible exhibition. We approached The Photographers Gallery in London. This was late 2012.

Yes, I remember we had long discussions about this whole question of whether the project could be transformed and re-articulated while keeping the same goal in mind. The Photographers' Gallery is

From : Peter Deckard
Sent : 04 November 2011 15:39:42
To : info@markneville.com
Subject : Deeds Not Words

Dear Mark,
Thank you for your book 'Deeds Not Words' which I have read with interest and I thought I should bullet point a few comments for you as feedback. As follows:

1. Local Authority Contaminated Land Officers are very much aware of the risks of developing sites that are heavily contaminated specifically managing risks to human health and the environment and what is often overlooked how this is communicated to stakeholders. Local Authorities on the whole are fairly unaware of the magnitude of these issues although the Corby case has certainly raised awareness.

2. As Roger Braithwaite's testament states resources are dwindling across all departments which for Land Quality here has meant a reduction in staff from 2.5 full time equivalent to 1. For industrialised areas such as Wakefield District this does put a strain on the effective management of contaminated land.

3. I would consider your book to be slightly biased in that you have not included the statements etc from the defendant's side [even if it was that you approached them and they declined to comment].

4. Being brutally honest here I would not take the book into meetings due to mainly the front cover and art which Is far from what is normally referred to in meetings i.e. technical guidance. I fear the perception this would give may reduce my credibility as principally a scientist / engineer. I do however honour the principle messages laid out in the book and I recognise the importance of socio-economic factors and risk communication issues during the safe re-development of land.

Peter Deckard

Land Quality Officer

E-mail response from a contaminated land officer to receiving a copy of Deeds Not Words, 2011

E-mail response to the book
Deeds Not Words

From : Janie MacMillan
Sent : 01/05/2014 12:22
To : info@markneville.com
Subject : Deeds Not Words

Dear Mr. Neville

I live beside beside what was the Ravenscraig steelworks in North Lanarkshire and am involved in a protest against putting a "super school" on that toxic tip. The Craig closed in 1992 with the towers coming down in 1996 and the first big plan was unveiled in 2001 but here we are in 2014 with a council so desperate to Kick start the New Town of Ravenscraig that they want and are determined to put a "super school" there to get it kick started!

I am aware that your book was set to every council but North Lanarkshire do not seem to have a copy and most certainly have not debated it: in a way that is proof that your book got under their skin when they will not even acknowledge that they have it.

Thank you for your interest in such a vital topic.

Yours sincerely

Janie MacMillan

interesting because it's not necessarily an art gallery. Its commitment is to the medium of photography in all its forms and institutional manifestations. It does show art but also documentary, archival projects, scientific projects, domestic photography, fashion, all kinds. So why not this project?

> Yes, why not? Could we use it as a platform for this project? The gallery took it on.

Which was adventurous and honourable of them.

> Despite the book not having the effect I was hoping for, the Wellcome Trust funded the production of an exhibition. We ended up with a show of around 35 large-scale photographs, plus a twenty-minute film exploring the court case and the project. There was also a large, colour poster on heavy paper, which had several images and a summary of the project. This was given away free.

What are your feelings about this second life of *Deeds Not Words*?

> The book was one thing. I was trying to arm local health authorities with information about the environmental risks of land reclamation. It was a tool kit that could be taken into meetings and boardrooms in the hope of changing policy in a very direct way. This was my fantasy of the book's role. The reality was very different. So when we went to meet The Photographers' Gallery I felt at that point that the project had failed. OK, I'd made a nice book, a "committed book", and I had delivered it in a targeted way but, really, it had failed. So the opportunity for a second life couldn't be turned down. It was hugely appealing but it was a very different approach. I thought the show worked really well, moving between prints, poster and the short film, but the key to it was the symposium. The Photographers' Gallery has a significant public talks programme. Could this be used to convene a discussion of the case? We invited politicians, scientists, lawyers and environmental health officers, with the help of a pressure group called ClientEarth. It was an important day. We also got great coverage from the journalist Katie Razzall at *Channel 4 News*. Out of all that, we put together a clear and intelligent manifesto that could be presented to the British parliament. So there is a sense in which this project is finally beginning to have the effect I had wanted, to impact on government policy. It looks likely to happen but it's been a very long process. Part of me wonders if the book's dissemination was in any sense integral to the project's success. In other words, if I had just come to you with a bunch of photos, some science, the history of the court case and some testimonies, could we have got the show and symposium at The Photographers' Gallery and had the same impact?

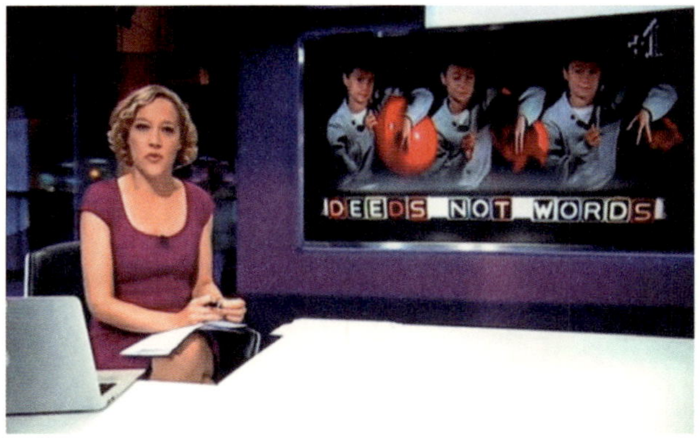

Still from *Channel 4 News* report on *Deeds Not Words*, 5/9/2013

That's a big question. Earlier you said that often the world of art and the world of exhibition come knocking on your door if you ignore them. They like to feel they've "discovered" something. So when we approached the gallery it wasn't just with a set of photos and

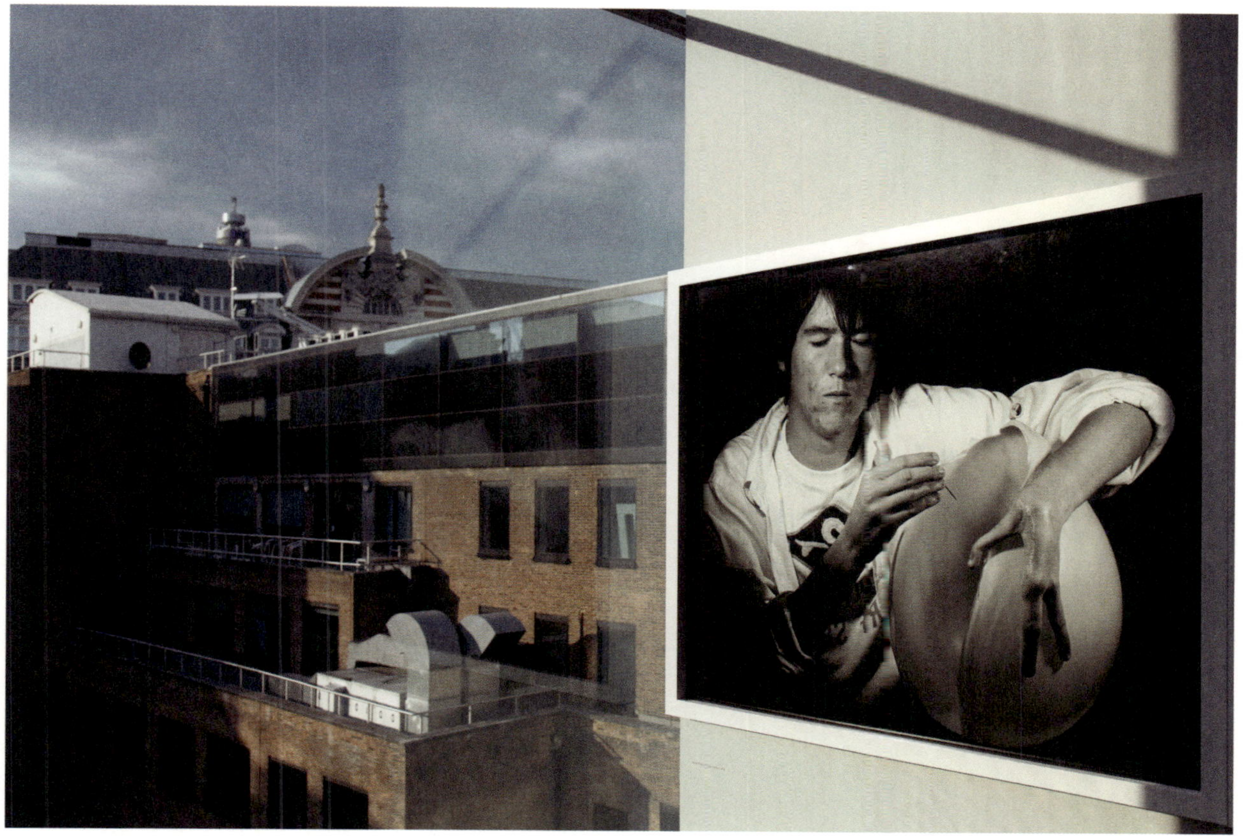

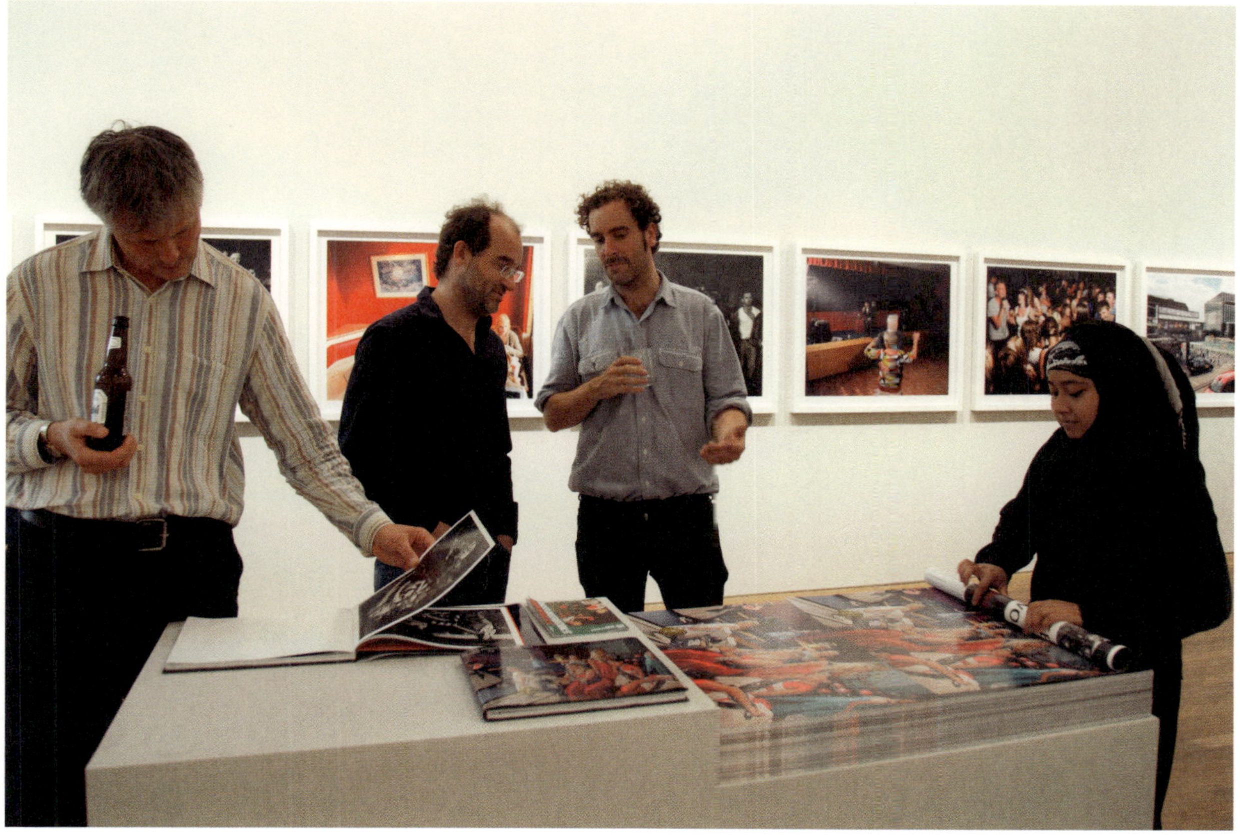

Deeds Not Words, exhibited at The Photographers' Gallery, London, 2013

From : Pam O'Connell
Sent : Tue, Sep 24, 2013 at 6:18 PM
To : info@markneville.com
Subject : Deeds Not Words

Hi Mark

I went to see your exhibition at the Photographers Gallery today. I would like to say that I found it profoundly moving, and it brought tears to my eyes to hear the warm affection you showed when talking about the people of Corby. I was born in Corby and lived there until I was nineteen - I am now in my fifties and have lived in London ever since.

I remember when I first heard about the court case for the children affected by the waste from the toxic ponds in Corby. At first I was shocked but in my heart I was not in the least surprised. In Corby we were used to the fact that some members of the local council were more interested in lining their own pockets than in working to make things better for people in the town. The worst thing is that they fought this case so hard and for so long, and that they had the gall to appeal the first judgement.

Growing up in Corby, we were all used to air pollution. No-one complained, we were used to the orange air and smuts all over any clothes we hung out on the line. But the shambles of the clean up operation and the cavalier attitude of the local council in their handling of the removal of the toxic waste is one of the worst things I have ever heard of. I can hardly believe that this happened in living memory. It "feels" more like something in a painting by Lowry in the 30s.

Who knows what the long term affects will be on people in Corby. Corby people are tough as nails and look after their own, but there has never been much of a culture of protest, so we all took what was dished out to us with very little complaint. No-one deserves to be treated like this, and when I think about it, I feel very angry.

Pam O'Connell

E-mail response to *Deeds Not Words*, exhibited at The Photographers' Gallery, London, 2013

documents: it was with a book, a very unusual book, that had a very unusual genesis and purpose. I think that new strategy interested the gallery. Now, is the making of a book that doesn't achieve its goals a logical way to get a show, that might have a symposium, which might have government impact? Probably not. But then we live in very illogical times, in which nobody really knows which methods, means and strategies are going to be effective. Documentary is, necessarily I think, an experimental practice. Experimental in its forms and experimental in its modes of distribution. I remember when you gave a talk at the gallery, an environmental health officer in the audience said that if he had received the book he would not have taken any notice of it because it did not look like campaign material. It was too confusing. But then another person said that typical campaign information often goes straight into the trash precisely because it looks like everything else! It left me very confused.

Yes, strange times do require strange approaches.

And there's no guarantee that anything will work.

But you have to try, and they may work in unforeseen ways.

It comes down to a real split in documentary and campaign work, between sticking to conventions and trying to find new approaches. On the one hand there is the notion that there is a set of tried and tested conventions; on the other a there is Bertolt Brecht's conviction that "realism must be sovereign over all conventions" because the world is changing so fast. Finding the right form for what you want to say is a struggle and it must come out of an engagement with the subject. There is no pre-packaged, guaranteed convention. Experimentation is a necessity, not an artistic indulgence.

My feeling is that the door to experimentation should always be left open.

The

Helmand

Work

2011

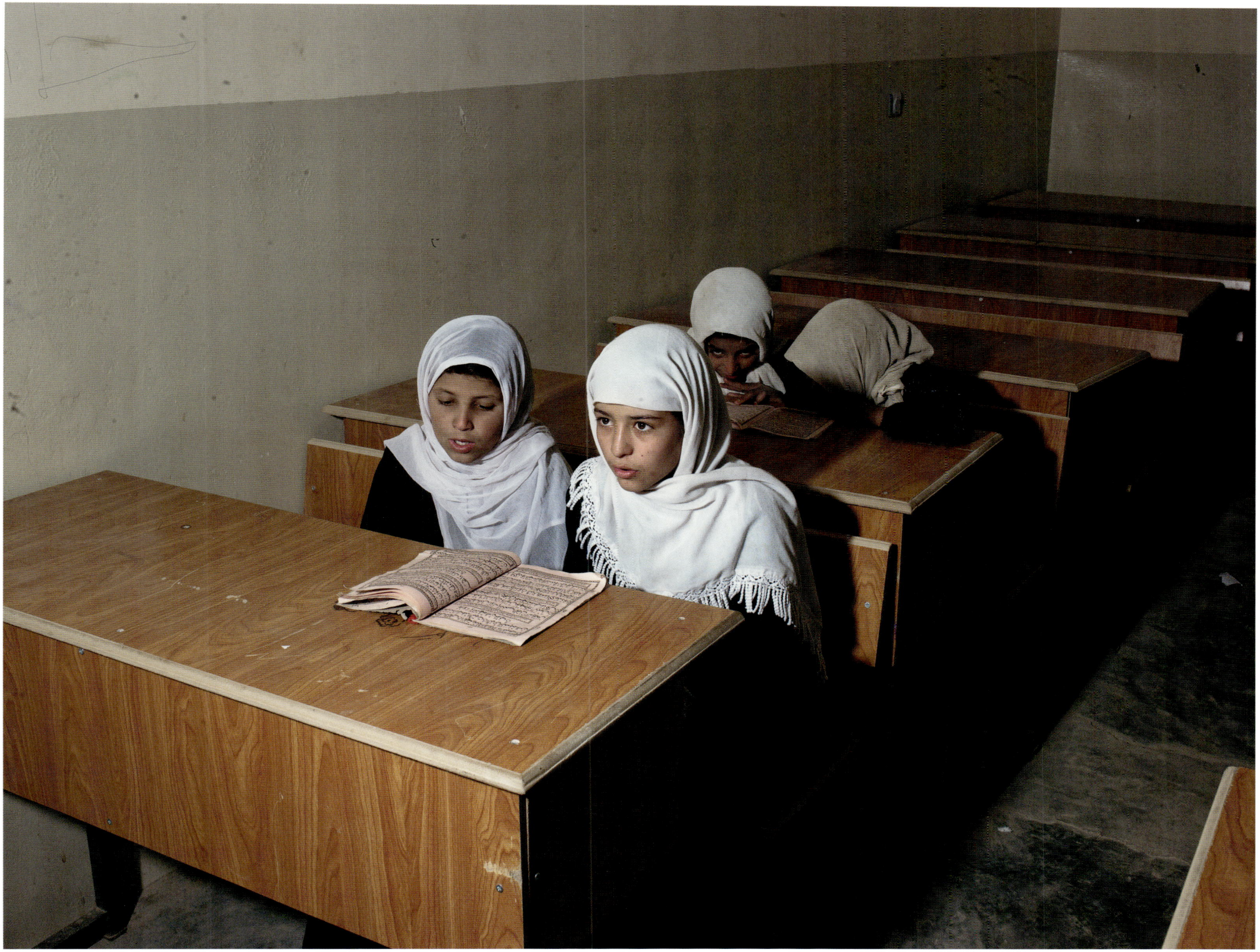

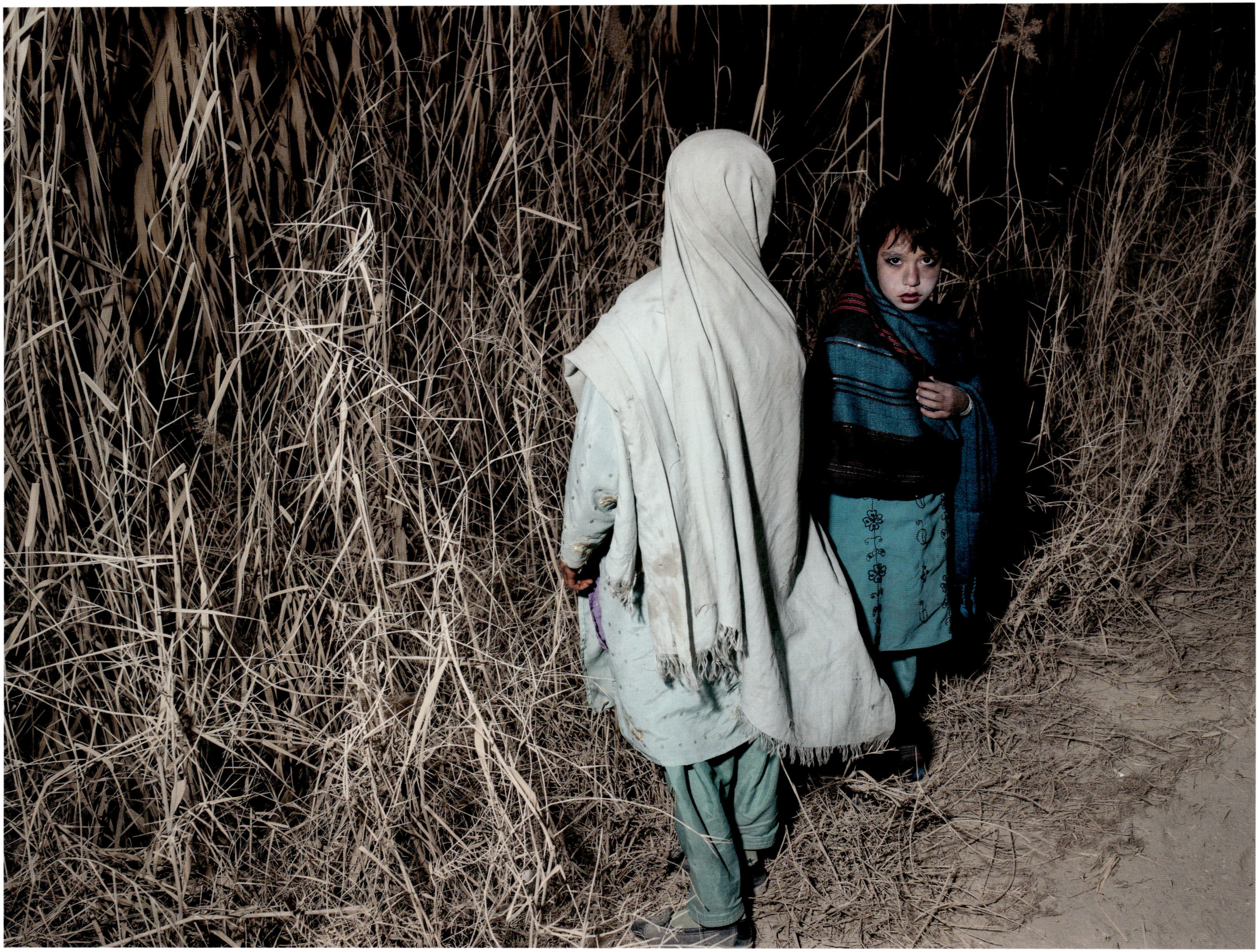

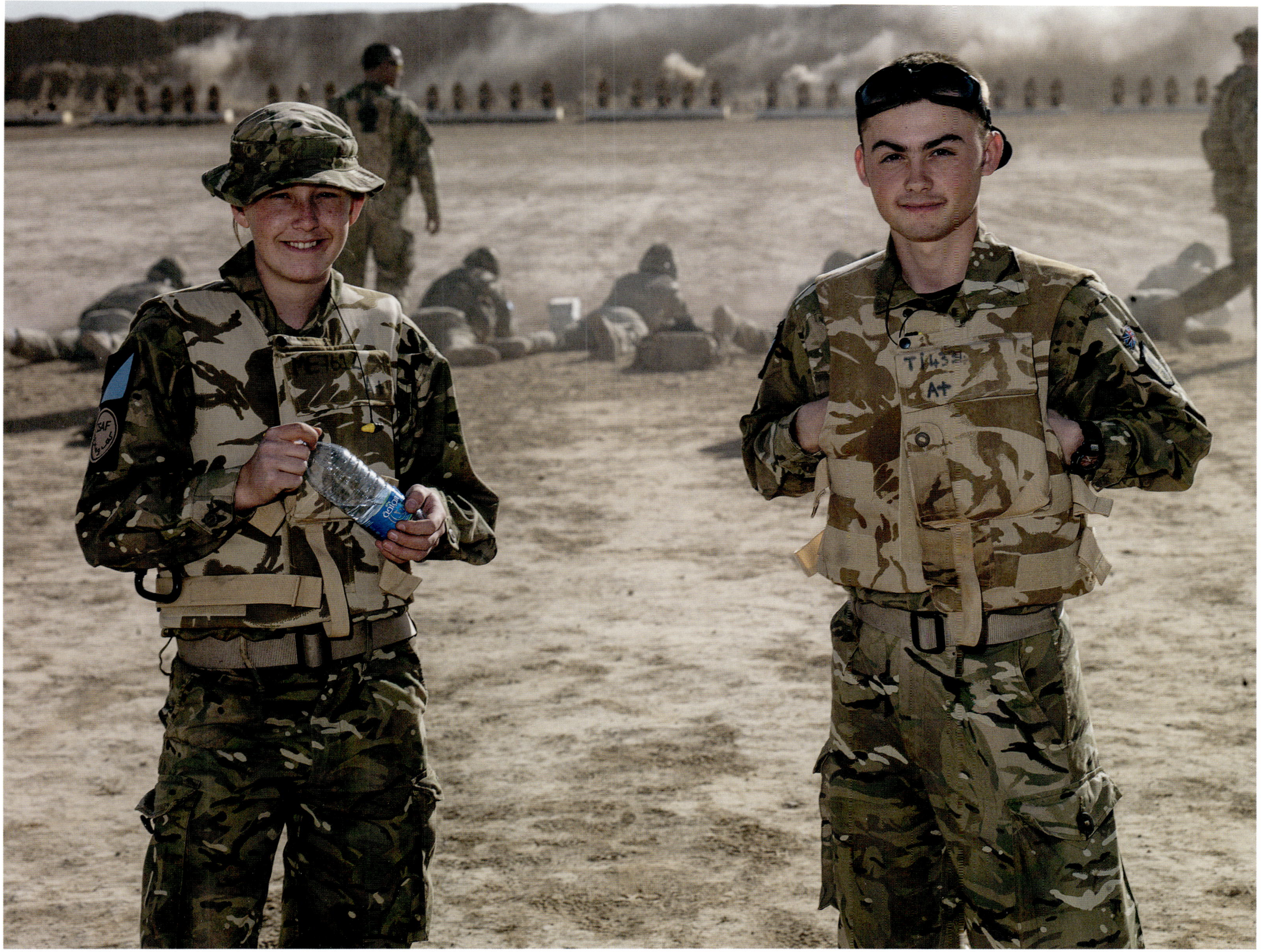

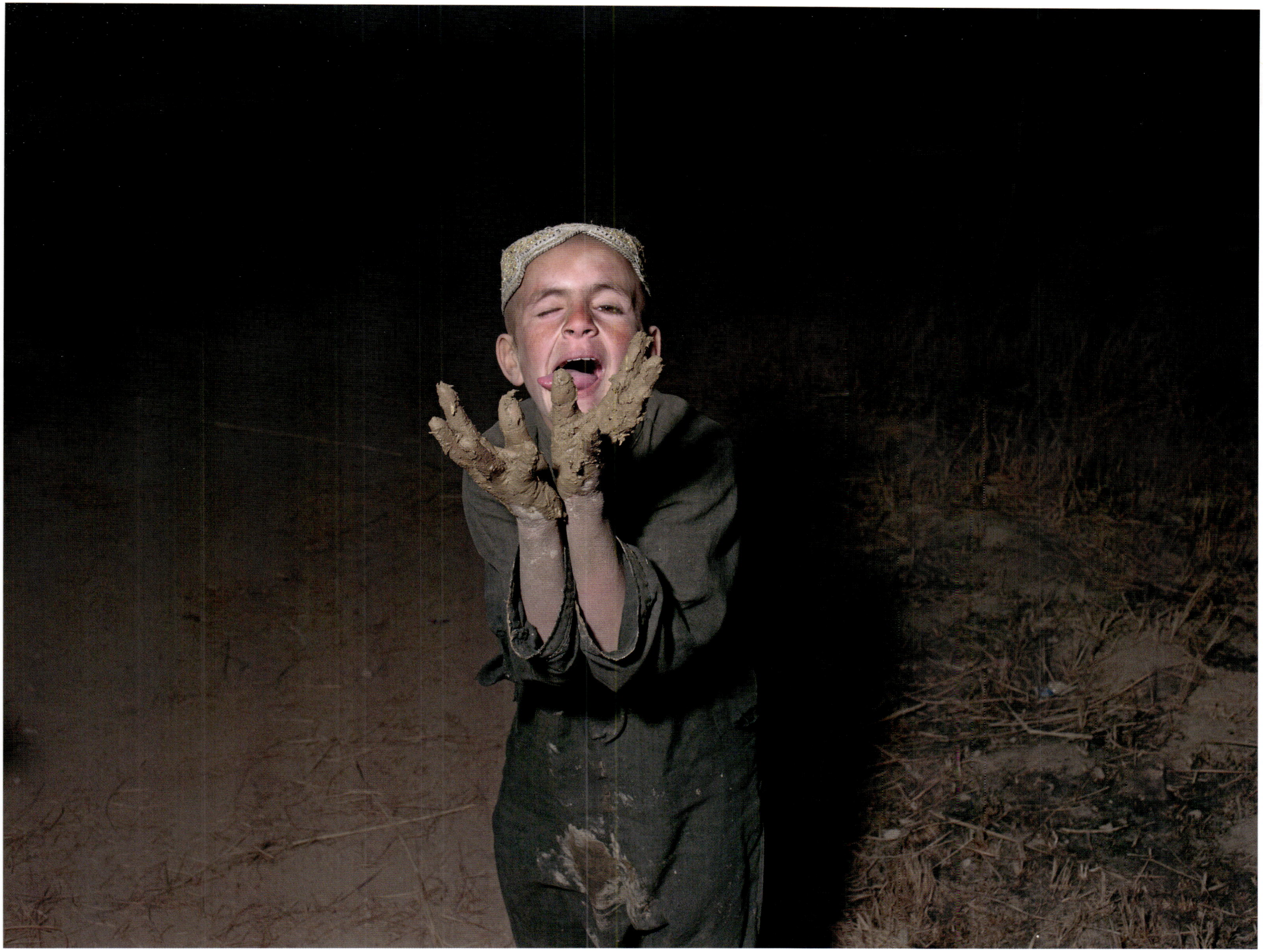

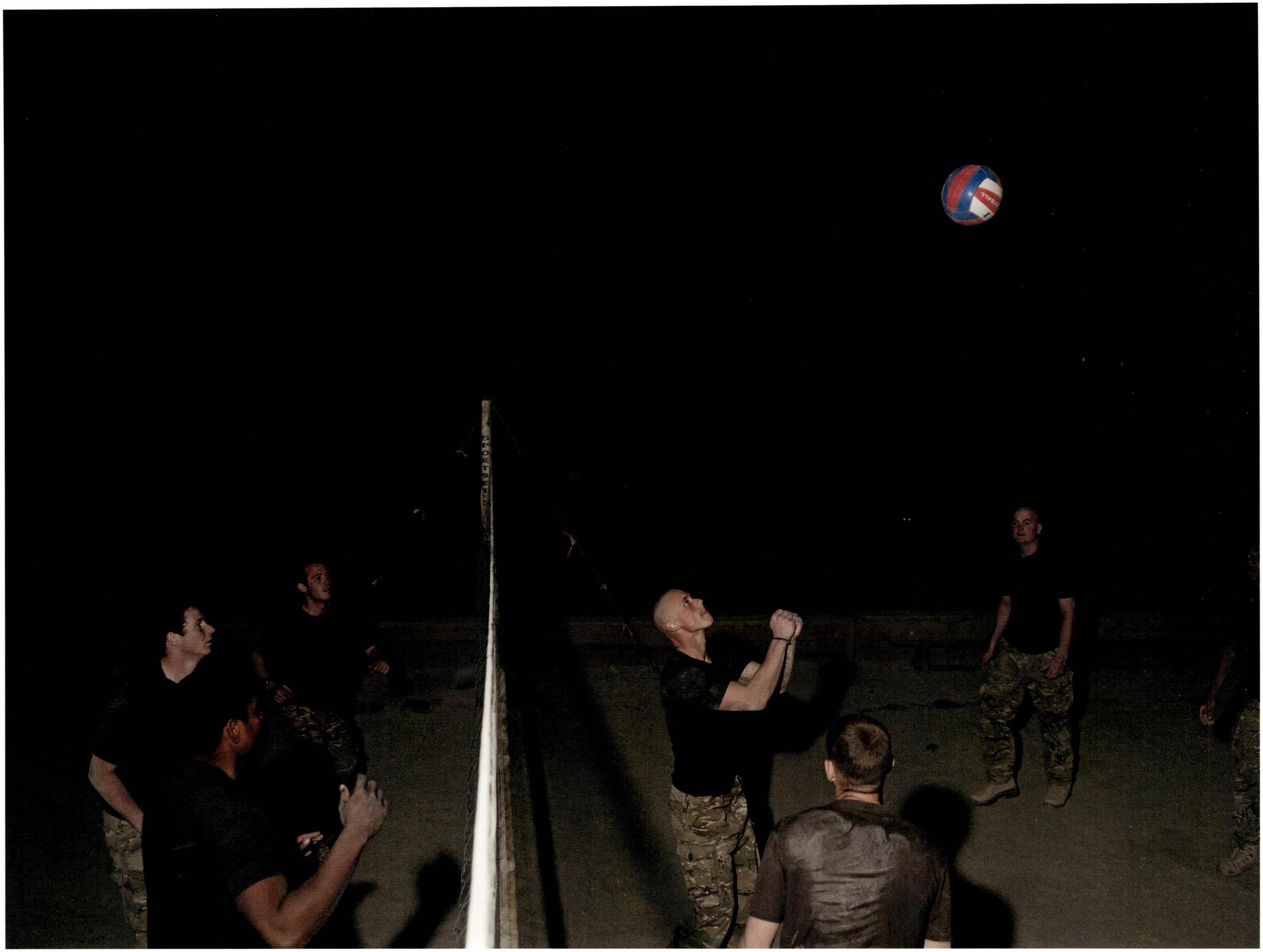

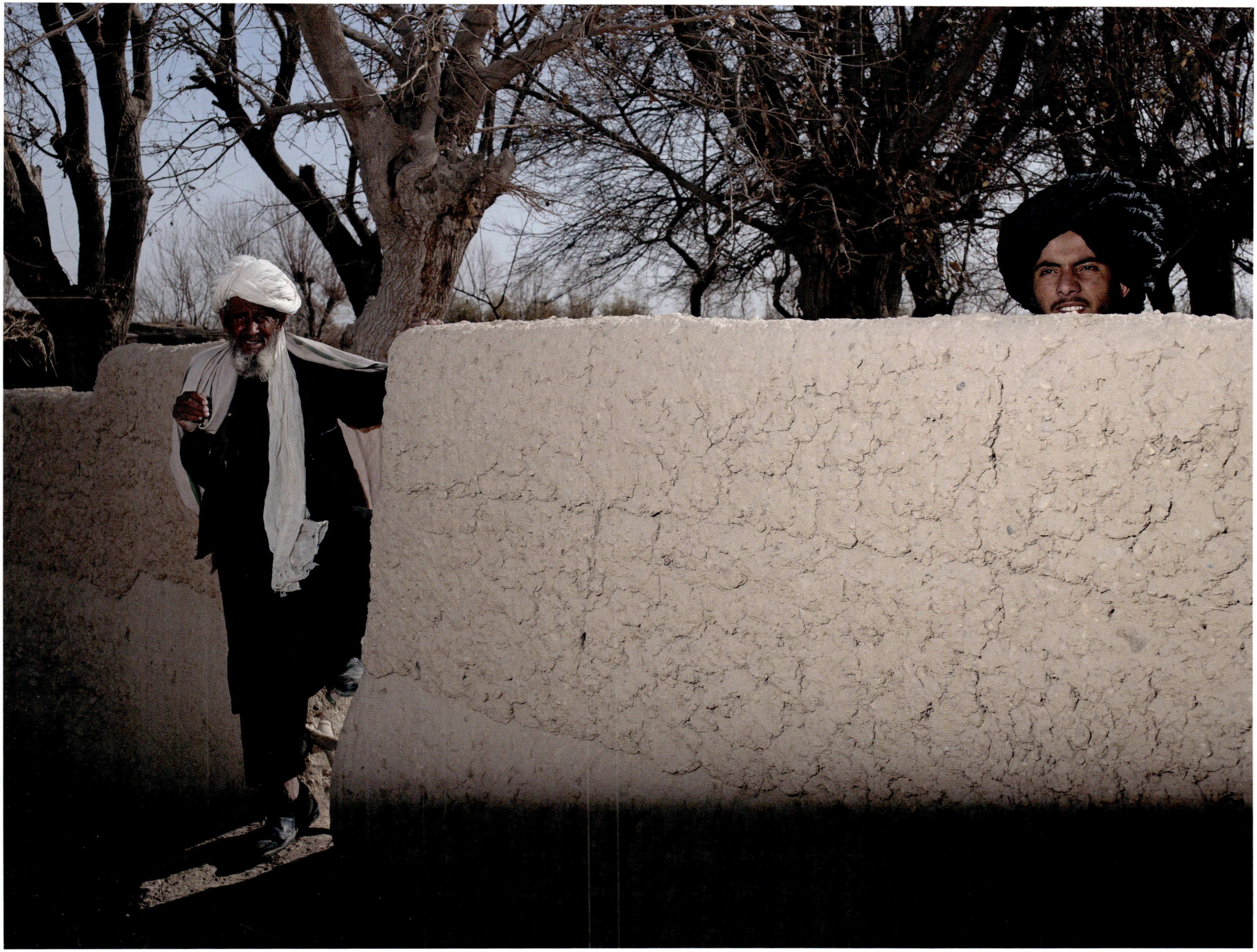

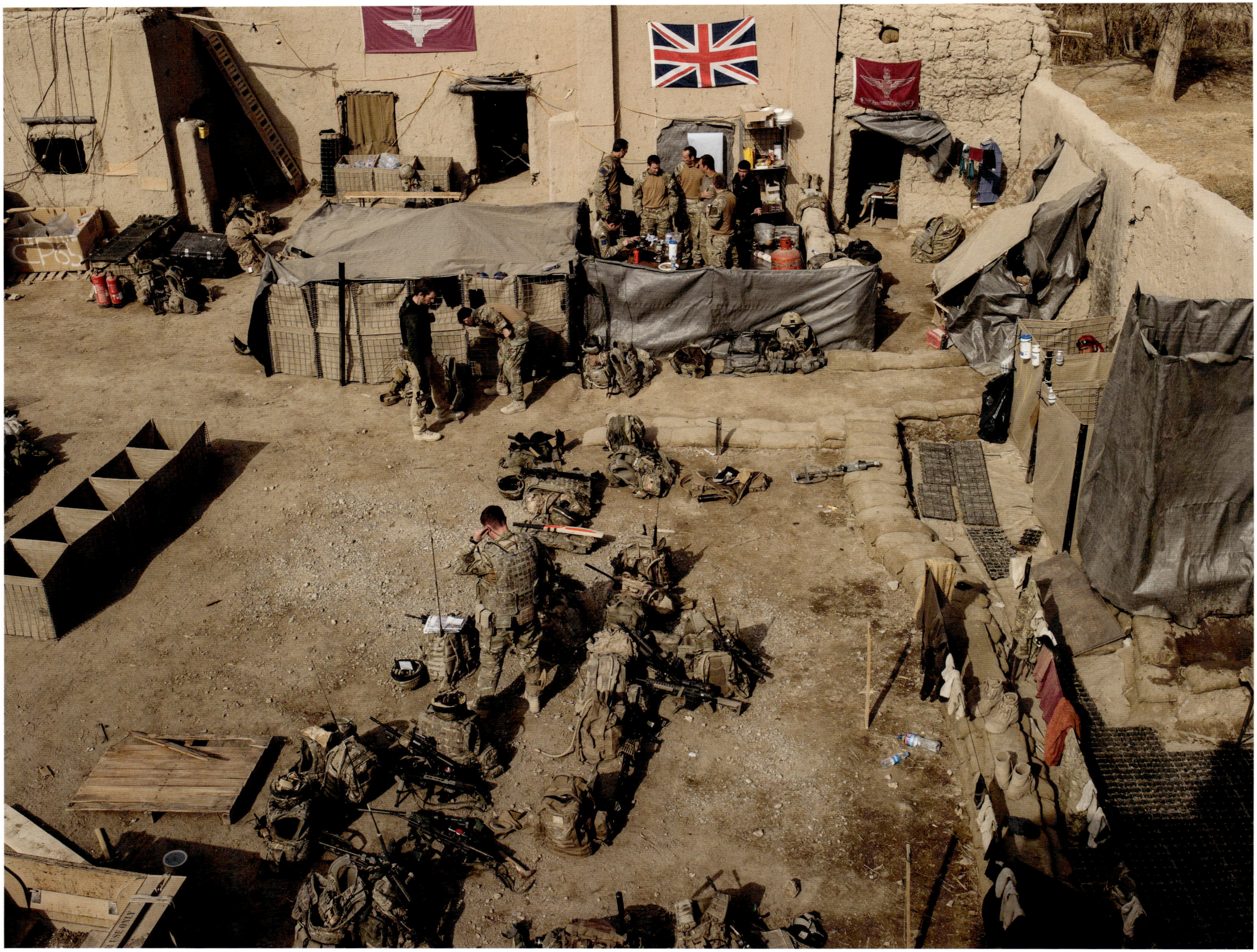

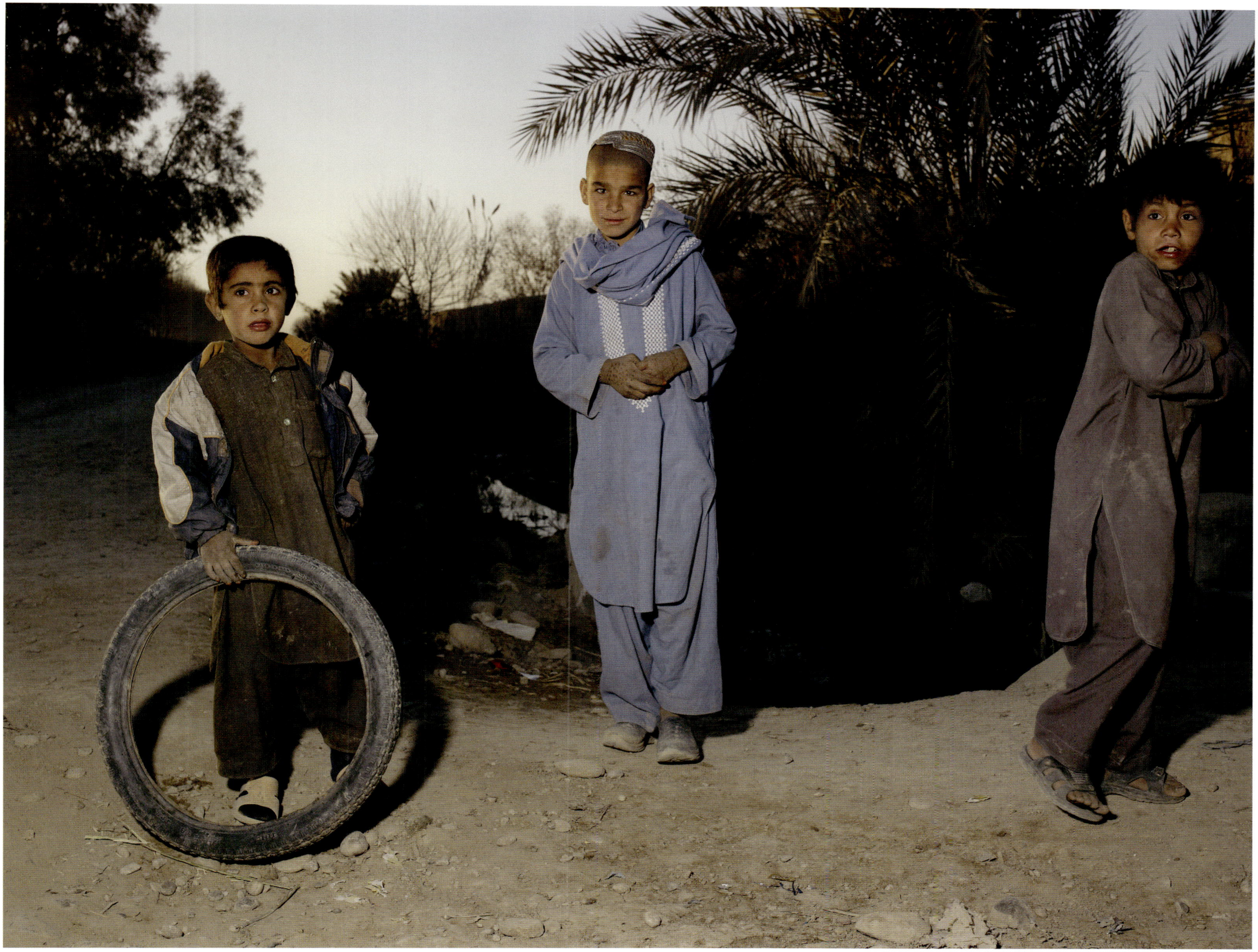

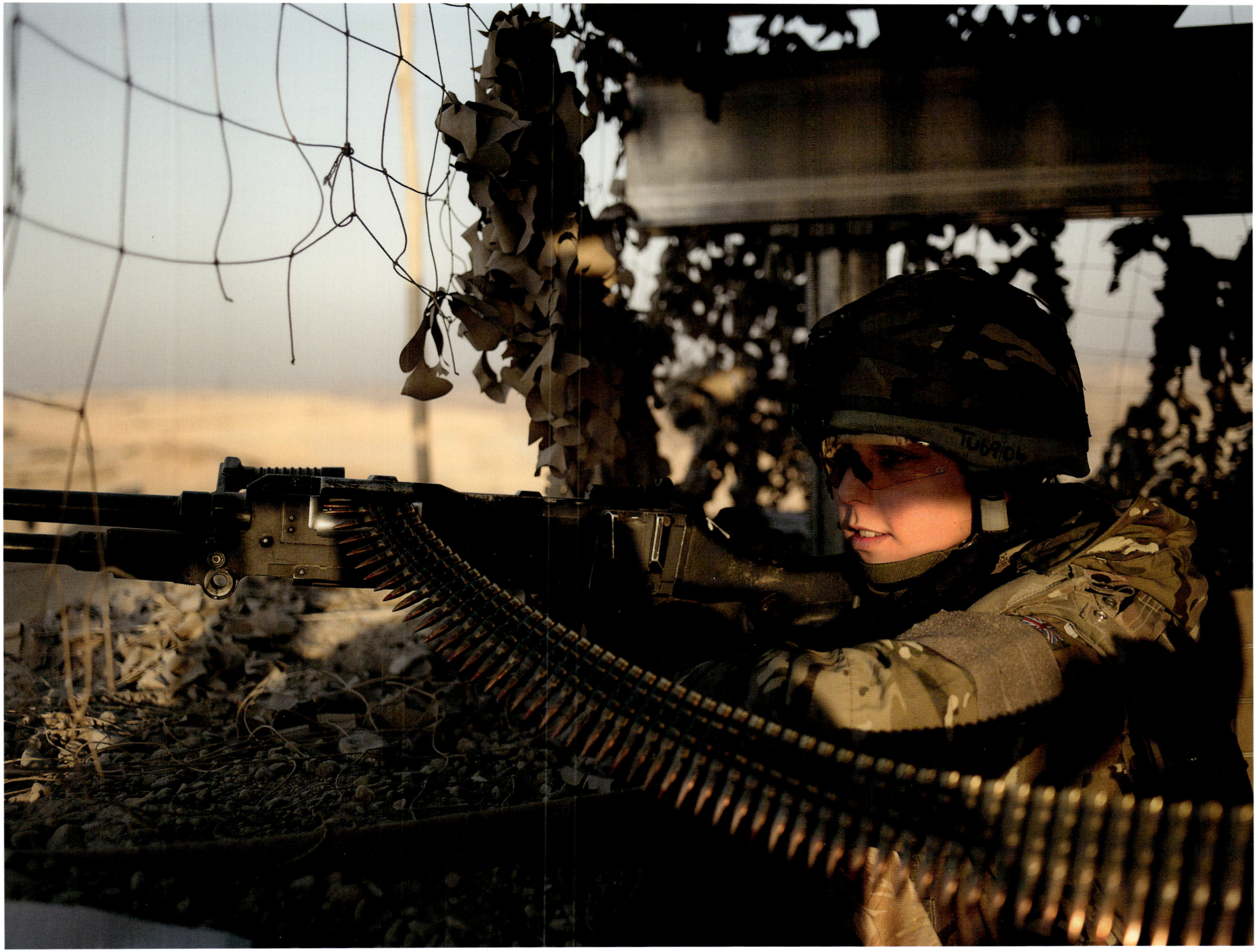

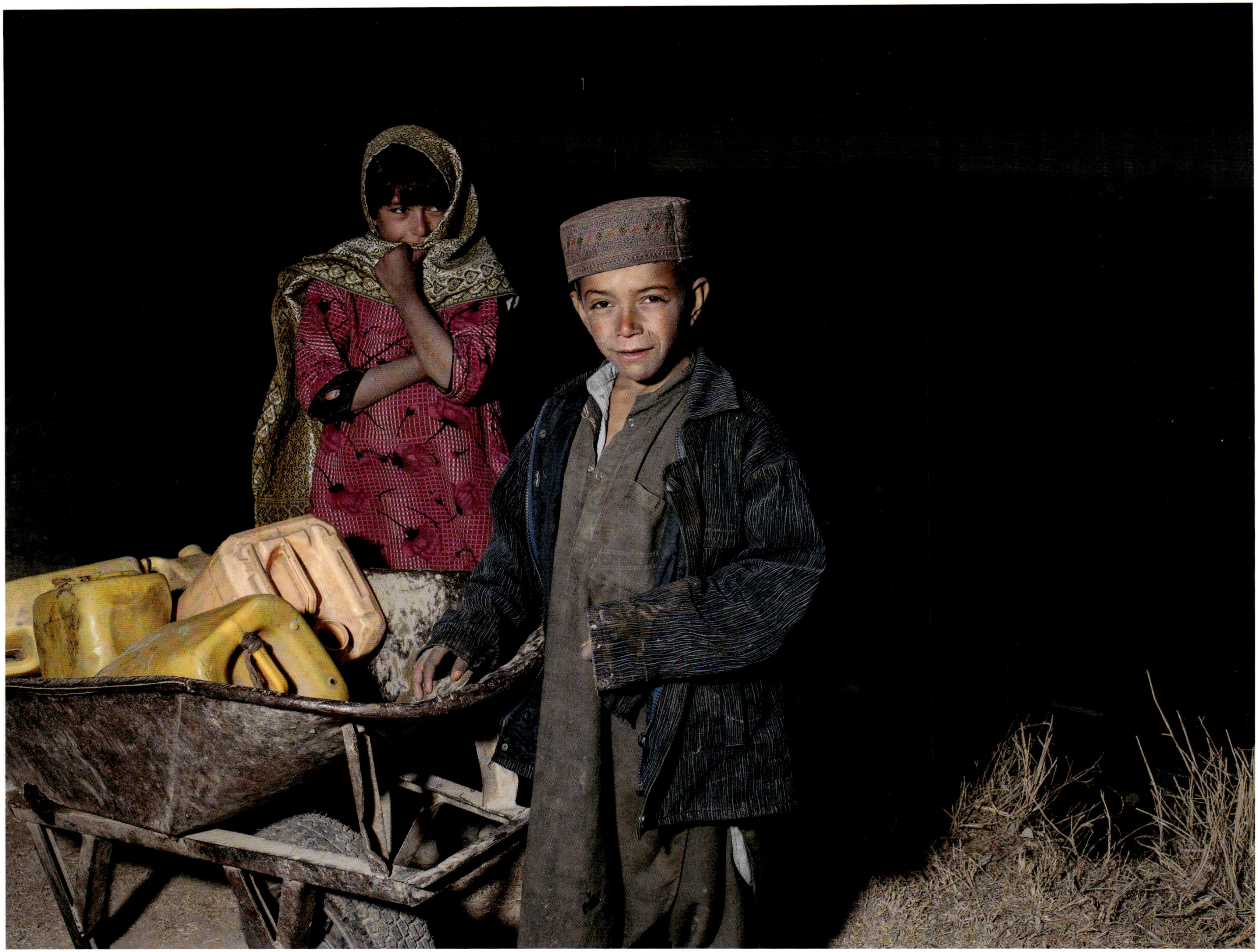

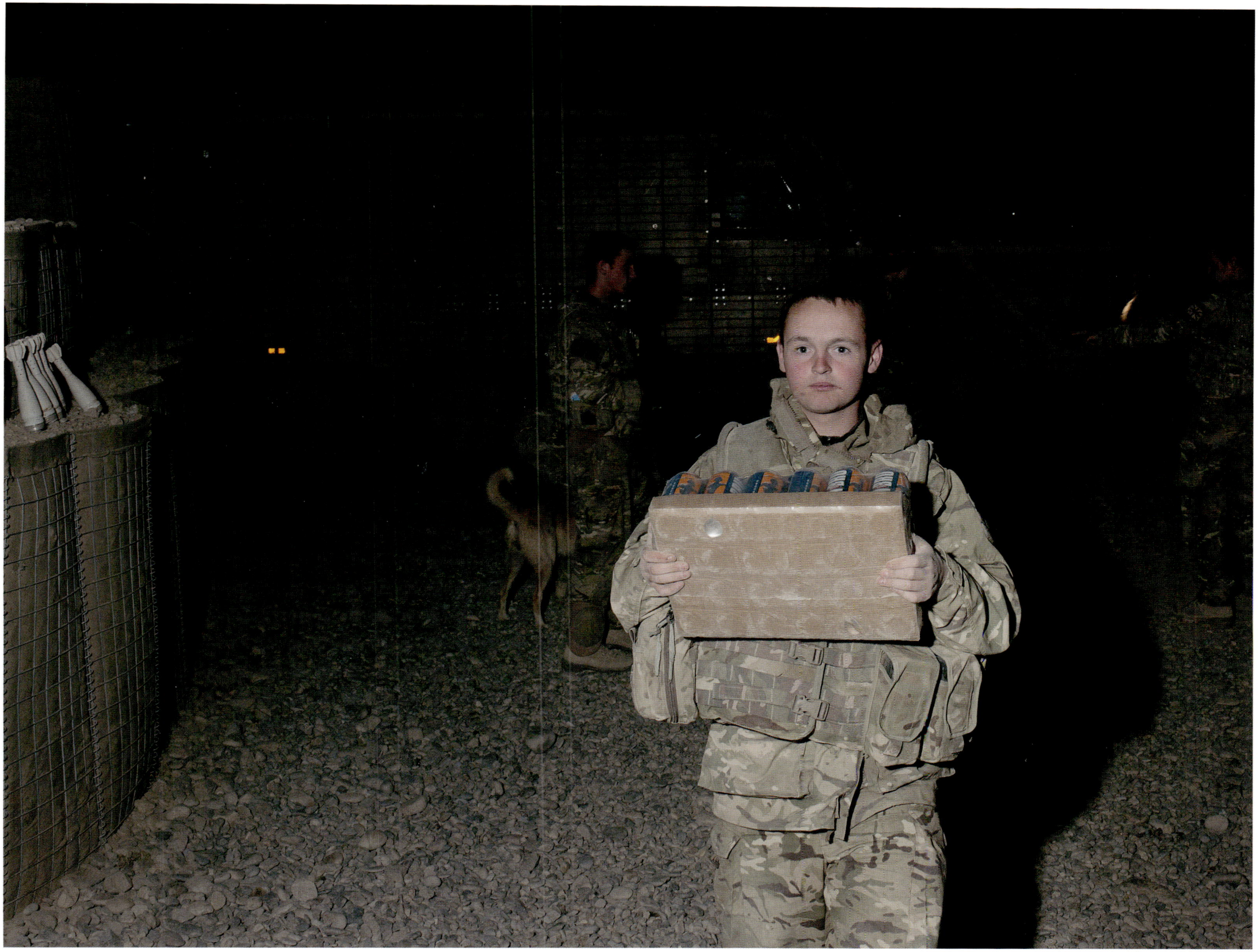

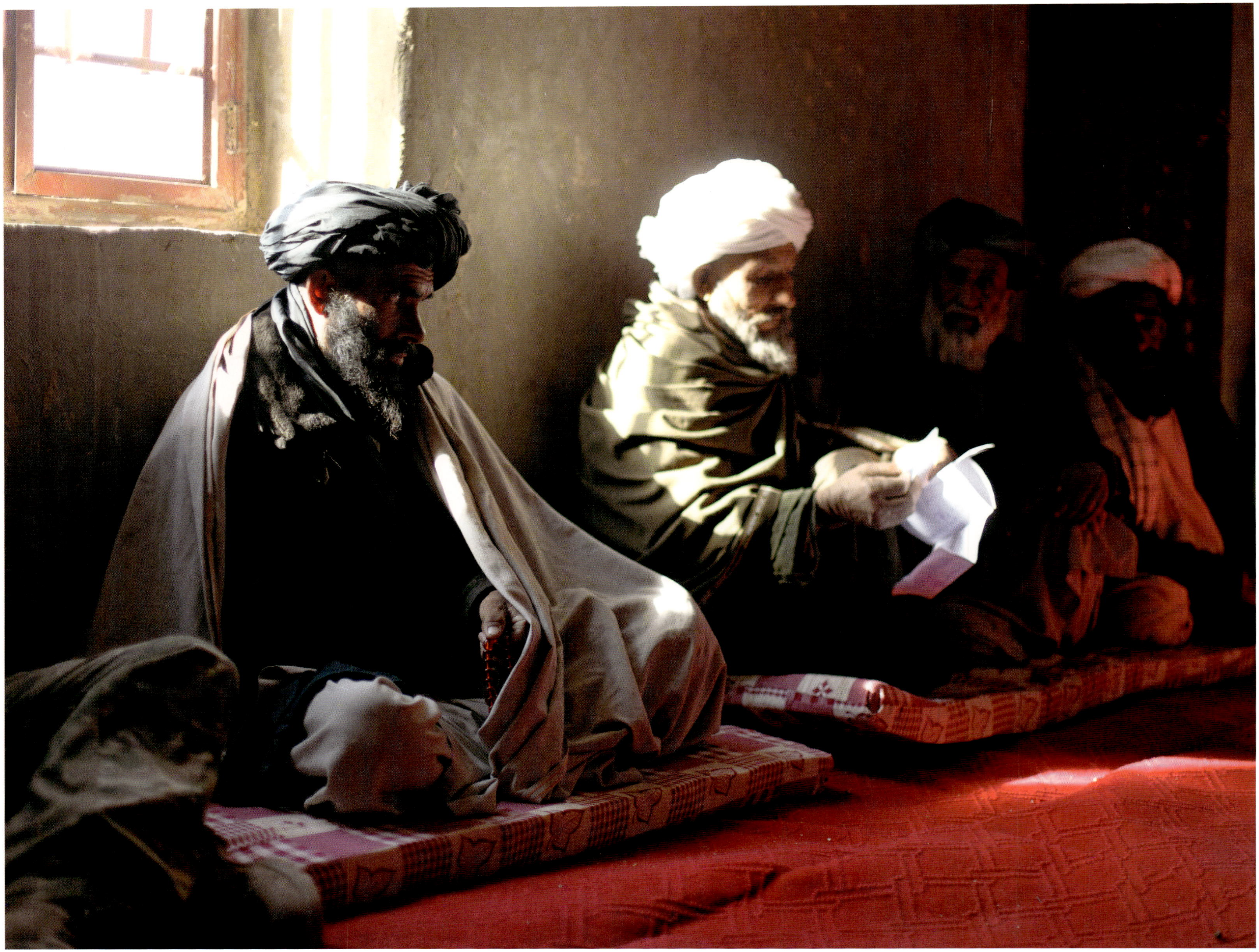

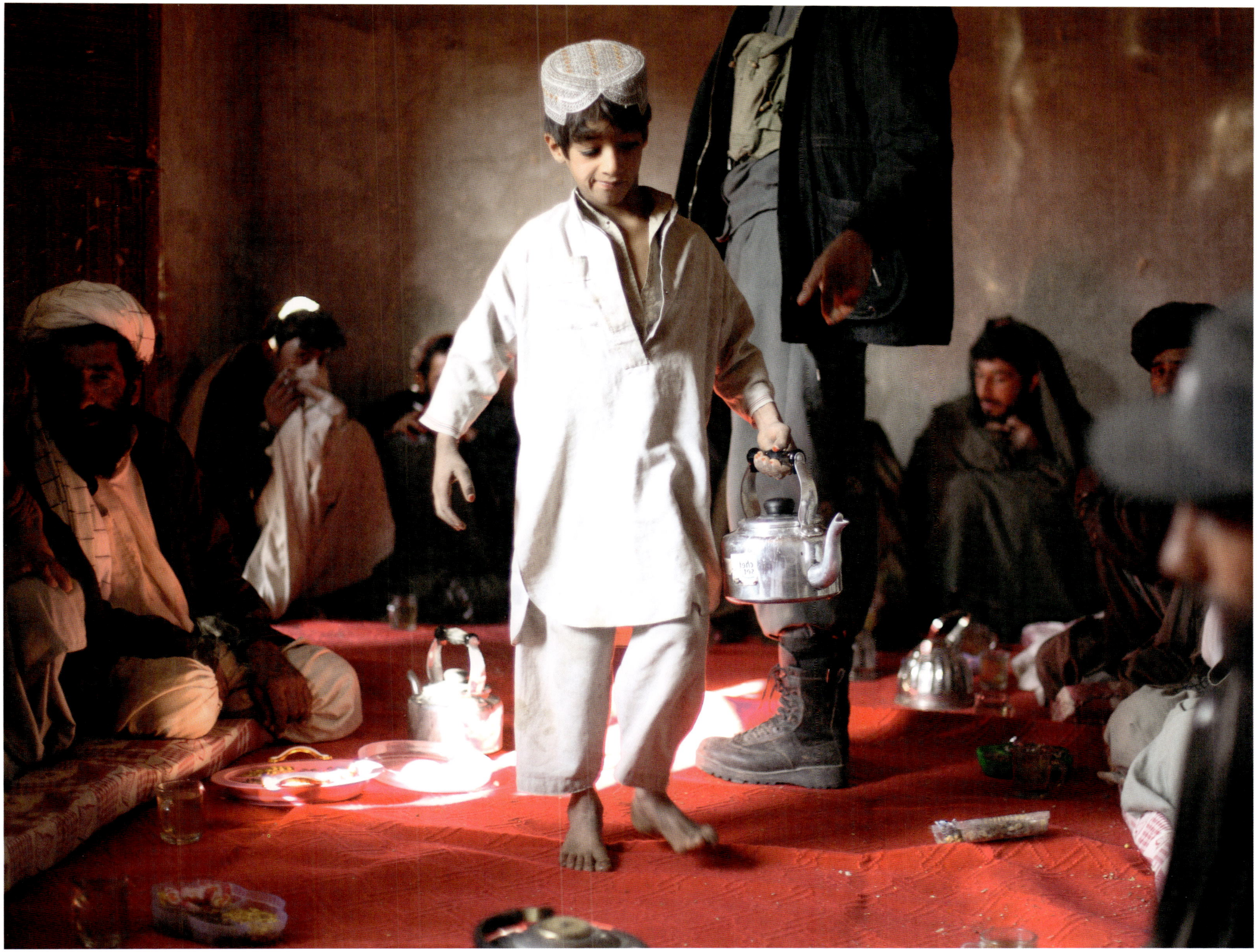

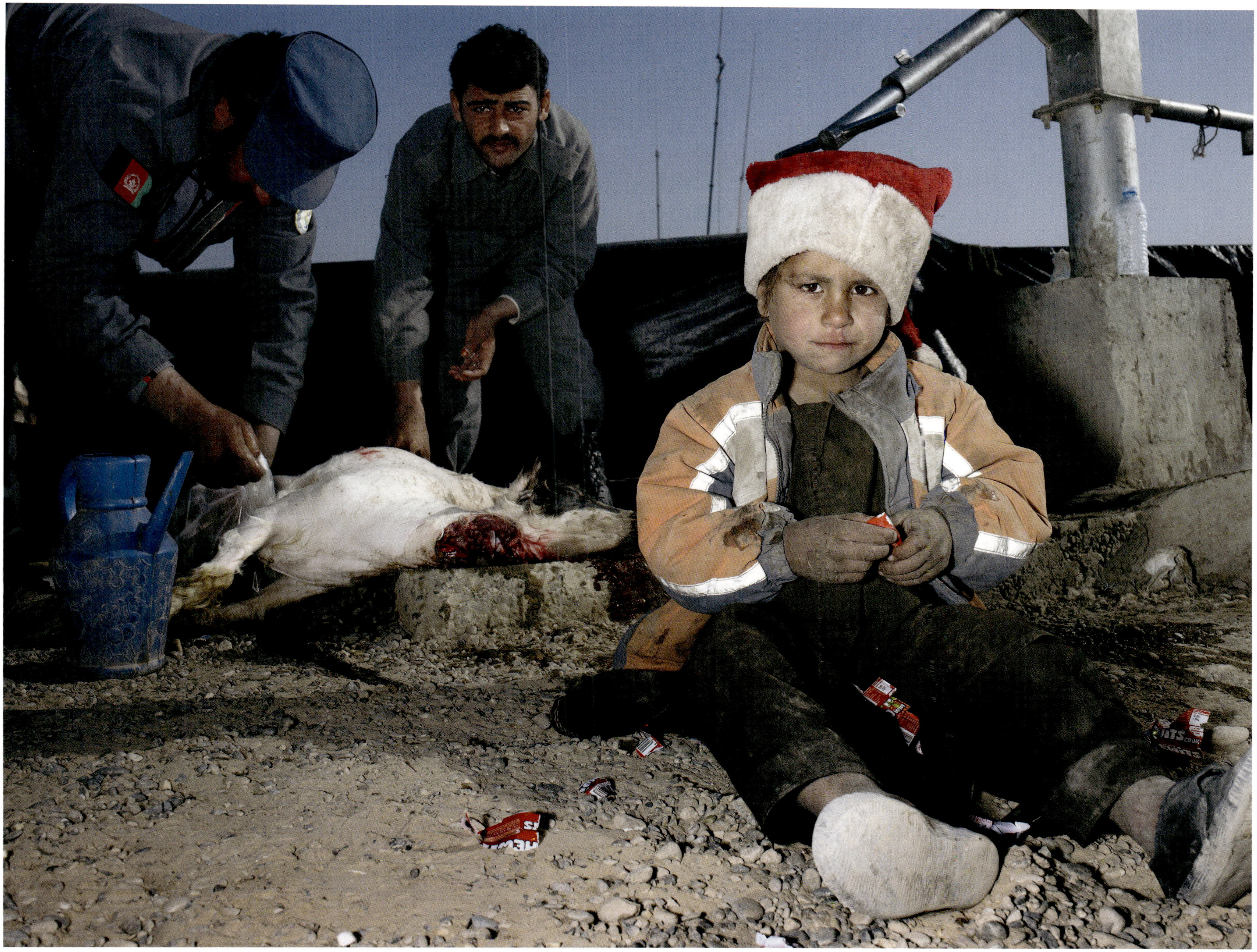

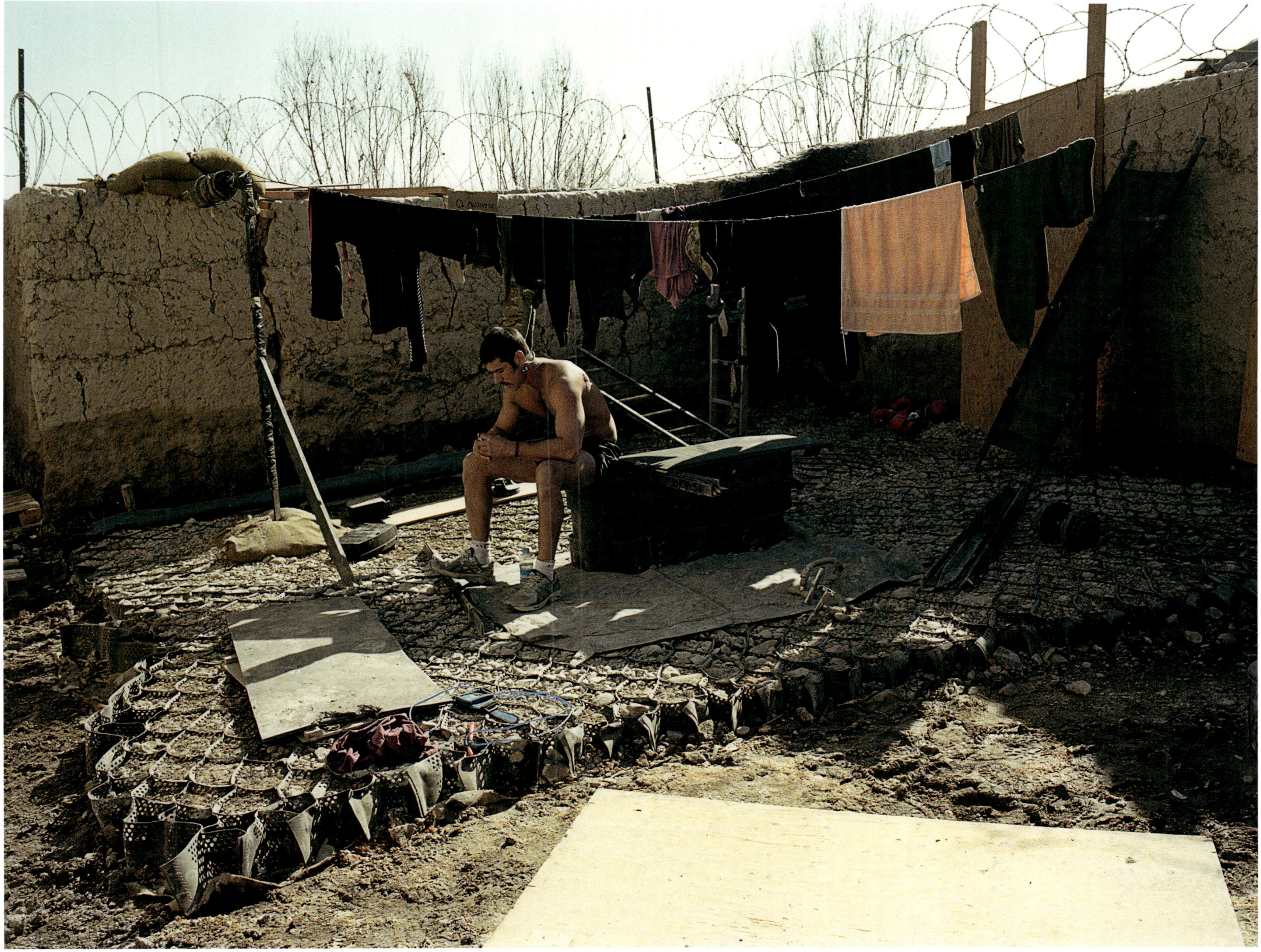

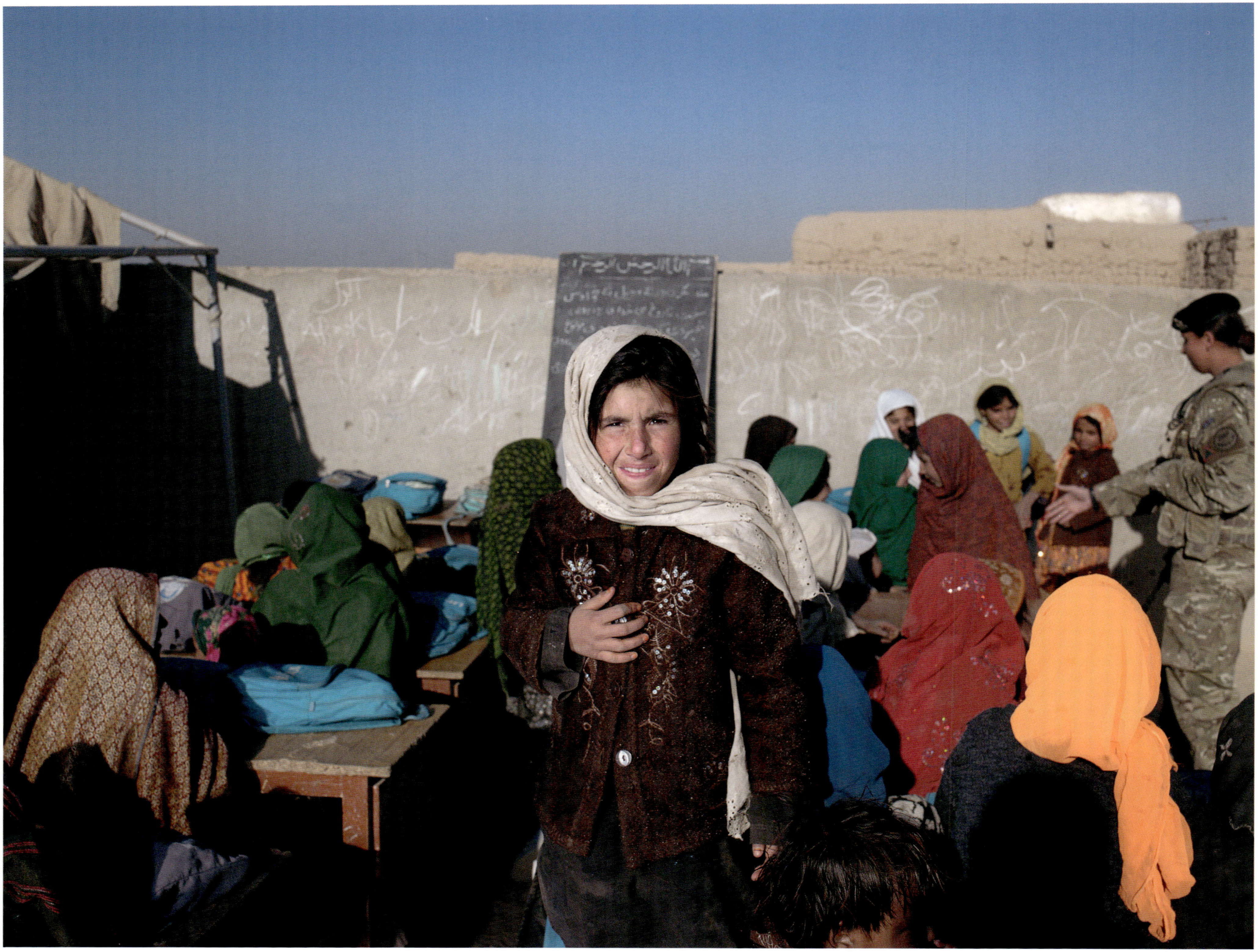

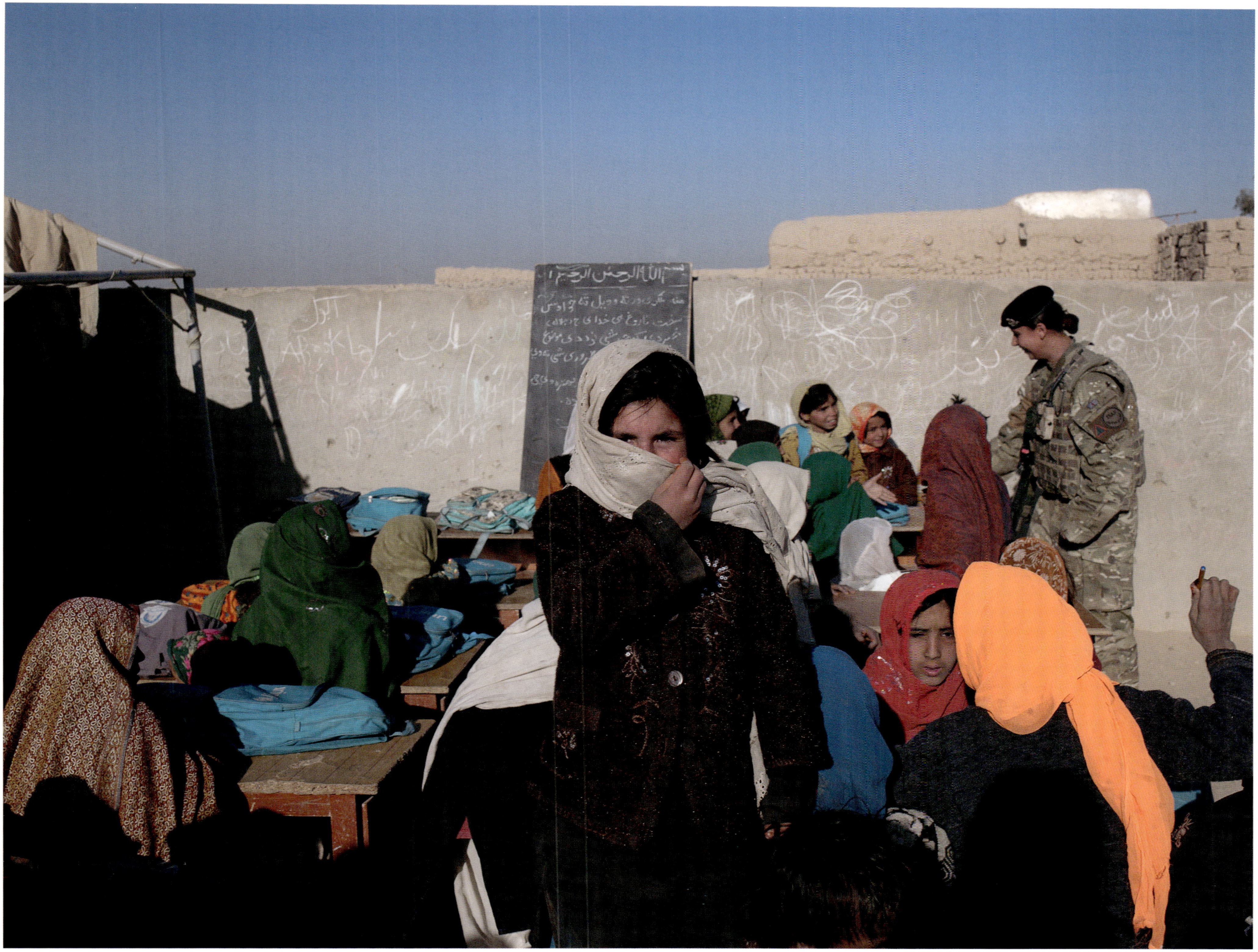

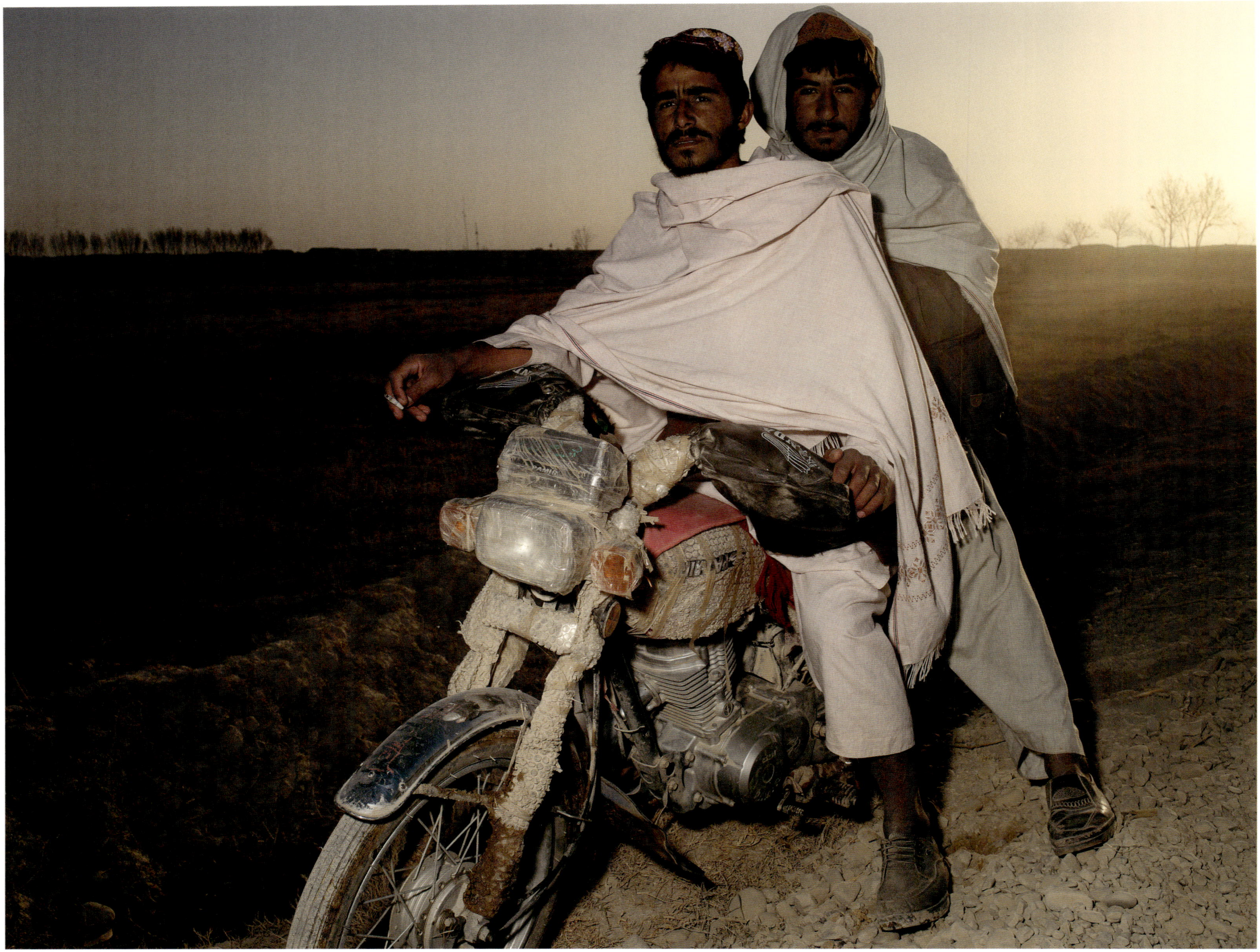

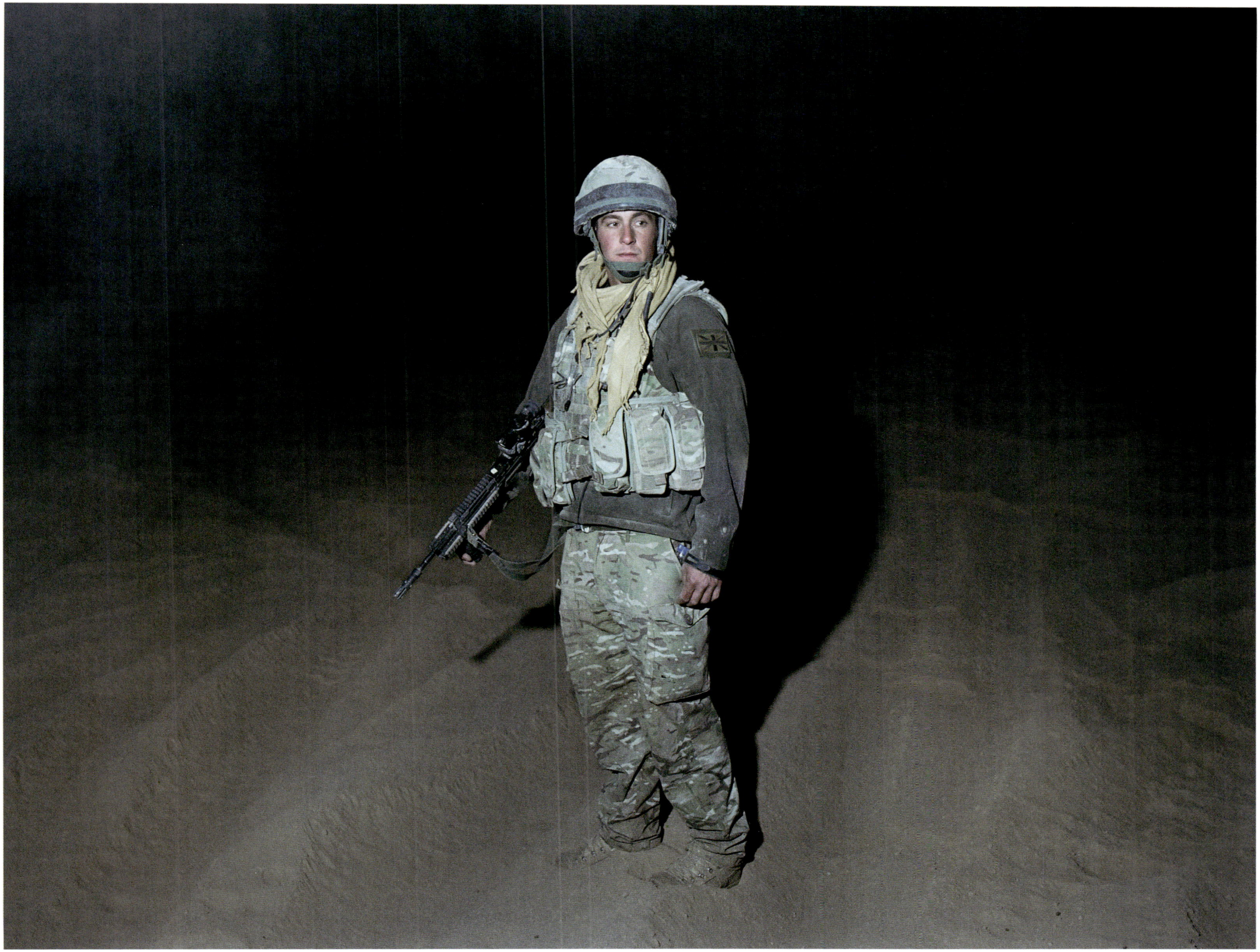

117. Lashkar Gah Girls School, 2011
118. On Patrol in Gereshk, 1, 2011
119. Firing Range, 2011
121. On Patrol in Nad Ali, 2, 2011
122. Camp Bastion Volleyball, 2011
123. On Patrol in Lashkar Gah, 2011
124. View on Checkpoint Perkha, 2011
125. On Patrol in Sangin, 2011
127. Watchtower, 2011
128. On Patrol in Lashkar Gah, 2, 2011
129. Supplies for Scots Regiment, 2011
130. Meeting of the Village Elders, 1, 2011
131. Meeting of the Village Elders, 2, 2011
133. Child, Jacket, Slaughtered Goat, Sweets, Painted Nails, Xmas Day, Helmand, 2010
135. Checkpoint Mail Delivered, 2, 2011
136. Lashkar Gah Girls School, 1, 2011
137. Lashkar Gah Girls School, 2, 2011
138. On Patrol in Lashkar Gah, 5, 2011
139. Out in the Desert, 2011

The Helmand Work

David Campany: While you were shooting *Deeds Not Words* you got the opportunity (the invitation?) to go to Helmand Province in Afghanistan.

Mark Neville: Yes, I was immersed in life in Corby and getting near the end of the photographic part of that project when I got an email in October 2010, asking if I would be interested in coming for an interview, along with five other artists, for a commission to be a war artist in Helmand.

Who was asking?

It came from an organisation called firstsite in Colchester, Essex, which was involved in commissioning site-specific projects of various kinds. Helmand was the most ambitious, I guess. 16 Air Assault Brigade, the biggest brigade in the British Army, is based in Colchester and it was about to do its tour of duty in Afghanistan. The head of firstsite met with the head of the Brigade, Brigadier James Chiswell, and hatched the idea of sending an artist to the war zone in Afghanistan. Cut to me in my studio one day wondering what I'm going to do after *Deeds Not Words*. On the basis of past projects it was assumed I somehow flourished making work with communities in extreme or closely-knit circumstances. Interestingly 16 Air Assault Brigade has eight thousand personnel, which is very roughly the population of both Port Glasgow and the Isle of Bute. That's big enough to explore and get to know but not unmanageable. That size also fosters quite a specific kind of community, I think.

Did you have to describe what it was you planned do in Helmand?

Not specifically, no. I came up with a series of strategies. I had three or four rounds of interview, including psychological screening by the Ministry of Defence, which established I was "fit for purpose"…

…or mad enough to go.

Exactly, "catch 22". Once accepted, I had only four or five weeks to plan and prepare. I knew I wanted to do as much preparation as possible, especially concerning the making of the work. I knew I would not have time to really get to know people, to learn the local languages—Pashto and Dari—so I gave up on doing that. But what was important for me was to go out with the right kind of camera equipment. Even though I knew I was going into the unexpected, I didn't want to come away with nothing. I wanted three or four working methods to fall back on, just in case.

You knew you did not want to be a "frontline photographer".

No, I didn't want to do that. I wanted to get away from the conventions of the mass media and the newsroom. I wanted to make films and photographs that on some level, maybe indirectly, were a critique of those ways of reporting. In fact it was shocking to me to find such a huge discrepancy between what we see on the TV about Helmand and the reality on the ground. I don't just mean in terms of dead bodies, blood and guts. I mean in terms of social and political situations on the ground everyday. So one of the biggest surprises for me was the huge amount of reconstruction going on in Helmand, all engineered by British forces—clinics, schools, roads. So little of this activity was being reported in the media. Why? It doesn't sell newspapers? It was just as significant as reports of shootings or casualties. But even in terms of casualties, when I was there, every day you would hear of British soldiers losing limbs, being blinded, day in and day out. Very little of that was reported back in the UK. Only if you die does it make the TV news back home. This collusion between the media, the government and the Ministry of Defence seems to manifest itself in this whole tacit cover up of how many soldiers lost limbs. We were so good at keeping people alive no matter the damage to the body. Even if you lost four limbs there was a good chance the hospital—Camp Bastion had the busiest trauma hospital in the world—could keep you alive. We were pumping huge amounts of money into Afghanistan. Obviously it was doing good on lots of levels but, if we're doing that, why wasn't it covered in the press? Maybe it was because the UK was going through such a deep economic recession, and the government was worried about the backlash about the spending in Afghanistan. But they owe the British public an explanation about how our money is spent.

So what did you plan to do?

For me the only way forward was to provide some kind of fresh perspective, visually, on the war experience. Personally, I knew I was pretty numb to any images of Helmand after ten years. The news coverage was kind of like wallpaper, invisible after a while. The media images are nearly always clichés. As soon as you see a line of soldiers backlit on the horizon, or a low camera angle showing advancing soldiers, you know exactly what you're going to get. War reporting is so easily reduced to a predictable and cheap coinage that says nothing about history and nothing about real suffering.

So in the end I had three main strategies. One was just to film interviews: talking. People knew I wasn't from the media and might be prepared to talk openly and candidly, which they often were. It was a conventional interview approach but, because of who I am and what I do, I got different responses. I was able to open a more honest dialogue, I think. Secondly, I shot with high-speed 16mm movie cameras, the technology I had been using since *The Jump Films.* One was a super slow-motion camera used in car crash-tests, which needed a tripod and a generator to run it. The other was a hand-held camera which shot at up to five hundred frames per second. I could just about manage to hold it on my shoulder with a battery pack around my neck. The third approach was to use backdrops. Prior to leaving the UK I had various images enlarged to use as backdrops, two meters wide. These included John Piper and Paul Nash's paintings from the First World War and John Burke's photographs of Afghanistan from the 1870s. Burke was the first photographer in that country and he had gone with the British military. Using these backdrops would be an almost graffiti-like, crude, obvious way of making basic connections between conflict now and conflict then. In some ways these works were about the cyclical nature of war and the long, repeated British presence in Afghanistan, which has never worked out well.

There is a long history of using montage techniques as a commentary on war, going back at least to John Heartfield's anti-Nazi work.

Yes. I chose images with the right scale, so that with foreground action that they would make sense in terms of perspective. It's a trick we know from cinema and theatre. The background is noticeably fake but the viewer makes the imaginative leap. Alfred Hitchcock would use back projection, even when he didn't need to, creating that strange psychological disruption within the realism.

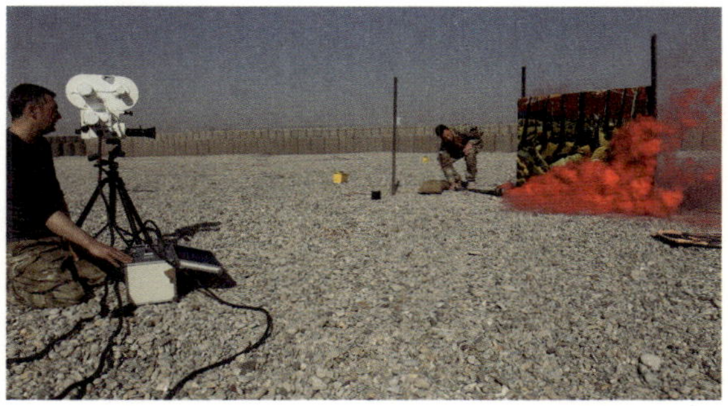

Neville filming *Backdrops* in Helmand Province, 2011

So you took a lot of equipment.

Cameras, tripods, lights, batteries, film stock, backdrops and the rest. Once there I began with vignettes such as the head of the Afghan National Police (who was killed in a bomb blast just weeks after) sitting tying his turban against the backdrop of the Afghan National Police from the 1870s. Or a soldier firing a gun in front of a Paul Nash battlefield. We know that even Nash's paintings have been reduced to quickly consumable images (I remember John Berger writing about this). But I felt that bringing one cliché into a relation to another might produce something new.

Not unlike Martha Rosler's mixing of Vietnam war reportage images with interior design advertising?

Yes. Through this I might be able to provide a new experience. I was that naïve or arrogant. Either way there is something extremely subversive in hearing a bomb go off two hundred metres away but pointing your camera not in its direction, but at a man sitting in front of a backdrop. It tells the viewer "you are no longer affected when you look at reportage of destruction on the front line, so I'm going to present some other visual material that may help you think about conflict again".

You took still photographs too, and in many of these images you focus on youth once again, looking at Afghan children and at just how young the British soldiers are.

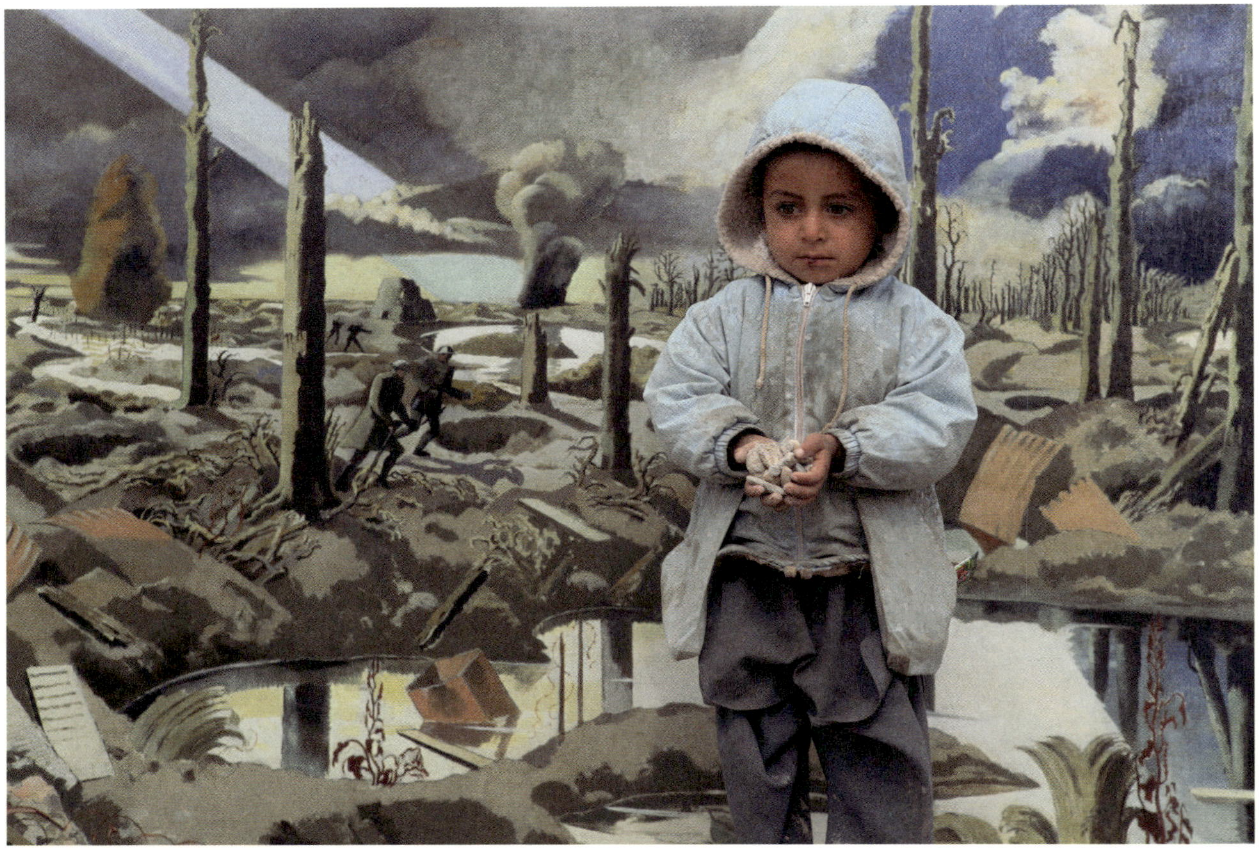

Production still of *Backdrops*,
9 mins, 16mm film, 2011

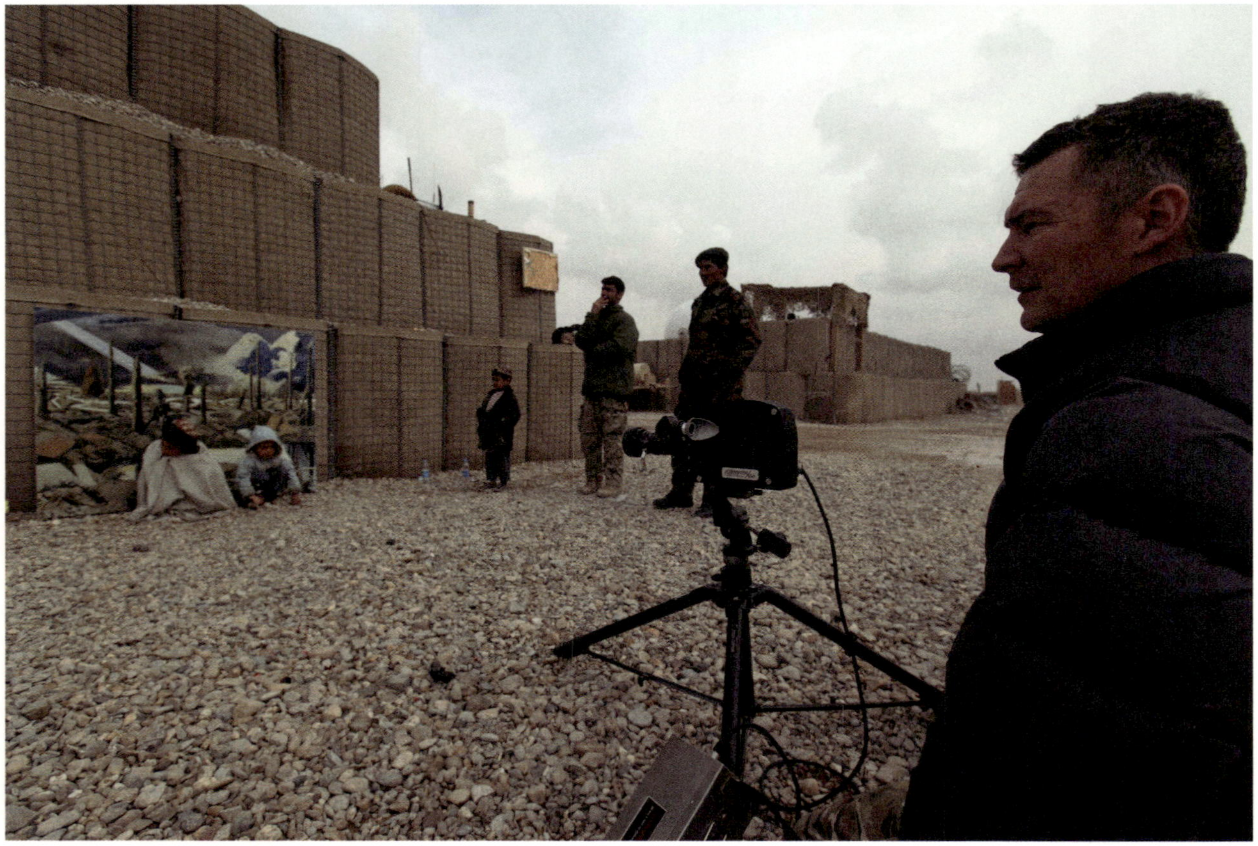

Neville filming *Backdrops* in
Helmand Province, 2011

When I got to Helmand I was struck by how old I was—more than old enough to be the father of many of these soldiers. To serve, you have to be eighteen but many looked a year or two younger than that. They were kids, basically. Out on patrol, Afghan children would appear out of nowhere, pushing a wheelbarrow or carrying food, with no adults for miles around. Where have they come from? Where are they going? What are they doing? It was clear they'd taken on adult responsibilities very early in life. You can see it in their faces, prematurely aged. This was in contrast to the baby-faced British troops, the boys not even shaving yet. But in both cases the youth was wholly inappropriate.

And the hand-held high-speed camera?

I wanted to make long, silent, panning or tracking shots, just documenting what I saw. I think the most powerful sequence I made, visually and emotionally, was a tracking shot from a tank in Bolan Market. The night before, I had loaded two rolls of 16mm film into the cartridges for this camera. I remember doing this in a sleeping bag with a flashlight in my mouth. At about 6am, I was picked up by an armoured vehicle called a Husky, which is armed with a big machine gun. Bolan Market was several hours away. I was taken there in order to witness a success story for British and ISAF (International Security Assistance Force) troops. The market was previously Taliban-run territory but now commerce was beginning to flourish again. Cars and mobile phones were being traded, alongside food and fabric. Most of the time you don't see this in Helmand, which is largely in abject, almost medieval, poverty. Subsistence farming. But here at Bolan you see the beginnings of trade. So you can understand why I was taken there. The troops were proud of their achievements.

What did you film?

Well, I was in the Husky and was told if I got out I could well be shot or kidnapped within ten minutes. It might be Taliban-free but that place still had highly complex relations between locals—ravaged for centuries by poverty and war—and the occupying forces. So this huge, threatening armoured vehicle passed through the market and I filmed from a turret in front of the mounted machine gun. I had the camera in the crook of my arm, trying to hold it steady and focused as we went. And going through the market I was struck by how deeply inappropriate my presence was. You can see in the film that people are shocked, not just at me with a camera but at the huge presence of the tank. It must have been like a spaceship landing in Peckham, south London. Some people would have seen tanks before, in the market, but most wouldn't have. So as the camera passes they are looking in awe, or fear, or resentment, or curiosity. You can really feel the ambiguity in the film. Are they waving in welcome or waving us away? Are they doffing their hats as a gesture of respect or fear? Are they turning their backs and walking away because they are Taliban

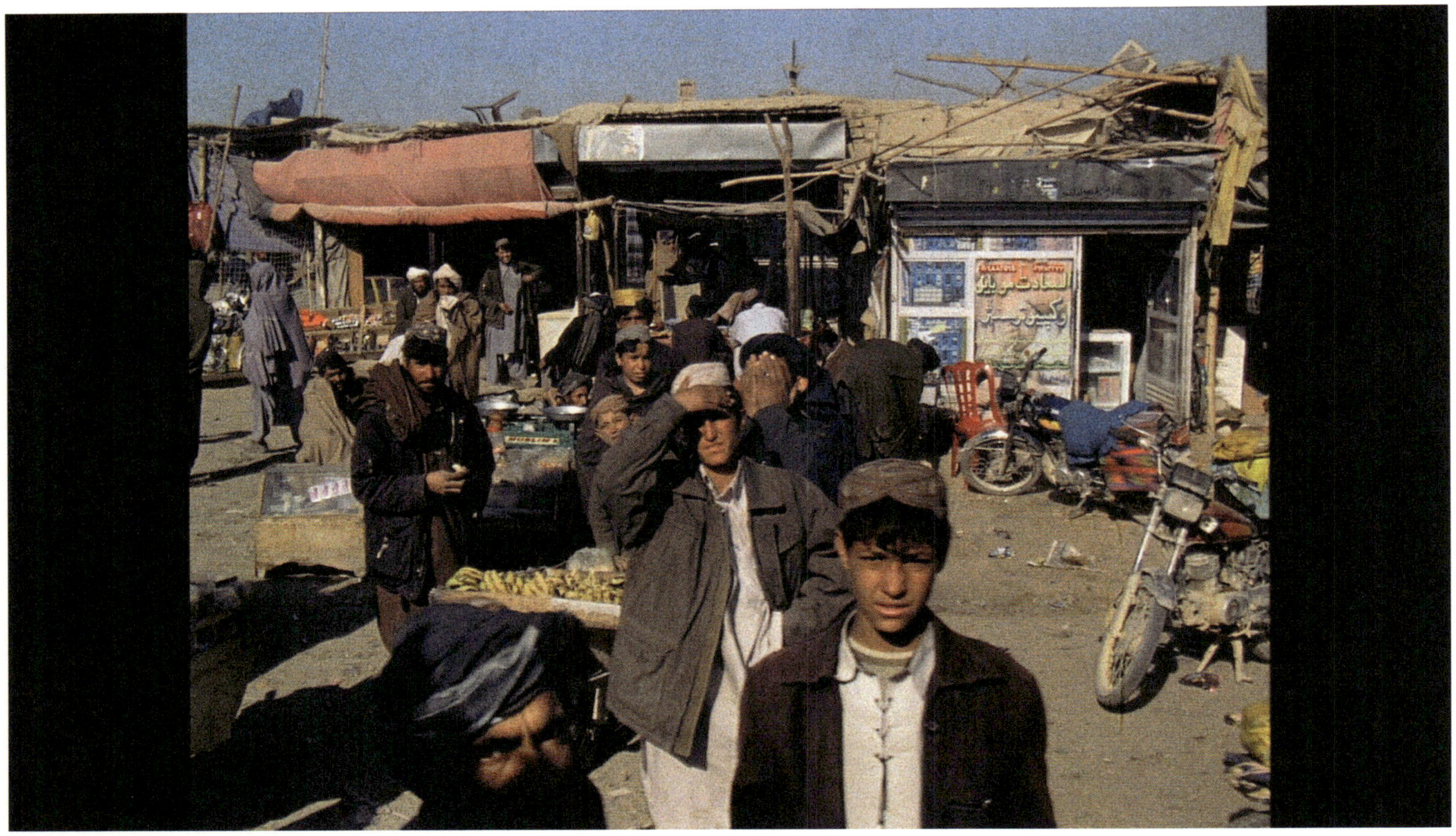

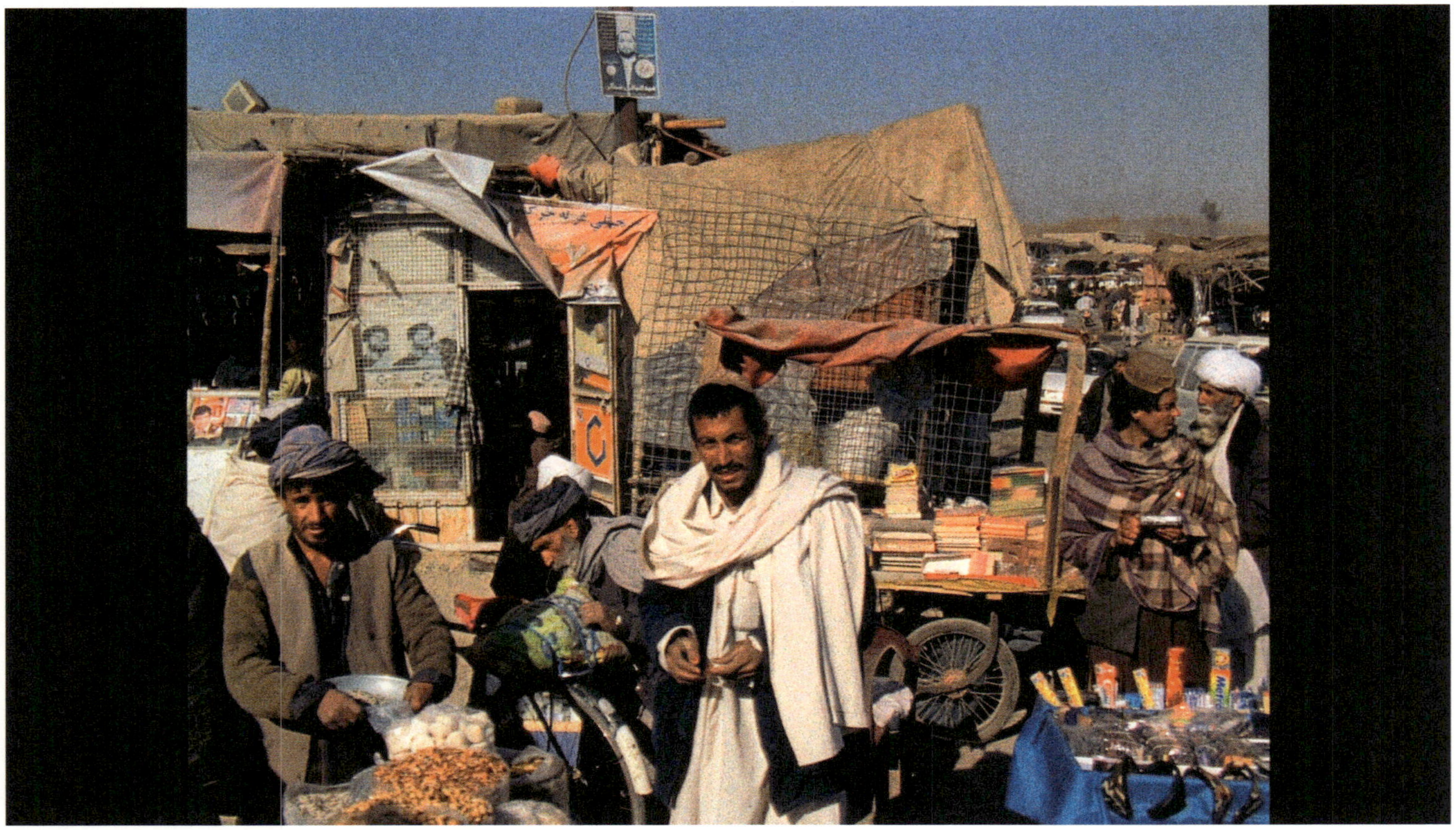

Stills from *Bolan Market*, 6 mins, 16mm film, Mark Neville, 2011

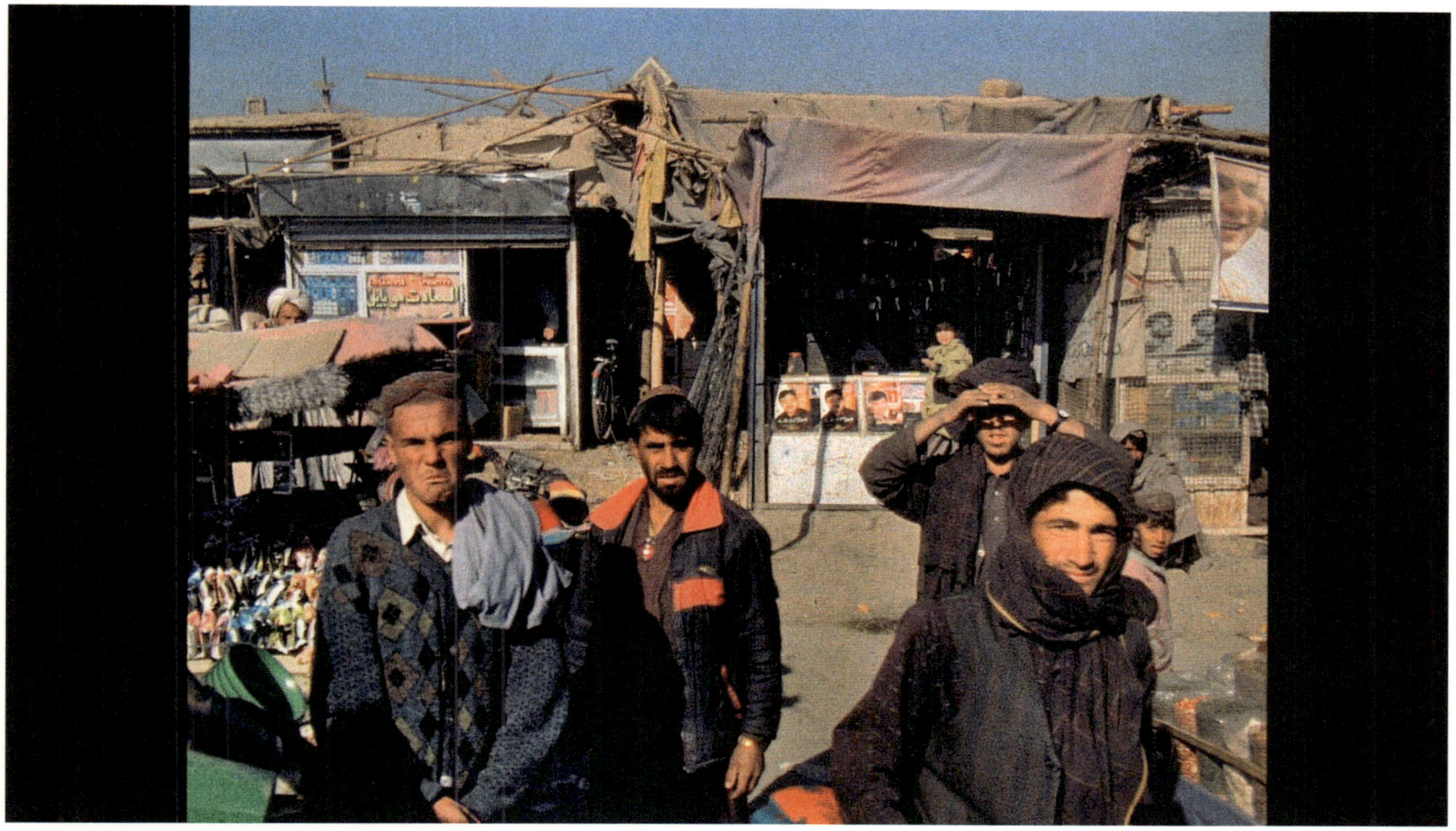

Stills from *Bolan Market*, 6 mins, 16mm film, Mark Neville, 2011

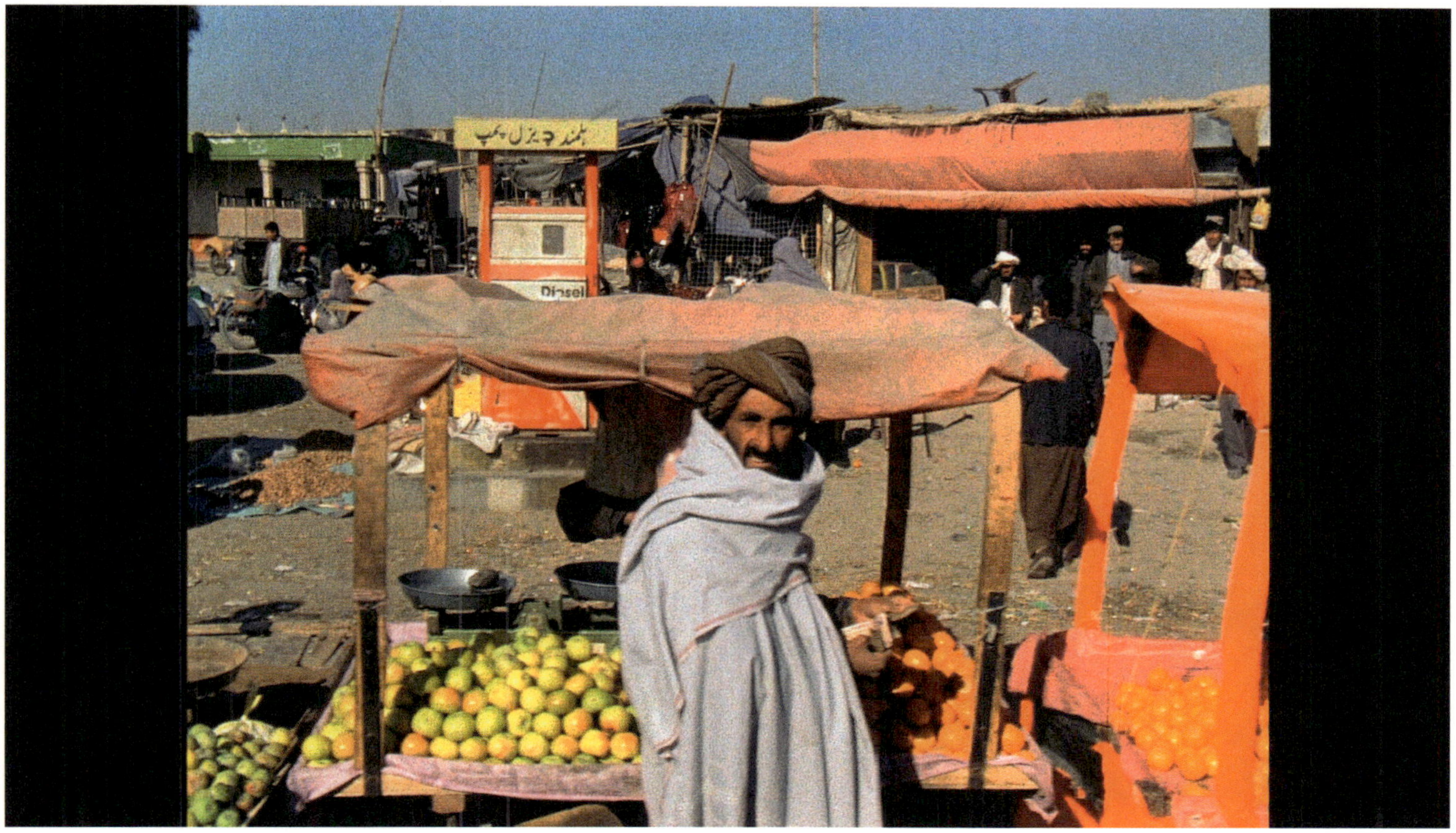

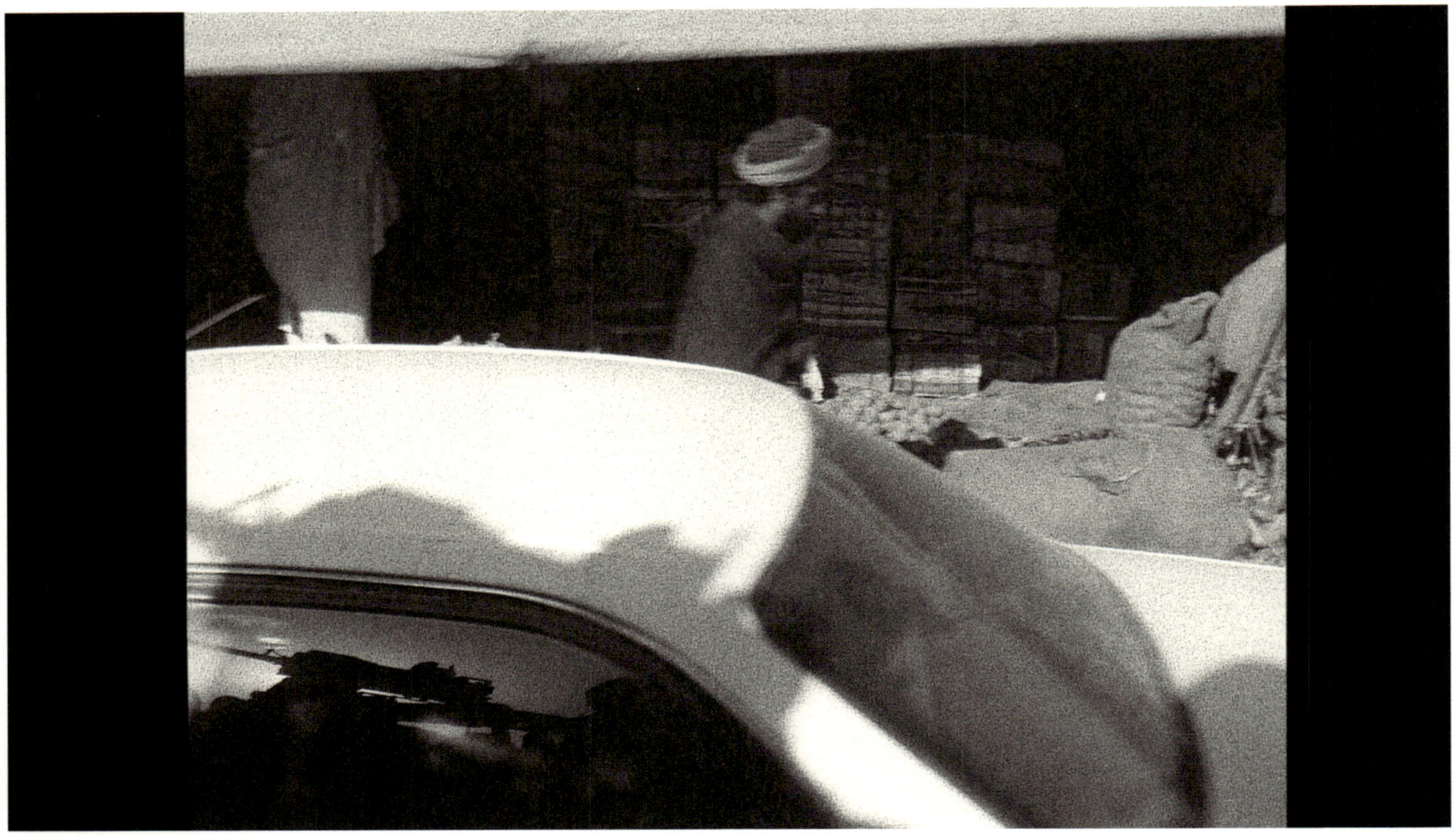

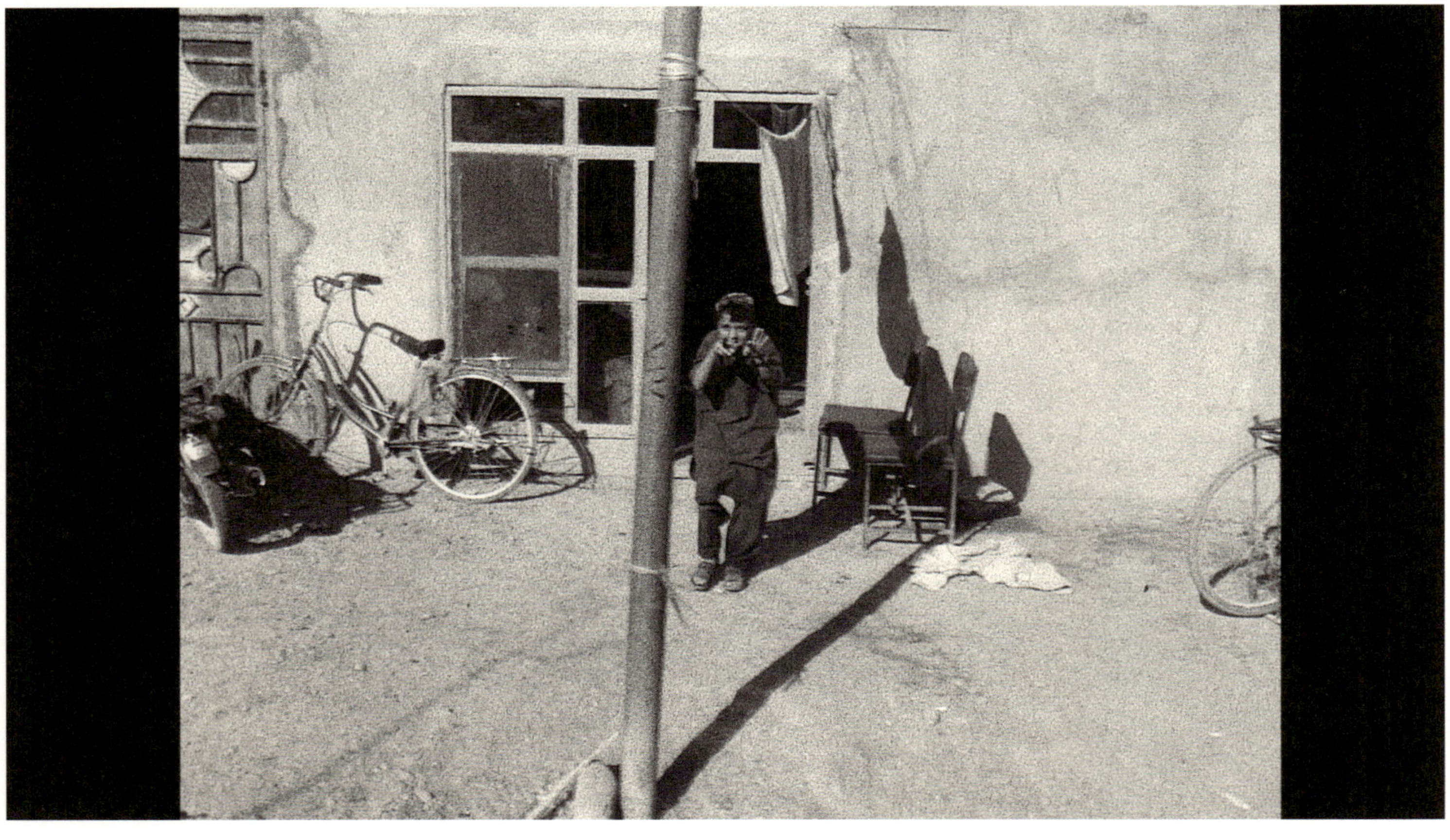

Stills from *7.62mm*, 11 mins, 16mm film, Mark Neville, 2011

sympathisers or because they've got better things to do? So lots of fear and mistrust, and lots of things we cannot even hope to understand.

And there is no sound. The film plays in complete silence.

I felt I was in a silent nightmare. But also the silence really helps the viewer to concentrate on the ambiguous details of what they are seeing. Moreover the silence seemed to point to the unbridgeable gulfs between me and what I was seeing, and between the various parties involved: the locals and the occupying forces.

It's unbridgeable but it is picturable and that's what you ended up doing. Picturing that gulf.

I think it was only in that tank that I truly realized how inappropriate my presence there really was...and by extension how inappropriate the British occupation was. From then on I felt the mismatches and the misunderstandings all the time. Afghanistan is barely a nation, it's a series of tribes. Britain has always misread this.

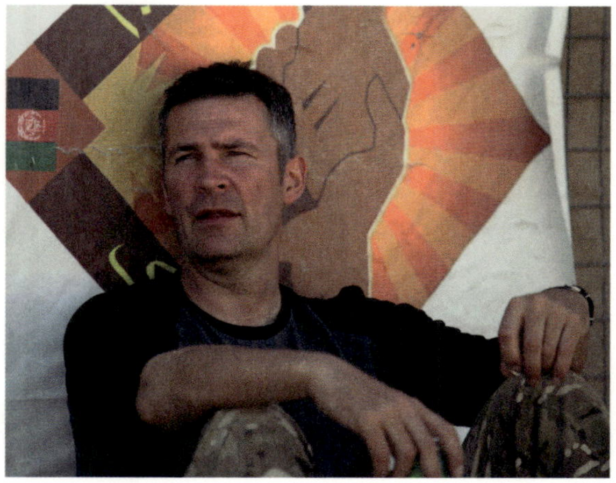

Neville in Helmand Province, 2011

When one thinks of the pressure and danger everyone is under in a war zone, you can understand why all experimentation in reporting gets dumped in favour of the tried and tested formulas. Experimentation looks odd to those around you. It needs a contemplative, thoughtful approach. While it is completely necessary to experiment it is next to impossible to do it under such circumstances.

That's very true.

When you returned there were difficulties getting that work shown.

I wanted it shown while it was fresh and contemporary, so that it would be some kind of intervention in an ongoing situation.

Images that are documentary at root have a different meaning when they are contemporary. They are judged against immediate experience. Once they are old, they stand in for that experience, which is not always helpful.

Quite. Before I left for Helmand I made it clear that I was not going for an experience and then coming back and making work in response: I would be making work there and then, on the ground, and it would be ready for publication or exhibition soon after my return. I definitely wanted what I did to be contemporary, and not an "alternative looking back". Anyway, for many complicated reasons, some of the films and photographs were finally shown at the London's Imperial War Museum in 2014, three years and four months after they were made.

That was after the announcement of British withdrawal from the occupation.

I had wanted my material to be seen as if it were news: the report from a war artist just returned. Plus, just like many troops, I had a

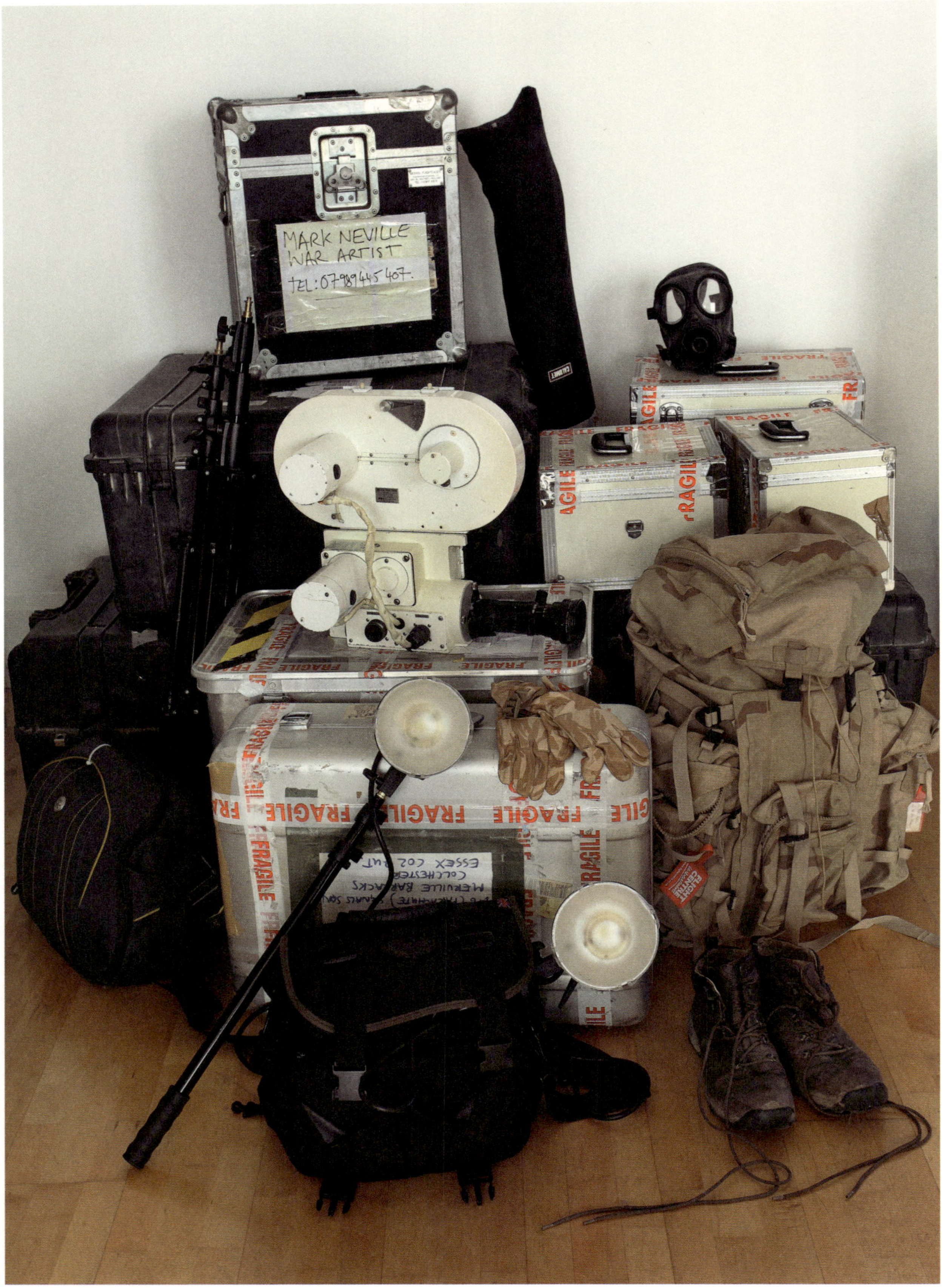

Neville's kit for use in Helmand, photograph taken prior to departure, 2010

really difficult time adjusting to civilian life when I got back. I needed some closure and without being able to show the work I wasn't getting that closure. It was emotionally and psychologically very hard. I'm sure this happens to many sincere photographers and filmmakers. They return home and editors sit on their stories and don't publish them or, when they are published, they are sexed-up and distorted.

I can see how the Helmand project completely fits with your interest in tightly-knit communities living in extremes. But it's a very different project in that you weren't able to conceive of the audience as a structural part of the making of the work.

Well I was, in the sense that I felt I was going against the grain of the typical images that western audiences see of the Afghan war. I knew about those interventionist works by Martha Rosler and Robert Heinecken, reworking existing media images into collages and giving them back to unsuspecting audiences. There was something of that in my approach. I wanted something of that collision with the general public. I went out there on those conditions. When those conditions weren't met I felt personally very tangled up in that work, cocooned in the experience, until it was finally shown. But it never had the chance to have the impact it might have had in 2011.

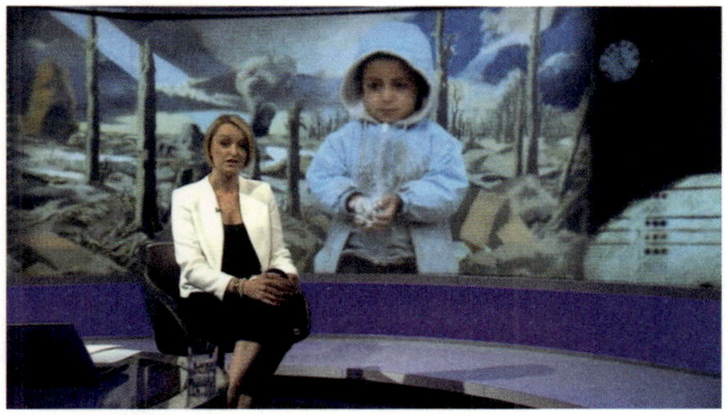

Still taken from Neville's self authored television feature about the war artist experience in Helmand, BBC2 *Newsnight*, 15/7/2014

But as we discussed earlier, you work in a way in which there can be few certainties. So much is unpredictable.

I do accept that, and welcome this aspect of what I do. I learned a lot from the Helmand project. I do not think that the work has a shelf life, despite the agonising delays.

BBC *Newsnight* allowed you to write and present your own assessment of being a war artist, which I thought you did clearly and strongly. And the BBC crew resisted the temptation to put your voice over the long clip of that silent tracking shot. I thought that itself was a very powerful moment in the television coverage of the war. Television gets anxious about long silences.

Thank you. I was working with Katie Razzall again, the same journalist who covered *Deeds Not Words* for *Channel 4 News*.

It's good to know there are still supportive people working in television.

I think the public has an appetite. They are frustrated by the coverage of such wars, just as governments are worried about telling the truth.

Here

Is

London

2011

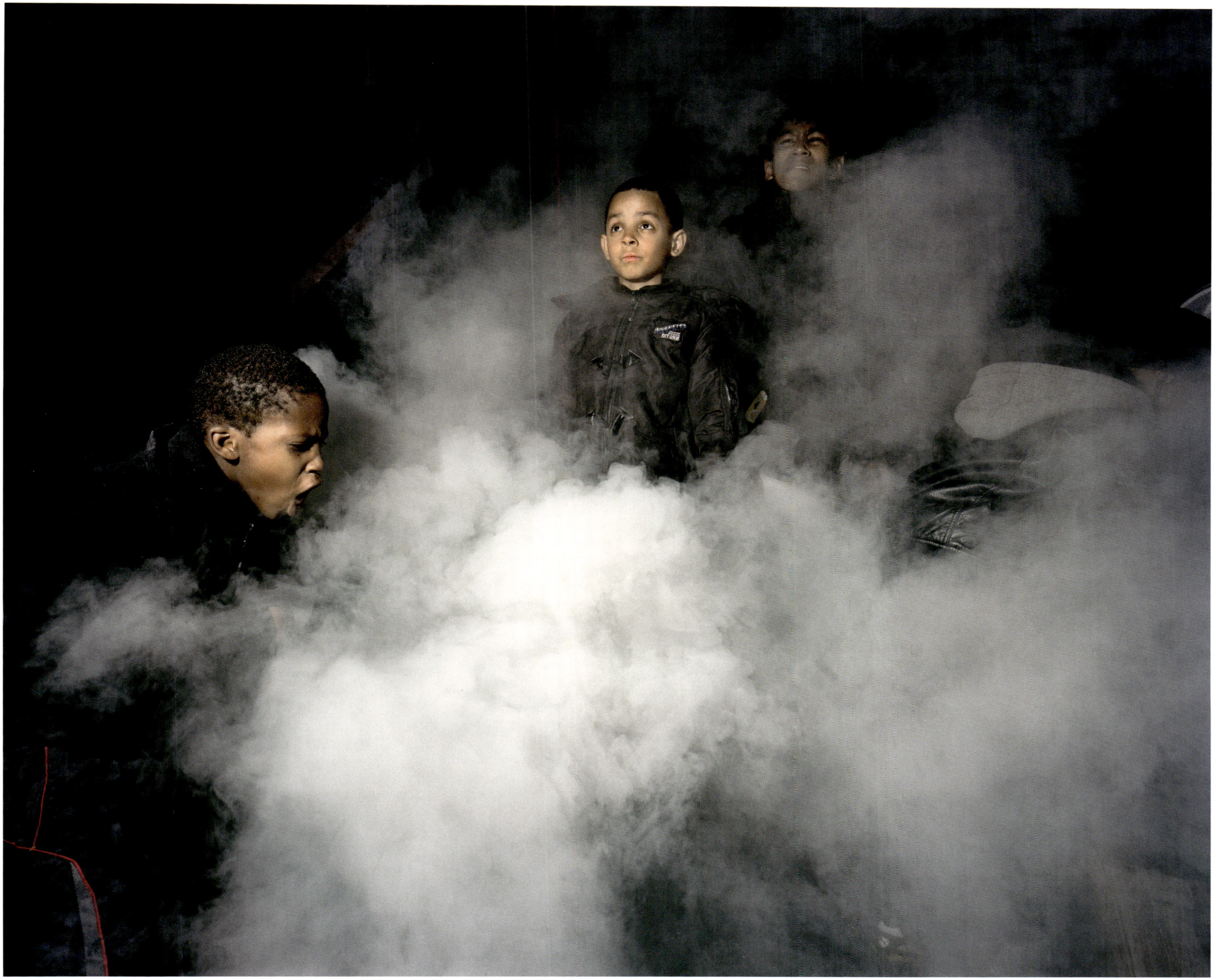

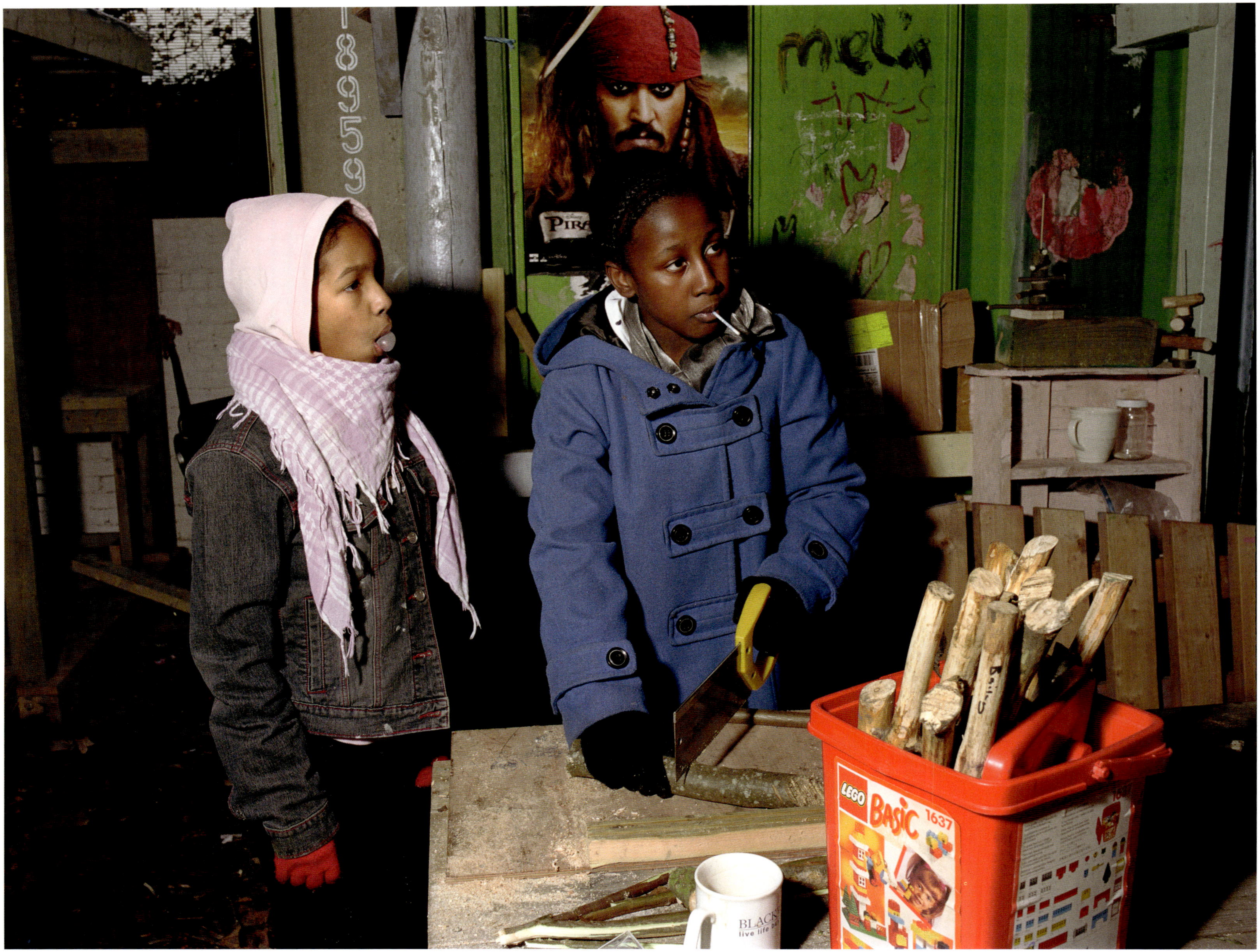
LEGO
BASIC
1637

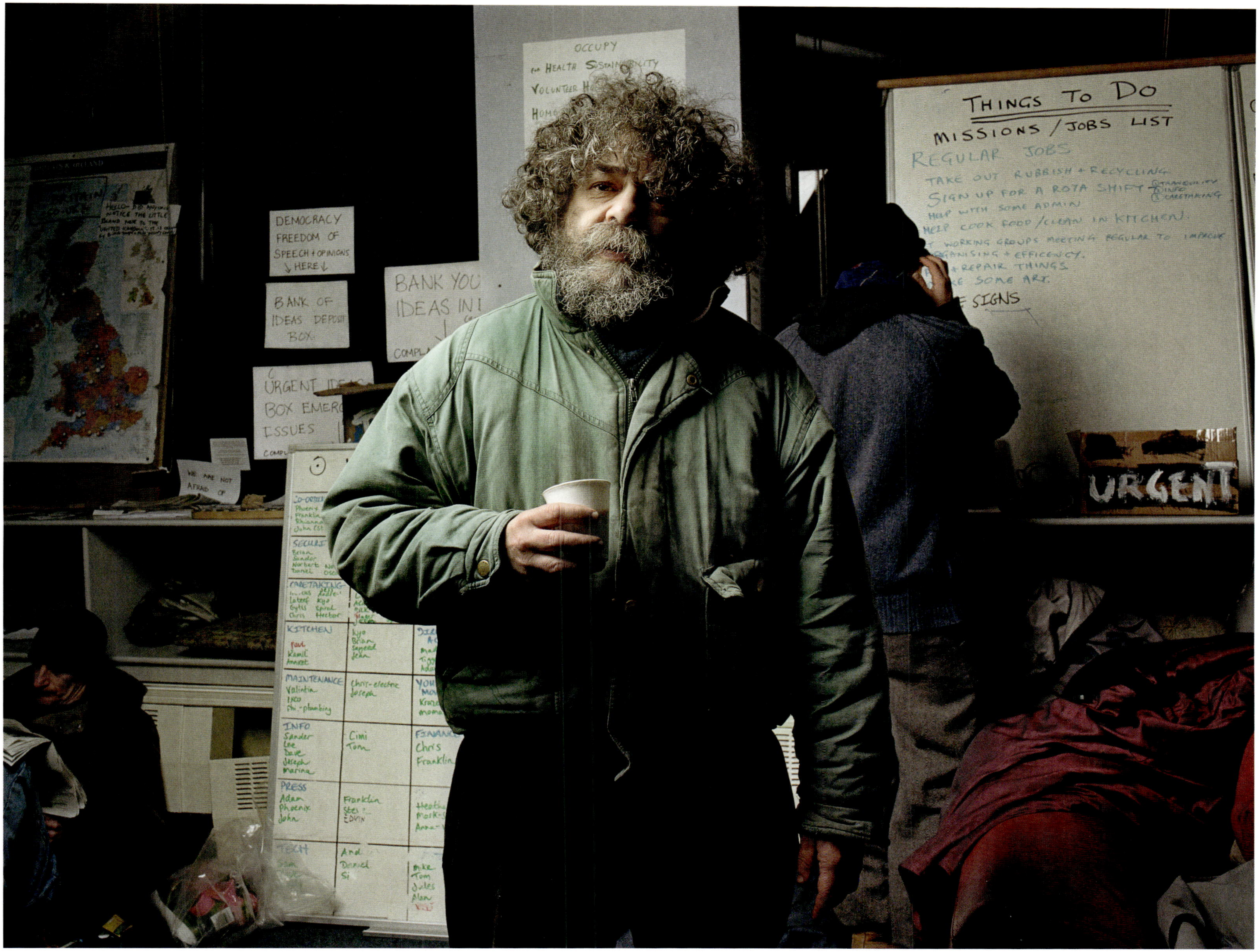
OCCUPY
DEMOCRACY
FREEDOM OF
SPEECH + OPINIONS
HERE
BANK OF
BOX.
THINGS TO DO
MISSIONS / JOBS LIST
REGULAR JOBS
TAKE OUT RUBBISH + RECYCLING
SIGN UP FOR A ROTA SHIFT
HELP WITH SOME ADMIN
HELP COOK FOOD / CLEAN IN KITCHEN.
URGENT

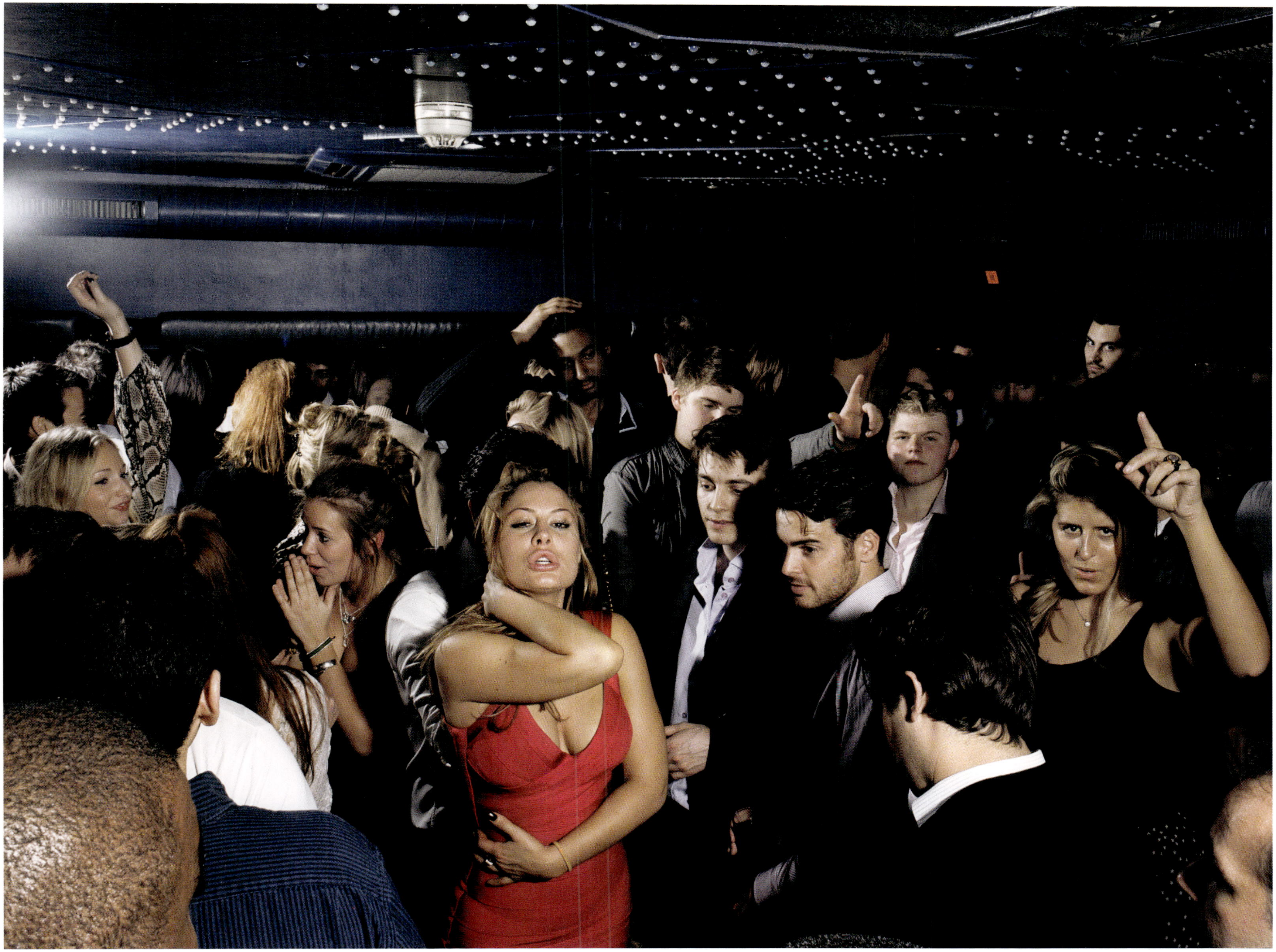

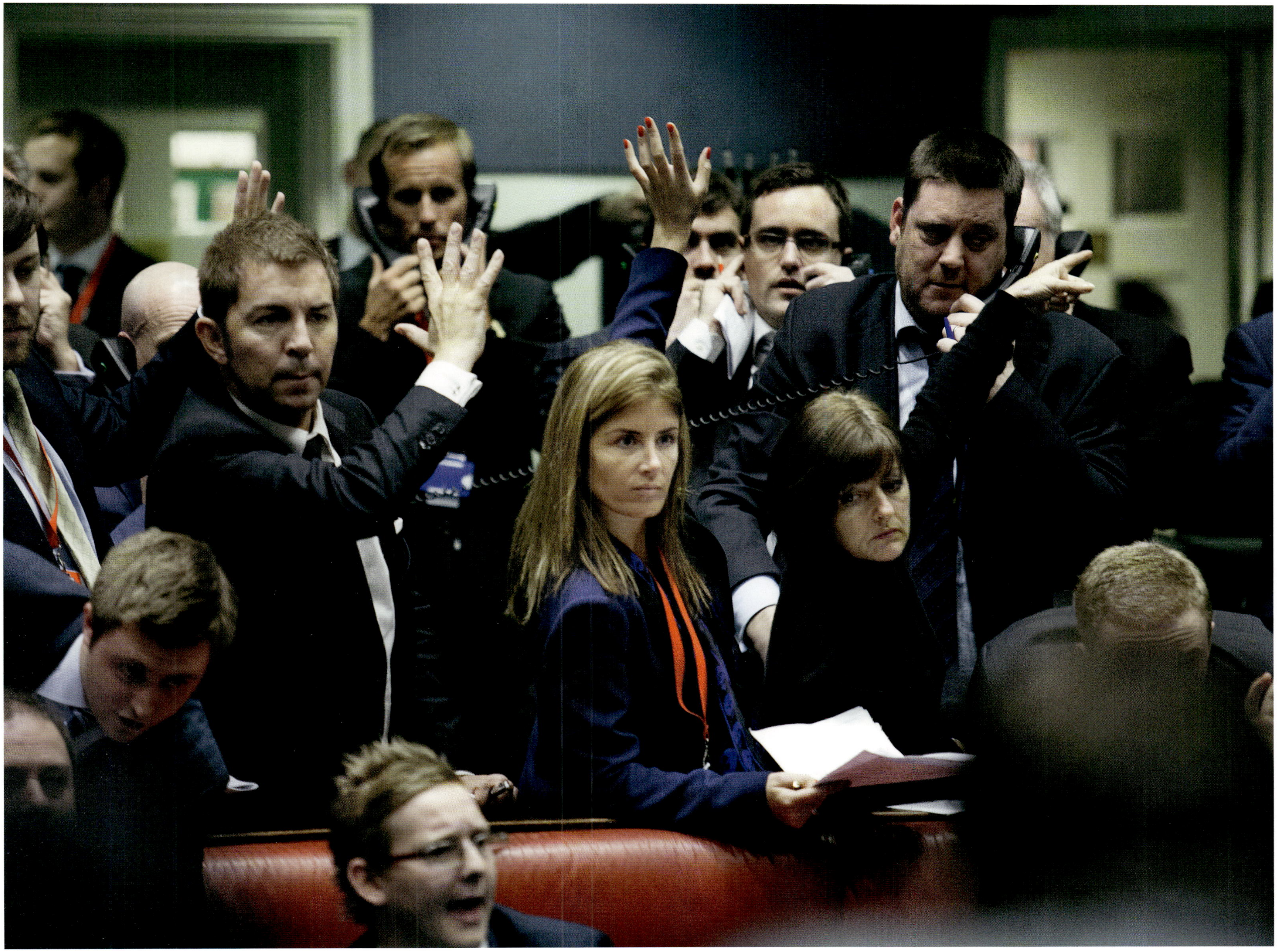

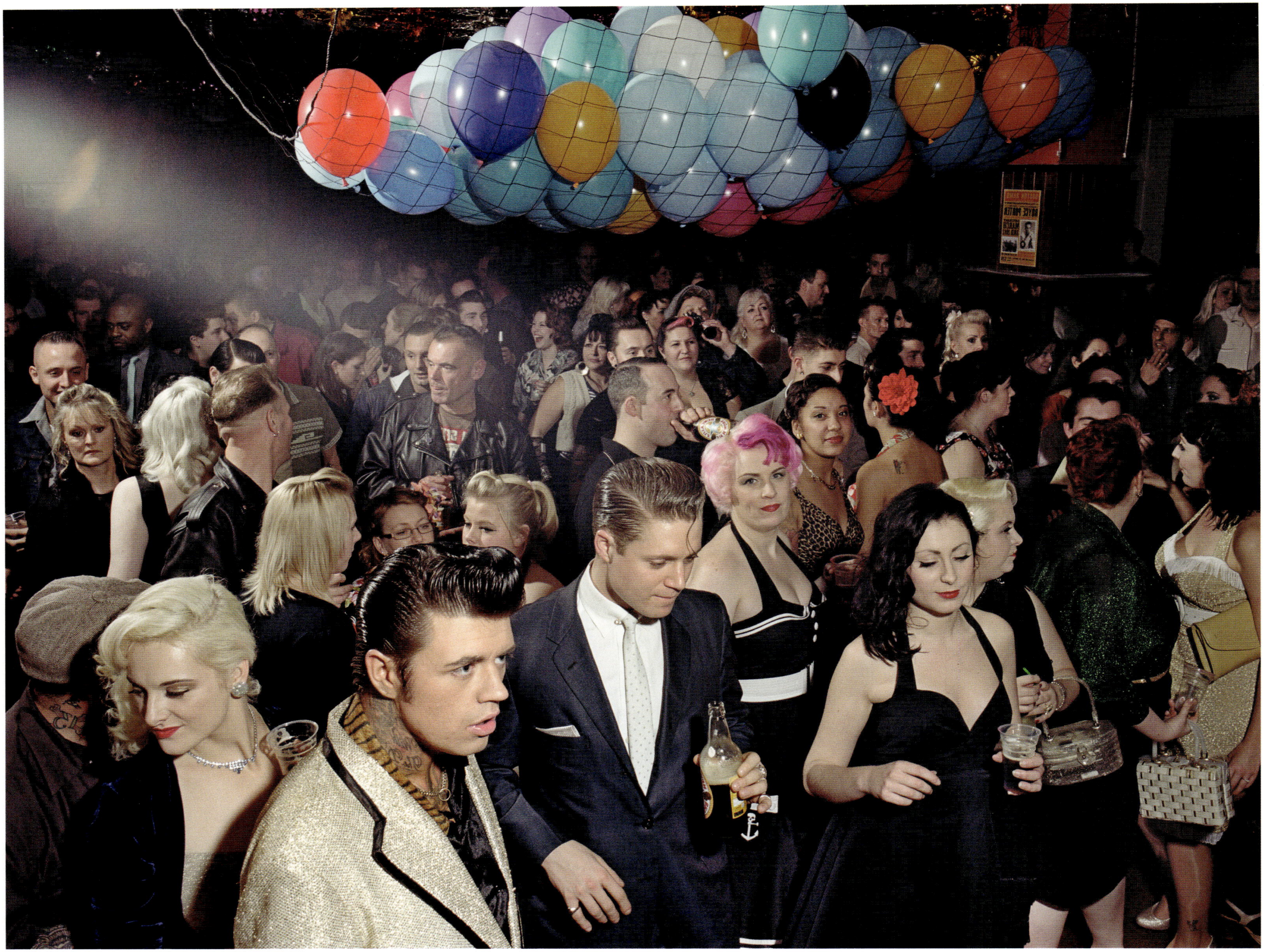

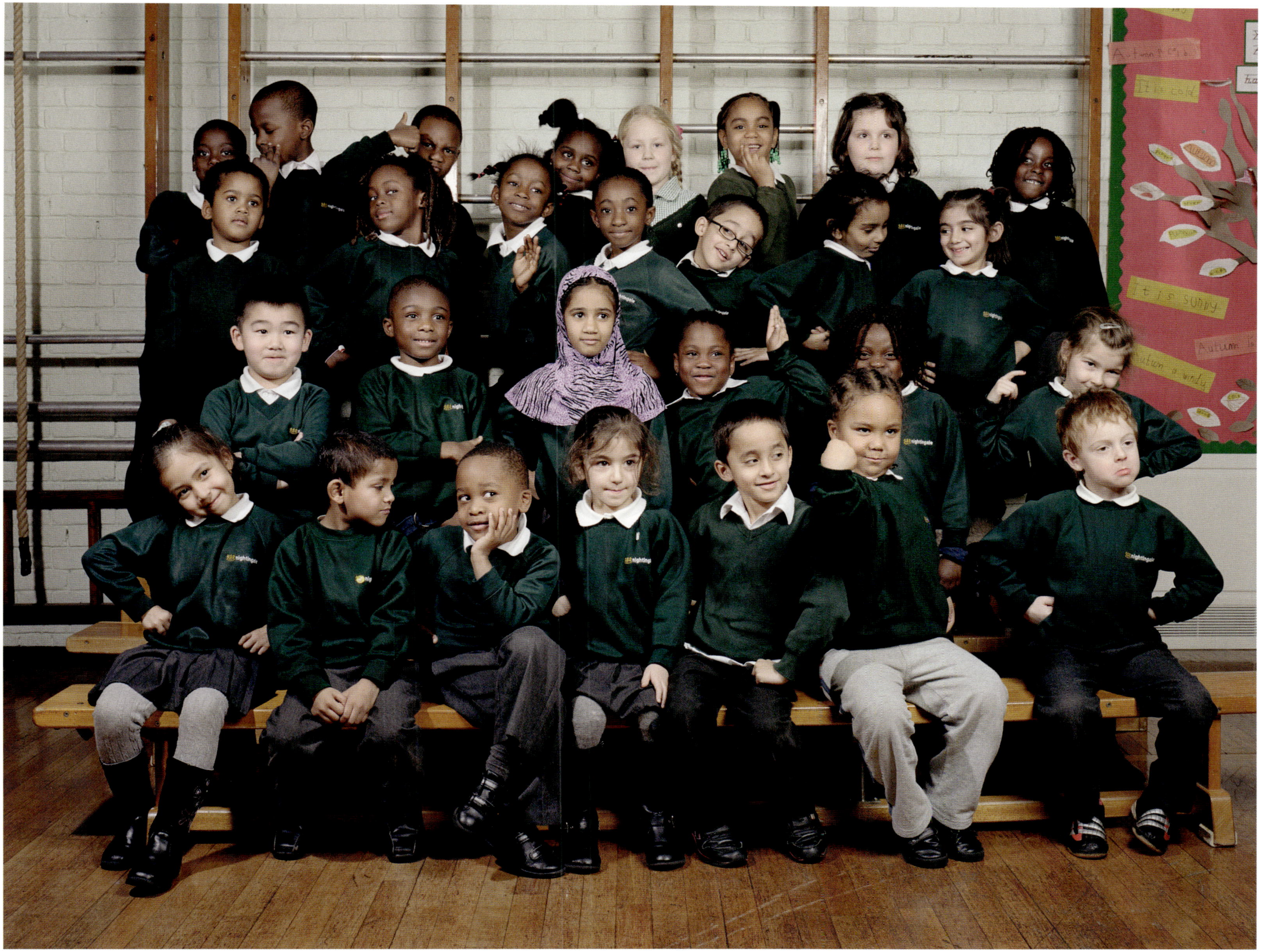

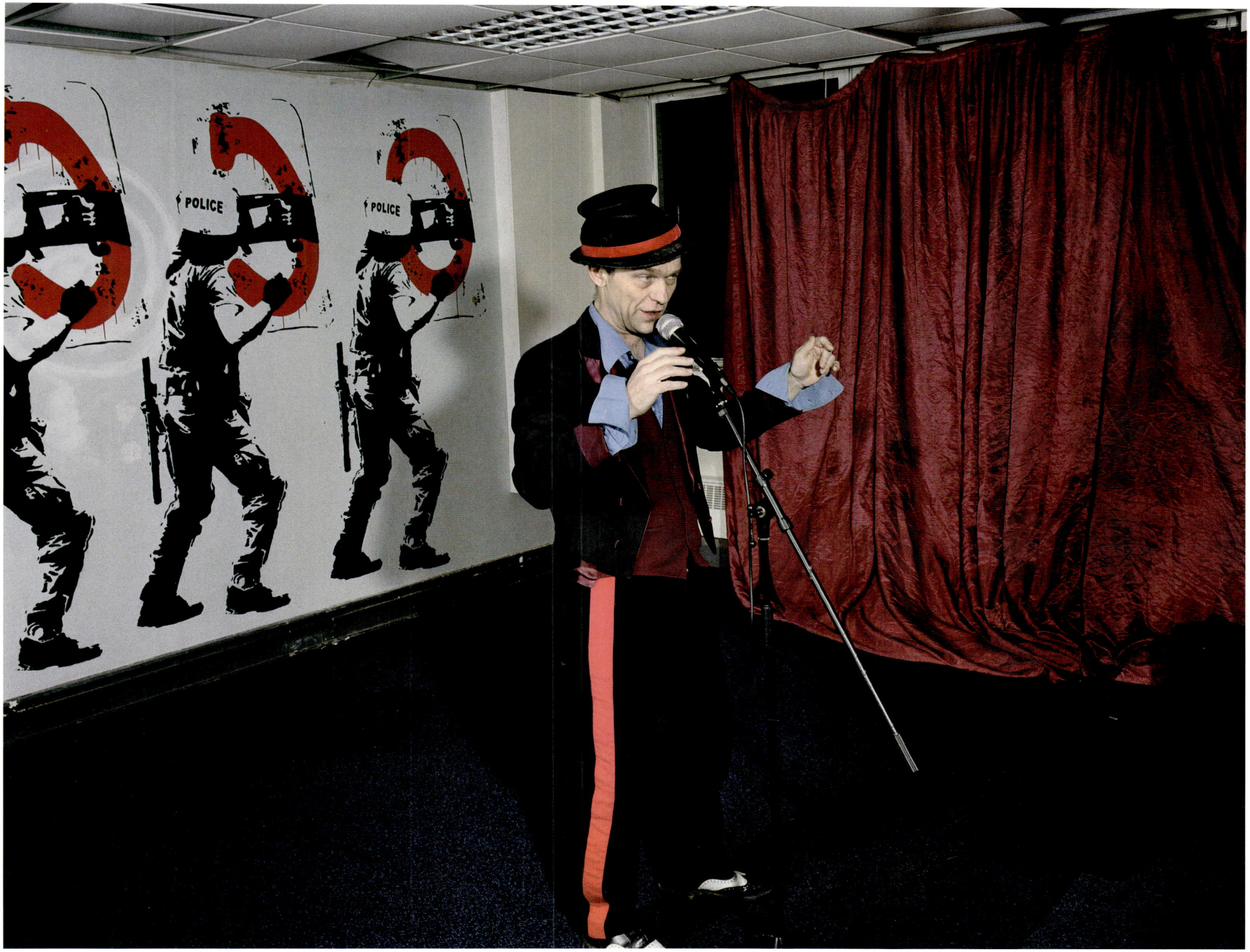
POLICE
POLICE

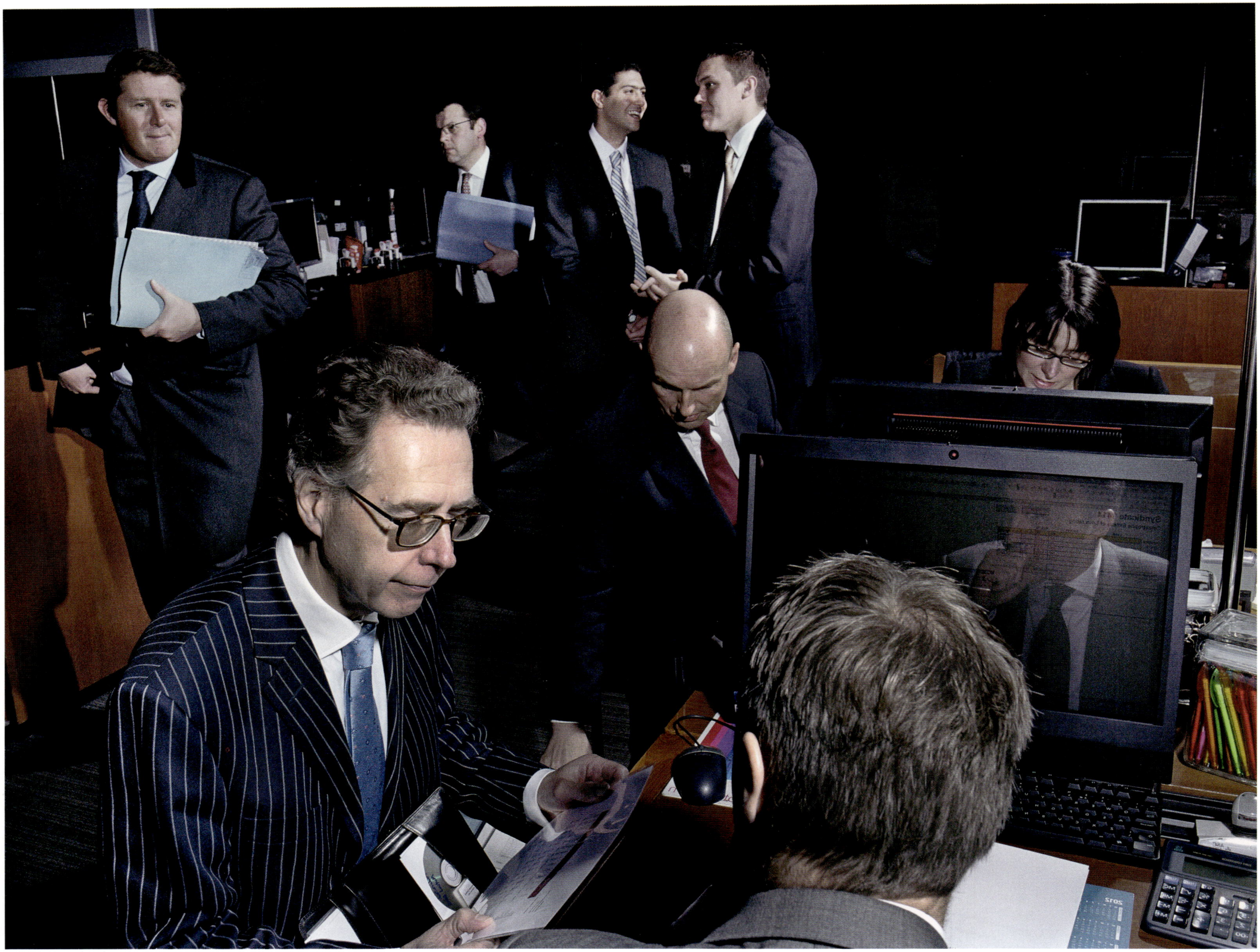

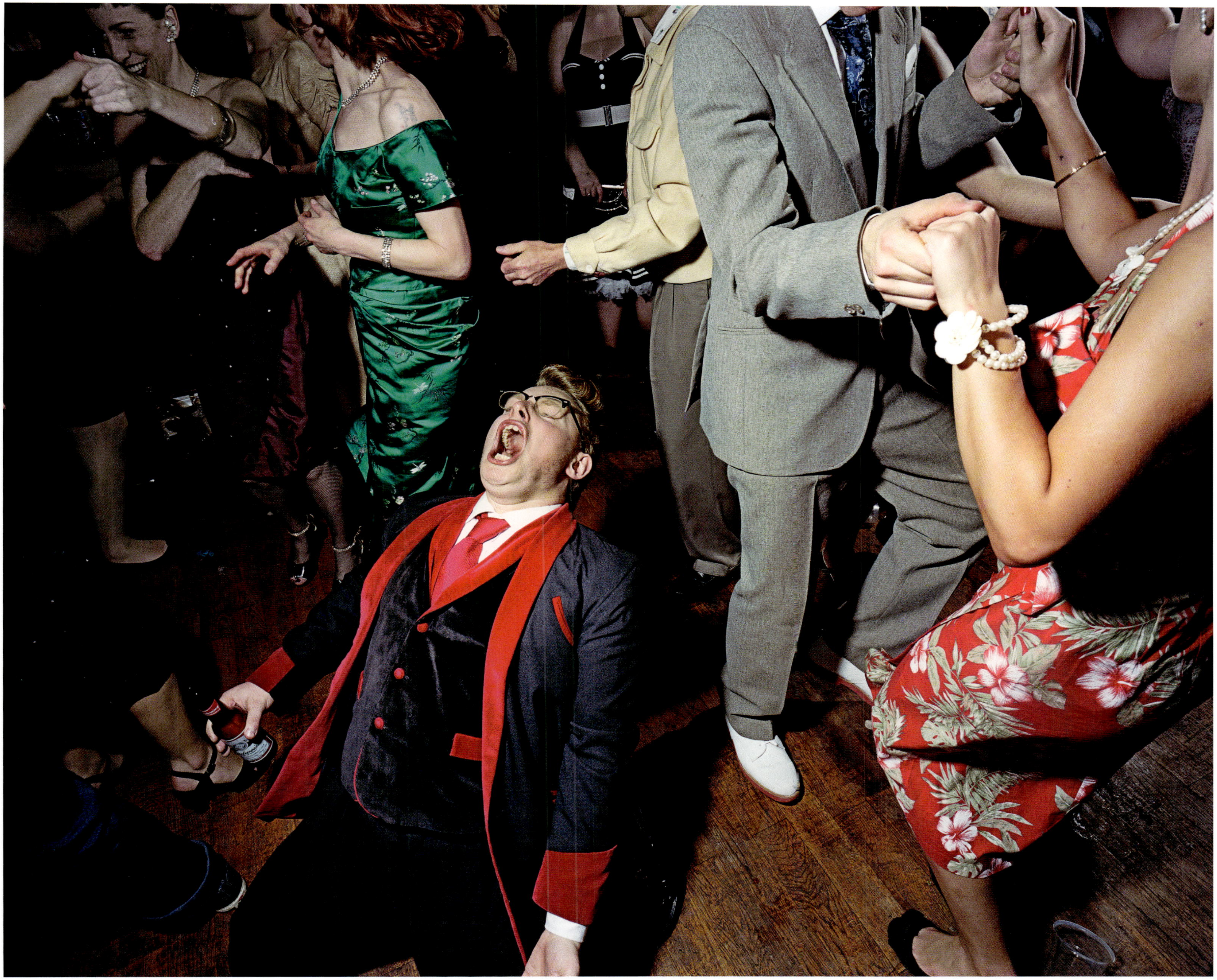

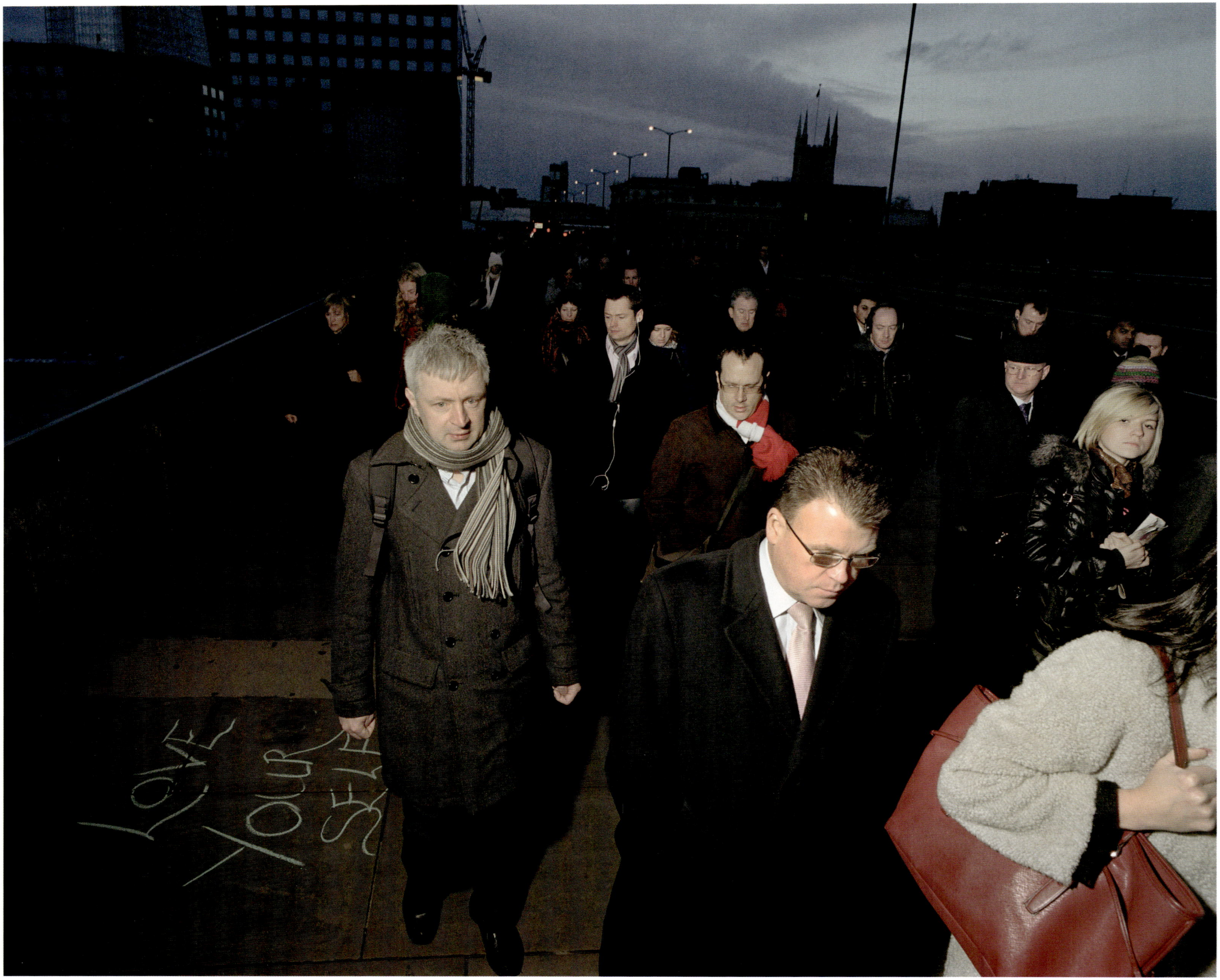
LOVE YOUR SELF

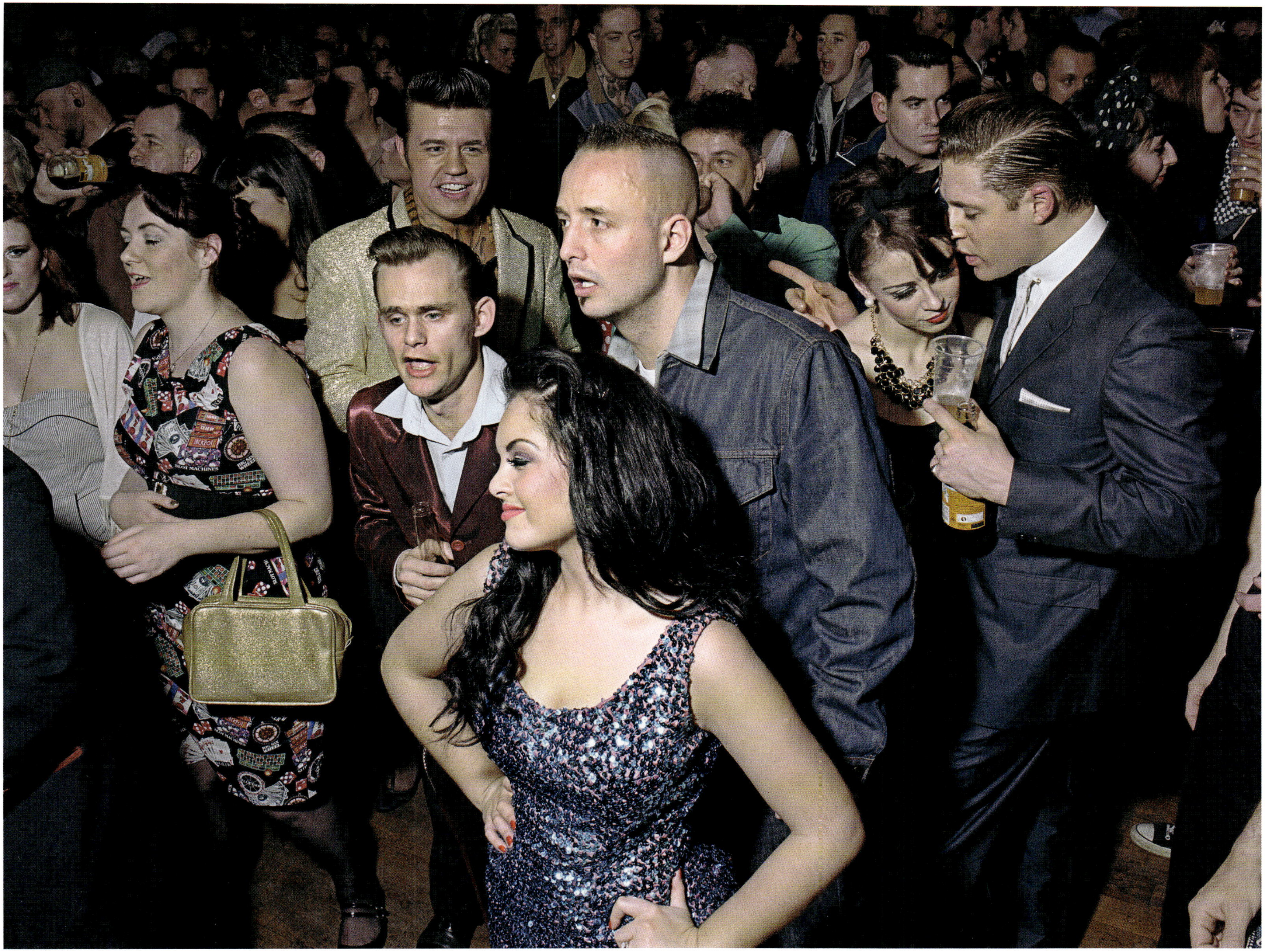

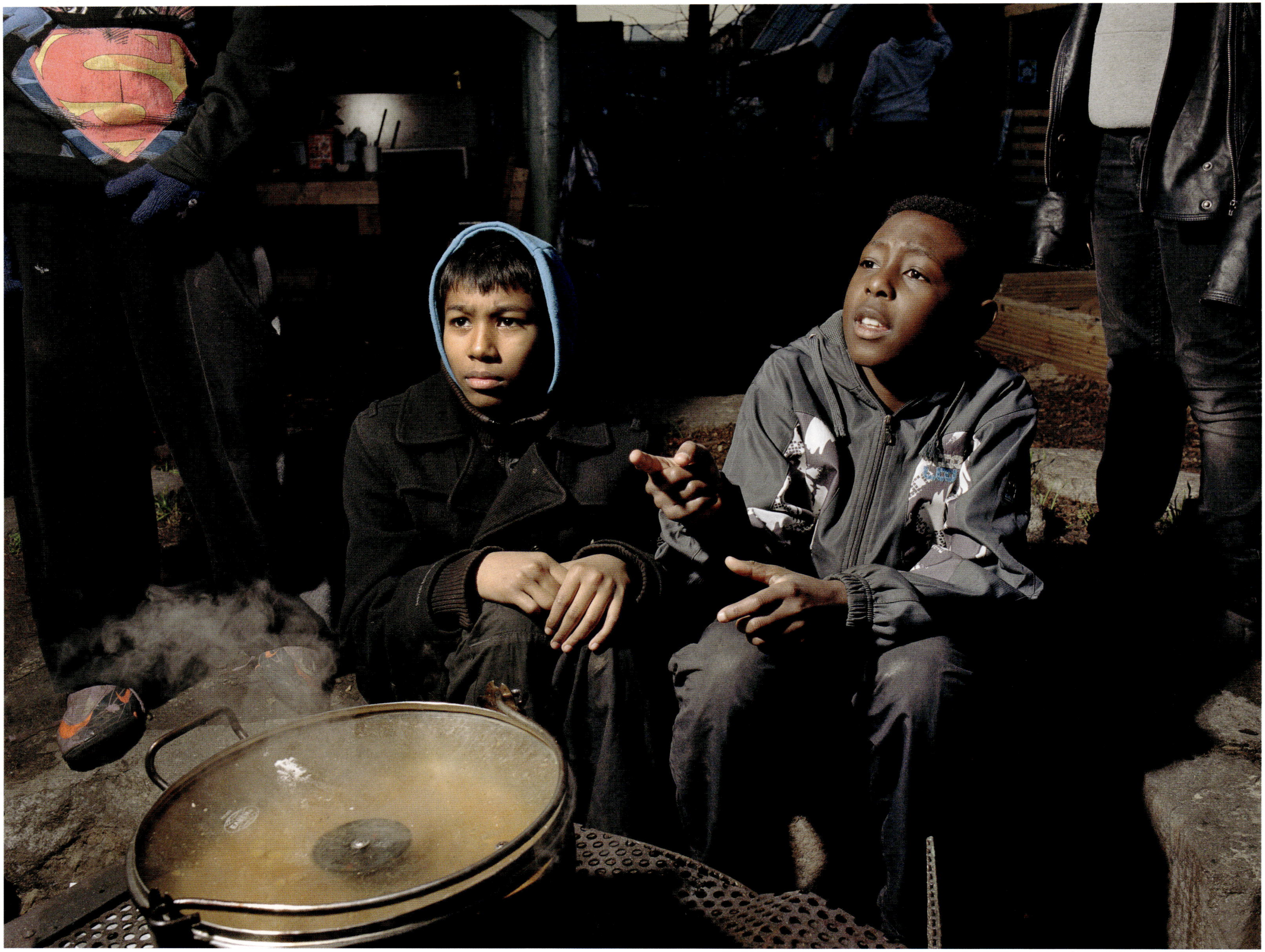

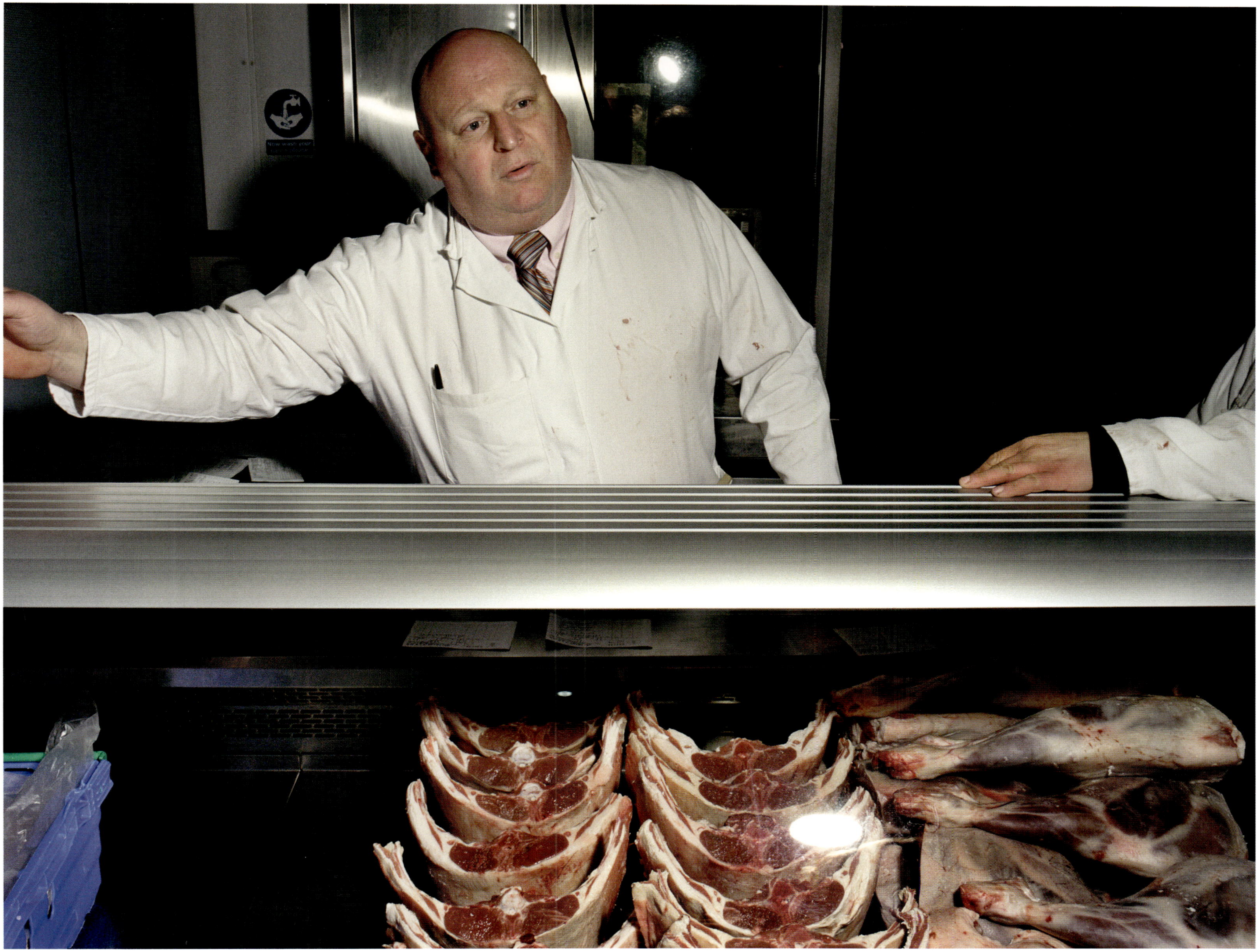

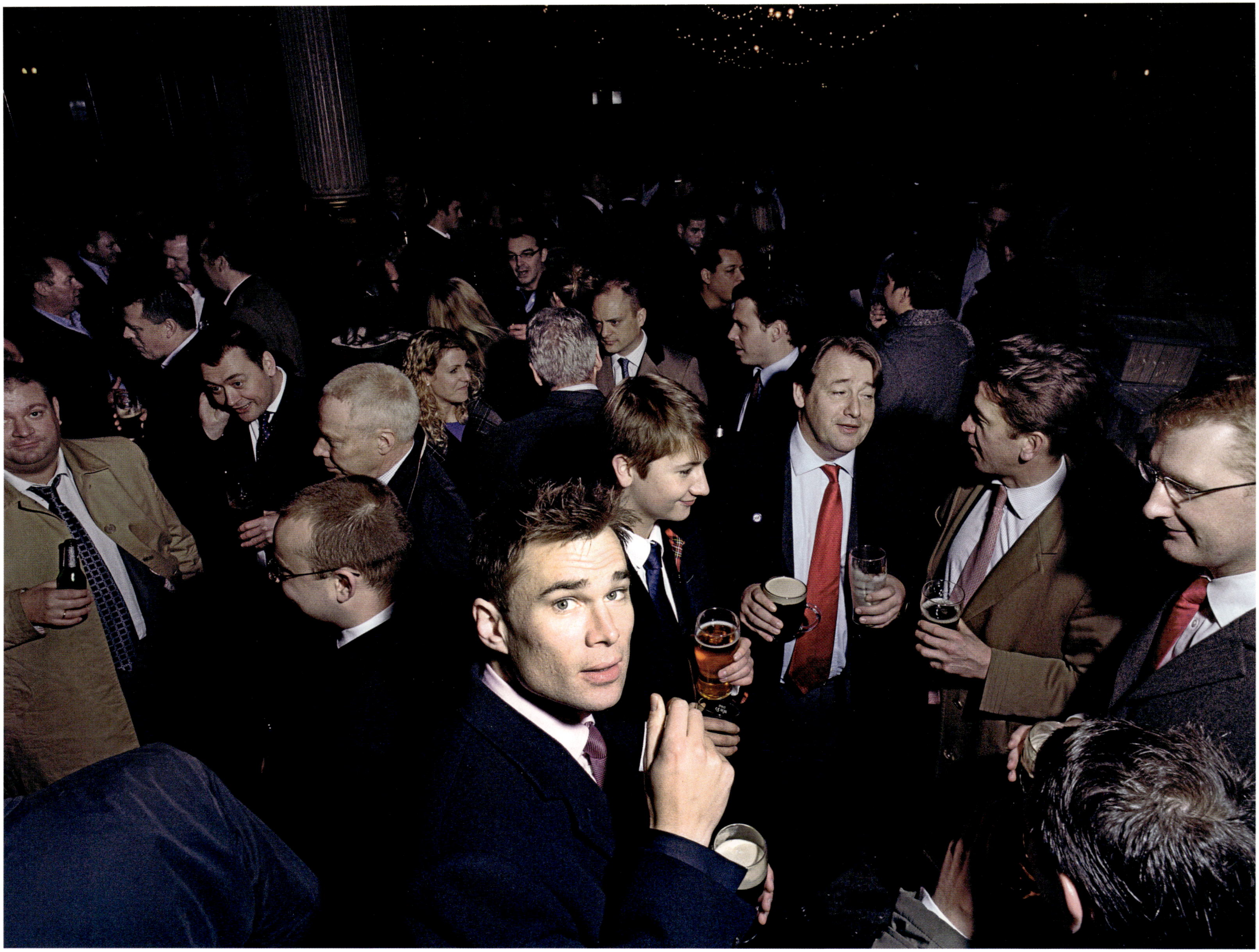

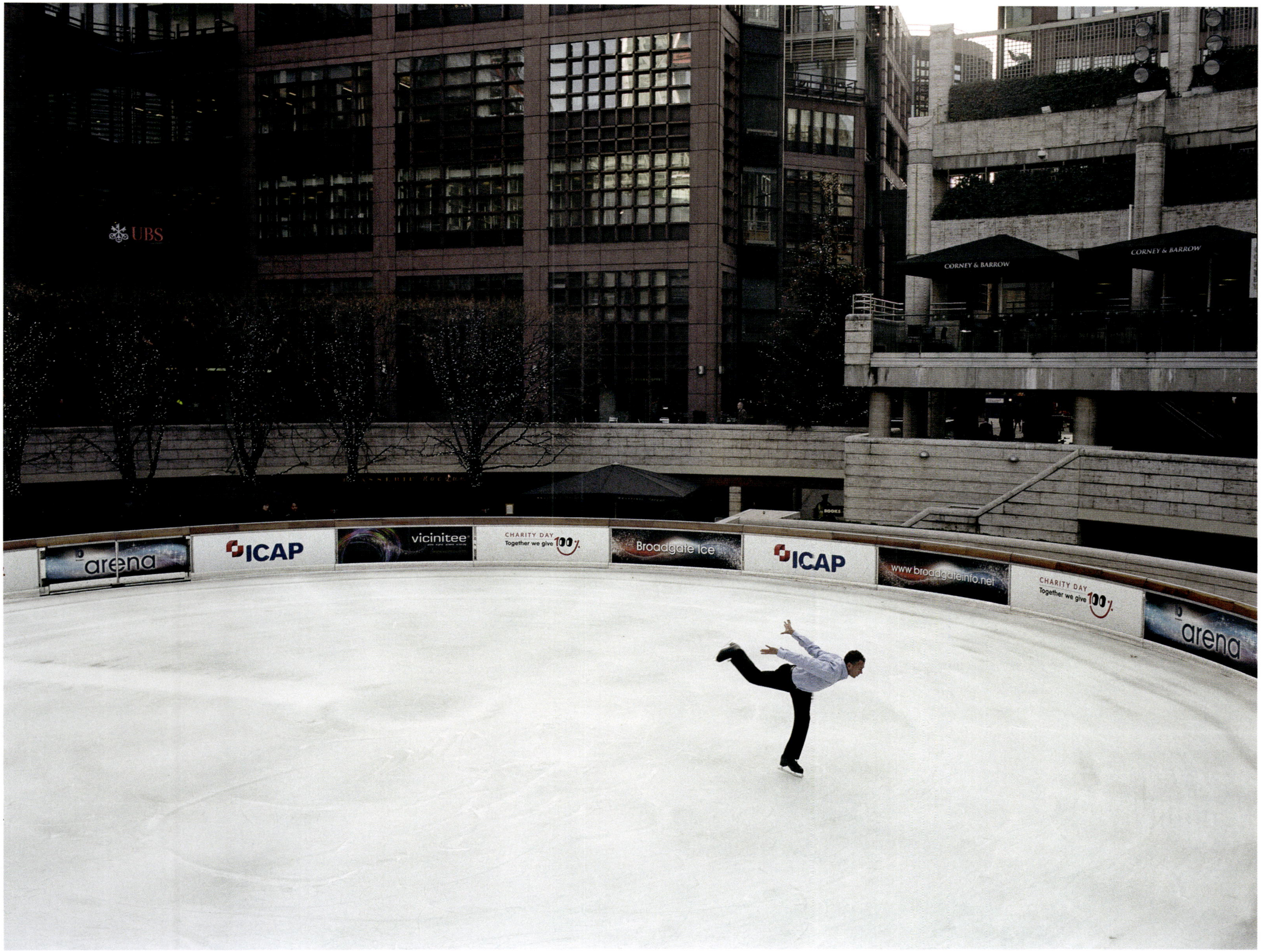
UBS
CORNEY & BARROW
CORNEY & BARROW
arena
ICAP
vicinitee
CHARITY DAY
Together we give 100%
Broadgate Ice
ICAP
www.broadgateinfo.net
CHARITY DAY
Together we give 100%
arena

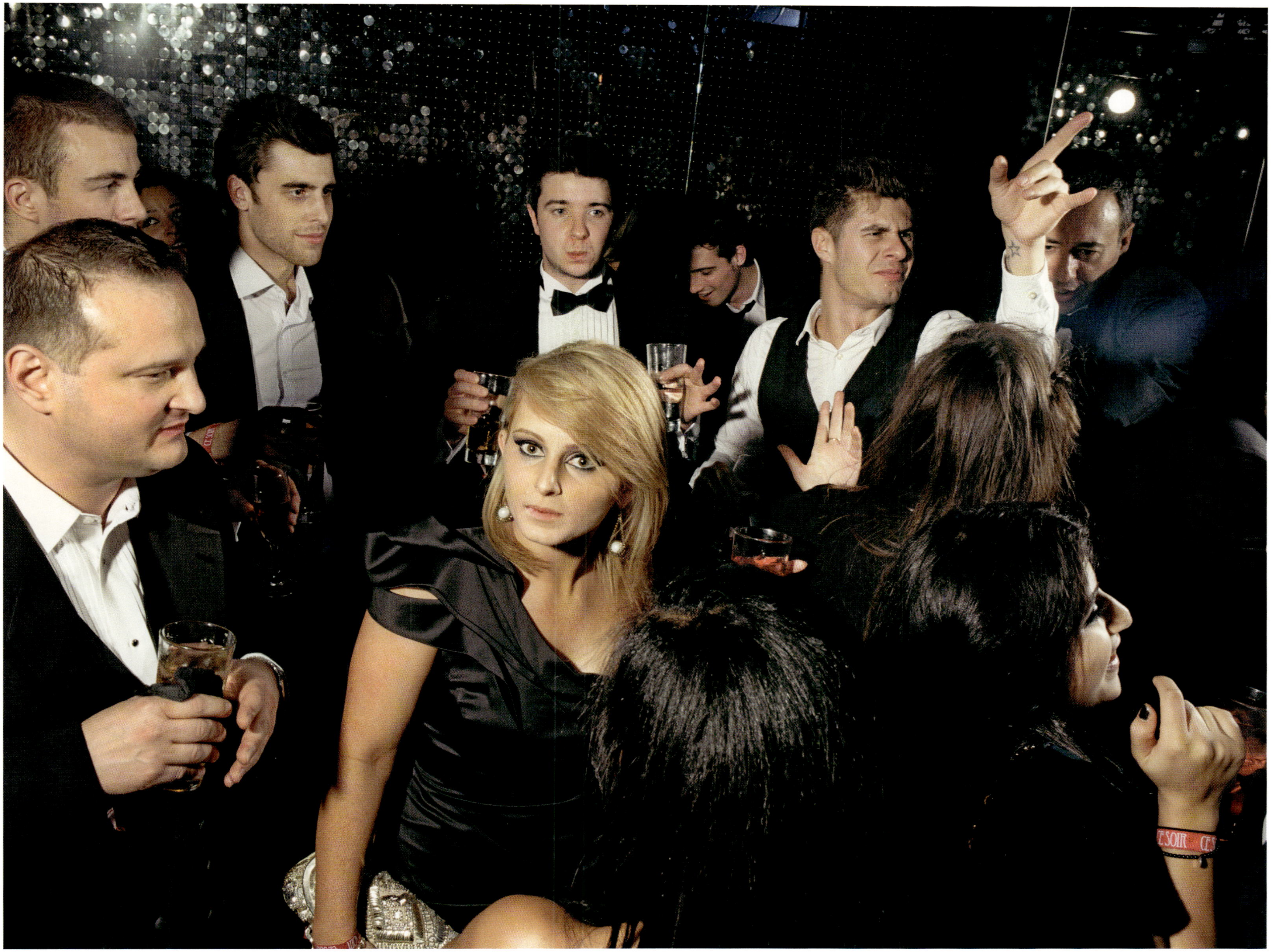

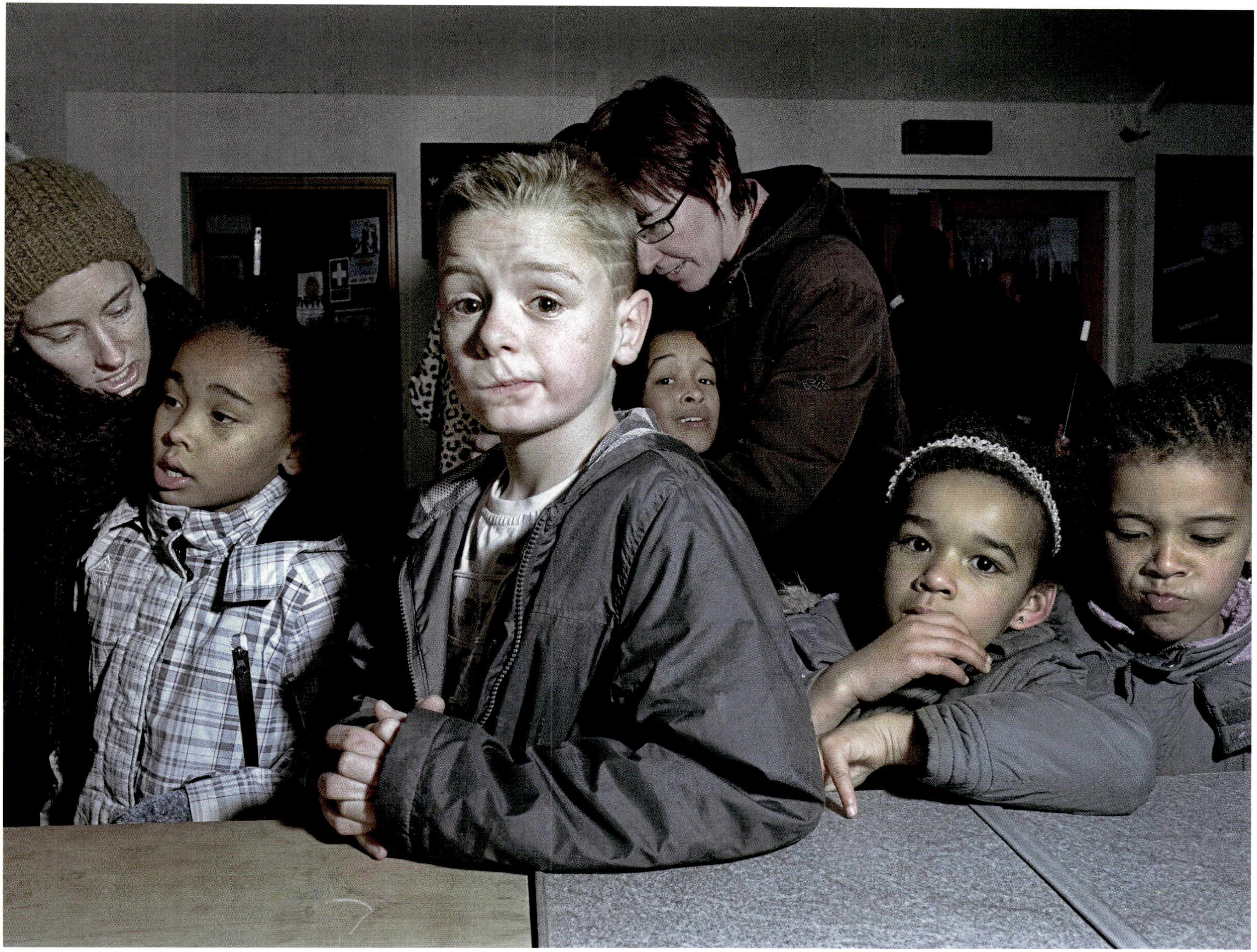

Titles

153. Kids at Somerford Grove Adventure Playground, Tottenham, put out the barbeque fire, 2011
154. Arts and Crafts at Somerford Grove Adventure Playground, 2011
155. 'Bank of Ideas', Occupy London, 2011
157. The dancefloor at Boujis Nightclub, South Kensington, 2011
159. London Metal Exchange, 2012
160. The Boston Arms, New Years Eve, 2011
161. Nightingale Primary School, 2012
163. A performer from Occupy London at the 'Bank of Ideas', 2011
164. Lloyd's Insurance Market, 2012
165. The Boston Arms, 2011
166. Commuters crossing London Bridge, 2011
167. The Boston Arms, Rockabilly Night, 2011
168. Cooking at Somerford Grove Adventure Playground in Tottenham, 2011
169. Smithfield Market, 2011
170. Bankers at Leadenhall Market, 2011
171. Businessman ice skating, 2011
173. Bankers at Boujis Nightclub, South Kensington, 2011
175. Somerford Grove Adventure Playground in Tottenham, 2011

Here

Is

London

David Campany: While you are immersed in these projects, your practice continues to gain a reputation outside of the communities you are working in. Museums, galleries, editors, curators and writers. For example the photographer Martin Parr, who has become a big advocate of photo books, got very interested in your *Port Glasgow* book. He exhibited it. Word got out. And suddenly you get a call from the *New York Times Magazine.* Kathy Ryan, the quite experimental Director of Photography at the magazine, wants you to shoot for a special issue on London.

Mark Neville: That was my first journalistic commission! For the first time the frame was conventional in a way, from the nature of the commission to the format of the magazine and its audience. But yes, Kathy does have a reputation of breaking conventions where she can, working with artists, "cross-commissioning" as she calls it. I was asked to make work synchronously with the writer/journalist China Mieville. He's somewhere between Marxism and science fiction. A commission to be a newspaper photographer for six weeks was an exciting possibility. I was living in Glasgow but came down to London and stayed in university halls over Christmas and New Year 2012. I worked solidly, shooting on film. I would get my material processed in an east London lab and scan it on my cheap scanner to see how I was doing. I showed Kathy as I went along.

How did you decide what to photograph?

Well, because the context was fixed in advance I had to work in a much more straightforward way. I wanted to explore the great divide in London between the rich and the poor, which is getting worse all the time. And I wanted to be pretty explicit. "Caricatures" is the wrong word and "stereotypes" is definitely the wrong word but there was an element of deliberate contrast and exaggeration between socio-economic extremes. Rich and poor. The establishment and subculture. Tradition and the new. The class system and racism too. Obvious themes to begin with. I shot in Lloyds of London and the London Metal Exchange. I also shot in Tottenham, a working class part of north London, and I shot the Occupy movement. In many ways the ridiculous social inequalities we associate with the 1970s and 1980s are still with us and are in many ways worse. It's as bad as it's been since the 1920s.

It's just that the media don't show this any more.

That's right. Britain and America are in the top five countries in terms of wealth inequality. If you are born into poverty it's becoming increasingly difficult to break out of it.

The money goes to money.

The proportion of working poor—those who work fifty or sixty hours a week and are *still* in poverty—is enormous and growing. This was the context in which I shot London for *The New York Times Magazine*.

The pictures are, as usual, incredibly immersive, for you and for the viewer. You're very involved with all those different groups and communities. But you don't have a year or eighteen months to do this. You have just a few weeks.

It was very intensive. Back in Port Glasgow when I shot the town hall Christmas parties I spent a week just rigging the lights in the ceiling. And I spent a week shooting. In London I had to shoot pubs and clubs in one night by myself, holding a portable flash sometimes with an assistant. My entrée into these places was "I'm Mark Neville from *The New York Times*." This had great power. It really did open doors where normally I would spend months building up trust and confidence.

Your photographs seem to be referencing the look and film stock of iconic colour documentary work from the 1970s and 1980s.

Definitely, that was a point of reference, to get that feel in a very contemporary setting, the look of "recession Britain" that you see in the work of Tom Wood from Liverpool, for example.

It's interesting that the London Metal Exchange is the last live trading floor in the city. It's still photogenic. The rest of city trading has gone completely electronic and thus invisible to the camera.

Yes, trading floors always seem to refer back to the 1980s.

The boom before the bust when the iconography was stripy shirts, slick hair, materialism and arrogance. The *Wolf of Wall Street* and all that.

Nothing much has changed. You have to look twice at my pictures. Again they're historically indeterminate. Are those kids gathered around a cooking pot in Tottenham in 2013, or am I looking at Depression-era America? Are they putting out a barbecue with water or are they starting a riot?

Before the Second World War, appearances were more clearly codified, from how people dressed to the language of architecture. Today appearances level out. Everyone looks like they shop at Gap and buildings look much the same. Where once the rich used to be fat and the poor thin, often it is now the other way around. Today the world discloses itself to the camera in much more complex ways.

We have to look much more closely, at the small details, I think.

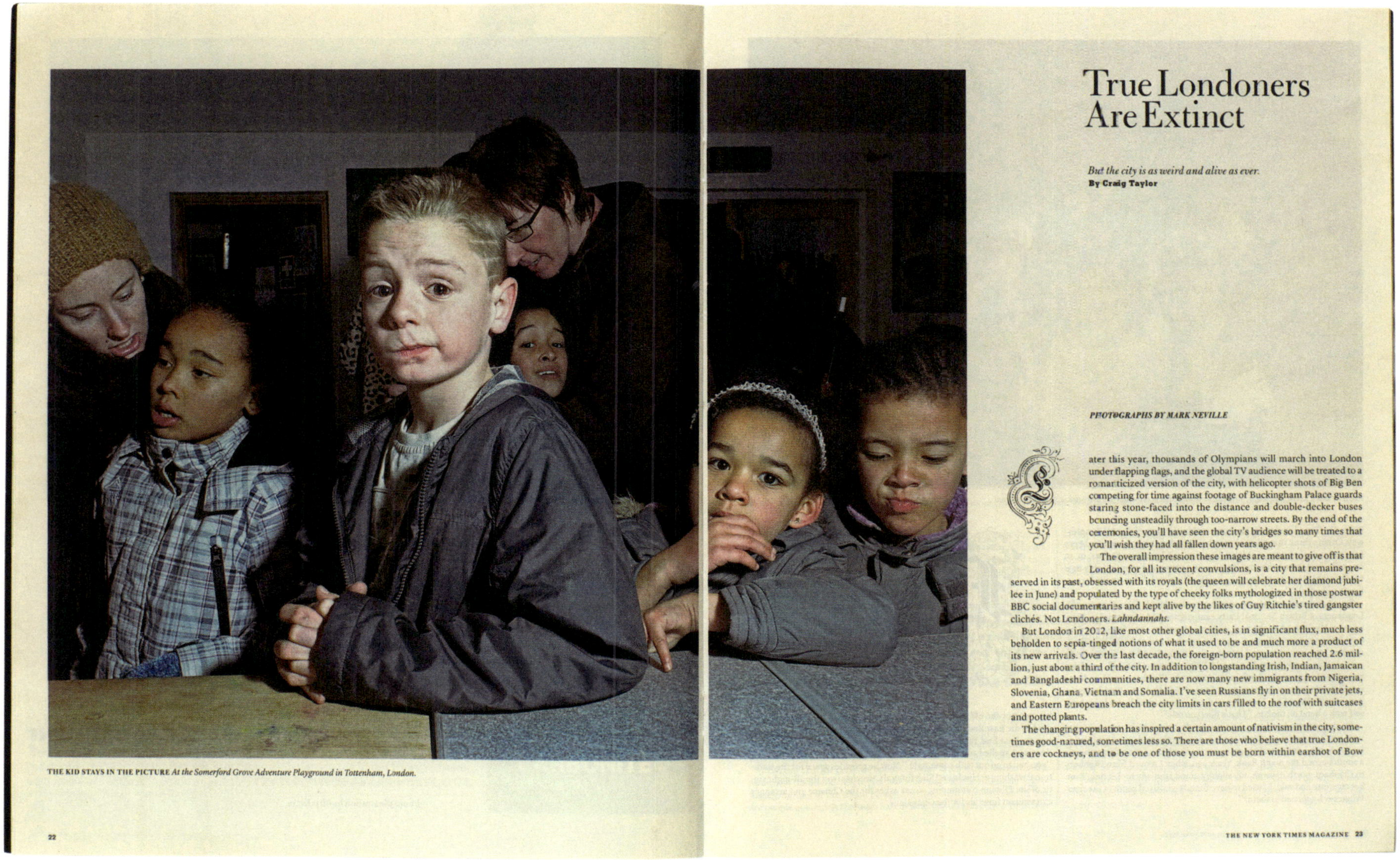

THE KID STAYS IN THE PICTURE *At the Somerford Grove Adventure Playground in Tottenham, London.*

22

True Londoners Are Extinct

But the city is as weird and alive as ever.

By Craig Taylor

PHOTOGRAPHS BY MARK NEVILLE

Later this year, thousands of Olympians will march into London under flapping flags, and the global TV audience will be treated to a romanticized version of the city, with helicopter shots of Big Ben competing for time against footage of Buckingham Palace guards staring stone-faced into the distance and double-decker buses bouncing unsteadily through too-narrow streets. By the end of the ceremonies, you'll have seen the city's bridges so many times that you'll wish they had all fallen down years ago.

The overall impression these images are meant to give off is that London, for all its recent convulsions, is a city that remains preserved in its past, obsessed with its royals (the queen will celebrate her diamond jubilee in June) and populated by the type of cheeky folks mythologized in those postwar BBC social documentaries and kept alive by the likes of Guy Ritchie's tired gangster clichés. Not Londoners. *Lahndannahs.*

But London in 2012, like most other global cities, is in significant flux, much less beholden to sepia-tinged notions of what it used to be and much more a product of its new arrivals. Over the last decade, the foreign-born population reached 2.6 million, just about a third of the city. In addition to longstanding Irish, Indian, Jamaican and Bangladeshi communities, there are now many new immigrants from Nigeria, Slovenia, Ghana, Vietnam and Somalia. I've seen Russians fly in on their private jets, and Eastern Europeans breach the city limits in cars filled to the roof with suitcases and potted plants.

The changing population has inspired a certain amount of nativism in the city, sometimes good-natured, sometimes less so. There are those who believe that true Londoners are cockneys, and to be one of those you must be born within earshot of Bow

THE NEW YORK TIMES MAGAZINE 23

Spread from *The New York Times Magazine*, 4/3/2012

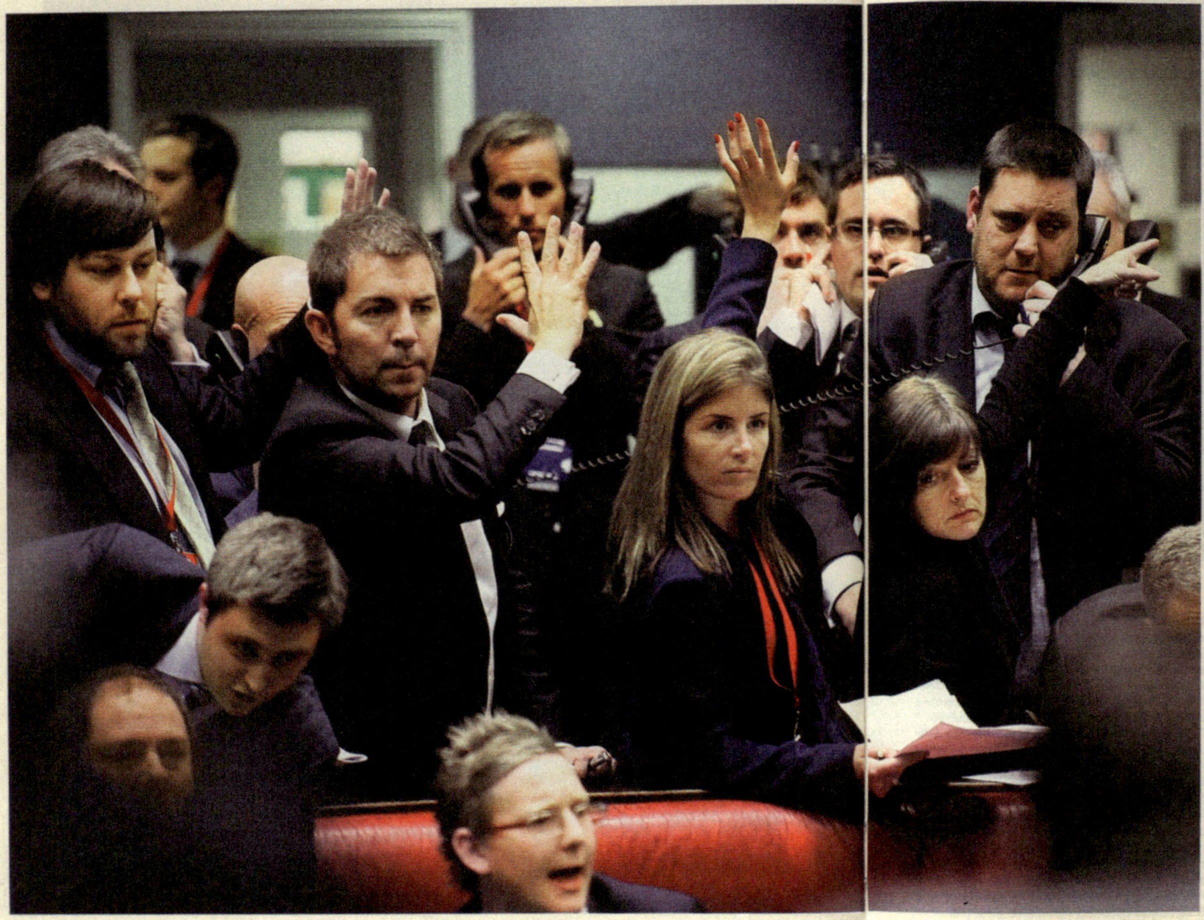

COMMERCE *Traders at the London Metal Exchange, a commodities market with a daily volume of more than $60 billion.*

42

'Oh, London, You Drama Queen'

Life in the world capital of wealth and worry.
By China Miéville

PHOTOGRAPHS BY MARK NEVILLE

An invisible bridge spans the Thames at Blackfriars. Victorian pilings jut from the river, the railway they once supported long gone. Dangling above them on this cold day, helicopters surveilled thousands of strikers and supporters processing loudly through central London. It was Nov. 30, 2011, and two million public-sector workers were on strike.

Mary Ezekiel, staff nurse at University College London Hospital, itemized the baleful effects that pension cuts — the cause of the day's action — will have. She flattened down her T-shirt. Many British tchotchkes are emblazoned with the cloying World War II propaganda slogan "Keep Calm and Carry On." "Get Angry," Ezekiel's shirt demanded instead, "and Fight Back." "All the speakers have been amazing," she said. "That's what I feel positive about. I just hope that it reaches Mr. Cameron" — she said the prime minister's name disdainfully — "in his mansion."

Cameron first denounced the day's action, then dismissed it. For the Right, strikes are both devilish and pathetic, have both terrible and absolutely no effects.

"The perils of marching!" a young woman said with a laugh, pushing banners out of her face. "Lashed by flags!" She was surrounded by bobbing cloth and cardboard. The logo of the Society of Radiographers wobbled near placards of the Worker-communist Party of Iran. Under a huge pink triangle, a young Ugandan man called Abbey said, "We are helping gay asylum seekers from over the world, especially Uganda, Nigeria, Cameroon, Senegal." He was there to support the workers. It's all linked, he explained. Cuts to social spending, soaring university tuition fees, scapegoating.

There's strife beyond the public sector. Several days after the strike, electricians working for the construction company Balfour Beatty walked out in protest against aggressive new contracts. People are fighting to stand still, whatever line of work they're in.

Stratford, East London, is being reconfigured on a biblical scale. It's December, and from the acres of mud and blue wrapping of the Olympic Park juts the city's new monument, the ArcelorMittal Orbit, by the artists Anish Kapoor and Cecil Balmond, a vast sculpture of knotting girders like a snarled Gaian hernia. Its name is a corporate grandiosity on the part of its donor, Lakshmi Mittal, the richest man in Britain. Near

Spread from *The New York Times Magazine*, 4/3/2012

It always shows in human bodies. The body of someone who does hard manual work looks very different to the body of someone who does not. That said, many of the super-rich bankers work seventy-hour weeks and it shows.

> It's brutal. Their bodies are stressed, definitely. To some extent, at the level of the body, everyone is trapped in the system. The bank traders I talked to were expecting to be done by the age of forty. Their bodies and their nervous systems can't take any more.

Do you think your work as a photographer is like that? From what you say it's exhausting.

> Yes, it's punishing physically. I work really hard to get the pictures and to develop a "better eye", for want of a better expression.

When I look at your photographs they do suggest a hyper-aware eye. Those compositions are so complicated. I know the lens takes in everything but there's something about the amount of social detail and information in those compositions ...it's not all visible by accident.

> I'm often in physical discomfort while shooting. Standing on a chair holding the camera up to my eye for several hours, in a busy environment, waiting for a great shot. And often I am feeling uncomfortable about my presence. Sometimes that's an imagined impropriety, and sometimes it's not. Photography is a highly intrusive activity and I have to do my best to minimise that intrusion, not just for my subjects but for me, because I want to feel comfortable making the photographs.

You talked at the beginning about your work being intensely personal. Can you say something more about your personality and how your pictures actually look?

> There are several things there. Although I do as much as I can to hand over authorial control to the subjects (I want to talk to them, hear from them, involve them, build up a relationship, suggest poses and locations, consult with people before reproducing an image) for myself I do need to make the most powerful and expressive image I possibly can. I feel that's my obligation. In the end the images mean as much to me as the ideas behind them.

Perhaps "behind" is the wrong word, although I hear it used all the time. Ideas are *in* things. In objects. In gestures. In locations. In images. The ideas are not "behind". I think that notion of the "idea behind" comes from conceptual art and its legacies in teaching. You know, where you have an idea, then you go and execute it. And maybe the work doesn't make much sense unless the viewer knows the "idea behind it". But that notion barely holds for documentary practice or it forces it into insensitive shapes. I can see you have a strategy of a kind but its open to what is in front of the camera.

Observation, affection, fascination, responsiveness. Those are not "ideas behind".

Sure. Good point. But it's interesting how ideas about dissemination feed into how one reads, or takes, an image. That picture of Betty on the dance floor in Port Glasgow—full of joy and freedom and self-expression—symbolises everything I wanted the project to be about. In that sense it is a coming together of image and a concept about the communal.

That's true. Another artist could have carried out the *Port Glasgow* project and produced a bad, boring book and the "concept" would have been the same in both cases. The concept doesn't guarantee the success. The same with *Here Is London.* The pictures exceed the idea.

I would hope so.

Front cover of the
International Herald Tribune,
3/3/2012

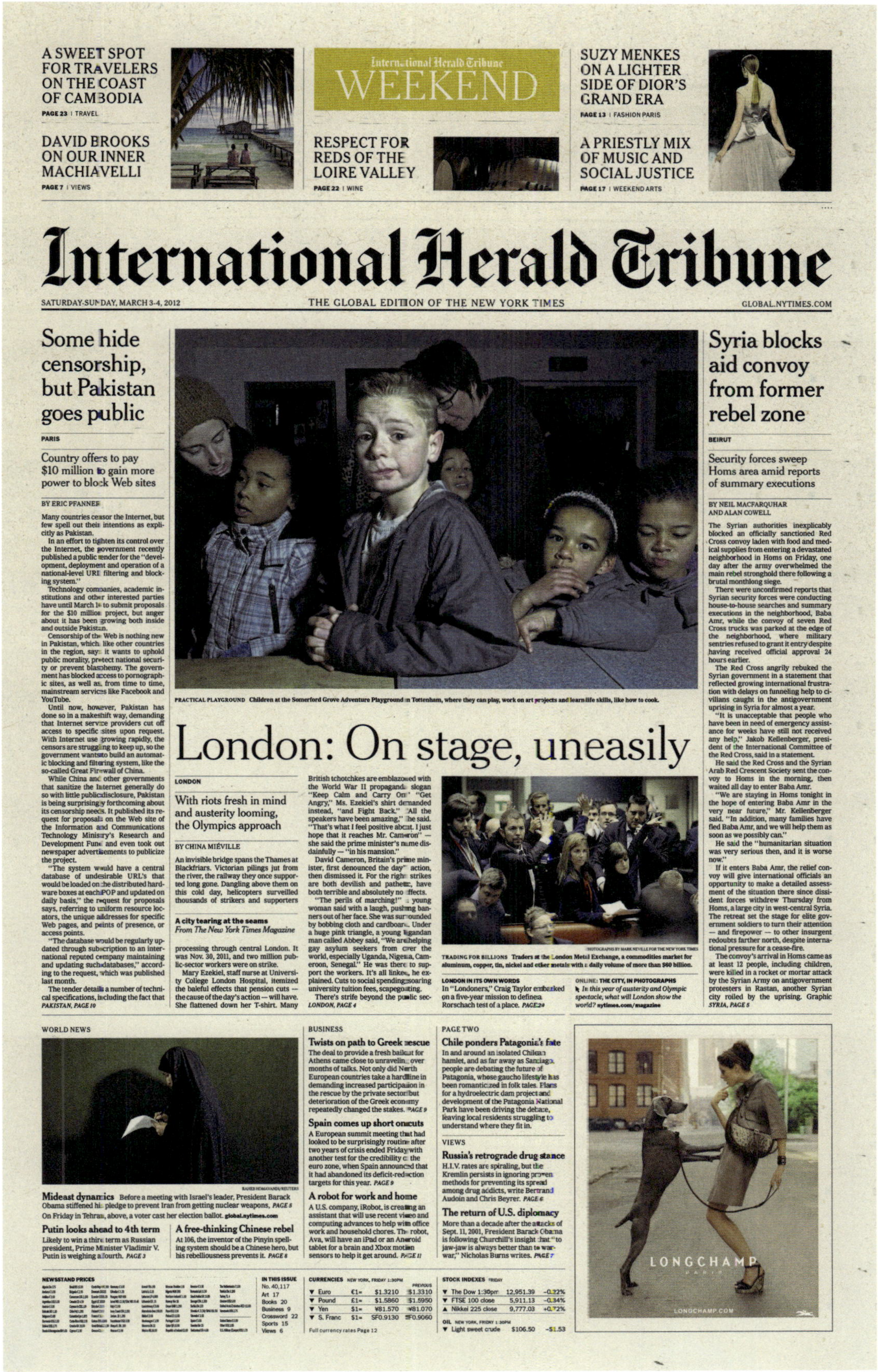

A SWEET SPOT FOR TRAVELERS ON THE COAST OF CAMBODIA
PAGE 23 | TRAVEL

DAVID BROOKS ON OUR INNER MACHIAVELLI
PAGE 7 | VIEWS

International Herald Tribune
WEEKEND

RESPECT FOR REDS OF THE LOIRE VALLEY
PAGE 22 | WINE

SUZY MENKES ON A LIGHTER SIDE OF DIOR'S GRAND ERA
PAGE 13 | FASHION PARIS

A PRIESTLY MIX OF MUSIC AND SOCIAL JUSTICE
PAGE 17 | WEEKEND ARTS

International Herald Tribune

SATURDAY-SUNDAY, MARCH 3-4, 2012 | THE GLOBAL EDITION OF THE NEW YORK TIMES | GLOBAL.NYTIMES.COM

Some hide censorship, but Pakistan goes public

PARIS

Country offers to pay $10 million to gain more power to block Web sites

BY ERIC PFANNER

Many countries censor the Internet, but few spell out their intentions as explicitly as Pakistan.

In an effort to tighten its control over the Internet, the government recently published a public tender for the "development, deployment and operation of a national-level URL filtering and blocking system."

Technology companies, academic institutions and other interested parties have until March 16 to submit proposals for the $10 million project, but anger about it has been growing both inside and outside Pakistan.

Censorship of the Web is nothing new in Pakistan, which, like other countries in the region, says it wants to uphold public morality, protect national security or prevent blasphemy. The government has blocked access to pornographic sites, as well as, from time to time, mainstream services like Facebook and YouTube.

Until now, however, Pakistan has done so in a makeshift way, demanding that Internet service providers cut off access to specific sites upon request. With Internet use growing rapidly, the censors are struggling to keep up, so the government wants to build an automatic blocking and filtering system, like the so-called Great Firewall of China.

While China and other governments that sanitize the Internet generally do so with little public disclosure, Pakistan is being surprisingly forthcoming about its censorship needs. It published its request for proposals on the Web site of the Information and Communications Technology Ministry's Research and Development Fund and even took out newspaper advertisements to publicize the project.

"The system would have a central database of undesirable URL's that would be loaded on the distributed hardware boxes at each POP and updated on daily basis," the request for proposals says, referring to uniform resource locators, the unique addresses for specific Web pages, and points of presence, or access points.

"The database would be regularly updated through subscription to an international reputed company maintaining and updating such databases," according to the request, which was published last month.

The tender details a number of technical specifications, including the fact that
PAKISTAN, PAGE 10

PRACTICAL PLAYGROUND Children at the Somerford Grove Adventure Playground in Tottenham, where they can play, work on art projects and learn life skills, like how to cook.

London: On stage, uneasily

LONDON

With riots fresh in mind and austerity looming, the Olympics approach

BY CHINA MIÉVILLE

An invisible bridge spans the Thames at Blackfriars. Victorian pilings jut from the river, the railway they once supported long gone. Dangling above them on this cold day, helicopters surveilled thousands of strikers and supporters

A city tearing at the seams
From The New York Times Magazine

processing through central London. It was Nov. 30, 2011, and two million public-sector workers were on strike.

Mary Ezekiel, staff nurse at University College London Hospital, itemized the baleful effects that pension cuts — the cause of the day's action — will have. She flattened down her T-shirt. Many British tchotchkes are emblazoned with the World War II propaganda slogan "Keep Calm and Carry On." "Get Angry," Ms. Ezekiel's shirt demanded instead, "and Fight Back." "All the speakers have been amazing," she said. "That's what I feel positive about. I just hope that it reaches Mr. Cameron" — she said the prime minister's name disdainfully — "in his mansion."

David Cameron, Britain's prime minister, first denounced the day's action, then dismissed it. For the right, strikes are both devilish and pathetic, have both terrible and absolutely no effects.

"The perils of marching!" a young woman said with a laugh, pushing banners out of her face. She was surrounded by bobbing cloth and cardboard. Under a huge pink triangle, a young Ugandan man called Abbey said, "We are helping gay asylum seekers from over the world, especially Uganda, Nigeria, Cameroon, Senegal." He was there to support the workers. It's all linked, he explained. Cuts to social spending, soaring university tuition fees, scapegoating.

There's strife beyond the public sec-
LONDON, PAGE 4

PHOTOGRAPHS BY MARK NEVILLE FOR THE NEW YORK TIMES

TRADING FOR BILLIONS Traders at the London Metal Exchange, a commodities market for aluminum, copper, tin, nickel and other metals with a daily volume of more than $60 billion.

LONDON IN ITS OWN WORDS
In "Londoners," Craig Taylor embarked on a five-year mission to define a Rorschach test of a place. *PAGE 24*

ONLINE: THE CITY, IN PHOTOGRAPHS
In this year of austerity and Olympic spectacle, what will London show the world? nytimes.com/magazine

Syria blocks aid convoy from former rebel zone

BEIRUT

Security forces sweep Homs area amid reports of summary executions

BY NEIL MACFARQUHAR AND ALAN COWELL

The Syrian authorities inexplicably blocked an officially sanctioned Red Cross convoy laden with food and medical supplies from entering a devastated neighborhood in Homs on Friday, one day after the army overwhelmed the main rebel stronghold there following a brutal monthlong siege.

There were unconfirmed reports that Syrian security forces were conducting house-to-house searches and summary executions in the neighborhood, Baba Amr, while the convoy of seven Red Cross trucks was parked at the edge of the neighborhood, where military sentries refused to grant it entry despite having received official approval 24 hours earlier.

The Red Cross angrily rebuked the Syrian government in a statement that reflected growing international frustration with delays on funneling help to civilians caught in the antigovernment uprising in Syria for almost a year.

"It is unacceptable that people who have been in need of emergency assistance for weeks have still not received any help," Jakob Kellenberger, president of the International Committee of the Red Cross, said in a statement.

He said the Red Cross and the Syrian Arab Red Crescent Society sent the convoy to Homs in the morning, then waited all day to enter Baba Amr.

"We are staying in Homs tonight in the hope of entering Baba Amr in the very near future," Mr. Kellenberger said. "In addition, many families have fled Baba Amr, and we will help them as soon as we possibly can."

He said the "humanitarian situation was very serious then, and it is worse now."

If it enters Baba Amr, the relief convoy will give international officials an opportunity to make a detailed assessment of the situation there since dissident forces withdrew Thursday from Homs, a large city in west-central Syria. The retreat set the stage for elite government soldiers to turn their attention — and firepower — to other insurgent redoubts farther north, despite international pressure for a cease-fire.

The convoy's arrival in Homs came as at least 12 people, including children, were killed in a rocket or mortar attack by the Syrian Army on antigovernment protesters in Rastan, another Syrian city roiled by the uprising. Graphic
SYRIA, PAGE 5

WORLD NEWS

RAHEB HOMAVANDI/REUTERS

Mideast dynamics Before a meeting with Israel's leader, President Barack Obama stiffened his pledge to prevent Iran from getting nuclear weapons, *PAGE 5*
On Friday in Tehran, above, a voter cast her election ballot. global.nytimes.com

Putin looks ahead to 4th term
Likely to win a third term as Russian president, Prime Minister Vladimir V. Putin is weighing a fourth. *PAGE 3*

A free-thinking Chinese rebel
At 106, the inventor of the Pinyin spelling system should be a Chinese hero, but his rebelliousness prevents it. *PAGE 8*

BUSINESS

Twists on path to Greek rescue
The deal to provide a fresh bailout for Athens came close to unraveling over months of talks. Not only did North European countries take a hard line in demanding increased participation in the rescue by the private sector, but deterioration of the Greek economy repeatedly changed the stakes. *PAGE 9*

Spain comes up short on cuts
A European summit meeting that had looked to be surprisingly routine after two years of crisis ended Friday with another test for the credibility of the euro zone, when Spain announced that it had abandoned its deficit-reduction targets for this year. *PAGE 9*

A robot for work and home
A U.S. company, iRobot, is creating an assistant that will use recent video and computing advances to help with office work and household chores. The robot, Ava, will have an iPad or an Android tablet for a brain and Xbox motion sensors to help it get around. *PAGE 11*

PAGE TWO

Chile ponders Patagonia's fate
In and around an isolated Chilean hamlet, and as far away as Santiago, people are debating the future of Patagonia, whose gaucho lifestyle has been romanticized in folk tales. Plans for a hydroelectric dam project and development of the Patagonia National Park have been driving the debate, leaving local residents struggling to understand where they fit in.

VIEWS

Russia's retrograde drug stance
H.I.V. rates are spiraling, but the Kremlin persists in ignoring proven methods for preventing its spread among drug addicts, write Bertrand Audoin and Chris Beyrer. *PAGE 6*

The return of U.S. diplomacy
More than a decade after the attacks of Sept. 11, 2001, President Barack Obama is following Churchill's insight that "to jaw-jaw is always better than to war-war," Nicholas Burns writes. *PAGE 7*

NEWSSTAND PRICES

IN THIS ISSUE
No. 40,117
Art 17
Books 20
Business 9
Crossword 22
Sports 15
Views 6

CURRENCIES NEW YORK, FRIDAY 1:30PM

				PREVIOUS
▼	Euro	€1=	$1.3210	$1.3310
▼	Pound	£1=	$1.5860	$1.5950
▼	Yen	$1=	¥81.570	¥81.070
▼	S. Franc	$1=	SF0.9130	SF0.9060

Full currency rates Page 12

STOCK INDEXES FRIDAY

▼	The Dow 1:30pm	12,951.39	-0.22%
▼	FTSE 100 close	5,911.13	-0.34%
▲	Nikkei 225 close	9,777.03	+0.72%

OIL NEW YORK, FRIDAY 1:30PM

▼	Light sweet crude	$106.50	-$1.53

Braddock /

Sewickley

2012

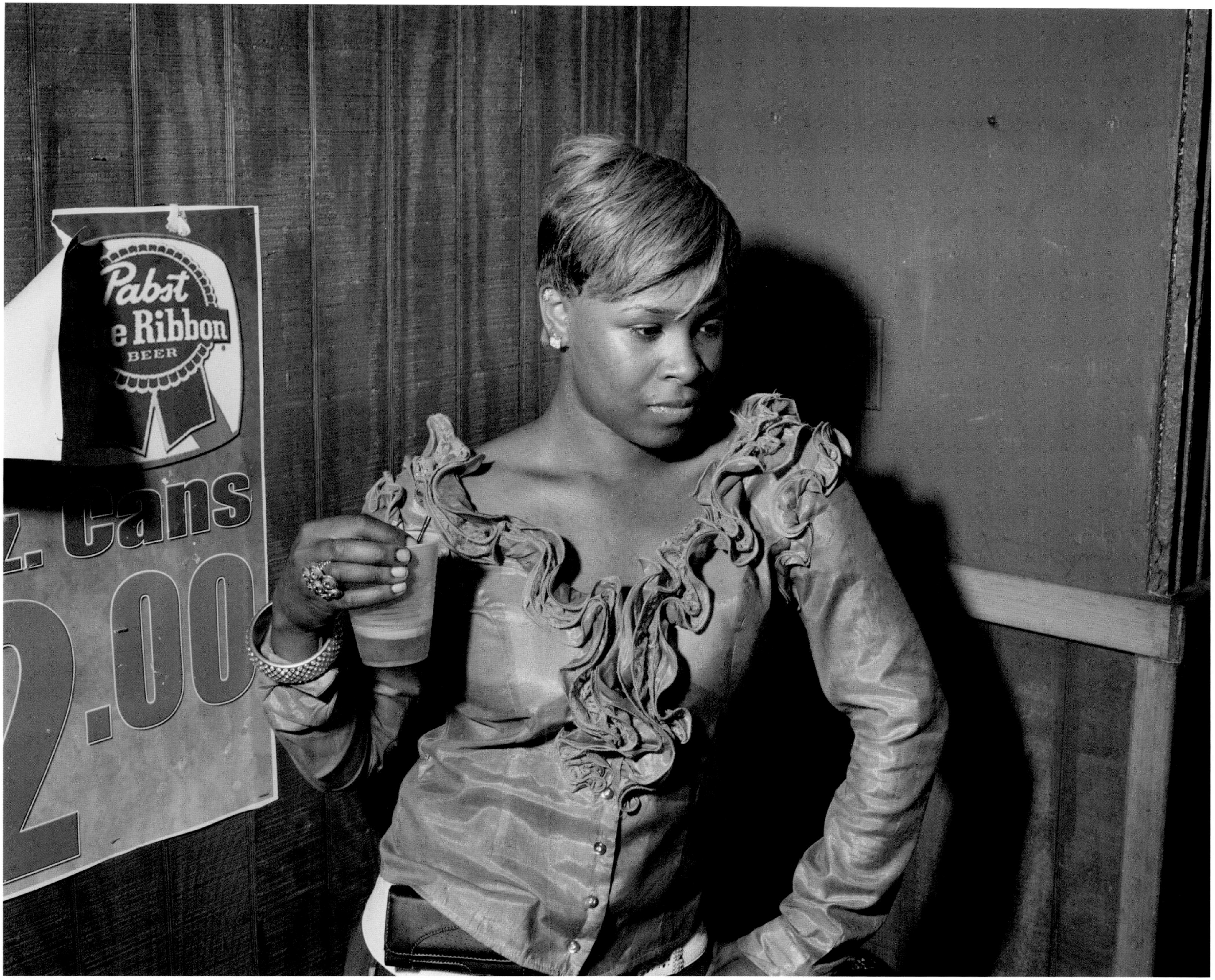
Pabst
e Ribbon
BEER
z. cans
2.00

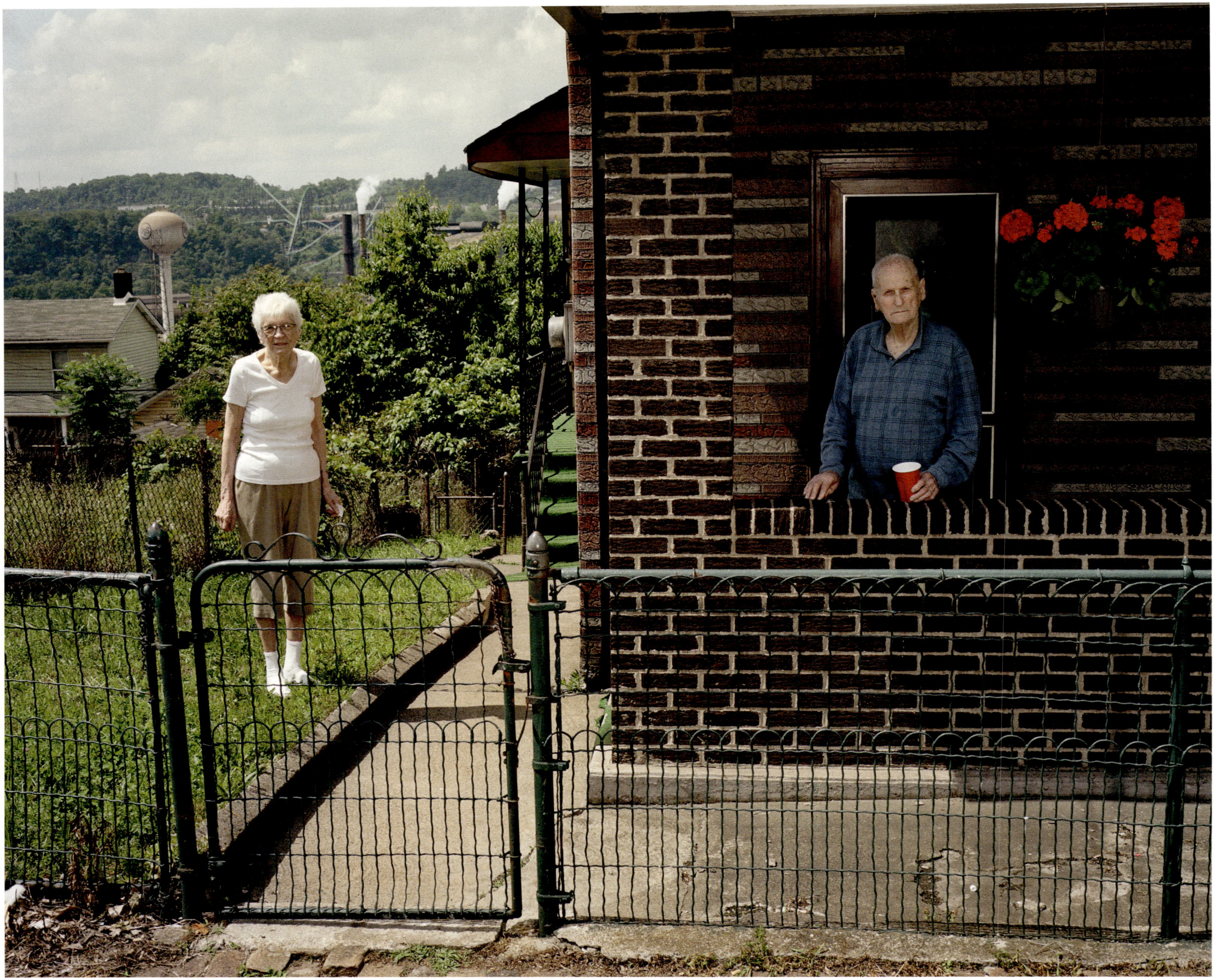

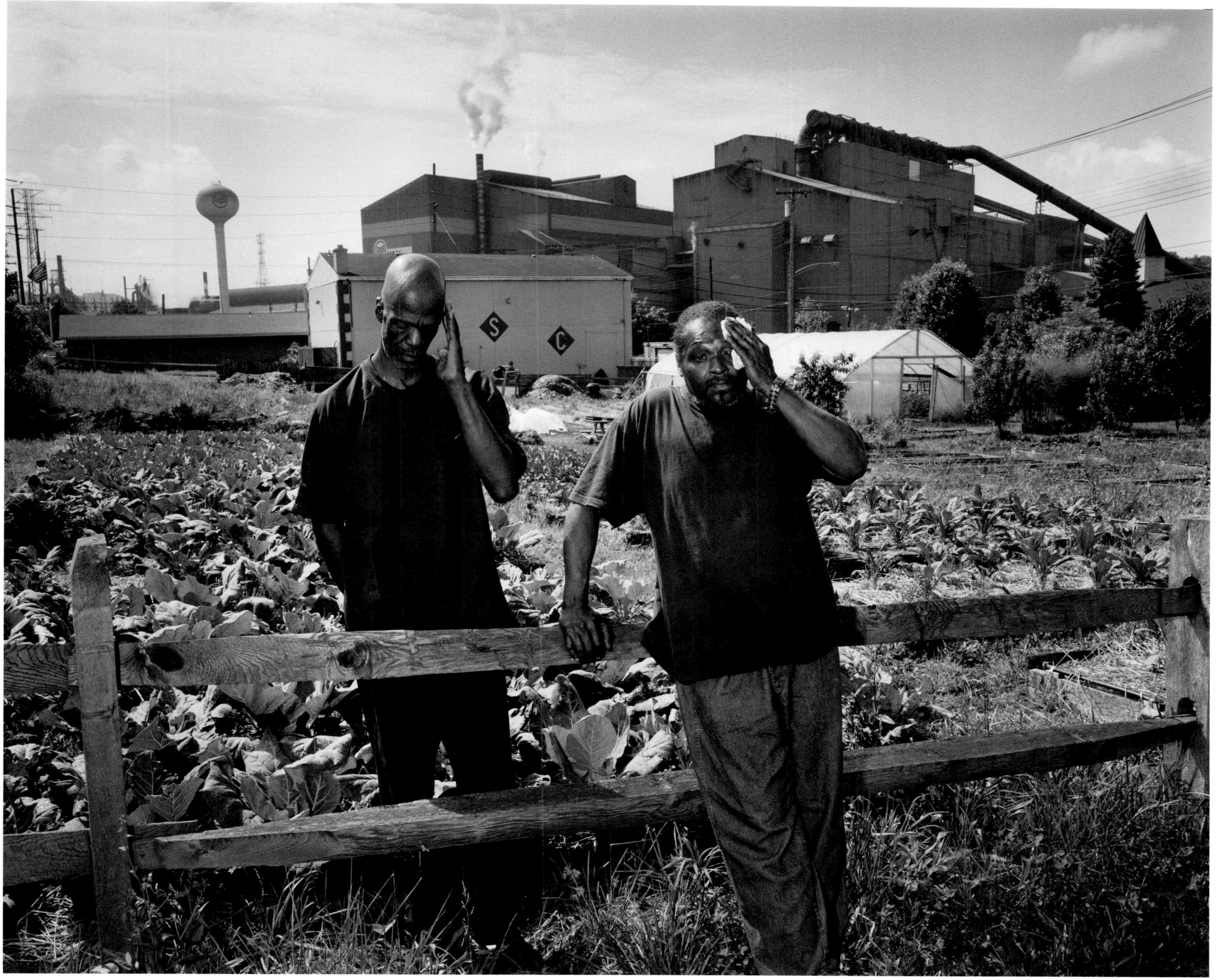
S
C

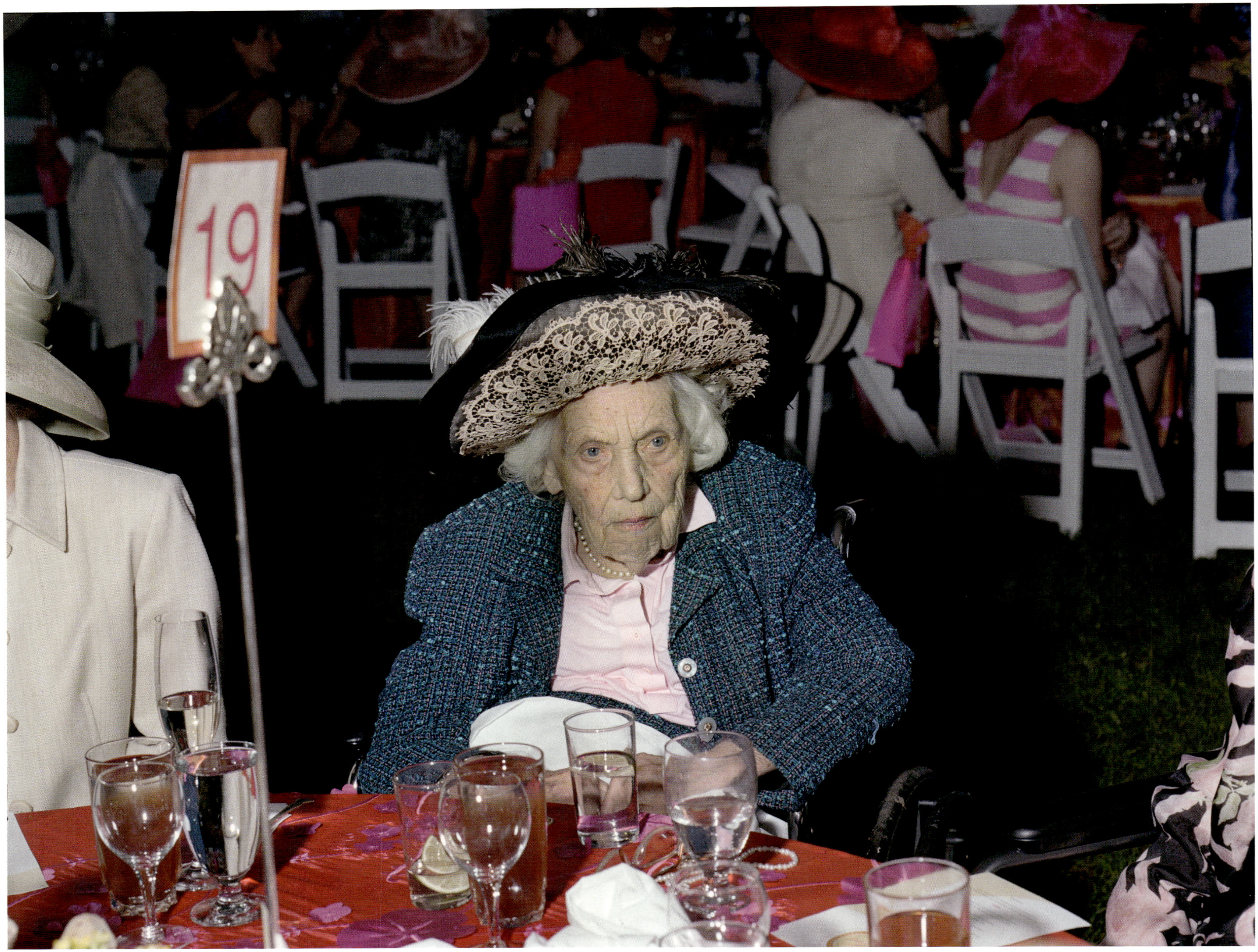
19

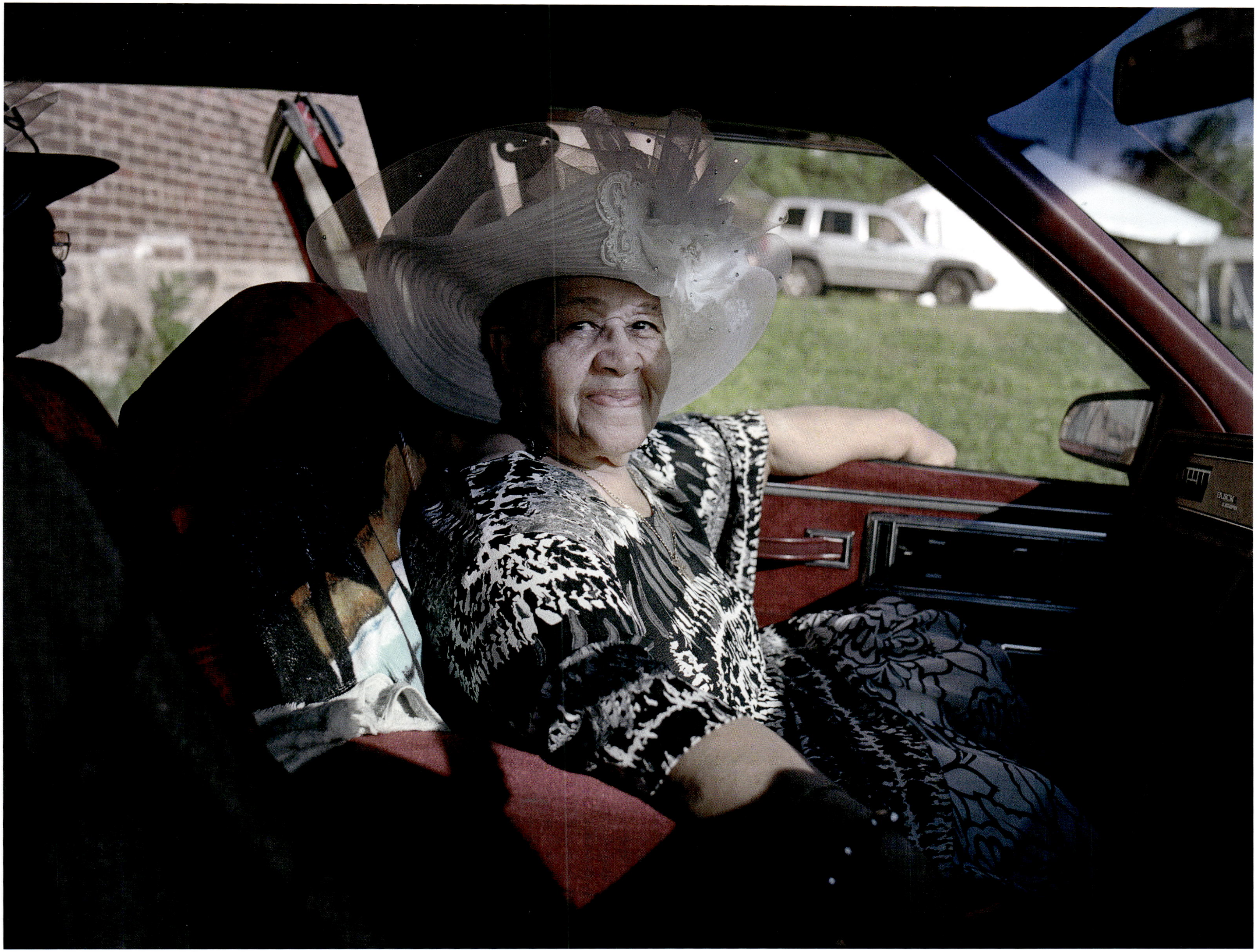

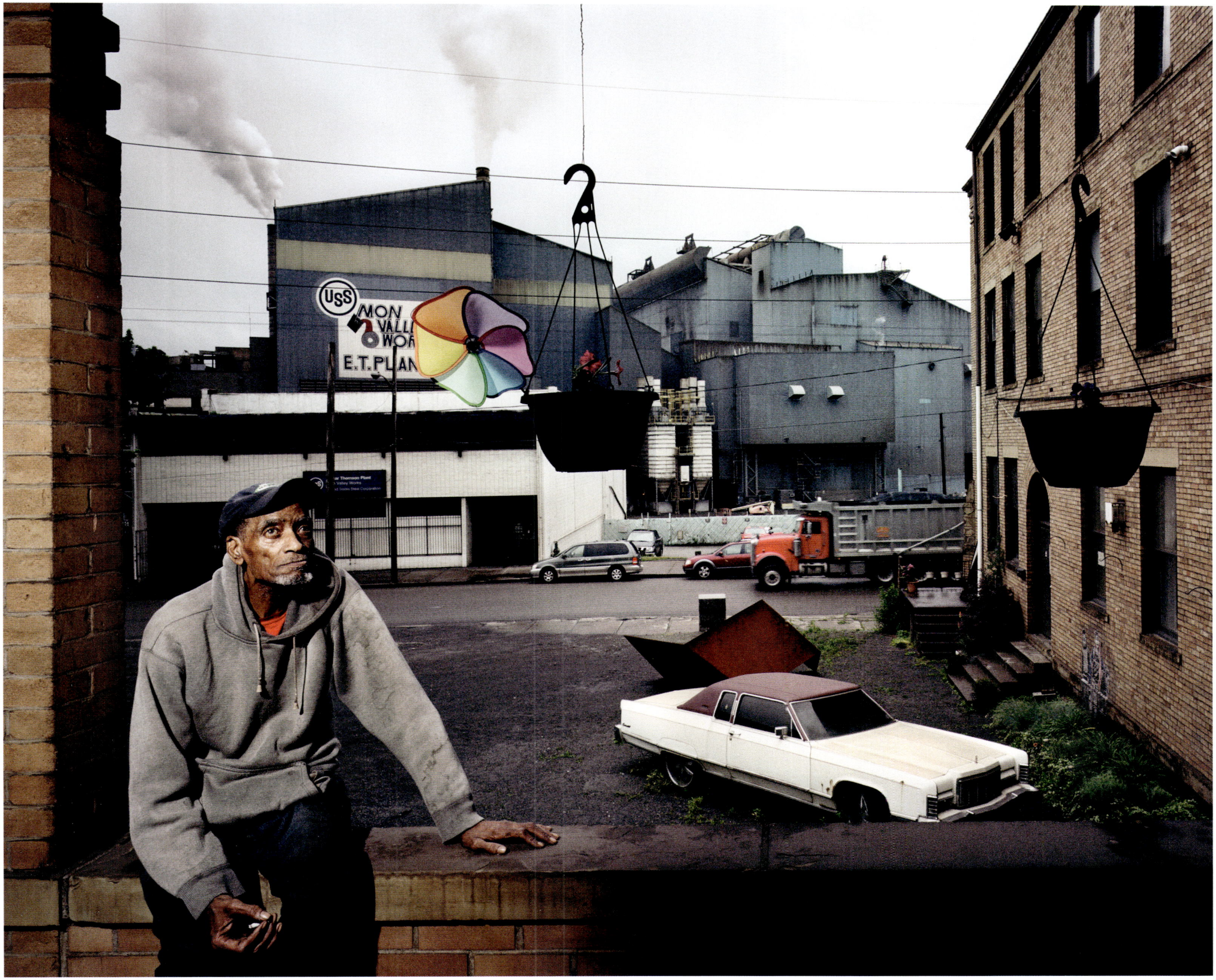
USS
MON

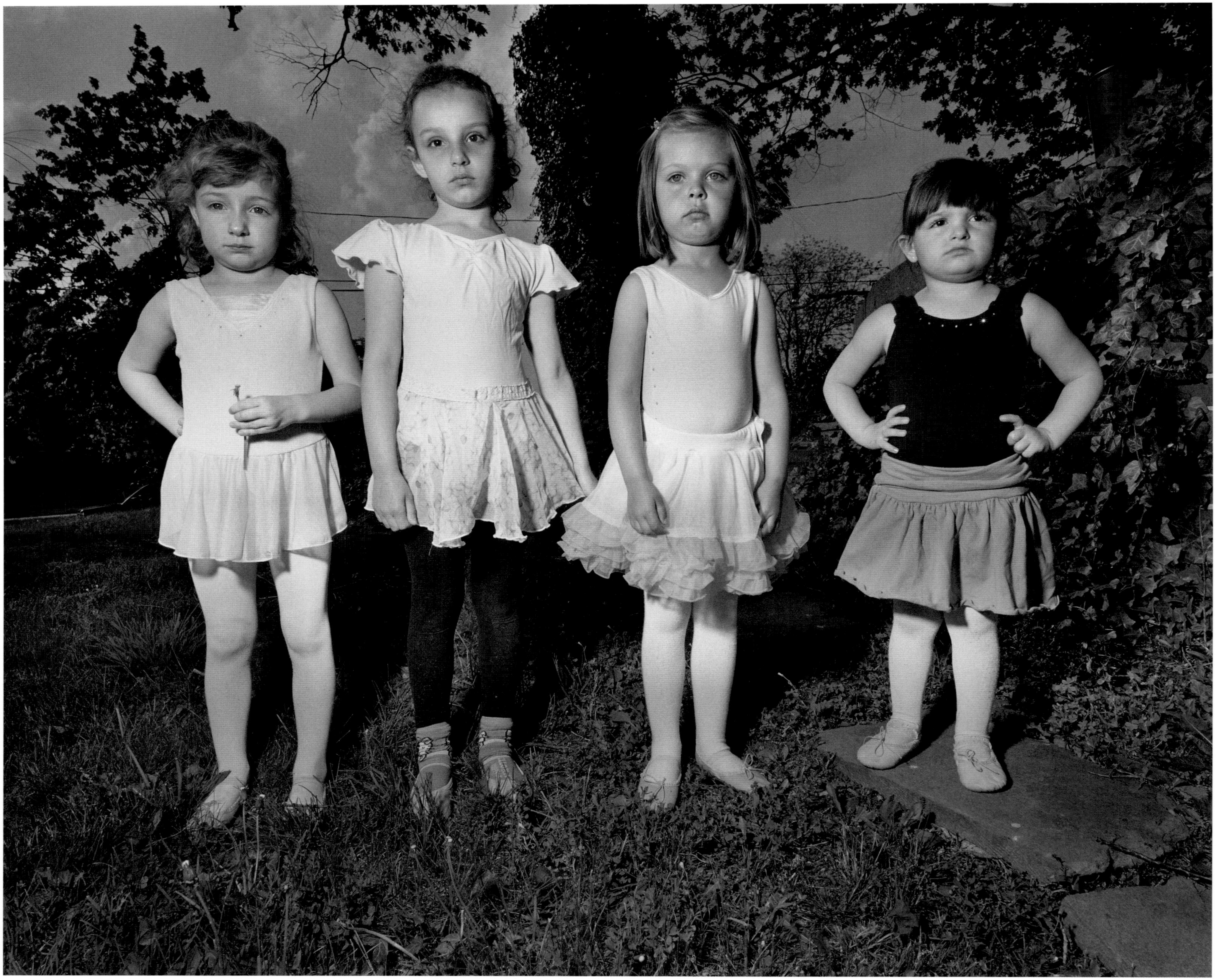

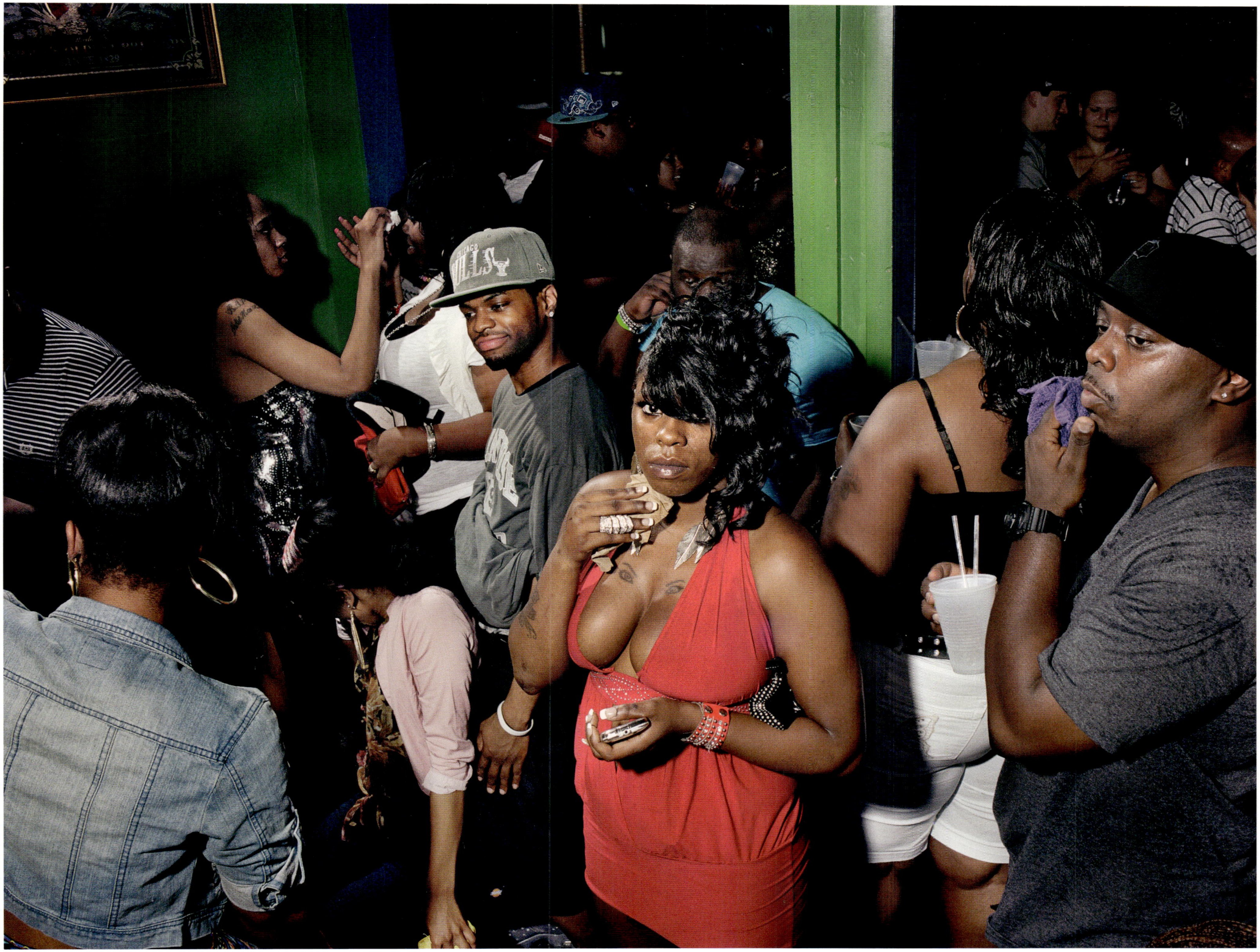

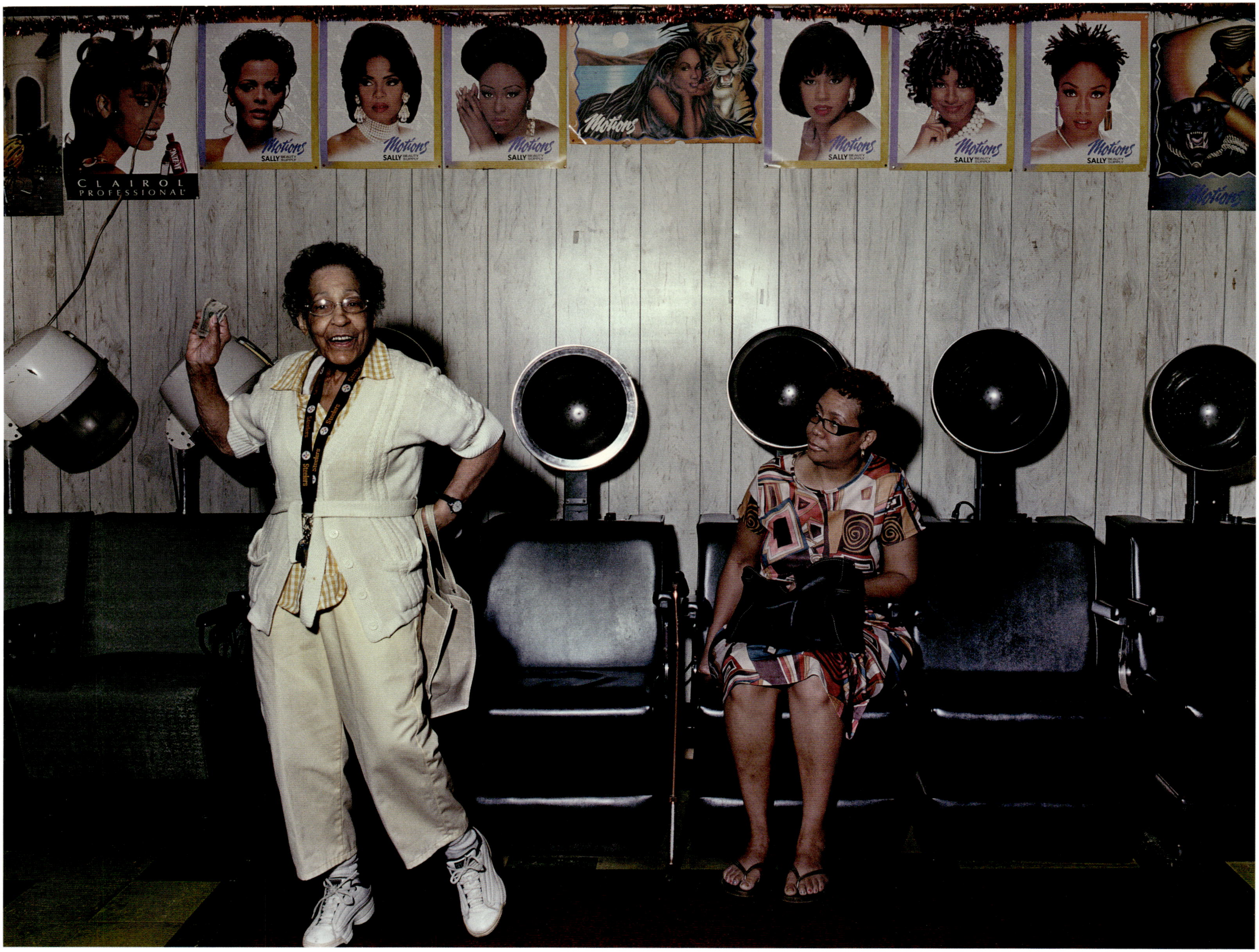
CLAIROL
PROFESSIONAL
Motions
SALLY

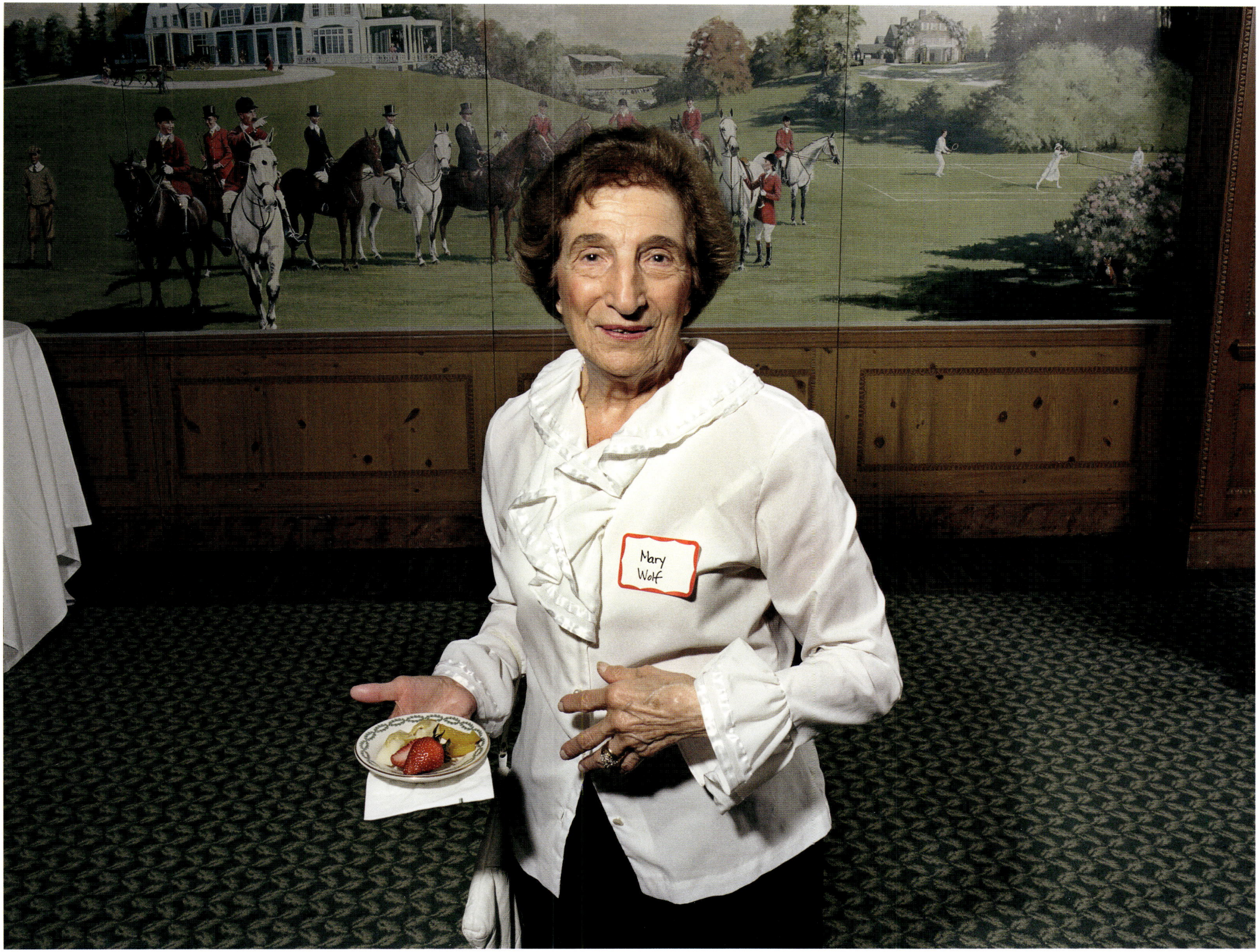
Mary
Wolf

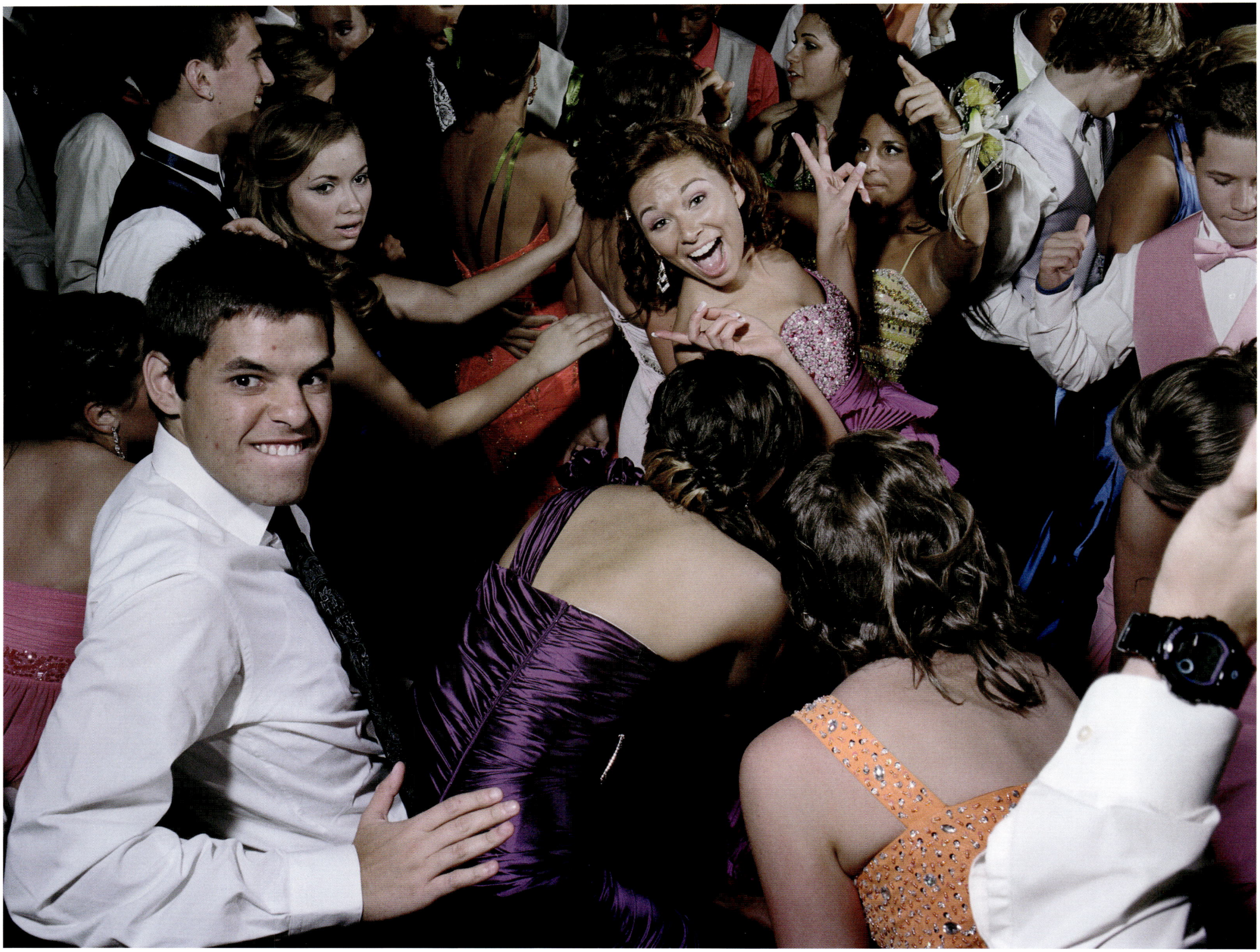

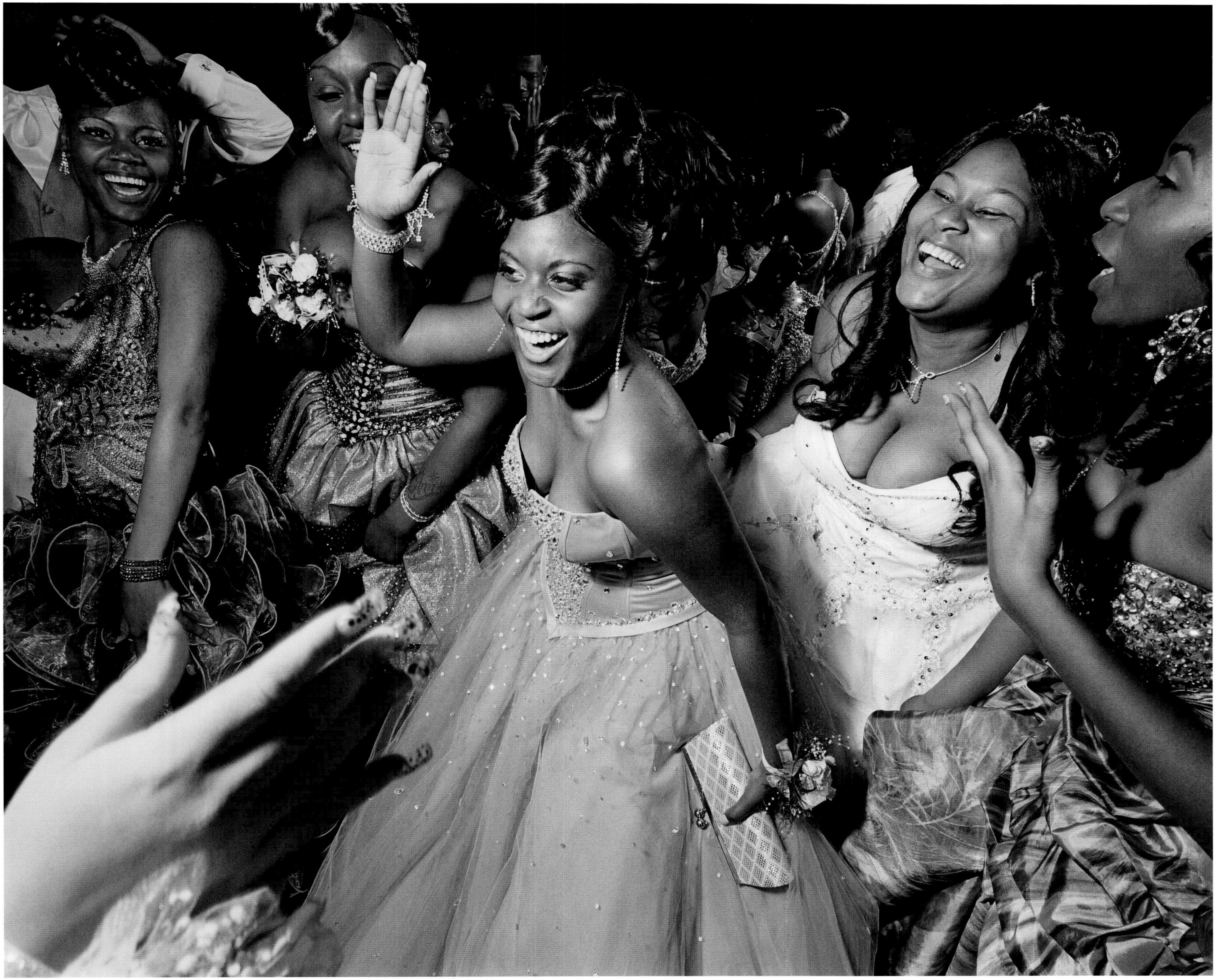

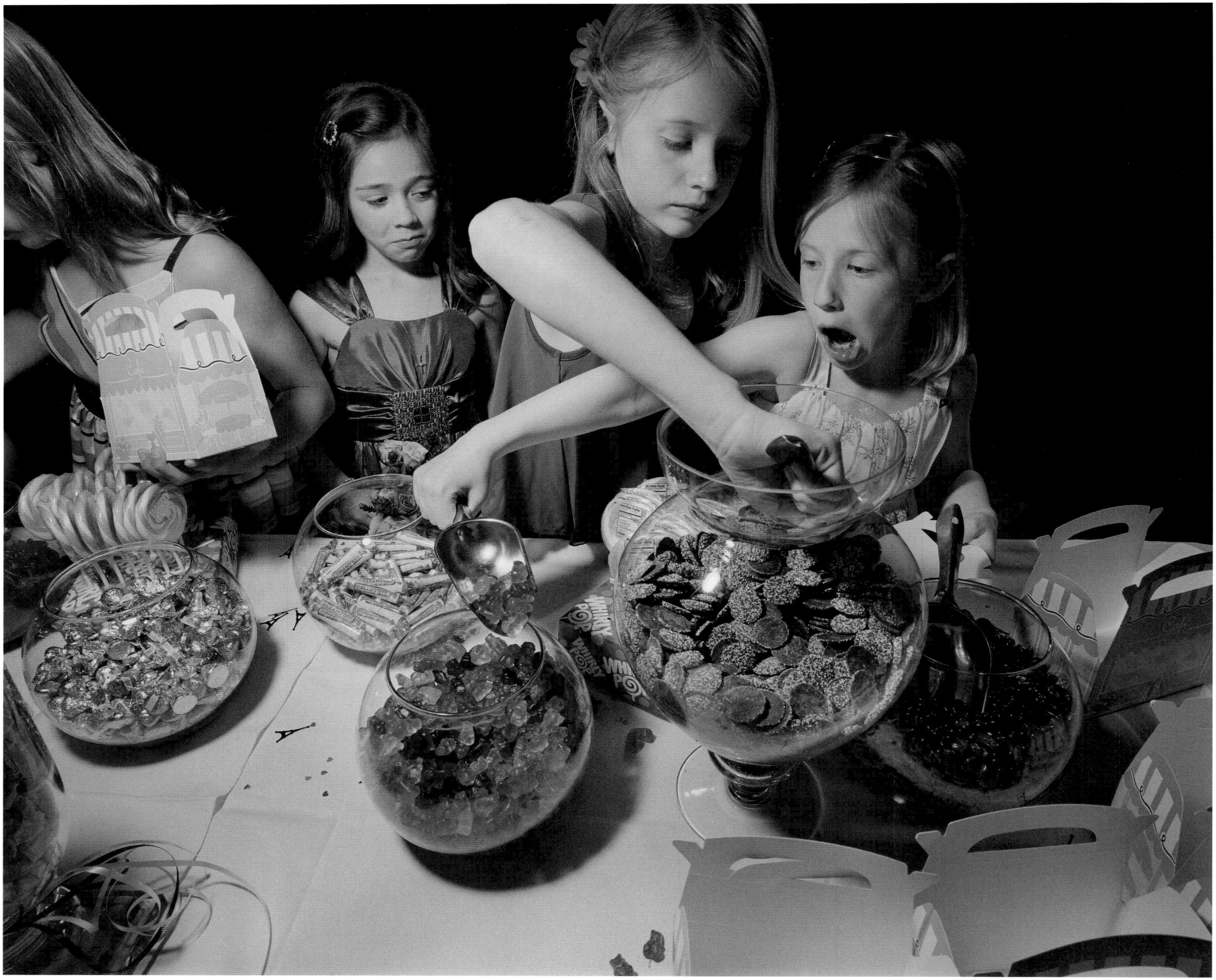
WHIRLY POP

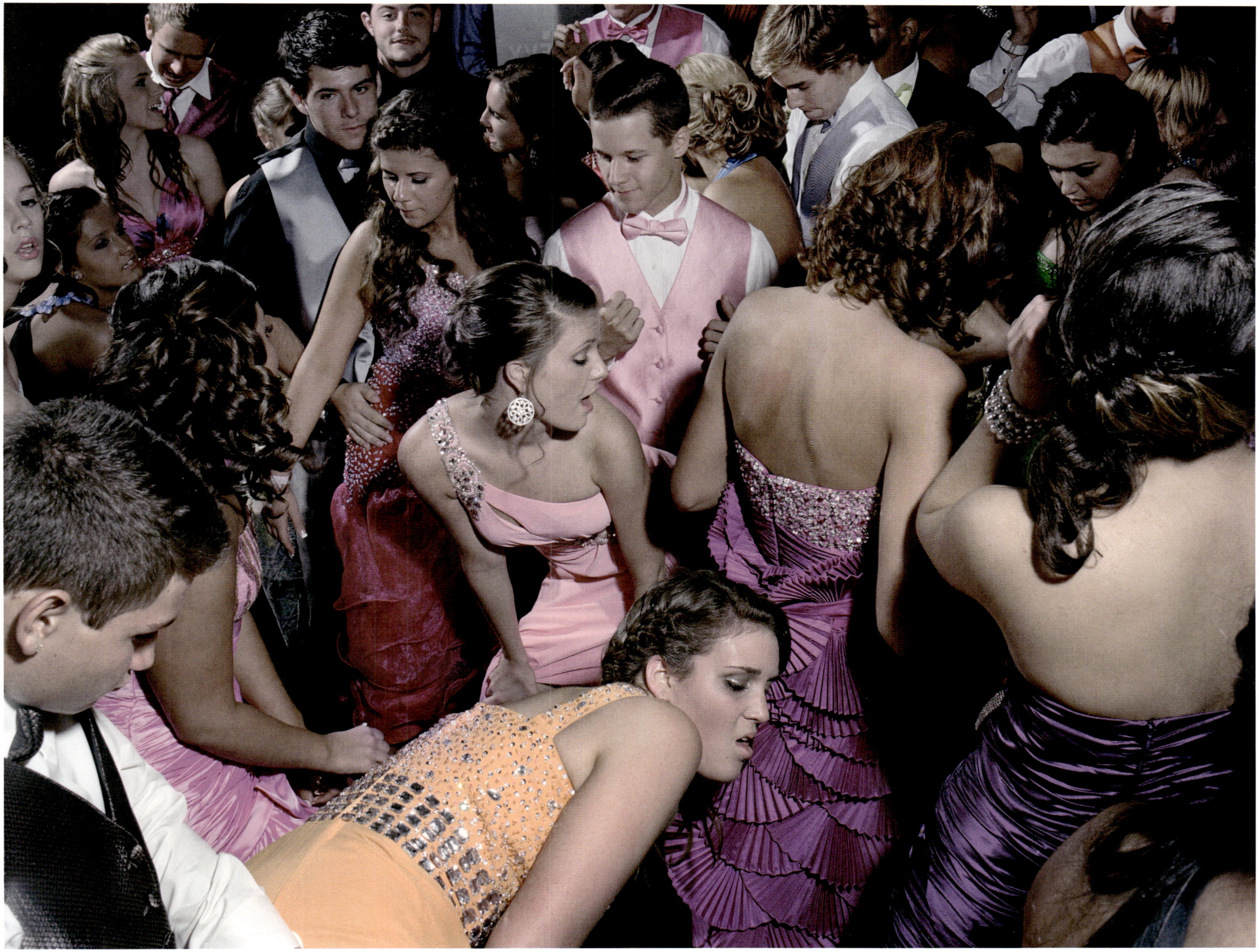

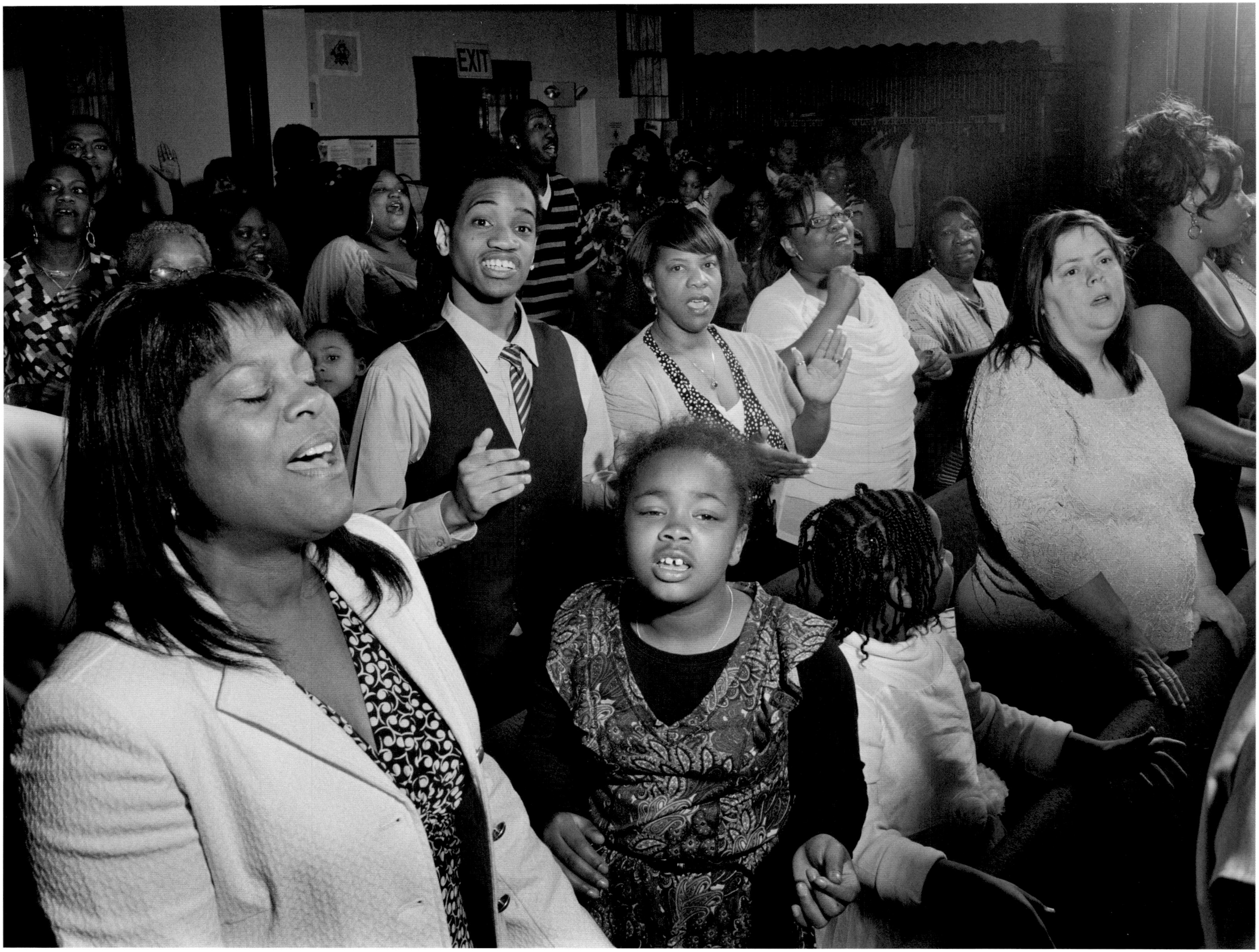
EXIT

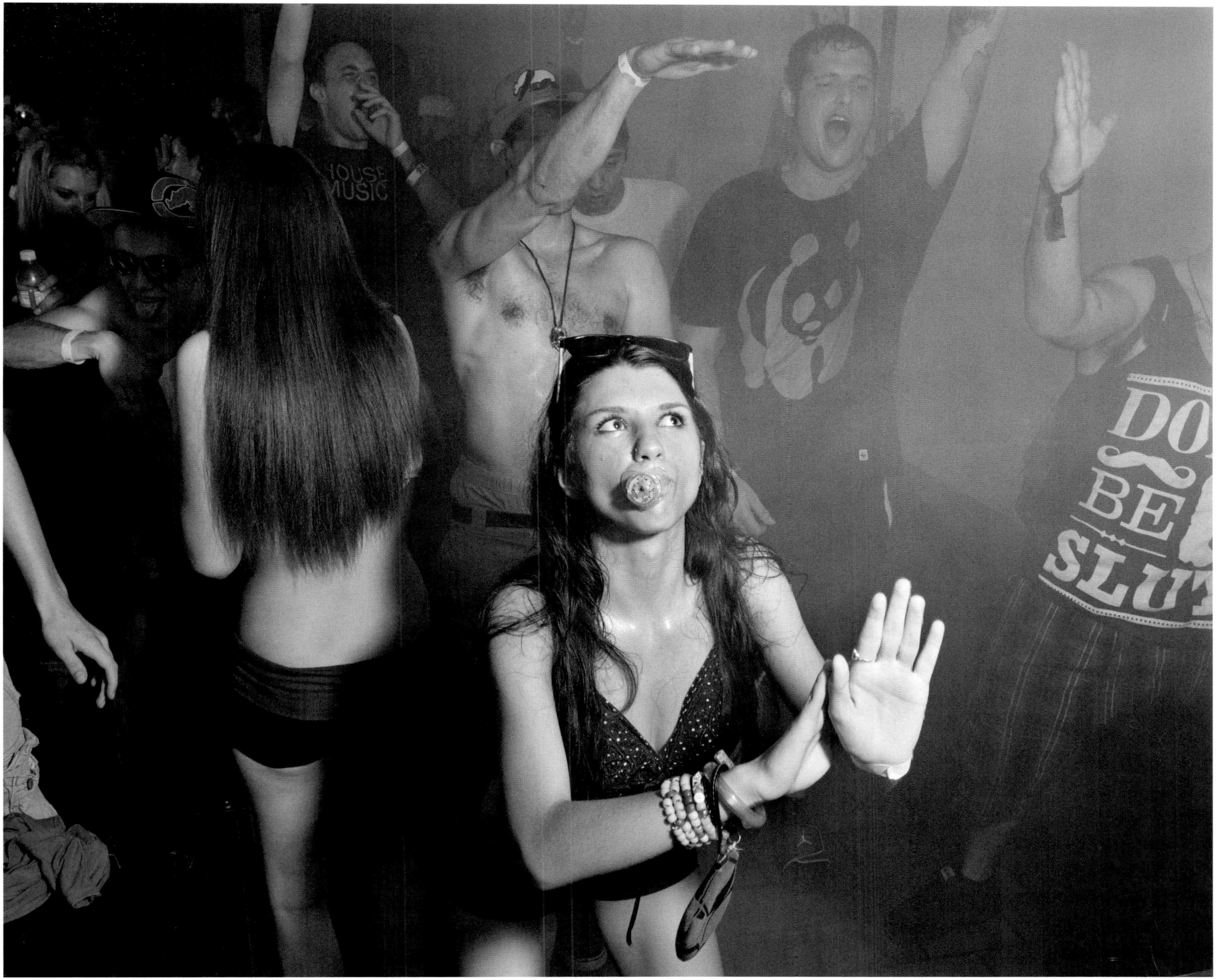
HOUSE
MUSIC
BE

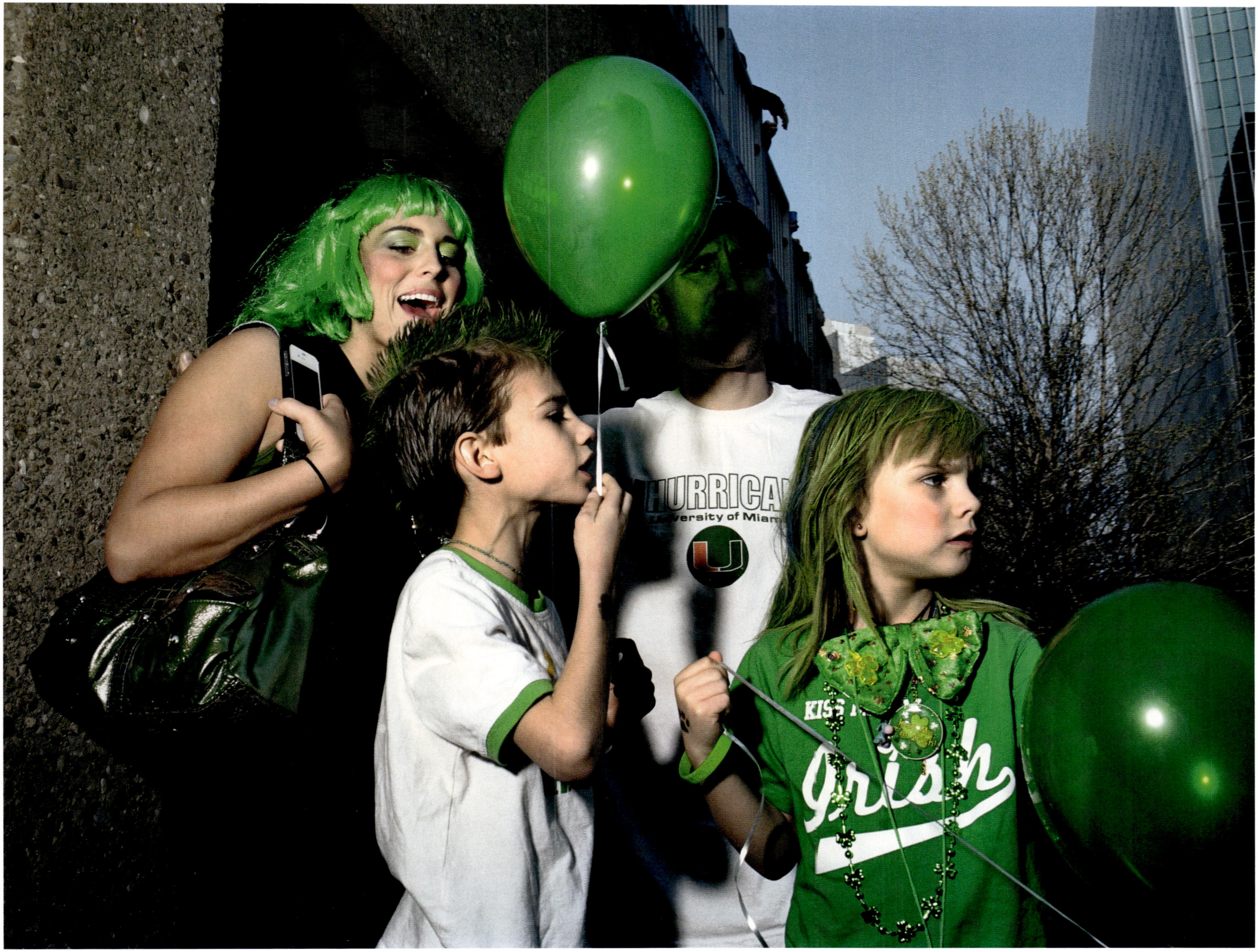
HURRICA
KISS
Irish

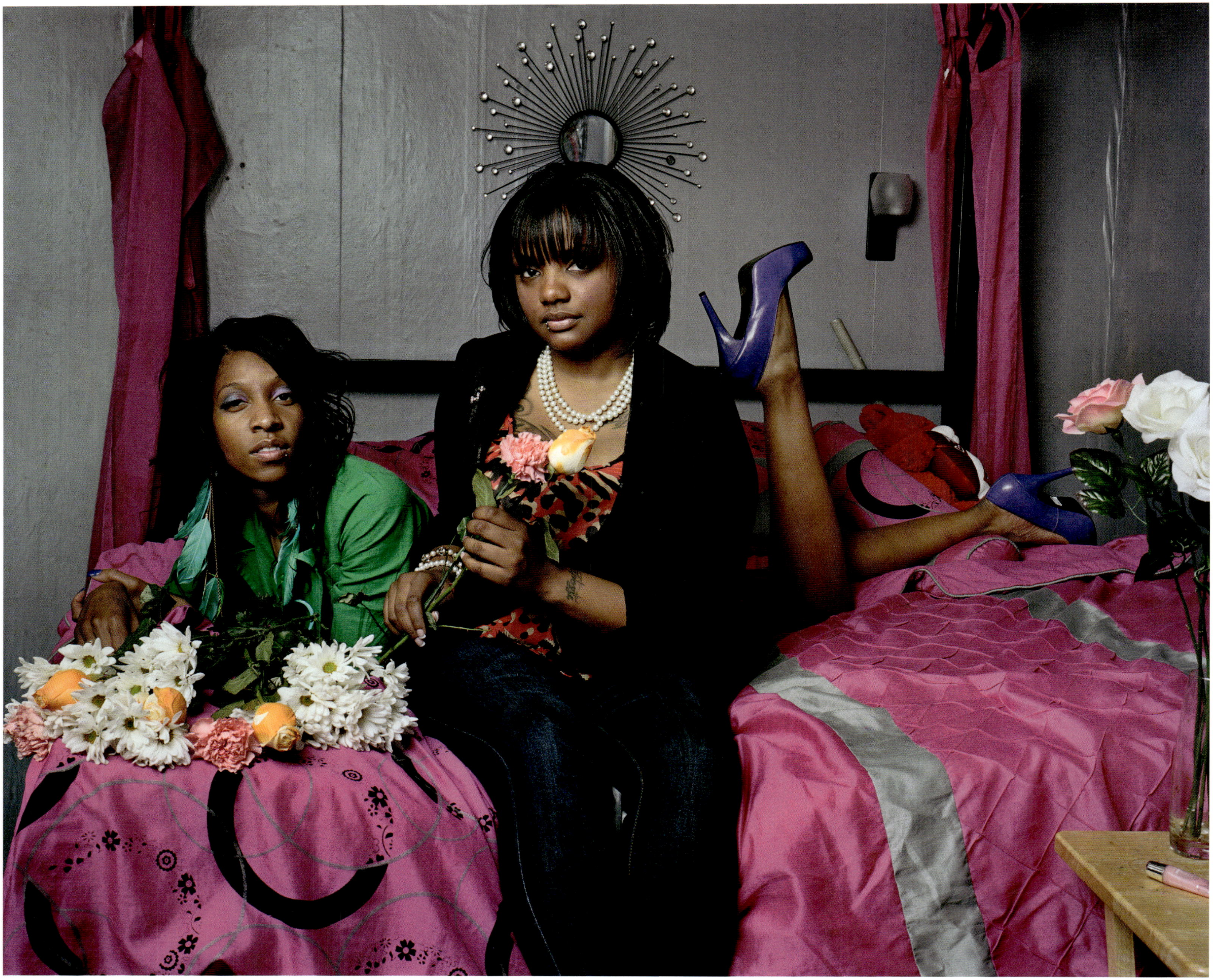

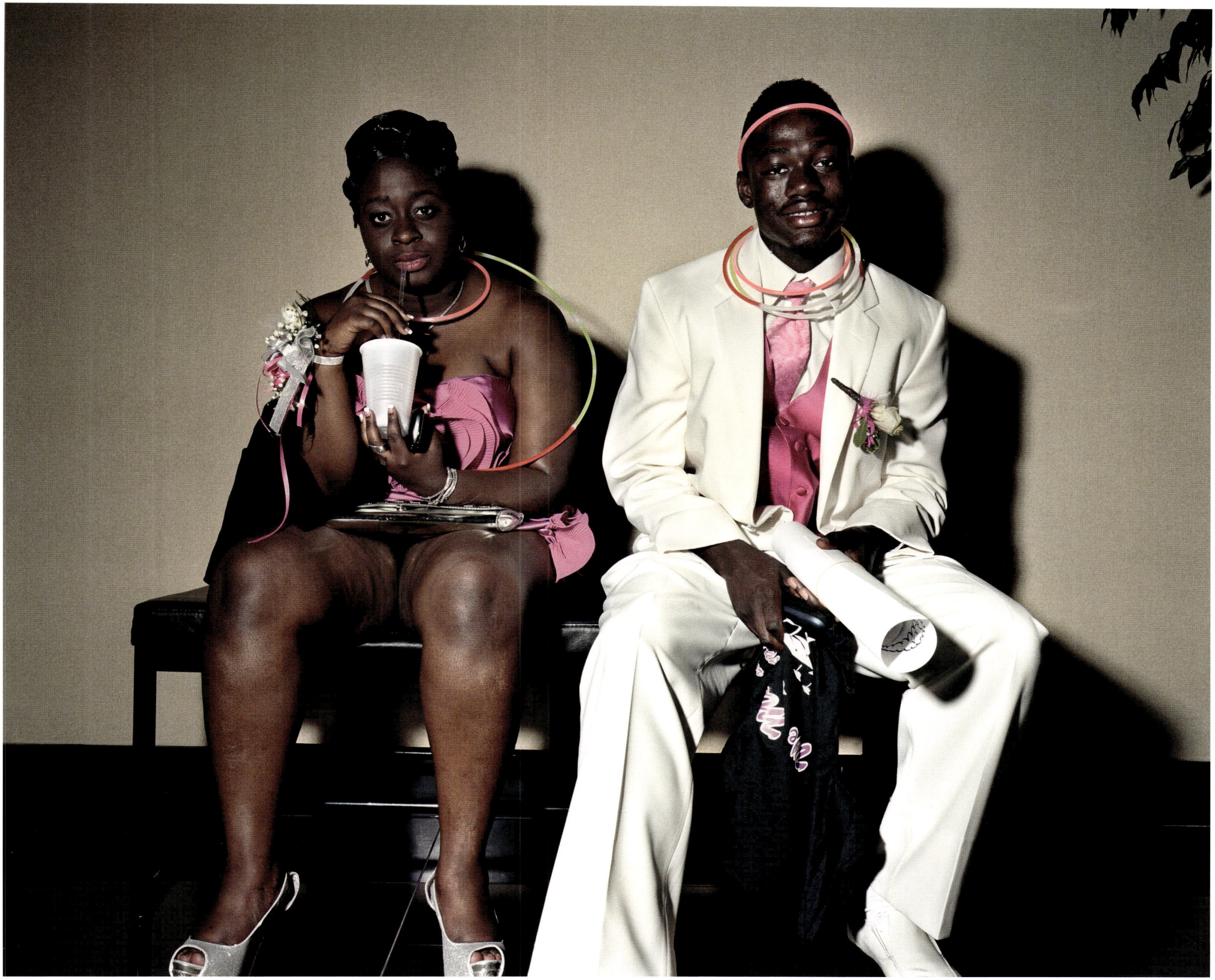

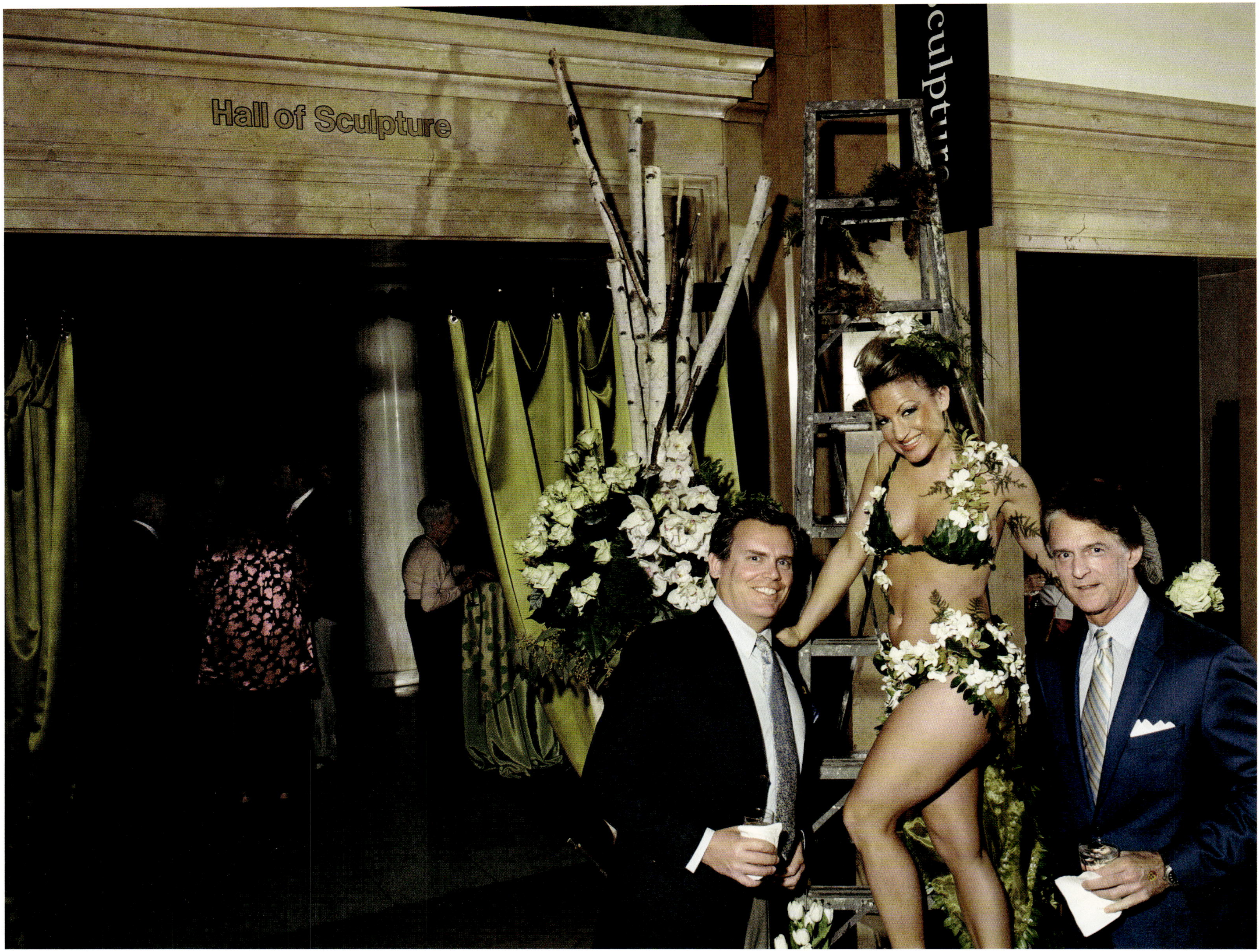
Hall of Sculpture
culpture

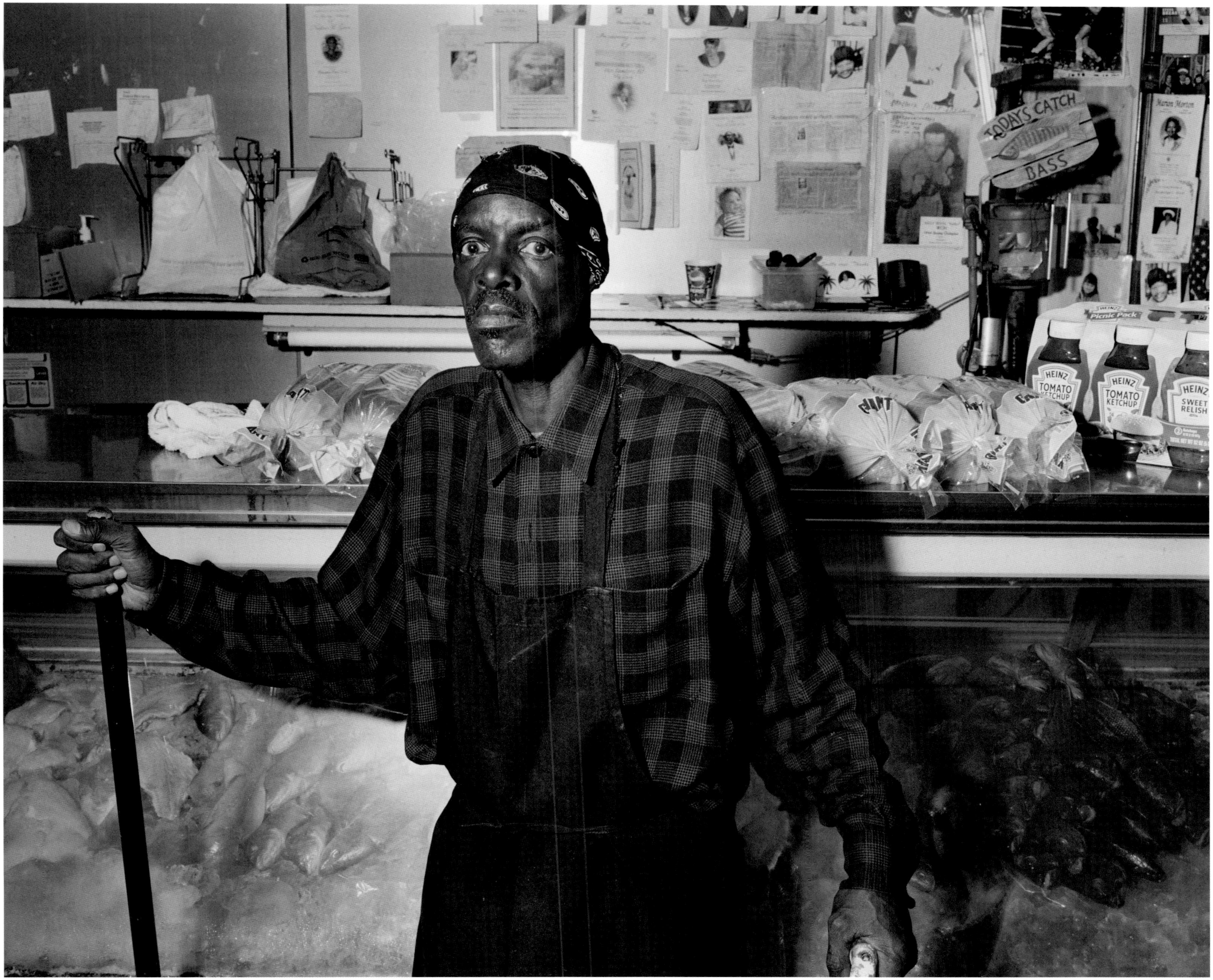
TODAYS CATCH
BASS
HEINZ Picnic Pack
HEINZ TOMATO KETCHUP
HEINZ TOMATO KETCHUP
HEINZ SWEET RELISH

185. Rumshakers Nightclub, 1, 2012
186. Begonias, 2012
187. Braddock Organic Farm, 2012
188. Parks Conservancy Hat Luncheon 1, 2012
189. Hat Parade in Braddock, 2012
191. My Neighbour Joe with our view on the Edgar Thomson Steel Mill, 2012
192. Sewickley Ballerinas, 2, 2012
193. Rumshakers Nightclub, 3, 2012
194. Braddock Beauty Parlour, 2, 2012
195. Republican Fundraiser at the Allegheney Country Club, 2012
196. Woodland Hills High School Prom, 2, 2012
197. Woodland Hills High School Prom, 3, 2012
198. Confectionary Stand at the Edgeworth Club, 2012
199. Woodland Hills High School Prom, 1, 2012
200. Triumph Baptist Church, Sewickley, 2012
201. Rave in the basement of the Elks Lodge, Braddock, 2012
203. St.Patrick's Day, Pittsburgh, 2012
204. Tiffany and Jessica in Braddock, 2012
205. Woodland Hills High School Prom, 4, 2012
206. 'Art in Bloom' Fundraiser at the Carnegie Museum, 2012
207. Dave cleaning up at Braddock Fishmongers, 2012

Braddock / Sewickley

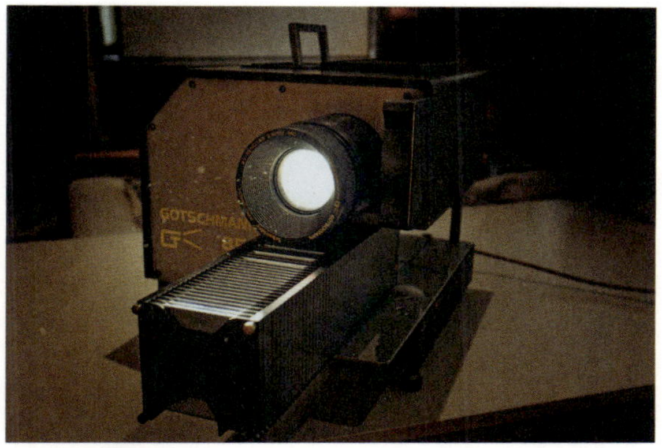

Medium format slide projector
in Neville's studio

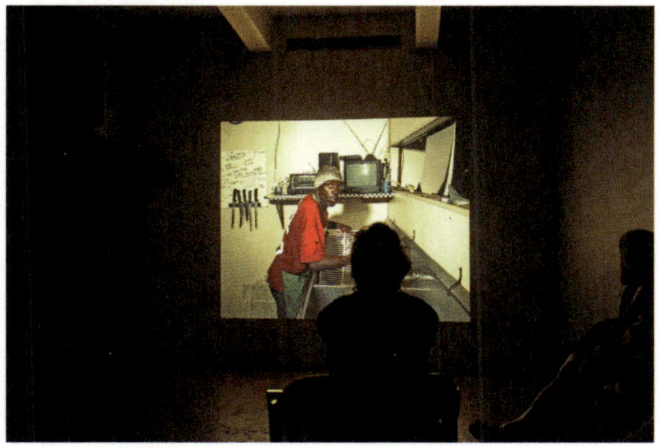

Medium format slide installation
of *Braddock/Sewickley* at the Andy
Warhol Museum, Pittsburgh, 2012

David Campany: In 2012 you went to Pittsburgh for several months. How did that come about?

Mark Neville: A curator at the Andy Warhol Museum in Pittsburgh had been to see *Fancy Pictures* on the Isle of Bute in 2008. He contacted me back then and said he wanted to work with me somehow. It took four years to bring the project together. He commissioned about fifteen artists worldwide. Orlan and many others contributed to a big project called *Factory Direct*. They would either make work in direct response to Pittsburgh or come to Pittsburgh and make work there. There were also two or three local artists involved. So suddenly this commission came up and, within four weeks of me finishing *Here Is London,* I was on the plane out to Pittsburgh. Somehow the two projects became implicated in each other. Both had their origins in American commissions for establishment institutions and both ended up exploring wealth, poverty and inequality. Also the dissemination of the work was fairly conventional: the magazine in the case of *Here Is London*, and an exhibition with the Andy Warhol Museum. In fact it would be the first time I'd made work directly for a museum show, certainly in the USA. So again I decided that because I had no or little control over the framing context, I had to make the images very powerful social documents, again talking about recession, boom and bust. Somehow the images themselves had to work harder than in the previous projects where I had control over dissemination.

And of course Pittsburgh is a highly polluted steelworks town, so it has much in common with Corby and Port Glasgow.

That was a coincidence but it was, of course, part of the attraction for me. The big difference in America, and in Pittsburgh especially, is that the lines of inequality are drawn along racial differences, ethnicity. So once I got there I lived in two very different communities. Braddock is predominantly African-American. It was a centre of the steel industry. Now there is only one steel mill left. The demise of the industry, combined with a crack epidemic in the 1980s more or less destroyed Braddock as a community. There were only about 1,100 people living there when I arrived. It has a terrible reputation for crime, drugs and shootings. I was there for a couple of months. I also stayed in Sewickley, in the north of Pittsburgh, which has the most extraordinary homes and golf clubs and country clubs. It was home to Carnegie and Mellon. I think three of the top five richest people in America had summer homes in Sewickley about a hundred years ago.

Industrialists?

Industrialists, who'd made huge amounts of money. They built these phenomenal homes. This was before income tax, so they would build their own private zoos, opulent Italian gardens, no expense spared. Those houses are still standing but today they're owned by DotCom millionaires and billionaires, baseball players: the modern day super-rich.

Where did *you* stay?

With a family called the Smiths in Sewickley who run an advertising agency. They have a grand house up in the hills with a smaller carriage house and I lived there. Every morning Lindsey Smith would drive me down in his convertible Audi, with the music on. I would go to the Warhol Museum sometimes or go to the centre of Sewickley village and try and gain entrée into the clubs and the very tight-knit, almost closed, social world. It's a world revolving around cocktail parties, Republican fundraising and salubrious affairs. It's a scene that relies on a constant flurry of social activities going on, the exchange of monies, phone numbers, funds, being seen, being seen to do good. So Braddock and Sewickley are two very contrasting communities and very much divided along racial lines. Very rarely does one see a black face in Sewickley, or indeed a white face in Braddock.

Were you equally comfortable shooting in both places?

Strangely enough yes. I found Sewickley people very welcoming although some of what was said was shocking to me, especially about race. At one point I was investigating moving to Pittsburgh permanently and buying a house there. I was advised by someone in Sewickley not to buy a house next to a black family. I was really shocked, especially coming from London where in some of the schools where I was photographing the children speak 27 different languages. Completely mixed, a fantastic sense of diversity. London is by no means perfect but it is quite well-integrated and coming to Pittsburgh was a shock.

So you photographed in Sewickley first, then in Braddock.

Yes, so in terms of material comforts I began with the easier experience. In Braddock I was right next to the steel mill. Every morning I would wake up coughing and you could see the dirt manifesting from the plumes of smoke of the steel mill just over the road. It covered everything with a gritty dust and sludge, like Corby had experienced. It's really tangible. And it starts to effect your breathing very seriously. Every morning I would get up and start shooting, walking around talking to people. I was told I would have problems doing this. One street has a reputation for being really rough and I made a point of walking down there each morning. And each morning there would be a particular group of guys on a stoop, drinking beers or smoking

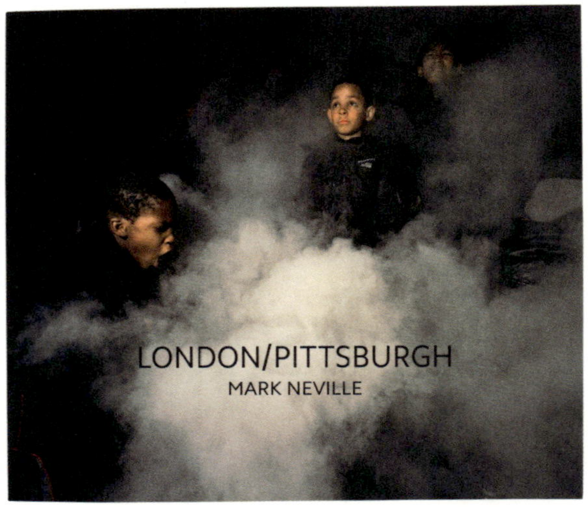

Cover of *London/Pittsburgh*, 2014

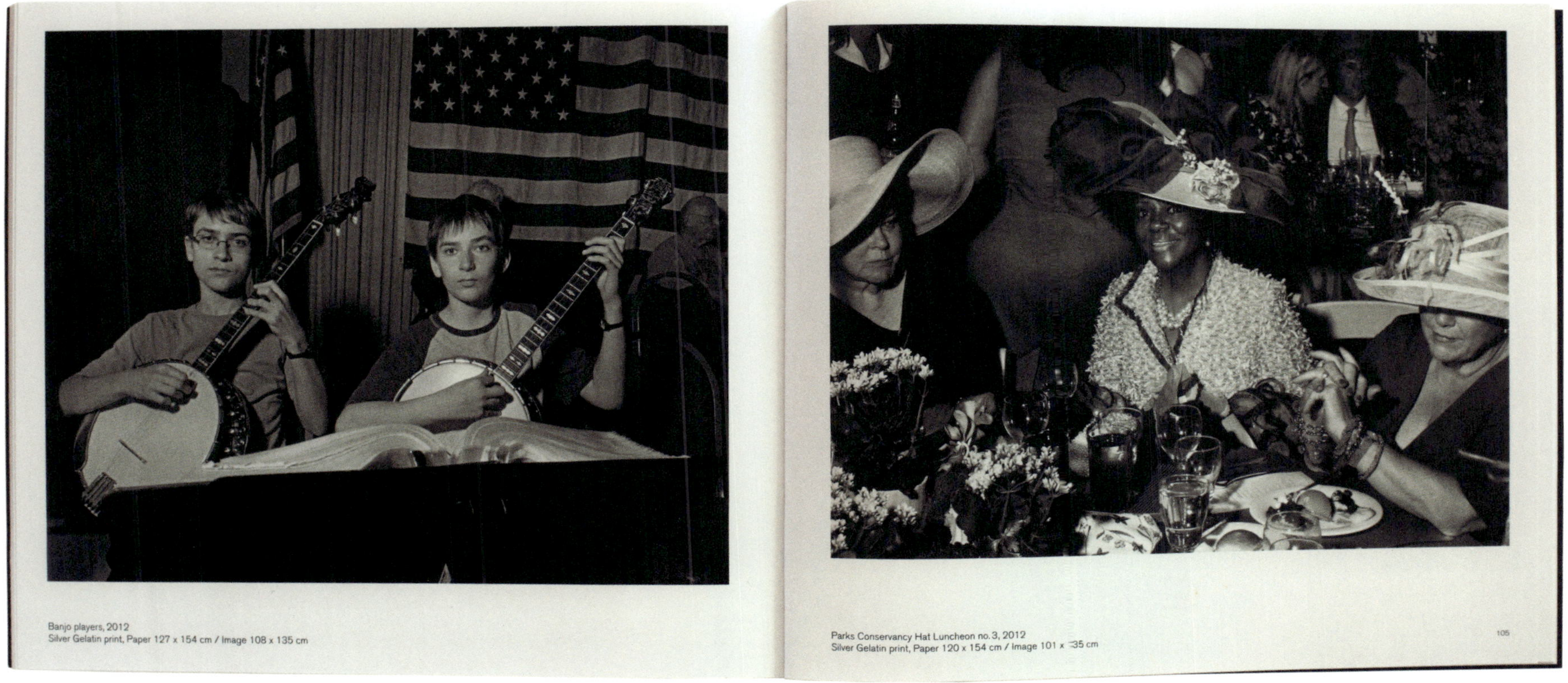

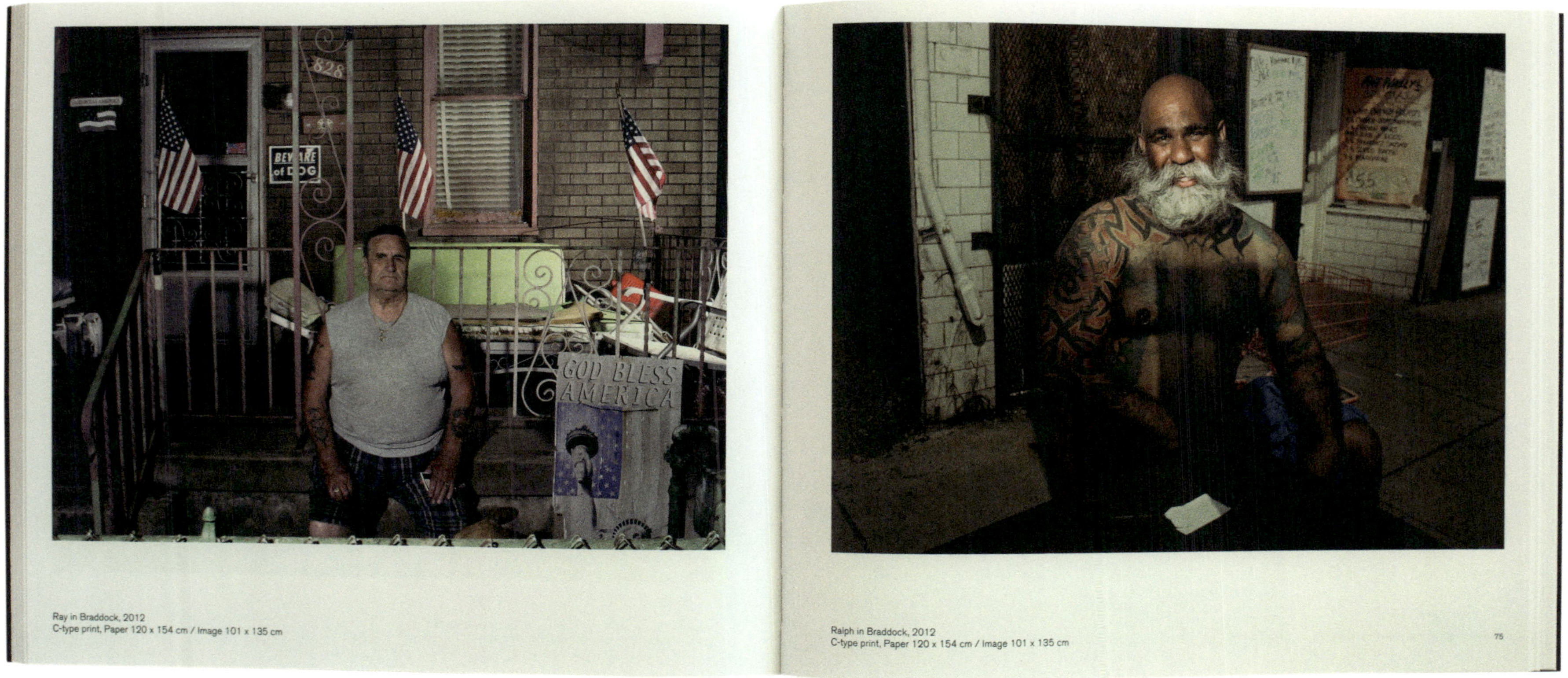

Spreads from *London/Pittsburgh*, 2014

crack or both. At nine in the morning with my camera kit I walked by and nodded to them. The next morning I said hello. The next morning one of them said hello back. The next morning I went over and started chatting to them and it turned out one of them was a war veteran. We ended up talking about Helmand. We looked at each other's dog tags and chatted.

What was his experience since the war?

He told me about how he had started drinking after leaving the army. We discussed PTSD, which is suffered by many returning soldiers. The next time I walked past I was invited in. And the next time they asked if I would take their picture. So rather than having some kind of confrontational experience, like quickly trying to grab a photograph, something just emerged between us. You need the luxury of time for those things to happen, and to show no fear. I was open and honest and patient with them. This way I find that people open up and talk, given time.

The Pittsburgh work has many things in common with your previous projects, most notably the party scenes. Those really busy group compositions lit by flash.

Well I had come straight out of the London project and this one was dealing with similar themes. But also in terms of looking at extremes of poverty and wealth one sees that both groups socialise quite a lot. The very rich and the very poor are often bound together for their identity by quite intense socialising.

...meanwhile the alienated middle classes stay home.

Ha-ha! That's so true.

Photographing in Sewickley and then Braddock were you looking to shoot similar kinds of scenes and situations? Did your Sewickley pictures provide the model for shooting Braddock?

Yes, to some extent. I was really looking closely at photography by Garry Winogrand, which talked so well about race and inequality in 1960s America, and Mitch Epstein, who documented the boom and bust of the 1980s. I was really studying them, looking at the lighting and the punch of those pictures and seeing if I could develop a similar strategy. By echoing the visual style of iconic photographers of the 1970s and 1980s, who also looked at an America or Britain undergoing recession, I hoped to communicate that the same economic and social forces present forty years ago are still with us. In fact all the statistics show that since the 1980s things have actually got *worse* in terms of the division of wealth.

Yes, not just in America and Europe, but worldwide.

Later I worked on an exhibition at the Alan Cristea Gallery in London, which brought together the *Braddock/Sewickley* and *Here Is*

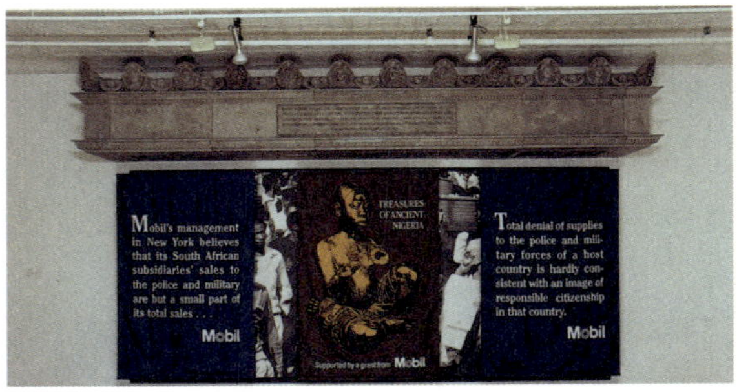

MetroMobilitan (Treasures of Ancient Nigeria), Hans Haacke, 1985, Courtesy Paula Cooper Gallery, New York

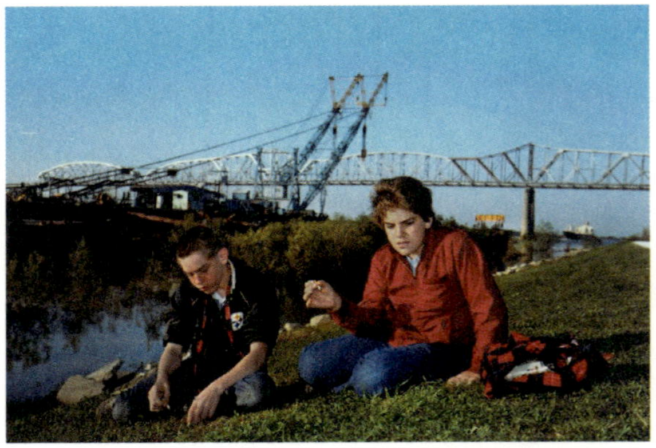

Bridge City, Louisiana, Mitch Epstein, 1984

London projects in an attempt to talk about this common experience of inequality. People imagine that equality is just good for the poor but many studies have shown that it's better for the rich too as there is less alienation, and a more realistic feeling of community.

Yes, the sense of community becomes open rather than defensive and anxious.

Right. So it's actually in everyone's interest that society is less divided. That's what we should be aiming for.

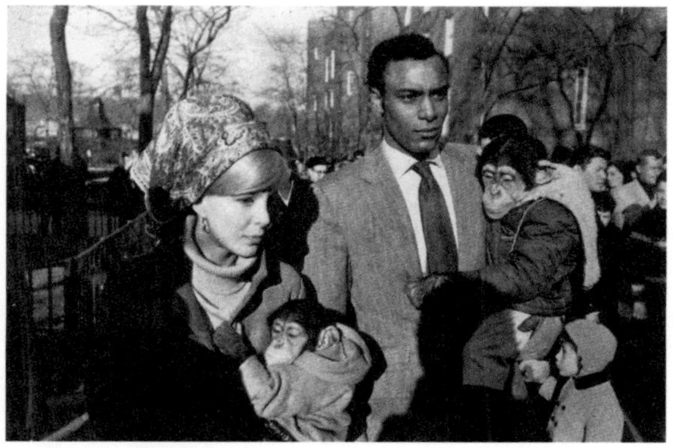

Central Park Zoo, New York, Garry WInogrand, 1967

Can you say something about wanting to make that kind of commentary and the visual experience of your pictures? You don't make point-scoring pictures. They are so layered, so rich and they include so much detail. You use deep focus, to allow the eye to wander all around, getting absorbed and even lost. That's very different from traditional campaigning photography that often tries to deliver quite a clear message. Sure, the contrast between Braddock and Sewickley, or between London bankers and working-class life in Tottenham is extreme, and would almost be a parody of extremes if it were not so true, but within that you want to accept as much visual complexity and social complexity as you can. I remember Jeff Wall's photograph *Mimic* (1982) in which a Caucasian man makes a racist gesture in the direction of an Asian man on the street. Wall said that it's often read as a picture about race and race relations, and in some ways it is, but that doesn't say much about the visual quality of the photograph as a picture to contemplate. It's easy to say that racism is bad. You just say: "Racism is bad." Pictures don't communicate so simply. They don't necessarily diffuse a central point like but they do lots of other things too. They embroider it, and expand it and make it truer in its richness.

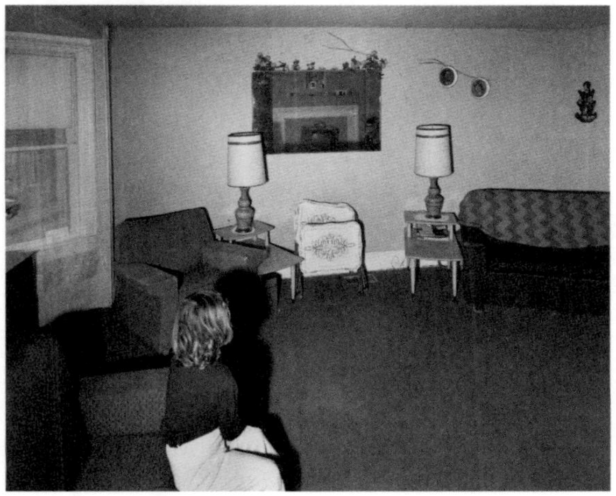

Wintersville, Ohio, Chauncey Hare, 1971

They do. And I like to explore the ways that they do. Although when I look at the London and Pittsburgh projects now they look aggressive in terms of their message.

Perhaps that's because the differences in the social settings are inescapable.

Maybe. I certainly felt the differences very strongly. All that took place in front of me. Those scenes happened. I experienced the differences. They weren't my fantasy about the life of the rich or the working class African-American life.

But the pictures can't be reduced to those differences.

Well I would hope not. We all know a photograph is not a window on the world. There is lighting, composition, timing, point of view. However the flip side of that coin is that I am ostensibly producing social documentary imagery and there *is* an external reality that is being recorded as it is being filtered. So part of my interest in basic technical things like a big depth of field is that I do want to record lots of detail. It is often detail that I cannot foresee or control, and the viewer senses this. It's a sort of visual democracy. I don't put any more importance on the colour of nail varnish, or the dirt on the street, or light hitting a glass. All of it is important, because it's a social document. So there are two things going on: a need to be objective and a need to have a voice.

Is it a dilemma that, on the one hand objectivity demands that there is no judgment made and, on the other hand social documentary has evolved through, if not revolutionary zeal, then a reformist agenda.

What I try to do is think about what use these photos can have in the real world, what function, whether that's a publication for a very specific audience or something less obviously targeted. So for example at this show at the Alan Cristea Gallery, I began with the framework, essentially a white cube with pictures in frames on the wall. But then we also organised a symposium at the London School of Economics called *Picturing Inequality* with speakers who did research into the London riots. We also arranged a bus trip excursion to the Gallery in Mayfair for kids who attend the Somerford Grove Adventure Playground in Tottenham (a location which features strongly in *Here Is London*). I also personally distributed the accompanying exhibition book to the chairs of the fifty wealthiest pension fund companies in the world. in the UK and the US, in order to try impact on one aspect of wealth inequality: the living wage issue. I sent it out with a cover letter encouraging them to invest their money, much of which comes from the working poor, in companies that endorse the living wage campaign. It's very difficult to talk to governments but you can talk to companies and chairs of companies via a photo book. So I see the exhibition as a way not just to bring two bodies of work together but to make a book that is an artefact that you can use in the world, socially and politically.

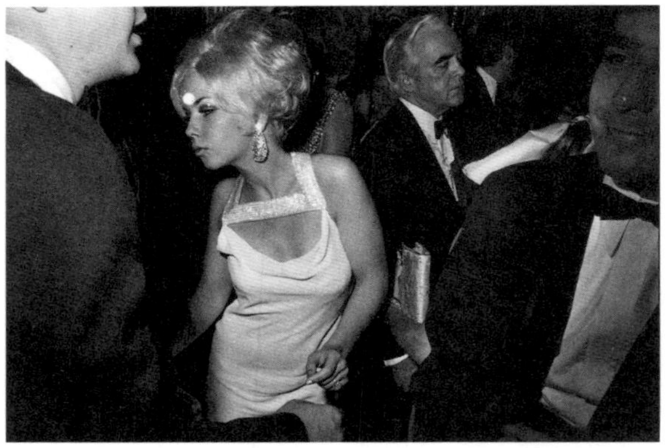

Centennial Ball, Metroplitan Museum of Art, New York, Garry Winogrand, 1969

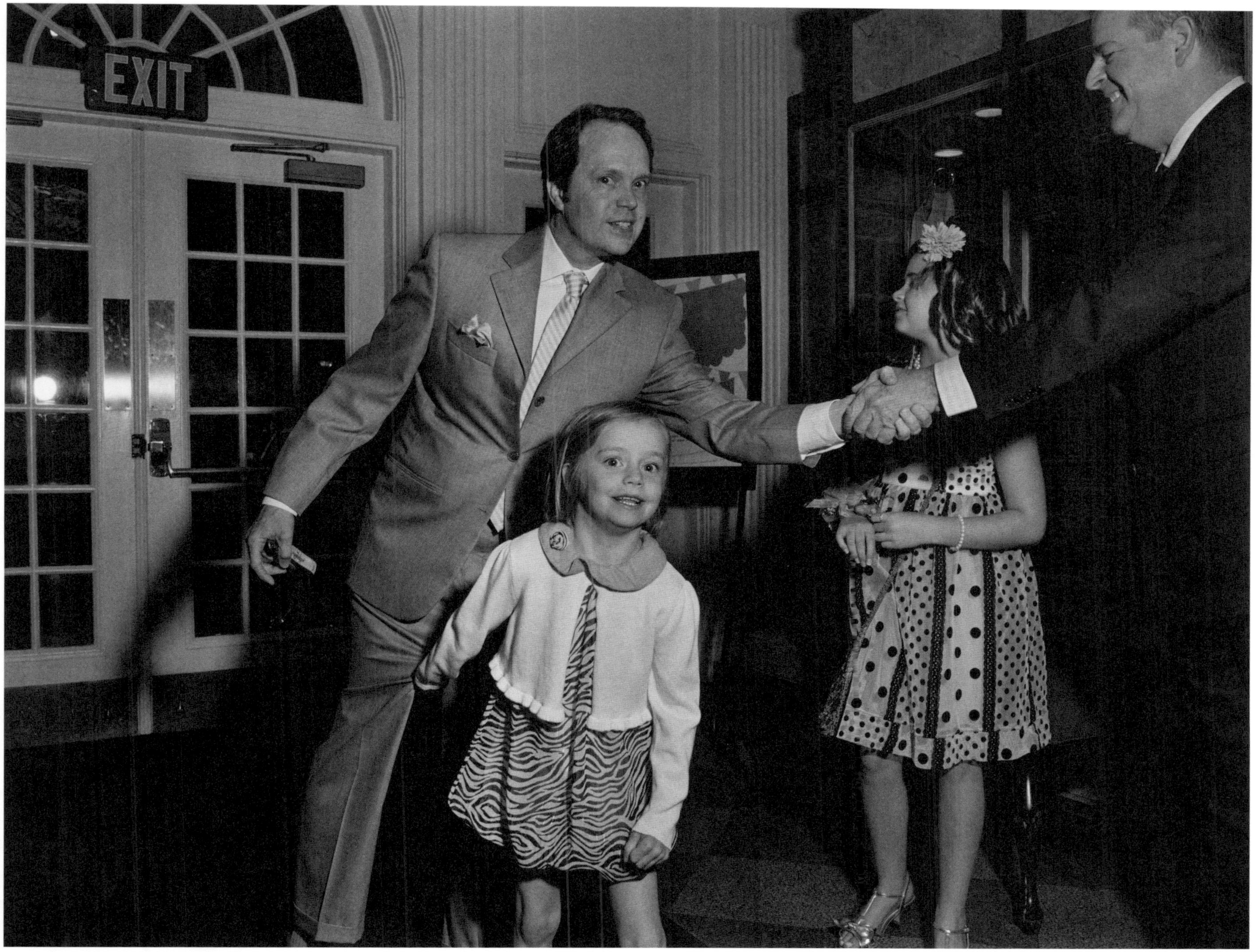

Arrivals at the Father/Daughter Dance,
Mark Neville, 2012

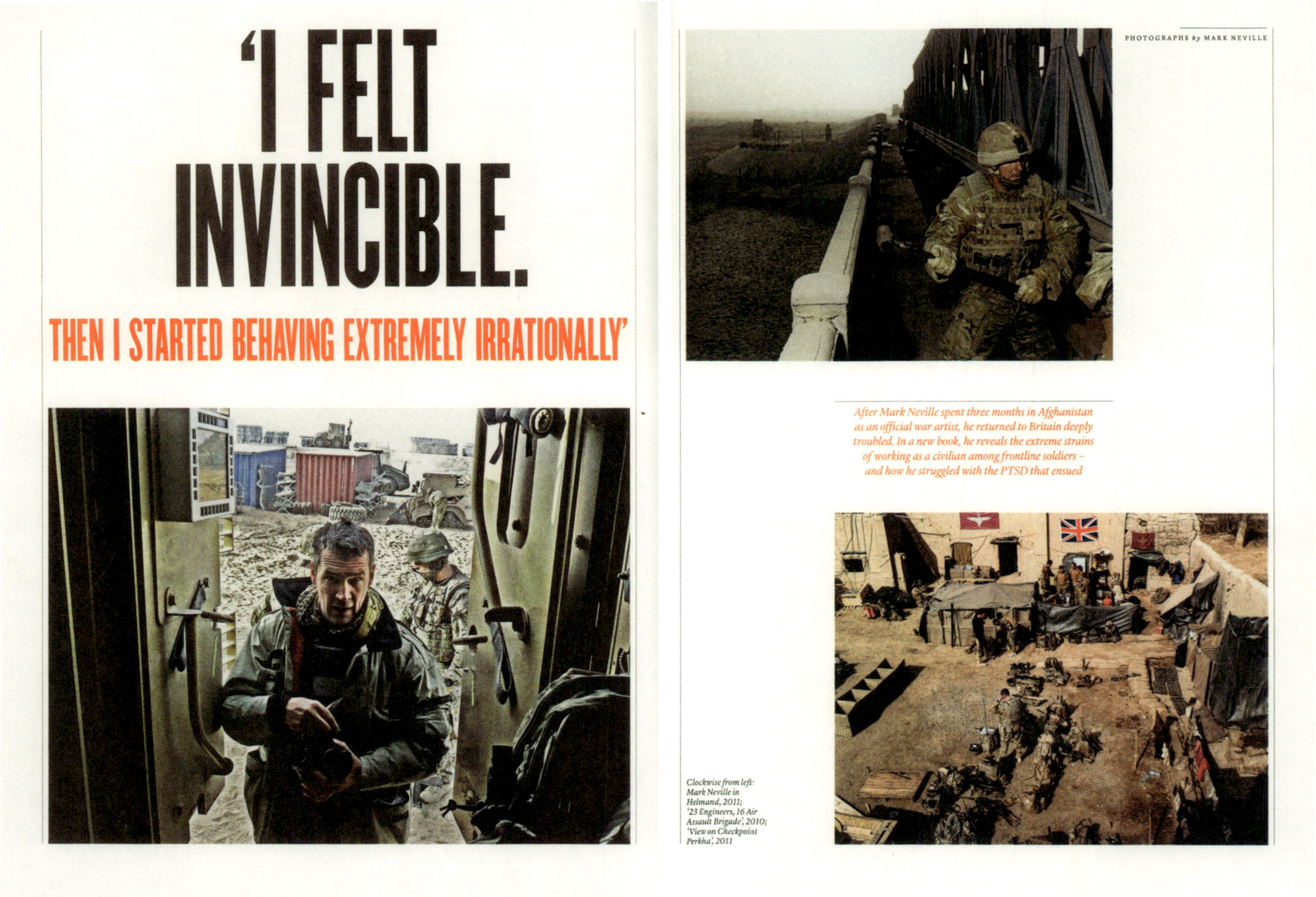

PHOTOGRAPHS *by* MARK NEVILLE

'I FELT INVINCIBLE.

THEN I STARTED BEHAVING EXTREMELY IRRATIONALLY'

After Mark Neville spent three months in Afghanistan as an official war artist, he returned to Britain deeply troubled. In a new book, he reveals the extreme strains of working as a civilian among frontline soldiers – and how he struggled with the PTSD that ensued

Clockwise from left: Mark Neville in Helmand, 2011; '23 Engineers, 16 Air Assault Brigade', 2010; 'View on Checkpoint Perkha', 2011

Mark Neville, Battling Stigma,
The Independent New Review, 24/5/2015

Battle Against Stigma

My most recent photo book project, *Battle Against Stigma*, is actually a book in two volumes, contained within one slip case. The first includes testimonies from military servicemen about their experience with adjustment disorder and PTSD, while the second volume combines photographs I made of troops in both Helmand and in the UK together with my own personal account of being a war artist. I combined my photographs and text as a way to give some insight into the issue of adjustment disorder which I found I had fallen victim to on my return from the war zone.. I sent the book out free to veteran mental health organisations throughout the UK, and it is also being used at Ruskin University by students studying a newly-established course on military mental health. That's a strategy I've used before in a different way.

What has the response been to *Battle Against Stigma*? Post-traumatic Stress Disorder is such a sensitive issue with the military institutions right now. It threatens to undermine the whole myth of the professional soldier who can cope with anything in the war zone and then slip back into civilian life.

The response to the book on every level has said something significant about the British fear of discussing mental health issues, and in particular the Ministry of Defence's desire to dismiss as insignificant the number of troops returning from war zones profoundly traumatised. I've personally stayed in touch with many of the troops I met in Helmand - they come and sleep on my sofa in my East End of London studio sometimes - all of them have now left the army, and all of them without exception are experiencing significant difficulties adjusting to civilian life. How can one go through that experience and not have problems afterwards? It's a normal reaction. I think of it like this: If I put a cat in a field and let bombs off all around it for several months, the cat may survive but it certainly won't be the same animal anymore…it is the same with people.

Before going to print with *Battle Against Stigma*, I had various meetings with the Ministry of Defence in Whitehall, London, to discuss the book..I gave them the opportunity to use my project as a way of celebrating their achievements in the area of treating PTSD..I asked them to write a chapter in the book and utilise the publication in any constructive way they wanted..My only interest was and is in reducing the stigma troops suffering with PTSD feel about coming forward and seeking help, it was never intended to point a finger of blame at the

MoD or anyone else. The MoD's first objection was that I intended to combine my images of soldiers in Helmand with accounts of PTSD from servicemen..their argument was that in so doing I would infer that everyone I photographed in Helmand is or was suffering from adjustment disorder. I explained that I had experience making photo and text books, and that I would clearly structure things so this inference was not made.

The MoD would not accept this however, and they then pushed me to use their own stock imagery of soldiers in Helmand taken from the MoD photo library instead of my own work in the book..pictures of heroic soldiers on patrol silhouetted against a setting sun..you know.. that kind of thing. I tried to explain that this ran counter to the whole meaning of the project, about the power of photography to change lives. These meetings, phone calls and e-mails with the MoD went on throughout 2013 and 2014. Finally the MoD said that they would not allow the written testimonies about PTSD from serving troops to be published if they were accompanied by my photographs of troops taken in Helmand and the UK. I agreed to this, and on that basis they gave the permissions. The idea I come up with in order to keep to my word whilst circumventing this obstacle (my strategy was unbeknownst to the MoD at the time) was to make a book in two volumes contained within one slipcase: one volume of testimonies from soldiers about PTSD, the second volume containing the account of my own adjustment disorder plus the photographs which I took in Helmand..It was an idea born out of a commitment to the photo book form and the concept of the project..and it was a kind of 'fuck you' to the MoD regarding freedom of expression. This format naturally proved to be much more expensive in terms of production costs, but I found a printer in Spain who was experienced making substantial slipcased books. The printer did a good job, and sent the 1500 copies over to the UK in two separate consignments.

Disturbingly, the first delivery of 500 copies of this book were seized at customs by UK Border Force (a special division of Customs with strong links to the Ministry of Defence) and have yet to be released. The second consignment of 1,000 copies entered the UK via a different route, thus escaping seizure, and arrived safely at my studio. I can only assume that this was a clumsy attempt at censorship by the powers that be..Nevertheless, it put the fear of God into me that the book, four years in the making, would never reach its target audience.. veteran PTSD sufferers who had never been treated. So for three months I personally disseminated the surviving 1,000 copies free to prison libraries, probation services, homeless shelters, veteran mental health charities and even Defence Mental Health Services at the MoD. Unlike the population of Port Glasgow, for example, this group of recipients for my book are, by definition, a demographic who have fallen through the cracks in British society, who are extremely difficult to locate, who are hard to reach. They are prisoners or homeless people who used to be in the military, who perhaps never had their PTSD treated, who started drinking or taking drugs in order to cope with their symptoms, and who perhaps ultimately became violent, lost their jobs and partners, and never managed to fully assimilate back into society after experiencing war. These are the people I tried to get the book to, in the hope that they will finally seek professional help and get treatment.

Then, in May 2015 a British newspaper, *The Independent*, published excerpts from the account of my own experience of PTSD from the book. At the end of my article I implored any veterans still suffering with PTSD to get in touch with me by email and I would send them a free copy of the book. To my astonishment I received e-mails from veterans every twenty minutes for about six weeks requesting copies and recounting their own heartbreaking experiences of adjustment disorder..some 1000 in total. So I replied in person to each of these e-mails, and spent a further few weeks packaging books and sending them out from my studio. Their overwhelming response made me realise that I had tapped into something significant and unspoken..a terrible indication of just how little support there is in Britain for veterans, and just how many suffering with PTSD have never received support or treatment…It also makes me think how frightening and threatening books can be to certain institutions and demographics, under certain conditions.. To date I've had my books burned (in Port Glasgow), and copies of *Battle Against Stigma* seized by border control..And yet, in my eyes, neither of these publications contained imagery or information which was inflammatory, and neither book employed shock tactics or 'sexed up' content. It makes me wonder what can possibly happen to my publications in future projects.

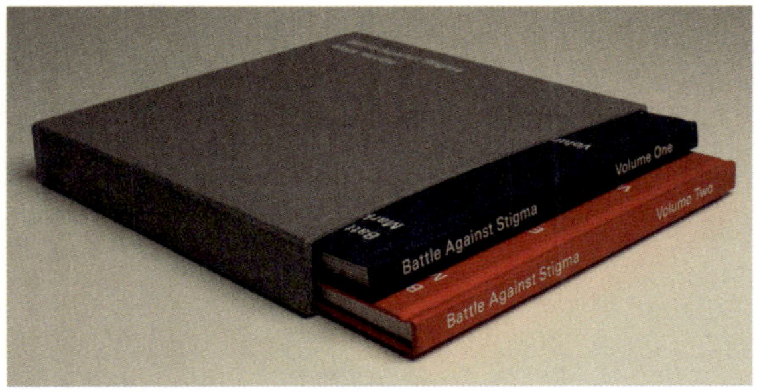

Cover of *Battle Against Stigma*, 2015

That's an extraordinary outpouring of emotion and support from soldiers.

Yes, and this mass of e-mail documentation really constitutes a major, new insight into the experiences of those suffering from mental illness following service in modern warfare. One particular e-mail stays with me..it was from an ex RAF Tornado navigator whose view of the war in Afghanistan was through a TV screen measuring 8x6 inches in the back of a Tornado jet. "Death tv" he called it. Where he was affected was not by seeing an attack once, but repeatedly…Part of his job was to write a report on what had happened during the sortie. He would have to go through his video tapes again and again. He didn't watch these guys die once..He saw them die seven or eight times. Repeatedly viewing these pixilated images had clearly burnt the trauma into him…*The Battle Against Stigma Book Project* was even discussed in the House of Commons in a debate about the mental health of our veterans…It might turn out to be the most effective of all my works. I just don't know. But right from the beginning of making work at art school I knew I felt uncomfortable with the muteness of the static image.

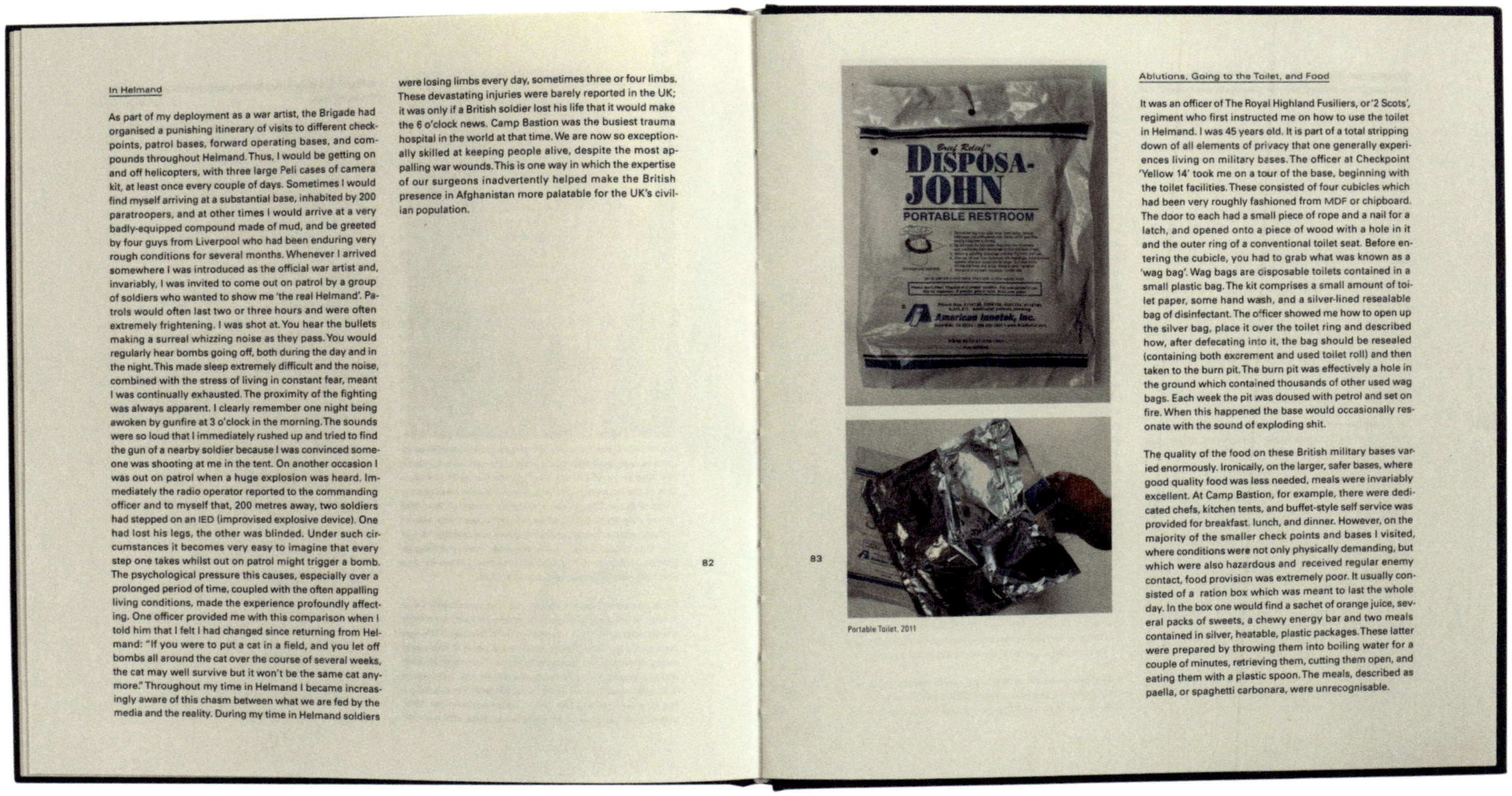

In Helmand

As part of my deployment as a war artist, the Brigade had organised a punishing itinerary of visits to different checkpoints, patrol bases, forward operating bases, and compounds throughout Helmand. Thus, I would be getting on and off helicopters, with three large Peli cases of camera kit, at least once every couple of days. Sometimes I would find myself arriving at a substantial base, inhabited by 200 paratroopers, and at other times I would arrive at a very badly-equipped compound made of mud, and be greeted by four guys from Liverpool who had been enduring very rough conditions for several months. Whenever I arrived somewhere I was introduced as the official war artist and, invariably, I was invited to come out on patrol by a group of soldiers who wanted to show me 'the real Helmand'. Patrols would often last two or three hours and were often extremely frightening. I was shot at. You hear the bullets making a surreal whizzing noise as they pass. You would regularly hear bombs going off, both during the day and in the night. This made sleep extremely difficult and the noise, combined with the stress of living in constant fear, meant I was continually exhausted. The proximity of the fighting was always apparent. I clearly remember one night being awoken by gunfire at 3 o'clock in the morning. The sounds were so loud that I immediately rushed up and tried to find the gun of a nearby soldier because I was convinced someone was shooting at me in the tent. On another occasion I was out on patrol when a huge explosion was heard. Immediately the radio operator reported to the commanding officer and to myself that, 200 metres away, two soldiers had stepped on an IED (improvised explosive device). One had lost his legs, the other was blinded. Under such circumstances it becomes very easy to imagine that every step one takes whilst out on patrol might trigger a bomb. The psychological pressure this causes, especially over a prolonged period of time, coupled with the often appalling living conditions, made the experience profoundly affecting. One officer provided me with this comparison when I told him that I felt I had changed since returning from Helmand: "If you were to put a cat in a field, and you let off bombs all around the cat over the course of several weeks, the cat may well survive but it won't be the same cat anymore." Throughout my time in Helmand I became increasingly aware of this chasm between what we are fed by the media and the reality. During my time in Helmand soldiers were losing limbs every day, sometimes three or four limbs. These devastating injuries were barely reported in the UK; it was only if a British soldier lost his life that it would make the 6 o'clock news. Camp Bastion was the busiest trauma hospital in the world at that time. We are now so exceptionally skilled at keeping people alive, despite the most appalling war wounds. This is one way in which the expertise of our surgeons inadvertently helped make the British presence in Afghanistan more palatable for the UK's civilian population.

82

83

Brief Relief™
DISPOSA-JOHN
PORTABLE RESTROOM
American Innotek, Inc.

Portable Toilet, 2011

Ablutions, Going to the Toilet, and Food

It was an officer of The Royal Highland Fusiliers, or '2 Scots', regiment who first instructed me on how to use the toilet in Helmand. I was 45 years old. It is part of a total stripping down of all elements of privacy that one generally experiences living on military bases. The officer at Checkpoint 'Yellow 14' took me on a tour of the base, beginning with the toilet facilities. These consisted of four cubicles which had been very roughly fashioned from MDF or chipboard. The door to each had a small piece of rope and a nail for a latch, and opened onto a piece of wood with a hole in it and the outer ring of a conventional toilet seat. Before entering the cubicle, you had to grab what was known as a 'wag bag'. Wag bags are disposable toilets contained in a small plastic bag. The kit comprises a small amount of toilet paper, some hand wash, and a silver-lined resealable bag of disinfectant. The officer showed me how to open up the silver bag, place it over the toilet ring and described how, after defecating into it, the bag should be resealed (containing both excrement and used toilet roll) and then taken to the burn pit. The burn pit was effectively a hole in the ground which contained thousands of other used wag bags. Each week the pit was doused with petrol and set on fire. When this happened the base would occasionally resonate with the sound of exploding shit.

The quality of the food on these British military bases varied enormously. Ironically, on the larger, safer bases, where good quality food was less needed, meals were invariably excellent. At Camp Bastion, for example, there were dedicated chefs, kitchen tents, and buffet-style self service was provided for breakfast, lunch, and dinner. However, on the majority of the smaller check points and bases I visited, where conditions were not only physically demanding, but which were also hazardous and received regular enemy contact, food provision was extremely poor. It usually consisted of a ration box which was meant to last the whole day. In the box one would find a sachet of orange juice, several packs of sweets, a chewy energy bar and two meals contained in silver, heatable, plastic packages. These latter were prepared by throwing them into boiling water for a couple of minutes, retrieving them, cutting them open, and eating them with a plastic spoon. The meals, described as paella, or spaghetti carbonara, were unrecognisable.

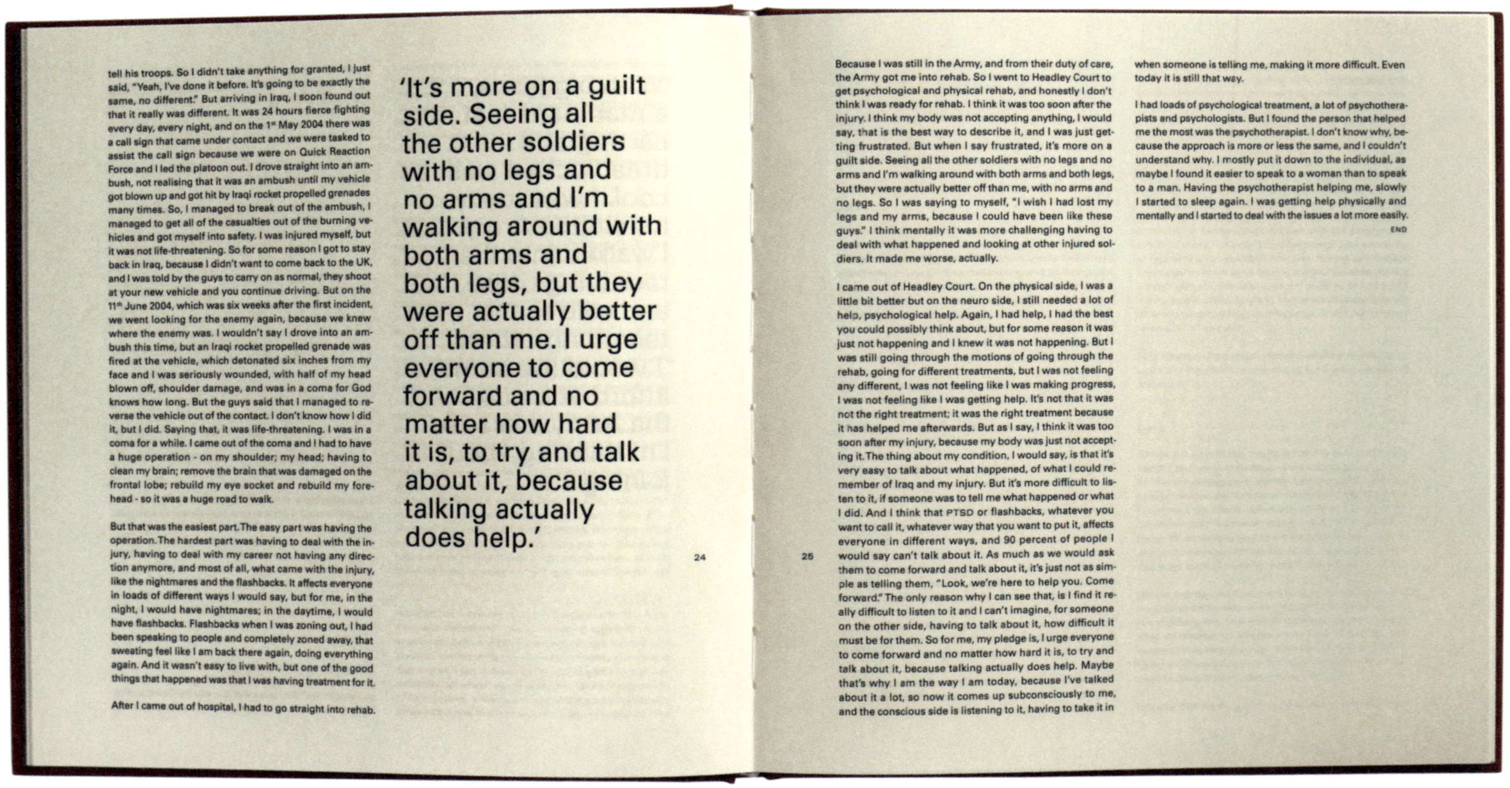

tell his troops. So I didn't take anything for granted, I just said, "Yeah, I've done it before. It's going to be exactly the same, no different." But arriving in Iraq, I soon found out that it really was different. It was 24 hours fierce fighting every day, every night, and on the 1st May 2004 there was a call sign that came under contact and we were tasked to assist the call sign because we were on Quick Reaction Force and I led the platoon out. I drove straight into an ambush, not realising that it was an ambush until my vehicle got blown up and got hit by Iraqi rocket propelled grenades many times. So, I managed to break out of the ambush, I managed to get all of the casualties out of the burning vehicles and got myself into safety. I was injured myself, but it was not life-threatening. So for some reason I got to stay back in Iraq, because I didn't want to come back to the UK, and I was told by the guys to carry on as normal, they shoot at your new vehicle and you continue driving. But on the 11th June 2004, which was six weeks after the first incident, we went looking for the enemy again, because we knew where the enemy was. I wouldn't say I drove into an ambush this time, but an Iraqi rocket propelled grenade was fired at the vehicle, which detonated six inches from my face and I was seriously wounded, with half of my head blown off, shoulder damage, and was in a coma for God knows how long. But the guys said that I managed to reverse the vehicle out of the contact. I don't know how I did it, but I did. Saying that, it was life-threatening. I was in a coma for a while. I came out of the coma and I had to have a huge operation - on my shoulder; my head; having to clean my brain; remove the brain that was damaged on the frontal lobe; rebuild my eye socket and rebuild my forehead - so it was a huge road to walk.

But that was the easiest part. The easy part was having the operation. The hardest part was having to deal with the injury, having to deal with my career not having any direction anymore, and most of all, what came with the injury, like the nightmares and the flashbacks. It affects everyone in loads of different ways I would say, but for me, in the night, I would have nightmares; in the daytime, I would have flashbacks. Flashbacks when I was zoning out, I had been speaking to people and completely zoned away, that sweating feel like I am back there again, doing everything again. And it wasn't easy to live with, but one of the good things that happened was that I was having treatment for it.

After I came out of hospital, I had to go straight into rehab.

'It's more on a guilt side. Seeing all the other soldiers with no legs and no arms and I'm walking around with both arms and both legs, but they were actually better off than me. I urge everyone to come forward and no matter how hard it is, to try and talk about it, because talking actually does help.'

24

25

Because I was still in the Army, and from their duty of care, the Army got me into rehab. So I went to Headley Court to get psychological and physical rehab, and honestly I don't think I was ready for rehab. I think it was too soon after the injury. I think my body was not accepting anything, I would say, that is the best way to describe it, and I was just getting frustrated. But when I say frustrated, it's more on a guilt side. Seeing all the other soldiers with no legs and no arms and I'm walking around with both arms and both legs, but they were actually better off than me, with no arms and no legs. So I was saying to myself, "I wish I had lost my legs and my arms, because I could have been like these guys." I think mentally it was more challenging having to deal with what happened and looking at other injured soldiers. It made me worse, actually.

I came out of Headley Court. On the physical side, I was a little bit better but on the neuro side, I still needed a lot of help, psychological help. Again, I had help, I had the best you could possibly think about, but for some reason it was just not happening and I knew it was not happening. But I was still going through the motions of going through the rehab, going for different treatments, but I was not feeling any different, I was not feeling like I was making progress, I was not feeling like I was getting help. It's not that it was not the right treatment; it was the right treatment because it has helped me afterwards. But as I say, I think it was too soon after my injury, because my body was just not accepting it. The thing about my condition, I would say, is that it's very easy to talk about what happened, of what I could remember of Iraq and my injury. But it's more difficult to listen to it, if someone was to tell me what happened or what I did. And I think that PTSD or flashbacks, whatever you want to call it, whatever way that you want to put it, affects everyone in different ways, and 90 percent of people I would say can't talk about it. As much as we would ask them to come forward and talk about it, it's just not as simple as telling them, "Look, we're here to help you. Come forward." The only reason why I can see that, is I find it really difficult to listen to it and I can't imagine, for someone on the other side, having to talk about it, how difficult it must be for them. So for me, my pledge is, I urge everyone to come forward and no matter how hard it is, to try and talk about it, because talking actually does help. Maybe that's why I am the way I am today, because I've talked about it a lot, so now it comes up subconsciously to me, and the conscious side is listening to it, having to take it in when someone is telling me, making it more difficult. Even today it is still that way.

I had loads of psychological treatment, a lot of psychotherapists and psychologists. But I found the person that helped me the most was the psychotherapist. I don't know why, because the approach is more or less the same, and I couldn't understand why. I mostly put it down to the individual, as maybe I found it easier to speak to a woman than to speak to a man. Having the psychotherapist helping me, slowly I started to sleep again. I was getting help physically and mentally and I started to deal with the issues a lot more easily.

END

Spreads from *Battle Against Stigma*, 2015

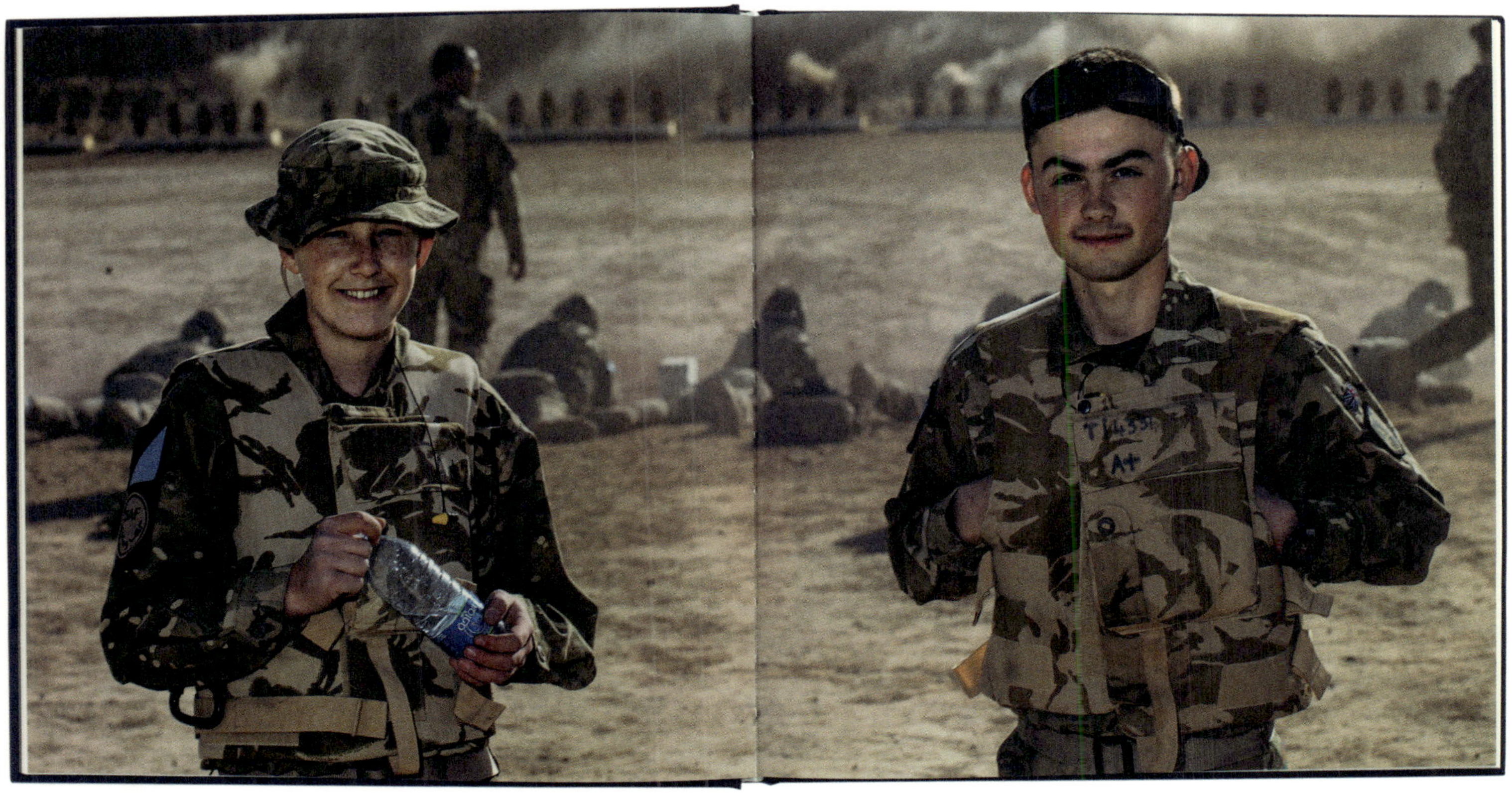

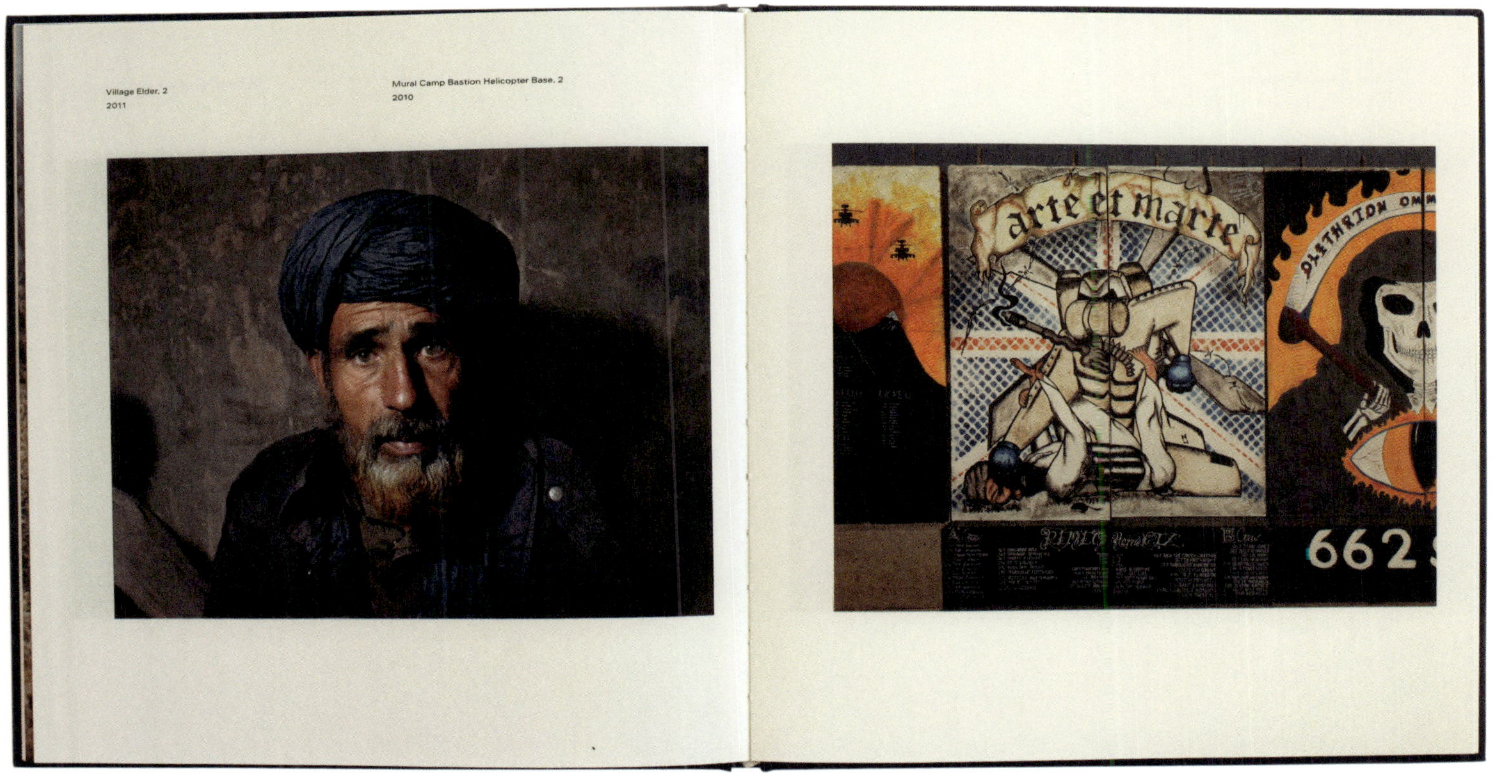

Spreads from *Battle Against Stigma*, 2015

I needed to do more with it, around it. Photographers are often lazy with their ambitions for their work, in terms of how the images are contextualized. I believe that images should have a very ambitious, ethical function in the real world because they deal with reality.

Photographs are eminently usable, so in the end photographers are eminently usable too, unless they are careful and vigilant. I agree that it's not enough to make the images. One has to think about the right framework for their reception and that might mean inventing a completely new kind of framework.

As you said earlier this often involves being experimental. Trying things out. We are first and foremost social and political beings. Albert Camus said that if he was only a writer he would cease to be *even* a writer. Chauncey Hare does not define himself as a photographer, but instead an engineer, a family therapist and, especially, a protester. All work is social and political. Sometimes it's explicit; sometimes it's implicit. But I do think that "witness art", art that bears witness to the evils of conflict or injustice, is the most important, even if it is the most complicated.

Even if it is the most complicated. So often "political" art is marginalised as difficult or it is idealised for doing the dirty work we should all be doing. I also notice that as soon as work is seen as political it's assumed that the artist knows exactly what they're doing, that they have a completely watertight argument or strategy. Again this rules out the necessity of experiment and play.

There is no perfect strategy. It is always messy.

One of the 933 e-mail responses to
Battle Against Stigma, 2015

From : Oliver Lovejoy
Sent : 28 May 2015 14:21
To : info@markneville.com
Subject : 'Battle Against Stigma'

Dear Mark,

I read your article in the Independent with tears in my eyes. My son served in Afghanistan with the Special Forces Support Group and has been struggling with PTSD since his return and since leaving the Army. His relationship with his partner broke down shortly after his return, he ran up significant debts and he won't speak to me (for over a year) as I seem to be some sort of representation of the demons in his life. I was an Army officer for many years and an obvious 'authority figure' with whom he is struggling. Maybe there is blame on my part. This has at least allowed him to focus his anger and whatever else on me and we no longer fear that he might take his own life, and so as hard as it it, it is something that I can bear in the hope that it gives him the room he needs to become well again. Fortunately he still maintains a relationship with my wife and that is how we stay in touch, but he, like you, is definitely struggling to readjust and is resisting help. He had a small amount of therapy, which seemed to start him on a journey that he is now unable to continue, and he refuses to take anti-depressants.

Please can you send me a copy of your book. I hope that if we give him the book (via my wife) that he might identify with it and gain some insight which might help him.

What you are doing is important. Thank-you. I don't have a God of my own, but if you do then may he or she or they bless you for what you are doing.

I wish you well and hope you continue to thrive.

Regards,

Oliver Lovejoy

I owe a huge debt of gratitude to Gerhard Steidl for his remarkable work and patience. I am deeply grateful to my friend David Campany who has understood and cared about the work since its very beginning. David continues to write about and curate the work with real insight. I want to thank Duncan Whyte for his superb book design.

Meroe Candy, David Cahill-Roots, and especially Marie-Lise Sheppard at the Wellcome Trust, have been instrumental in supporting my work and ideas, often making brave decisions to fund projects which deal with sensitive, important issues. Without Marie-Lise Sheppard, much of the work contained in this book quite simply would not have been made.

I feel exceptionally fortunate to have had the support of the many communities in which I have lived and worked, as well as from the curators, writers, patrons, editors, museums and galleries who have gone on to present these projects. These are too numerous to list, but include Roza Wlodarczyk, Midge Palley, Kay Pallister, Rachelle Cousineau, Jason Tasker, David Curtis, Caroline Douglas, Andrew Nairne, Carey Young, Mike Schofield, Simon Clarke, Duncan Hedges, Jamie Hacker Hughes, Kathy Ryan, Stacey Baker, *The New York Times Magazine*, 16 Air Assault Brigade, the thousands of veterans who requested copies of *Battle Against Stigma*, everyone at Port Glasgow Town Hall, Ferguson's Shipyard, The Corby 16, Katie Razzall, Liliana, Liu Gang, Mark Sealy, Andrew Hoskins, Nicola Freeman, Caro Howell, Jerome Sother, Gwinzegal Art Centre, Heidelberg UK, Janice Hiller, Sergio Bechelli, Reka Koszta, Robert Epstein and *The Independent on Sunday*, Liz Jobey, John Kobal Foundation, David Thomson, Tim Prus, Barbara and everyone at the Archive of Modern Conflict, Aminatta Forna, Indre Cukuraite, Gemma Marmalade, Lindsey Smith, everyone at The Photographers' Gallery, Imperial War Museum London, The Andy Warhol Museum, Modern Art Oxford, Kunstmuseum Bern, Scottish Parliament, Luisa Summers, Marichka Varenikova, Ailbhe Clyne, National Galleries of Scotland, Creative Scotland, Metro Imaging, Antonio de Luca, the British Council, The Arts Council Collection, Jill Constantine, SK Kultur Köln, Brian Lang, Graham Shearing, the Silver Eye Centre, Street Level Gallery, Eric Shiner, Stephanie Flower, Len Thornton, Martin Parr, Annie MacDougall, Sophie Crichton-Stuart, Mount Stuart Trust, Johnny Bute, Wendy Law, Malcolm Dickson, Duncan Forbes, Gwen Sasse, and finally my heartfelt thanks go to Helen Waters, Alan, David Roberts, Kathleen Dempsey, Gemma Colgan, and everyone at the Alan Cristea Gallery.

Mark Neville
London
June, 2016

First edition published in 2016

Book design: Duncan Whyte
Scans by Mark Neville
Separations by Steidl's digital darkroom

Production and printing: Steidl, Göttingen

Steidl
Düstere Str. 4 / 37073 Göttingen, Germany
Phone +49 551 49 60 60
Fax +49 551 49 60 649
mail@steidl.de
steidl.de

ISBN 978-3-86930-908-8
Printed in Germany by Steidl